André Laurendeau

André Laurendeau

French-Canadian Nationalist

1912-1968

Donald J. Horton

Toronto
OXFORD UNIVERSITY PRESS
1992

Oxford University Press, 70 Wynford Drive, Don Mills, Ontario M3C 1J9

Toronto   Oxford   New York
Delhi   Bombay   Calcutta   Madras   Karachi   Kuala Lumpur
Singapore   Hong Kong   Tokyo   Nairobi   Dar es Salaam
Cape Town   Melbourne   Auckland   Madrid

and associated companies in
Berlin   Ibadan

This book is printed on permanent (acid-free) paper

To Louise

Canadian Cataloguing in Publication Data

Horton, Donald James
    André Laurendeau: French Canadian nationalist, 1912-1968

Includes bibliographical references.
ISBN 0-19-540917-5

1. Laurendeau, André, 1912-1968.   2. Canada – English-French
relations.   3. Journalists – Quebec (Province) – Biography.   I. Title.

FC2925.1.L38H67 1993   971-4'04'092
F1053.25.L38H67 1993   C92-094921-5

OXFORD is a trademark of Oxford University Press

1   2   3   4   5   –   95   94   93   92

Printed in Canada by John Deyell Ltd.

Contents

Acknowledgements

All photographs were provided courtesy of Fondation Lionel Groulx, Centre de recherche Lionel Groulx. 1. André Laurendeau the ballet student, photograph by Albert Dumas. 2. Blanche Hardy and Arthur Laurendeau, photographer unknown. 3. Laurendeau and Ghislaine Perrault, photographer unknown. 4. With a friend at the countryside, photographer unknown. 5. En route to Europe, photographer unknown. 6. With Maxime Raymond and Henri Bourassa, photograph *La Presse*. 7. Speaking for the Bloc Populaire at the Jean Talon market, photograph by Lew McAllister. 8. At the Cercle Juif de la Langue Française, photographer unknown. 9. Interviewing Abbé Pierre, photograph by J. Marcel. 10. The Royal Commission on Bilingualism and Biculturalism, photograph Ville de Québec.

The endnotes attribute all material quoted from other sources.

Every effort has been made to determine and contact copyright owners. In the case of any omissions, the publisher will be pleased to make suitable acknowledgement in future editions.

Preface

André Laurendeau is a figure from Canada's past whose personality and thought have become more, rather than less, intriguing with the passage of time. During his life (1912-68) he was widely known in Quebec as a political editorialist for the French-language newspaper *Le Devoir*, although his nationalist activism and theorizing stretched back through the conscription crisis of the Second World War to the radicalism of the Depression years. English Canadians, on the other hand, became aware of him only in the 1960s, when as co-chairman of the Laurendeau-Dunton Commission he tried to define and promote a bilingual and bicultural Canadian identity. During that decade, when a gallery of colourful French Canadians—Jean Lesage, René Lévesque, Pierre Elliott Trudeau, Jean Drapeau—etched their images into the Canadian consciousness, Laurendeau was a less flamboyant presence. In the quarter of a century that has elapsed since his death, however, the different facets of his life story have aroused considerable interest because they so closely reflect the stages of French-Canadian nationalism's own emergence into the modern era. In addition, his thought-provoking writings, many of which attempt to plumb the depths of French Canada's cultural and political identity, have been published in several collections, in both English and French. Although a French-language biography of Laurendeau appeared in 1983, this is the first in English.

The Association of Canadian Studies supported this book in its research phase with an award intended to bring the achievements of important twentieth-century Canadians to the attention of their fellow citizens. The Association called pointedly for a biography of 'reasonable length', written for 'the general public'. I have tried to remain true to these original terms of reference, and in my struggles I owe a great deal to others. Madame Juliette Rémillard and her gracious staff at the Fondation Lionel Groulx in Montreal helped to guide me through the superb collection of Laurendeau materials assembled there. The staff of the Public Archives of Canada greatly facilitated my work with the forbidding collection of documents there pertaining to the Royal Commission on Bilingualism and Biculturalism as well as related collections on key figures.

The research assistance of John Bonar and Anthony Horton was most welcome, as was the work on translations provided by Suzanne Tomek and Kristine Jantzi. I am especially grateful to William Halverson for his excellent comments at various points in the manuscript's preparation. Mrs Gail Heideman was the indispensable person, as she has the habit of being, behind the production of the original text, and I was blessed with a very talented editor, Sally Livingston, who was also kind and calming. Finally, I would like to thank Brian Henderson of Oxford for his encouraging and patient support. With this sort of assistance there shouldn't be any errors, but those that have persisted are mine.

1

The Notable Tradition, 1912-1931

What is it that makes us French Canadians? . . . Is it our history? The vision
so often conjured up by the term is that of heroic figures: but I have more
fundamental things in mind, such as the accumulation of lived and shared
experiences which imprint a stable character upon a nation and those social
forces acting in time and space to build up our environment and thus condition our natures. This continuing aspect of history . . . finds its expression
in a national culture.

André Laurendeau, 1951[1]

At the Laurendeau house in Montreal's Outremont district, music was
always playing. Virtually everyone who has recalled the period of André
Laurendeau's youth, especially during the 1920s, has spoken of a home
filled with musical sounds. He remembered it that way himself: 'I was
born into an atmosphere of scales and arpeggios, of vocal exercises and
musical theory, of ballads and extracts from operas. . . .'[2] At five André was
made to sit and listen while his father Arthur sang the melodies of
Debussy, Ravel, and Mussorgsky, with his mother Blanche accompanying
on the piano. A close relative has described how the little boy's 'fluty'
voice could be heard passing from room to room, chanting the brooding
Latin phrases of Catholic hymns. As an adolescent he glued his ear to the
radio to pick up the 'crackling' new music on the Hits of the Week show
from New York—tin-pan alley songs such as 'Good Night Sweetheart'. In
spite of his father's warnings about mixing English words into the natural
rhythm of his French speech, he thought it 'chic' to memorize the lyrics of
raucous tunes like 'Yes We've Got No Bananas' as well as the latest jazz
creations. Besides, it was the only English he knew or cared to know, and
when relatives visited there were plenty of French-Canadian songs. In the
evenings classical music took over, either from the radio concerts André
listened to by the hour (with static as a perpetual accompaniment) or from
the parlour, where he and his mother took turns coaxing the old piano to

triumphs beyond its abilities. And then there was the day-to-day cacophony of youthful voices, breaking off and starting up again at a word from his father, a singing teacher of the no-nonsense, baton-tapping old school. In brief, it was a musical environment of devout and popular, traditional and modern, French and English influences that mirrored to a considerable degree the elements shaping the wider French-Canadian culture during the inter-war years.

In later life André frequently heard this culture described as outdated, the death rattle of a peripheral sub-group destined to be further marginalized by the forces of modernity in North America. Such an interpretation conjured up visions of the long-broken French culture of Louisiana or, at the very least, the scattered and dispirited Acadians. He feared such a development and fought to his dying breath against it. But he never did believe the negative, doomsday view of the French-Canadian past that it presupposed. Just as he always looked back on the musical bouillabaisse nurturing him in his parents' home as a mysterious factor that helped to mould his adult personality, so he believed French-Canada's past to be an inalienable and dynamic element of its present and future. Indeed, throughout his remarkable career as author, playwright, journalist, politician, and nationalist leader in Quebec, he was an always eloquent, sometimes wistful spokesman for what he called 'the active presence of the past among the living'.[3] This was the case, for example, during Quebec's Quiet Revolution in the 1960s, when a young generation of radical reformers dismissed French Canada's heritage as 'irrelevant'. Though sympathetic to the cause of reform, he used his position as editor of Montreal's French-language newspaper *Le Devoir* to caution against forsaking the best of French Canada's traditional culture. As one observer of his journalism aptly remarked: 'he established a context through constant reference to the past—a past in which, as he liked to make clear, he functioned as both participant and witness.'[4] It was in fact this deep historical consciousness, underpinning his symbiotic dual role as a man of action and of analysis, that made Laurendeau his generation's most respected interpreter of French Canada's national culture. And this in turn makes his biography a revealing study of how French Canadians, in Quebec especially, experienced the difficult transition from a traditional to a modern society.

It is not hard to understand, given his personal background alone, why Laurendeau had such great respect for the past. As he himself once explained, all the formative influences of his youth—familial, environmental, educational, and spiritual—focused on French Canada's traditional culture. It began with the French language. 'During this period of my life,' he wrote, 'we never heard another language spoken than French. . . . In daily life nearly everybody forgot they lived in North America.' His memories of childhood were inundated with images of French Canada's centuries-old heritage: colourful celebrations under the statues of well-remembered national heroes; annual festivals with hard-drinking men and peasant-garbed women spinning out the steps of two-hundred-year-old dances; black-frocked priests with thin wire spectacles reading the classics on park benches. He understood, of course, that memory is an imperfect witness, especially when recapturing childhood. 'The poetry of memory intervenes,' he noted; '. . . one embraces analysis—then the analysis does its mischievous work. It is found that we were not exactly as we have dreamed.' It was the poetry of memory, however, that he believed constituted the still living part of the past. This was the past that he tried to recapture in his charming novel *Voyages au pays de l'enfance*.[5] But even allowing for his tendency to idealize this period of his life, André was not far wrong in portraying himself as a child of tradition.

He was born on 21 March 1912 into one of the families known in Quebec as the 'notables'. Characterizing a certain elite social type located, for the most part, within the French-speaking professional middle class, the term conveys a general impression of the family's social position within the petty-bourgeois hierarchy from which the majority of French Canada's nationalist leaders came, prior to the Second World War. While the type still exists today, it does so only in isolated pockets, and has long since been robbed of its social potency, much as the small-town doctor and local clergyman have been bypassed as voices to be reckoned with elsewhere in North America. But in the first half of this century, as for much of the century before it, the notables exercised a powerful influence on the shaping of French-Canadian ideology.[6] They occupied important positions in education, in lay organizations of the Catholic church, in cultural bodies and in nationalist groups, and in most cases they could point to a long list of forbears who had done the same. They grew up knowing each other's families, attending the same schools, and, notwithstanding their many conflicts, sharing a general point of view. Above all they assumed, in an almost aristocratic manner, that it was both their birthright and their duty to maintain French Canada's national culture.

Nor was it merely a few quaint characteristics they wished to sustain, but a value system that they described as 'spiritual' and that was grounded—at least according to their mythology—in a Golden Age of the distant past when the language had been pure, the French laws unalloyed, the *canadien* family strong, and the Catholic church unchallenged in its moral leadership of society. From their bastions in Montreal and Quebec City, not to mention the professional enclaves of every small city and town, the notables had resisted challenges to this backward-gazing ideology—described in modern histories of Quebec as the *survivance* ideology[7]—for generations; like all true conservatives, they accepted change only when it had become overwhelmingly necessary. It was, furthermore, by weaving a seamless web of their own values and the broader cultural definition of the French-Canadian nation as a whole that the notables managed to perpetuate their role as indispensable nationalist leaders.

Perhaps because the Laurendeaus were not a prominent family but one firmly entrenched within the upward-striving second rank, they worked all the harder to emulate the lifestyle and uphold the values of the notables. This was particularly true with respect to the importance they attached to their rural background and to the emphasis they placed on preserving their extended family ties. The young André was encouraged to identify positively with the rural roots of which his parents spoke almost as if they were a token of the family's moral superiority. But he traced their lineage somewhat more prosaically: 'my father was a musician, my grandfather a country doctor in a small village. And then peasants and peasants until the first one who came from France'—this 'first one' having arrived in Canada in 1680. The 'small village' was Saint-Gabriel-de-Brandon, a farming community about seventy miles north of Montreal where the Laurendeau family had finally settled in the late 1800s after migrating from one rural region of Quebec to another over the preceding two centuries.[8] André's grandfather, Olivier, owned a house there in the early 1900s, out of which he operated a medical practice. André's father Arthur was born there, and it was the family's summer home throughout André's youth. On a Radio Canada broadcast many years later he reminisced: 'When I was young, I had the impression . . . of being lord of the place.'

He recalled how as a child he travelled to Saint-Gabriel by train each summer from Montreal's Lafontaine station 'with an exuberant joy in going and a romantic sadness upon returning'. Saint-Gabriel was the garden of his youth, and the eventful summers he passed there did a good deal more to nurture his idealistic impressions of rural life, it seems, than his parents' emphasis on the long, grey line of ancestral farmers. At age twelve he wrote home from school bemoaning the fact that 'the vacation has passed so quickly. Those fine swims I took in the lake; that fishing excursion I enjoyed so much; those pleasant picnics; in a word, that summer without equal.' It was only a short leap for his active imagination to paint the farmers toiling in the nearby fields, while he played, in the same arcadian hues. In fact, André's numerous letters and journal entries during adolescence were filled with romantic images of the 'noble peasant'. And when, as a young adult during the 1930s, he was taught by mentors like the historian Abbé Lionel Groulx that French Canada's very survival hinged on the perpetuation of rural virtues, he wrote even more lyrically on the subject. Looking back much later he observed:

> . . . I can truthfully say that we were taught an agricultural ethos, or more precisely, that we could not help but absorb it from the atmosphere around us. It often took the following form: agriculture was regarded as the only

completely normal and wholesome activity. Abandoning rural areas was considered immoral. By their very nature, big cities had something vaguely sinful about them.[9]

Long after he had abandoned his belief in French Canada's rural destiny, he continued to extol the wisdom and quiet confidence of the *habitant* as a model for all French Canadians. Describing his neighbours in Saint-Gabriel, he wrote: 'these people had the defects of all human beings . . . [they were] vain, quarrelsome, selfish . . . I'm not trying to paint utopia: But it was a milieu that felt sure of itself.' It was, moreover, a French-speaking environment: even the Eaton's catalogue had to be in French translation, or no one could have read it.

Although they lived in Montreal, André's parents endeavoured to keep up the extended family ties that were characteristic of their rural past. This is a normal tendency among first-generation urban families, but it was doubly important for the notables, who regarded the traditional family as French Canada's basic social structure. To maintain kinship ties, in their view, was also to strike a blow for national survival. André, an only child, was surrounded by cousins, second cousins, and suspected cousins who, together with their parents, thronged the Laurendeau household on special occasions in a mesmerizing tangle of comings and goings. At times it became too much for him. 'You're lucky to still have such a good impression of family gatherings,' he wrote to a friend in 1932. 'For me, it's become an obligation to prolong a dinner, to dance with aunts who dance very badly, and to listen to an indescribable din without wanting to make any noise myself.' As he grew older, however, his memory filtered out these negative impressions, and he wrote fondly about the advantages of the traditional family. Indeed, the problem of its survival in the face of French Canada's conversion to an urban value system was to become one of his most enduring concerns.

André grew up in Outremont, a district of Montreal—although he insisted it was much less so during his youth:

> I was born in a small town or so I would be inclined to say. As a matter of fact, the small town was Montreal. But then much more than now, the Metropolis was divided into districts, most of which were ancient villages that the city had annexed but not completely swallowed.

His part of Outremont was a drowsy residential area of two-storey houses, tree-lined streets, and quiet parks on Mount Royal. It was the tranquil refuge of Montreal's French-speaking professional middle class, and in those days, before it was invaded by *nouveaux riches*, immigrants including Hasidic Jews, and students—many of whom were English-speaking—it had a distinct character. Its inhabitants were self-consciously above what they saw as the obnoxious turmoil of the commercial world down the mountain, not to mention the working-class pell-mell farther on towards the waterfront. If they were forced to acknowledge the existence of these 'other' Montreals and, worse still, to descend into them in order to make a living, they could at least return to a place where the better things in life—manners, music, books—were still appreciated.

Although the Laurendeaus could not afford to live in one of the large, well-preserved older homes of the district, on Hutchison Street they were close enough to share in the rarefied atmosphere of the Outremont nota- bles—an atmosphere not so much of wealth as of tranquil solidity. It is not easily recaptured today, but personal memoirs and descriptions dating back to the 1920s do yield a composite picture. The atmosphere was most beguiling at twilight, when the soft notes of a piano or flute floated down from an open second-floor window to mingle with the tinkling of formal silverware from the dining room below. Beyond could be heard the voices of small children in darkening alleyways, calling softly back and forth. Through a parlour window a passerby could see heavy wooden bookcases with their compulsory burden of leather-bound classics and, just above them, a crucifix with its tiny red spot on the tortured side. And up around the shade of a floor lamp, in an amber halo of light, would almost certainly curl the pipe smoke of some lawyer-philosopher. In this Outremont of André Laurendeau's youth, there was still time to read history and liter- ature, to ponder religious mysteries, to savour the moments.

Outremont would remain André's home throughout his life, but it never influenced him more than in childhood and adolescence, when the world of the neighbourhood is often the only world we know. Although he freely acknowledged much later that it was an isolated bourgeois sanc- tuary, cut off from the throb and anguish of Montreal's economic and social mainstream, his most poignant recollections were of the unspoiled, self-sufficient French character of life there:

> The district, in the east end near Parc Lafontaine, offered all that was nec- essary to a child. . . .
> The remarkable thing [is that it was] located . . . 50 miles from the Amer- ican border . . . Neighbours, people you met in the streets, priests and pro- fessors and tradesmen: everybody spoke French. You were not handicapped because you did not know the English language . . . an English person would have felt completely lost.

Between them, Outremont and Saint-Gabriel provided Laurendeau with an unshakeable sense of his French-Canadian identity. He grew up con- fident that French Canada was more than just a cultural idea or an ethnic type sprinkled here and there. For him, it was a place where speaking French and having a sense of historical roots were the norm.

If André Laurendeau's family background and childhood environment both reflected the values of the French-Canadian notables, it was his father Arthur who was most responsible for incorporating those values in his upbringing. One of ten children, Arthur had moved to Montreal as a youth and studied singing while attending the classical college at Joliette. In 1908 he abandoned his law course and went to Paris for more advanced vocal training, where he fell in love with the works of the modern composer Claude Debussy—a passion he would pass on to his son. After returning to Montreal in 1910, he performed concerts with Léo Pol Morin, a pianist and composer who also had a taste for the moderns, and interpreted the works of Rodolphe Mathieu, another French-Canadian composer. These two family friends would become André's principal music teachers. Also in 1910 Arthur married Blanche Hardy, herself a concert pianist and a descendant of another long line of musicians. Her father, Edmund, owned a music store whose magical atmosphere André would later evoke in his fiction:

He is alone, and so behaving himself. A glance at grandfather, who . . . chats with a client. The child proceeds to inspect the musical instru ments. He remembers the word of warning: look, don't touch. Hands behind his back, he goes from case to case. He recognizes the beautiful full bodied shapes of the violin and cello but doesn't stop there: they are less mysterious, these instruments, since one has pulled a vibrating sound from their strings. Here on a garnet cloth are the clarinets, sober of line and colour. What is beautiful, what catches the eye, are the brass instruments: they look alive, the enormous tuba that would crush you, the cornet, and especially the slide trombone. 'Grandfather, can I try?' Yes, he can, from the corner of an eye, someone will be watching.[10]

In 1917 Blanche founded the César-Franck trio, and she played on the radio as a founding member of the 'Lady's Morning Musical Club' Except for teaching, however, she did not pursue her own career after marrying —the normal decision for a middle-class French-Canadian woman in that era. Instead she devoted herself to assisting Arthur's career, which included teaching in Montreal's normal schools, serving as organist and choirmaster at the Saint-Jacques Cathedral, and conducting the Montreal Orpheum Orchestra. In 1917 Arthur formed the National Society of Comic Opera, and over the years he put on several operas in Montreal.[11] No wonder, then, that André remembered music as the most absorbing aspect of his childhood. Recalling performances at 'a little Opera house in the east end of Montreal', he wrote:

I knew the melodies and the dialogue by heart. My father was in charge of voice. I used to attend performances where most of the soloists and all the chorus were amateurs. It would have been easy to sit back smilingly and demystify the whole performance. But each time it was pure magic, directed by my father's silhouette which I could distinguish in the dark orchestra pit. Somewhere down there in the blackness my mother played the piano and my maternal grandfather the bass—a real family enterprise.[12]

He was drawn into the family enterprise, primarily by his father, at an early age. Arthur gave very explicit instructions for his son's musical edification when, as a seven-year-old, the boy travelled with his mother to live in London, England, for a year; Blanche was to accompany her friend Sarah Fischer, an opera singer studying at the Royal Society of Music. Spending Christmas of 1919 in Paris, they attended the opera *Lakmé*, by Léo Delibes. Arthur must have been gratified to read his son's precocious commentary: 'Lakmé sang off-key in the first act, less off in the second, and not at all off in the third.'[13] His mother had already begun teaching him piano and introduced him to the major composers. Initially he was a poor student, detesting the Schmoll method he was trained by, and disliking Mozart and Bach. But 'the gods of music', to use his phrase, sent him a lively female cousin who convinced him that 'the piano is also music'. Thanks to his father he had an ear for the moderns, especially Debussy and Ravel, even before taking lessons. Instructors like Morin, who had known Ravel and who in 1927 organized North America's first Debussy festival, in Montreal, only reinforced this tendency.[14] André was soon composing some melodies and adaptations for the piano himself. Later, at twenty-one, he would compose an operetta, his friend Claude Robillard writing the libretto, with the title *L'Argent fait le bonheur*. Inspired by his love of jazz, it was performed in 1933, featuring the talented mezzo-soprano Jeanne Maubourg-Roberval.[15] Though his hopes for a musical career ended early on, in 1964 he would tell the Royal Society of Canada that whenever he thought about who he was, music came to his mind first:

> . . . considering my own life, I am able to conclude today that I fell first from music into literature, then from literature into action and journalism, without really knowing why. Yet in those obscure regions of the self where our true hierarchies of values are developed, the first word that springs out is music, and the first name Debussy.[16]

Although Arthur Laurendeau has been described by his friends and grandchildren as an enthusiastic and jovial spirit, his ideas were old-fashioned, and he was inflexible in his supervision of André's artistic, intellectual, and moral development. Though he enjoyed a good reputation and made a passable living from his musical career—one that even allowed him a certain entrée into high society—Arthur had hoped for much more. It had been his ambition to contribute something brilliant to the world of the arts, to add to French Canada's cultural legacy. When it became obvious that he was not sufficiently talented, and medical problems had developed,[17] he transferred his ambition to his son. He was convinced, long before André showed any such proclivity himself, that his boy would make a great contribution to literature. 'Do you know what I dream?' he wrote to the seven-year-old André, 'that you are a very educated man and that you write beautiful books. . . . If you are not a musician, I will not reproach you . . . I think rather that it is in literature that you will succeed. You have a very lively sensibility. . . .' Having planted the idea, Arthur was not one to let it germinate in mysterious ways. He hammered it home at every opportunity. André remarked later in life on the high level of literary expectation placed on him:

> My father didn't always know how to talk to children; he deliberately treated them as adults; thus he made me read the Iliad at age eleven in the Leconte de Lisle translation . . . as well as Le Cid, whose courage thrilled me. A little later I was horrified by Mademoiselle de Lespinasse, whose love letters my mother was devouring, and which she discussed at the table with her husband for interminable weeks, to be followed by months devoted to Balzac.[18]

Arthur was convinced that André would never attain any worthwhile goal without extraordinary self-discipline. In his traditional view of the father-son relationship, moreover, wherein customs like the paternal benediction were still fondly remembered, he considered it his duty to develop this quality through a rigorous stewardship. His correspondence suggests that he seldom thought of André as a child, but as an adult in the making. This is not to say that he never displayed affection; when André travelled with his mother to England, for example, Arthur's letters spoke lovingly of his little 'angel—with your wise, delicate smile and your little doe's eyes.' But those same letters were filled with stern instructions to the seven-year-old on how to control his passions and how to become learned and cultured. 'I always tell you the same things,' he wrote, a little self-consciously, '. . . to prepare you for a fine future as a vigorous, patriotic and Catholic man. . . .'

Nor did he leave any room for doubt that, in this triumvirate of virtues, Catholicism was the most important. Arthur regarded a son, much more than a daughter, as a special gift from God to be moulded spiritually for achieving the Creator's will on earth. He took care, therefore, to supervise his son's personal devotions closely, and well into his adult life André considered it normal to report to Arthur on how often he took communion or to consult him on which priest to select as his confessor. God, according to Arthur Laurendeau, was not a warm, friendly deity but a brooding punisher of transgressions. Everything hinged upon banishing evil thoughts. As Arthur explained it to eight-year-old André: 'God is all powerful and he has pity for little souls like you. . . . Avoid being disobedient, insolent and violent, because these are the things which to him are so bad—don't be afraid to try and improve your character.' A little later he noted that his own attitude wasn't much different from God's, for his love depended on André's behaviour: 'I love you more than . . . all pleasures, more than all happiness . . . art . . . intelligence, . . . more than myself . . . but I would prefer to see you dead than to see you wicked and vicious.' This, as we will see, was a moral training that would profoundly affect André's psychology in later life.

Not surprisingly, Arthur also believed that Catholic literature and philosophy were the best guides for André's intellectual development. Most of his own ideas were narrowly derived from the works of conservative French Catholic thinkers and he held up writers in this mould, like the ultramontane Louis Veuillot, for André to emulate. Uplifting works of French classical literature, particularly Corneille and Racine, and exemplary tales of pious knights like Le Cid were solemnly handed to André for Christmas, his birthday, and saint's day each year. They dominated the five-hundred-book library he owned by the time he was eighteen. Coupled with Arthur's endless haranguing, they filled him with religious idealism and made him abnormally concerned with repressing even the mildest intemperate urges in his own personality. As he wrote to his parents in 1923: 'I don't wish to say that I am a saint (you know that well anyway) but I wish to work at becoming one.' His model was Saint Francis Xavier, whose life he studied in every detail. Although he never considered becoming a priest himself, he was concerned well into his twenties with 'the idea that a good Catholic, who wanted to become better, ought to become a priest'. During his youth he consulted priests regularly on intellectual questions and he accepted their interpretations as final—for, as his father said, 'the priest's mission gives him a special authority'. No doubt Arthur was also primarily responsible for sowing the seeds of religious intolerance in his son. 'The innuendos about protestantism,' André wrote much later, 'though not numerous were not sympathetic. Talking of a protestant was talking of a stranger.' Jews, not surprisingly, fared even worse. For decades André could not conceive of a French Canadian who was not also a Catholic.

Arthur Laurendeau was a dedicated French-Canadian nationalist and worked from the earliest days to make André one as well. During the 1920s and '30s Arthur belonged to several nationalist organizations, including the Saint Jean Baptiste Society, and he wrote articles for nationalist journals. Between 1934 and 1937, he also edited one of those journals, *L'Action nationale*, which was to become important in André's life as well. Arthur particularly admired the right-wing French nationalist movement on which L'Action Nationale and its 1920s predecessor in Quebec, L'Action Française, were modelled.[19] 'With every mail delivery from Paris,' André recalled,

> my father communicated his enthusiasm . . . for the *Action française*, for [Charles] Maurras, Léon Daudet . . . and other stars of the monarchist heaven. This was how I became a monarchist before learning that my fervour was pointless, since a constitutional monarchy [like ours] could never glorify a Maurrist, and since in Canada the Crown was British.[20]

Arthur's writings demonstrate that he was an even more dogged follower of French-Canadian nationalist spokesmen like Henri Bourassa and Lionel Groulx. At the outset of the 1920s he was still under the influence of Bourassa's moderate nationalism, which emphasized mutual respect between the English and French in Canada. Thus he spoke not unenthusiastically to his son about the visit of the Prince of Wales to Canada in 1919, and when André was in England he urged him to study the great achievements of English culture: 'Try and listen as much as possible to beautiful music, look at the lovely paintings and the stately mansions, but see to it that your heart is in Canada, even when your eyes and ears are in London.' Like many French-Canadian notables, Arthur admired England much more than English Canada, which he viewed as a pale colonial imitation. But British imperialism was always the *bête noire* that stood in the way of genuine respect.

At this early stage, however, André was more influenced by Arthur's personal relations with the English minority in Quebec. 'My father had English students,' he noted at one point, 'and considered them like the others—except that it was harder to teach in English—but though he would not speak to me about it, I learned later that he had very solid reasons against the English group as such, reasons born of history.' Arthur was particularly concerned about preserving the French language from what he considered to be the mutilating effects of English and went to some lengths to protect his son in this regard. When André was in England, he instructed him to 'learn just enough English to love French better' and he sent an article to his wife that condemned bilingualism as destructive to the young. He added:

> You will see . . . the dangers of studying English at André's age. Without boasting, I had a premonition, even though I'm no pedagogue, that it is not good to fill a young person's head with too many words in two different languages. We need not worry if he learns a little English: but at this age, his intellectual formation would suffer badly from too much cerebral activity

When, on returning, André rapidly forgot all the English he had learned in London, Arthur was pleased, and took care thereafter to fight all English intrusions into the family's daily life. As André observed:

> The Bell Telephone Company was the occasion of the first practical lesson I received in patriotism. As there were no automatic phones, the operator asked, 'What number please?' Then my parents would act as if they did not understand: 'Pardon? Qu'est-ce que vous dites?' And if she repeated, 'What number please,' mother and father would insist, 'Parlez français Mlle.' To do only that during 20 years, 10 times a day, takes a lot of energy and solid conviction.

It is ironic but not astonishing, therefore, that André Laurendeau, the primary architect of official Canadian bilingualism, showed no inclination to learn English until his late twenties and could not speak it with any confidence until his forties. Although he met Americans from time to time at the fishing and hunting club near Saint-Gabriel, he knew few English Canadians and none intimately.

To what extent was André affected by his father's well-meaning but heavy-handed supervision? To answer this it is important to note that André was a delicate and sickly child with a personality that was naturally sensitive and introverted. He was not the type, in other words, who out of either stolid obliviousness or fierce independence rebels against adults. On the contrary, he exhibited a filial respect that even in his early adult life made him shrink from openly challenging Arthur. This respect was to play a key role in limiting the range of his intellectual growth during the early 1930s: he would have to leave the country, thereby removing himself from Arthur's direct influence, before a full flowering could occur. The situation was aggravated by the fact that he had no brothers or sisters; the closest he felt to another child was in his early teens, with a godson named Paul-André whom he rocked in his arms and entertained on the piano. The absence of siblings not only meant that there was no alternative target for his father's overbearing attentions, but deprived André of an intimate confidant for the exchange of views differing from or, at least, questioning Arthur's. A close associate from a later period in his life pointed out that André was always fascinated to learn what it was like for children to grow up in a large family, adding, 'I always suspected that what he lacked at the outset was a child's childhood rather than an adult's.'[21] Such considerations help to explain why he grew up striving always to meet Arthur's high standard without even asking if any other existed.

His mother was not much help in alleviating this pressure. She was an unusual woman, especially for that epoch, both in pursuing an independent and public musical career prior to her marriage and in embarking on adventures such as her year-long sojourn with André in London. It seems, however, that she was driven by the sort of demons that led her both to overprotect and to place great pressure on her son. She came from a family of disappointed marital relations, especially where her two sisters were concerned, and just before her marriage she herself was forced to cope with the sudden and humiliating arrival from Paris of Arthur's very pregnant lover. Apparently Arthur's brother paid the interloper a large sum to disappear and the marriage went ahead, but it scarred Blanche for life. Suffering from a severe asthmatic condition, she had always been high-strung and tormented; now she became jealous and overbearing as well. She had wanted many children, but André remained the sole object both of her attention and of her two childless sisters'. Blanche took the unusual step of having her son's bust sculpted at age eleven, perhaps in anticipation of his brilliant future, and he admitted that even after his marriage in 1935, when he went to Paris for two years, she wrote so persistently about missing him that it appeared she wanted to poison him against Europe. André's own son, Yves, has written that Blanche's influence undoubtedly played its part in his father's secretive disposition, his life-long struggle with guilt feelings, and his frequent bouts of agoraphobia. He and others have also speculated that it may have contributed to driving him towards a career in public affairs rather than in the music or literature for which he had so obviously been groomed—fields in which his dread of failure must have been severe.[22] Certainly there was no refuge from his father's long shadow in maternal love.

As one would expect, Arthur Laurendeau took pains to see that André's formal education reinforced the moral and intellectual precepts taught to him at home. André followed the prescribed educational path for a notable —a path illuminated by the Catholic-humanist pedagogical tradition that had been reproducing French Canada's elite for generations. This was a different education, in principle and in practice, from that found in English Canada or anywhere else in North America. It began for André in 1919, during the winter he spent with his mother in England. A tutor instructed him according to the curriculum of the Jardin des Enfants, a Catholic normal school in Montreal that was run by a teaching order of nuns, the Soeurs Muettes. Arthur explained to André in a letter what Sister Bernadette, the school's principal, expected of him that year: 'you should know your catechism up to the sacrament of penitence . . . arithmetic up to problems involving the four basic rules, and in French you should have some idea of what a verb is.'

From 1920 to 1923 André attended the Jardin des Enfants where the primary emphasis seems to have been on establishing a firm idea in each student's mind of how important discipline is to success. This was achieved in the curriculum proper by alternating lessons in languages, history, and geography with large doses of the catechism. Religious knowledge was reinforced by recitation and buttressed by endless repetition. As André recalled later:

> The nuns who taught me my catechism told me that my guardian angel stood invisible on my right, and the devil on my left. When temptations appeared, I remember practising an exercise both physical and spiritual, unknown to Saint Ignatius, which consisted of raining blows on the empty air—but the empty air to my left, where stood the enemy of mankind. The nuns, of course, had not intended any political undertones to their teaching.[23]

The sisters, it appears, did unto others as they had been done unto, severely punishing the most minor disobedience or laziness. Whether or not the children understood Catholic theology by the time they left school, there is no doubt that they could repeat lengthy passages from the Bible by heart. If nothing else, this training permitted the adult André to back up any point he cared to make with an appropriate biblical allusion.

While this period in his education was too early to permit many other conclusions, his report cards do show that he was precociously advanced in
literature—a mainstay of his adult intellectual life. They also reveal that
he was already launched on his life-long battle with mathematics. Referring dolefully to the latter, he told his parents: 'You know my weakness in
this subject; I don't know the basics of calculation; I fight with numbers
and I always lose.'

When he wrote these words, the battle was being fought at the
'classical college' of Sainte-Marie in downtown Montreal, where he was a
student from the age of eleven to nineteen. Although the classical college
system has gone the way of the notables, it hung on until the early 1960s,
and the influence of the last generation of French-Canadian leaders to bear
the unmistakable imprint of its training—Pierre Elliott Trudeau, Claude
Ryan, Jacques Parizeau—is still felt. The first colleges were established in
the reactionary climate of the early 1800s by Catholic orders either self-
exiled or expelled from post-revolutionary France.[24] Throughout their
history they were, with a few exceptions, strongly opposed to liberal
trends and dedicated to sustaining a conservative Catholic tradition.
Central to this aim was the conviction that a civilized society was always
led by an enlightened elite, ever alert to the spiritual and cultural needs of
the community. Hence it was expected that the best graduates of these colleges would go on to universities, which were even more elitist, to eventually become professionals, priests, and politicians. Those who were not
so successful—those whose formal education ended at the college—
often became the lesser lights and dutiful upholders of the tradition. The
graduates were encouraged to view themselves as rightfully privileged
and to fraternize with their college fellows throughout their lives—much
as graduates of private institutions do in English Canada. This was all the
more true if they had attended an elite college such as Saint Jean de
Brébeuf or Sainte-Marie.

Sainte-Marie was located in the eastern, French-speaking section of
the city and was operated by the Jesuit order. In the 1920s, when André
Laurendeau was a student, its curriculum and teaching methods faithfully
reflected the *raison d'être* of the classical college system as a whole. The
curriculum was based on the fundamental disciplines—theology, philosophy and classical languages—that for centuries had been the core of
Catholic humanist pedagogy, supplemented, though without much enthusiasm, by modern subjects like contemporary literature. It was simply
assumed that the most profound questions concerning the human predica-
ment had been posed and answered by the great classical philosophers,
particularly Catholic thinkers like St Augustine and especially Thomas
Aquinas, and the goal of a sound curriculum was to pass on their wisdom
to each new generation of students. A secondary goal was to acquaint
them with the best achievements of European civilization. Science was

taught in a rudimentary way and with a strong bias towards natural science. Although the social sciences were beginning to have an impact in the United States, they were unknown in the classical colleges and would remain so for decades. Industrial and commercial subjects, which were then making their mark in Ontario schools, were generally regarded at Sainte-Marie as a form of training that was best left to another, inferior level of education.

André's course of study closely reflected the main thrust of the curriculum. The subject areas were roughly the same from year to year and had titles like Great Literature, Rhetoric, Philosophy, Theology, and Syntax. He took Latin for eight years and Greek for seven. English, by comparison, was dropped after the second year. Much later, André commented on the cultural arrogance of his teachers:

> Our educators were sure of their superiority Their link with French culture gave them the conviction that they participated in the most perfect human culture—[which had] inherited the best of Greece and Rome. . . . [some days] we were told that we were America's Athens. True, the English possessed money, but we had the arts and culture and intelligence.

Optional subjects were most often in the creative arts—music, dance, and theatre. André frequently complained that he was not physically strong or adroit enough to participate in the vigorous playground activities also favoured by the Jesuits. He was one of those delicate, studious boys who are often harassed by their classmates. Earlier this sort of treatment had forced him to give up ballet lessons, which he took only at his mother's insistence,[25] to save himself from embarrassment at social occasions; as he observed ruefully years later, 'Opinion here in Quebec frowns on young boys taking classical dance classes'.[26] He was well into his twenties when he finally became reconciled to his physical weakness. 'I am always limited by my health, but it isn't a drawback: it prevents me from having great adventures in sport, but also from doing foolish things; I probably have the body best suited to my temperament. . . .'

The Jesuits' teaching methods were from the same 'tried and true' school as their curriculum. The Socratic dialogue of question and response towards the unfolding of a philosophic truth was the standard classroom practice. Correct answers were rewarded with more refined questions, and error was punished by that standby of the Soeurs Muettes, repetition. The development of logical thinking and interrogative probing was constantly stressed, along with the ability to express thoughts coherently with supporting facts drawn instantly from memory. These skills would play a vital part in the success of the future journalist. Courses in rhetoric, language, and method were intended to polish the delivery system for the higher thoughts of philosophy and theology. 'The method class,' he complained during his third year, 'is very hard, the most difficult, I think, of all.

... There is so much work to do, and above all it has to be done quickly: the latter is not my strong point.' Each student's writing ability was tested by constant practice and criticism. For instance, even though the school was only a few blocks from André's home, each month he was required to write his parents a long letter that was carefully scrutinized by a teacher. Referring to one of these letters as the 'antique', because his parents had already been told what was in it, he wrote sarcastically of the 'learned professor who must have something better to do than correct it'. At this point he was still too naïve to understand the practical value of this Jesuitical device. For those who attended Sainte-Marie, strict discipline was the order of every day. According to one of André's schoolmates, the students weren't even allowed to go to church with their parents on Sunday, but had to attend as part of the college in their much-hated black serge uniforms.[27] It was a stark change for André from the attention he had received as an only child, although the moral code was the same. As Denis Monière describes it, for the boarding student the school could be almost like prison:

> His life is henceforth regulated by a set of impersonal rules. He must submit himself to an abstract authority and a collective form of discipline. He is constantly under surveillance, from the study hall to the recreational yard, from the canteen to the chapel and dormitory, the priest is omnipresent. Isolation is virtually forbidden. The obsession with sins of the flesh perverts all human relations within the college, where mistrust and suspicion reign.[28]

As a student André performed well. His religious intensity, romantic ideals, and personal timidity dovetailed perfectly with the Jesuits' program. A fellow student who came to the college in the same year observed that 'he came out of an environment where it wasn't necessary to wait for the Jesuits to read Homer and Racine and Corneille. He was already very knowledgeable musically; he had what could be termed "culture" at the age of eleven or twelve.'[29] The one exception, it seems, was the study of Greek. His aversion for this subject began light-heartedly enough with comments like '*le grec est sec*'—'Greek is dry'—but as his grades plummeted he became more caustic: 'Greek: Never was a more difficult, irritating, discordant, dissonant, unloved language invented.' Nevertheless, he concurred fully with his teachers in his love of the classics and European culture, while holding North American achievements and most things modern in disdain. 'Europe . . . is overflowing with artistic monuments,' he wrote somewhat pretentiously to a friend, 'it constitutes the most gigantic effort of the human spirit to project itself outward . . . We have achieved almost nothing in this sense.' In another letter, near the end of his time at Sainte-Marie, he recommended dispensing with modern literature and history in favour of the classics: 'Repeat to yourself that you are in Paris and, trust me, immerse yourself in the classics. . . . Don't give in to a desire for what you think is originality, but is merely bizarre.'

Don't think that one can love the venerable tragedies only when one is past 40. I am 19, and I sincerely love them.'

The only modern history he considered worth studying at that stage was French-Canadian history. After standing second in this subject during his first year, he wrote home in words that were music to his father's ears: 'This is the subject in which I do best, I'm very interested in it. I want to know the history of my country in order to defend it when the time comes.' There could be no doubt that 'my country' meant French Canada alone. At Sainte-Marie he learned virtually nothing about English Canada, and even after completing his university studies he was forced to concede: '[I] read almost all that was available about Canadian history, by French-Canadian historians. But, to be frank, I did not completely read 3 books on [Canadian history] by English Canadian historians. This is not a rule, but I don't think I'm an exception.'

In 1962 Laurendeau pointed out how so much of French Canada's historical writing was centred on the earliest period of its history and how, in the young, it inspired a sense of romantic distinctiveness:

Here is a boy or a girl in their first years of high school. They study the history of their country, which begins with a century and a half of French regime. This boy and girl are French by culture and language and will identify themselves with the people of this period, which is a long struggle between French and English North America. Then come the last battles, all of which—except the most important one—are French victories. Certain individuals find these stories more exciting than a good hockey game. They know to what team they belong. At times, they could shout and burst into tears or into applause. The boy and the girl become these French generals, these French adventurers or missionaries, these French *coureurs des bois* or *habitants*, these soldiers or militia men. The final defeat will never become an accepted fact.[30]

During the 1920s the classical colleges in general and Sainte-Marie in particular were less militantly nationalist than they were to become in the following decade, but the Jesuits succeeded nonetheless in cultivating the notion that French Canada was, by virtue of its spiritual and cultural ties to Europe, isolated in North America. Father Thomas Mignault, whom André came to regard as his first nationalist mentor, even spoke of a future independent state of 'Laurentie'.[31]

The idea of French Canada as a society tied to the great cultures of Europe was reinforced in André's case by the intellectual elitism of his friends at Sainte-Marie—among them the poet Saint-Denys Garneau—who did their best to act out the role of European sophisticates in the grim college setting. Around 1927 they formed a literary club called the Cercle Crémazie,[32] which they talked about as if it were the equivalent of the great eighteenth-century French salons. They wrote and exchanged articles with an eye to publication and engaged in feverish discussions of the poems, plays, and novels they were working on. In 1931, André himself passed around a short play he had written entitled *Tenuto* (an Italian word meaning 'fragile', which in light of its reception was not inappropriate). Sometimes older friends like Robert Choquette and Rex Desmarchais, who would go on to have literary careers, came along to the Grille Restaurant on the avenue du Parc. As one member wrote later: 'We lived in a certain ferment, a fervour with respect to literature, to the word, to writing, to poetry and the uses one could make of poetry, to the novel, to the essay.'[33] The group was contemptuous of Montreal society's cultural banality: 'The ordinary people have only an intellectual snobbism,' André wrote, 'they are bourgeois at heart and prefer their cars and carpets to true artistic emotions.' While his thoughts on this subject would change, he always retained a preference for European literary and cultural models.[34] As his career increasingly propelled him into the hothouse of political and nationalist issues, moreover, he would often yearn for the quieter world of the creative arts—a world he periodically returned to. And even in his most stressful periods, he would keep alive the ties to the artistic community that began at Sainte-Marie.

The Jesuits viewed the activities of the Cercle Crémazie with a good deal of mistrust, suspecting its members of that worst of all sins 'unsupervised reading' as well as other nefarious activities. They also suspected that the group had been organized in direct opposition to their carefully controlled literary club, l'Académie France. This was, after all, still a time when the Catholic Index of forbidden books was taken seriously and works by writers like Mauriac, Gide, Proust, and Baudelaire were thought to be dangerous for young men. But while Laurendeau dutifully wrote the Bishop to obtain permission to read Montaigne, he could not resist the other books that members of the club obtained through a winking local bookseller.[35] According to Pierre Dansereau, who had come to Sainte-Marie in 1924 and was a fellow club member, the only thing he and André were guilty of was their passionate desire to write great literature. 'I think that if André had been able to write *Madame Bovary*, if I had been able to write *Les Hommes de bonne volonté*, we would have sacrificed everything else we might do in the course of our lifetime. This was what we wanted most at 17 and 20 years of age.'[36] Their growing frustration with the banality of life at Sainte-Marie became too much for the Jesuits. Expelled from the college just before their final exams, the two were required to employ the services of a certain Monsieur Sainte-Hilaire, who prepared students outside the classical college system for their baccalaureate exams. They passed nonetheless and were rather proud of having been singled out as rebellious spirits. They thought it a good sign for the future.[37]

To assess the influence of André's early education upon his character and career, one must keep in mind both its content and its instructional method. It is clear that his studies at the Jardin des Enfants and the

Collège Sainte-Marie reinforced the value system that he had been absorbing almost from the cradle. It was, on its best face, an education that cultivated a serious attitude towards personal intellectual growth and a respectful appreciation of cultural excellence. Both of these would be central to André's mentality throughout his life and would play an important part in his greatest achievements. On the other hand, in their preference for esoteric topics, remote in time and place, his teachers failed to inculcate in the young man a realistic awareness of the material and social world around him, and this was a shortcoming that would require a mighty struggle in later life to redress. As he confessed with respect to the onslaught of the Depression, 'I was completely unaware of the economic problem.' Furthermore, the unremitting stress of his clerical educators on inner discipline, moral uprightness, and duty—which they regarded as the correct training for those destined to become the elite—placed enormous pressure on his already fragile personality.

During his final few months at the Collège Sainte-Marie, Laurendeau experienced the first symptoms of a nervous breakdown. Of course it wasn't called that in 1931. In Quebec, as in most of Canada, psychology and psychiatry were still considered to be among the exotic, if no longer dark, sciences. They had their proper place in institutions, out of sight, but there were few practitioners among the populace at large, and the language associated with neurosis and psychosis -repression, paranoia, inferiority complex—had not yet percolated downward into common parlance. Emotional problems, especially for the rigidly Catholic notables, were seen as spiritual deviations and when they were spoken about at all, it was in the language associated with prayer, will power, and morality. Thus in the spring of 1931, when André began to lose interest in his studies and to slip into a morbid lethargy, he was instructed to see a priest and to work harder each day at developing the 'muscles of the will'. When this approach failed and some more worldly explanation was sought, he was sent to a dentist to have several teeth removed on the suspicion that his body was poisoned. Meanwhile the weight loss, migraine headaches and depression, which would plague him at various times through his life, only worsened. 'A sea of anguish,' he wrote as late as 1933; 'I find myself the way I was on certain days last year and through the terrible summer before. Anguish: everything is heavy and it goes on for days and days . . . to do anything seems impossible. All things appear long, endless, heavy.'

Arthur Laurendeau became more and more concerned, as well as impatient. He could not understand how such an intelligent and sensitive young man, so obviously destined for a leadership role, could be brought low by 'a bout of nerves.' He suspected, moreover, that at least part of André's depression could be attributed to the pangs of thwarted love. There was indeed a close parallel between the most severe attacks and particularly frustrating episodes in André's ardent courtship of Ghislaine Perrault. The courtship had begun at a relative's Christmas party in 1928, when he was sixteen and she just fourteen. From that moment until their marriage in 1935, André, the romantic idealist in all things, had eyes for no one else. Ghislaine, however, was the daughter of Antonio Perrault, a prominent lawyer who was a professor of law at the Université de Montréal. The Perraults were a clear cut above the Laurendeaus in the finely stratified hierarchy of the professional middle class and, still more to the point, Antonio Perrault had no use for the gaunt, dreamy-eyed youth who seemed to be constantly under foot. At first he tried to discourage André by imposing a strict code of conduct on his daughter: orders were issued, for example, that all of the lights in the house were to be on any evening young Laurendeau was about. When these measures failed, Monsieur Perrault sent Ghislaine to complete her education in Paris. She studied there for several winters, but her tenacious Romeo wrote unfailingly. Some of them running to twenty-five pages, the letters were tireless in urging her earliest possible return. Monsieur Perrault soon reached the end of his rope, and in an explosive confrontation he accused André of being a feckless dreamer who started many things but finished none. Adding that he was convinced André would not have a job until he was at least thirty and therefore could not support a wife, he forbade all further contact with Ghislaine. 'Your door is henceforth closed to me,' André wrote plaintively to his beloved, 'you are to stop writing me, if you obey.'

It is worth noting here that André's view of love, marriage, and women in general was firmly rooted in the role-oriented middle-class Catholic thinking of French-Canadian tradition. This was one element of his outlook that would be slow to change. As late as the 1950s he wrestled with the implications of the post-1945 sexual revolution and feminist-inspired reforms. As his creative writing in that period would reveal, he had dark feelings about certain types of domineering and/or jealous women. In fact, it was probably the challenge of trying to understand his 'liberated' daughters and his coming to grips at last with certain religious doubts during the 1960s, rather than some intellectual insight or broad social transformation, that finally converted him, and even then never totally. But if his thinking did adjust over time, in 1931 he was firmly in the grip of the 'pedastalizing' influence of Catholic teaching and chivalric literature with respect to women. He was certain that just one woman could be his perfect mate, a creature of remote high-mindedness, the ideal of the troubadour songs, whom it was his duty to adore and protect. He played down, for the moment, the third traditional male responsibility, the one that was most important to Monsieur Perrault: namely, to support.

André's tendency to idealize Ghislaine was heightened by his lack of experience with other women. He had no sisters and there were few young women in his masculine circle of classical college dilettantes. In addition his shyness had contributed to what was almost, if not quite, a reputation for avoiding the opposite sex. While he was a fine dancer—his ballet lessons had not been entirely in vain—and was known to play a sad tune late in the evening that attracted the more romantically inclined girls, he also had an aloofness about him, a reticence that made it difficult to break the ice. Thus to him Ghislaine was not just 'a' woman, or even 'the' woman. She was woman. To lose her would be to lose, almost before starting, a vital cornerstone of his future—his life-long companion, the mother of his children, the faithful supporter of his endeavours. Was this not, after all, the role that his mother played in his father's life? It goes almost without saying that there was no place for raw sexuality in his conception of love. Though seemingly endless, his overripe love letters rarely went beyond a few sighing references to some 'red pyjamas' to convey a hint of physical yearning. He sublimated all of those feelings by punctuating his letters with phrases from the love songs he listened to ten or twelve times over in order to get the most syrupy parts down pat — 'sweet and lovely', 'cheerful little earful', 'now that you're gone'. André flew into a rage, on the other hand, when Ghislaine dared to attend a dance in Paris. Holding himself up as a model, he noted his own refusal of an offer from some friends to visit a prostitute. He urged Ghislaine to regard their love as having the sanctity of a spiritual cause. 'Do you see, my dearest,' he explained, '. . . our love must be very pure, very detached; it must be our light and must sustain its flame in God.'

Yet another cause of André's severe depression in 1931—and one of even greater long-term significance—was his obsessive concern over his personal future. In this context the word 'career' would be too narrow. Apart from the pressure exerted by Antonio Perrault and in spite of the Depression, there was no need for him to find a job or make money. In fact, he would continue to show up on his father's tax return as a dependent until 1937, when he was twenty-five, married, and a father himself. The Laurendeaus, like most of the notables, regarded education as a good deal more than school achievements leading to a career path. One studied in the classics, the arts, and religion whether or not one happened to be at school. It was assumed, for instance, that André would not actually consider a long-term job until he had attended university and travelled to France and the other cultural centres of Europe. This 'grand tour', which the notables saw as a kind of polishing exercise, had been part of his father's education and would naturally be part of his too. Add to this André's personal conviction that his intellectual growth was a private responsibility that should continue throughout his life, and it becomes apparent that he was not worried about a vocation in the conventional sense. Rather, his obsession had to do with how and in what field he would make his great cultural contributions to French Canada. This, we have seen, had always been the not-so-hidden agenda of his father and his elitist educators.

Initially he believed he would make his mark in the field of music. Besides the obvious influence of family background, his teachers had convinced him that he had special gifts. At age thirteen he informed his mother: 'I think I have definitely decided on my future profession; I will devote myself to music.' He proposed dropping out of college, the way his father had abandoned law, but his parents persuaded him not to. For a year or so he spent every Saturday afternoon entranced as his teacher Léo Pol Morin introduced him to an ever more fascinating repertoire of modern composers.[38] In his letters home he spoke of 'my regime—my piano and my studies' and joked about eschewing the violent games of the playground in favour of piano or organ practice. At nineteen he was good enough to be invited to play as a guest recitalist for radio concerts. But in 1931, that year of so much disillusionment, he began to doubt his ability to go farther. He was at a loss to explain this himself, but he noted that Morin's interest in him seemed to decline.[39] He complained that his technique was flawed and was unlikely to improve even with more work; his fingers did not have the necessary delicacy. His son Jean, a clarinetist with the Montreal symphony, has pointed out that his father often admitted he never applied himself to technique; as André wrote, 'If I didn't become a musician, it was because I didn't work at the scales. I would have liked to become a musician without having to go through the technical apprenticeship.' But Jean believed there was another reason too: that André always responded to and wished to preserve the mystery he felt in the music, and thus avoided those aspects involving analysis: 'Beethoven's music was not a subject of analysis for my father, it was an active force. Debussy's music had nothing of the cultural flower about it, it was the air he breathed. . . .'[40]

About this time, André shifted the focus of his ambition to writing about music. As a student he had submitted a few articles on jazz. These efforts led his friend Saint-Denys Garneau to invite him to write an essay on Bach for Garneau's radio show. 'It's a corvée,' André explained, 'to which I would never submit myself; to study someone I hardly know and whose work I don't like. I accepted this time because it is a beginning, humble and honourable, of a reputation.' Later he prepared and read an essay on his favourite composer, Debussy, for radio station CKAC. The fourth in a series, it called for him to demonstrate certain points on the piano. He did it in spite of his depression and with great frustration. 'Tomorrow's broadcast worries me,' he wrote in February 1932, 'I practise a prelude or write a page of my talk and I'm all in a sweat, incapable of going any further.' After the broadcast, when his parents told him that his was the best in the series, he was only half appeased; 'I . . . played, without any style . . . this dear old master who has been my favourite since my first stirrings of musical emotion.'[41] It was one of his earliest experiences in broadcasting, and, after complaining that his voice whistled, he prophesied that he would never succeed in that field. A few weeks later he was asked to give a talk about Beethoven at the Salle de Saint-Sulpice. Once again morbid thoughts contended with his high hopes: '. . . all human undertakings are so unstable—I have already had sad experience of this—that I am trying not to get needlessly excited.' This time the illustrations on the piano and violin were strongly performed by a professional trio and his spirits afterwards were almost buoyant. He titled the lecture 'Beethoven, hero-musician' and his son Jean has speculated that music alone, during this dark period, could fulfil his idealistic yearnings.[42]

André's spirited defence of Debussy against the criticisms of Lucien Parizeau in the Montreal newspaper La Patrie impressed Parizeau so much that he invited the precocious upstart to write a regular critique of the Montreal symphony's Sunday concert series. This was a breakthrough that brought André to the attention of Montreal's musical community. 'I notice, a little amused,' he wrote, 'the change in the artists' behaviour towards me . . . since I began writing musical criticism for La Patrie. I exist . . . not only as papa's son, but as myself.' Soon there were more offers, among them one to become choirmaster at Villeray. But the door to a musical career slammed shut as quickly as it had opened. Requests to give radio recitals soon stopped, chiefly because he didn't play well enough. And after only a few months he was dismissed from La Patrie for some particularly cutting remarks he made about the predominantly English-speaking business sponsors of the Sunday concerts. As his confidence crumbled, he mocked his own ingenuous assumption that someone as young as he could have anything worthwhile to say about a Beethoven, or that he possessed the talent to achieve something truly extraordinary.

Although André's depression lasted off and on for several years, the summer of 1931 was an especially low point. He stayed in his room for weeks and barely spoke to anyone. Whether he contemplated suicide is unclear, but his letters were black with despair. 'In short,' he wrote in July, '. . . there is an age when it is very difficult to be oneself, and . . . this age is troubled and causes tremendous suffering.' It requires no deep psychological analysis to establish that his was a crisis of runaway idealism confronting the harsh world of reality. His introverted and serious personality was cracking under the weight of his own Olympian expectations, in addition to those placed upon him at home and at school. As his son Yves later described him at this moment: 'Only son of a father whose resonant voice, impressive bearing, and noble words made him a difficult model to emulate, and of a demanding, possessive mother who, moreover, placed enormous hopes in him, Laurendeau [passed] from a too-solemn childhood [into] a depression that lasted two years. . . .'[43] He survived this crisis, but its effects on his character were permanent. For example, while he would always have a witty sense of humour, his smiles were quick and furtive, and even as a young man he had the look of someone bearing more than his share of the world's burdens. Nor would he ever again be free of wrenching self-doubts. In fact, it was his anxiety on this account, more than the joy of work or discovery, that often drove him to labour beyond the limits of his endurance. No matter how carefully he weighed an issue, he was seldom confident in his conclusions, because he was always concerned that some vital aspect, some important qualification, still had to be taken into account. It was partly for this reason that, in the 1960s, he could never quite embrace separatism, nor fully approve of federalism. But if his angst-driven scruples were at times a curse, they also helped to keep him open to divergent views and to make his reflections on any issue a *tour de force* of analysis.

As for his future role as a nationalist leader, we have seen that Laurendeau's childhood and adolescence were shaped almost exclusively by the customs and the *survivance* ideology of traditional French Canada. His family background and petty-bourgeois social status, his father's iron ethics and conservative nationalist beliefs, the rarefied environment of Outremont and a Catholic humanist education—these were just a few of the influences that combined to imbue him with the precepts that had served the interests of Quebec's notables so well for so long. It was a formation that gave him confidence in French Canada's viability as a society. Even later, when he came to see that this viability had been undermined long before the 1920s by Quebec's urban-industrial revolution, and that the notables' ideology was both class- and culture-bound, he would not surrender all the old values. He would strive instead to bridge the gap between fathers and sons, to reconcile tradition and change. And one could often detect in the lingering melancholy of his mature thoughts a nostalgia for the relative simplicity and coherence of his youth, as well as its facile certainties.

2

Nationalism and Separatism, 1932-1935

Who are the citizens of our country? Is our nationalism designed to bind together Canadians, Frenchmen, or French Canadians?

* * *

Not simply Canadians. As soon as we begin to investigate the meaning of that word, it becomes clear that the 'Canadian nation' is nothing but a myth invented by the Fathers of Confederation. There is no such thing as a Canadian nation.

* * *

Our nationalism springs from the desire that our French-Canadian—or Laurentian—nation should fulfill its own truth completely, and embrace its own natural vocation, thus preparing itself for its supernatural mission.

André Laurendeau, *Notre nationalisme*, 1935[1]

The Gésu Hall on rue St Denis in Montreal was a familiar rallying place for French-Canadian nationalists during the inter-war years, much as the Paul Sauvé Arena has been since the 1960s. On the evening of 19 December 1932 the hall was packed with more than 2,000 people. Most of those on the platform and in the front rows were well-dressed professionals; petty-bourgeois notables who were used to occupying the front pews in church. Although the Depression was at its hollow-eyed worst on the east-end streets all around the hall, this crowd had not come to hear outraged proposals for radical economic reform. It had gathered instead to listen as the leaders of Quebec's young generation repeated time-honoured nationalist maxims about French Canada's cultural and political oppression with fresh enthusiasm. Particularly interesting was a serious-looking young man, in a baggy, narrow-lapelled suit, black shoes, and clashing white socks. He was the keynote speaker. At twenty André Laurendeau had already acquired the dark pouches under his eyes, the sensitive, melancholy expression around his mouth, and the habit of leaning forward intently through wisps of his own cigarette smoke that would capture his audiences' attention throughout his public-speaking career. He had recently helped to organize a militant nationalist organization called Jeune-Canada at the Université de Montréal. This was its first public rally, and he had been chosen both to write its manifesto and to read it to the crowd.[2]

Laurendeau did not disappoint the audience or the older nationalist leaders, like Armand Lavergne and Esdras Minville, who were with him on stage. He had gained a little experience in broadcasting, thanks to his short-lived musical career, and had learned to control his high-pitched speaking voice to the point where its periodic quaverings came across as a kind of sincere punctuation. By all accounts the tone he struck on this occasion was one of controlled but deeply felt anger. And the text of the manifesto matched this tone. It combined ringing denunciations of French Canada's traditional enemies both inside and outside Quebec—English Canadians, foreign trusts, and politicians, to name just a few—with a spirited call for the youth of the 1930s to inject an uncompromising new energy into the nationalist cause. On the matter of representation in federal institutions, for example, the manifesto stated:

> We are French Canadians; we constitute almost a third of the population of Canada, nearly three-quarters of Montreal, and four-fifths of the province of Quebec. We live in a Confederation, a political regime set up in 1867 in order to safeguard certain features of the various provinces. One particular feature, the existence of French Canadians, was indeed one of the main motivating reasons for the establishment of the Canadian Confederation. This was the aim of the Fathers of Confederation, and we do not intend to let it be distorted. We wish our own people to be adequately represented in the civil service. In some federal departments, particularly, we are determined to be content no longer with the crumbs that have been thrown our way so far, with purely subordinate positions, very often under superiors imported from Britain. We pay our share of taxes—it is our right to demand fair representation within all federal ministries. In Montreal, the third largest French city in the world, we shall no longer tolerate superiors of another nationality, especially if they are unilingual. This kind of servile position would never be tolerated in any English city in the entire empire.[3]

When the meeting ended and the audience shuffled out past the hungry poor in the nearby streets and up Mount Royal towards their quiet, well-ordered neighbourhoods, they could feel satisfied that yet another generation of French Canada's elite had mastered the nationalist catechism. The chant of *survivance*, repeated for nearly a century, would be heard in Quebec still. The nationalist newspaper *Le Devoir* said as much, while drawing attention to André Laurendeau as an up-and-comer, a young leader to be watched. Looking back later, Abbé Lionel Groulx, the guru of young nationalists during the inter-war period, went further: 'André Laurendeau [was] the hero of the evening; he [gave] the most moving speech, to the most applause.'[4] For his part Laurendeau shed tears of joy with the other Jeune-Canada members over the enthusiastic reception they had received. He could not have foreseen that this, his first public appearance, had launched him on what would turn out to be a thirty-six-year odyssey as one of French Canada's foremost nationalist spokesmen. What he did realize, however, was that he had found a cause that gave his life new meaning. As he pledged in his private journal: 'Ghislaine and I would give our lives for our national and religious ideal.'

How did Laurendeau, the delicate and sickly youth of his school days, the frustrated, love-struck musician on the edge of mental collapse, come to be swept up in this radical French-Canadian nationalist movement? We have seen, of course, that his family background and education had cultivated a strong loyalty to traditional French-Canadian values. The aim of this formation, both in his father's eyes and in his own, was to make a distinguished cultural contribution to his people. But while this helps to explain his positive aspirations with respect to the French-Canadian identity, it doesn't account for his militancy towards English Canada. His life had unfolded to this point in an isolated but confident French milieu. Outremont, Saint-Gabriel, the Collège Saint-Marie, the homes of his dilettante friends —all represented an elitist enclave formed from the upper strata of one of Canada's two solitudes. His personal anxieties, though severe, were contained within this environment, and the kinds of choices they involved— a musical or a literary career; Ghislaine or desolation— took little account of the outside world. He had shown no interest in Canadian politics and knew next to nothing about English Canadians, not even those living practically next-door in west-end Montreal. Until now, in fact, he and his friends had reserved the bulk of their scorn for their own culture, which they regarded as pedestrian. Their attention was focused on the splendours of Europe; that was where they wanted to go. There were exceptions, like Pierre Dansereau, who were interested enough in North America to want to explore it, like the voyageurs of old, but André and the others generally regarded it as impenetrable frontier.

And yet it was always there — a vast continent where another language was spoken and values were known to be different. Years later André tried to explain the impact that this vague awareness had on the formation of a young French Canadian's sense of identity:

When you are brought up inside the community, you speak the language of your parents. The family speaks French; so does the street in most of our cities; so do your schoolmates and professors. At some moment you meet l'autre—the Other One; he speaks English. The experience may be good or bad, but it gives you the feeling of your own identity. From now on, you know that you belong to a group and to a tradition. Then, if you go more deeply into the problem, you learn that you belong to a culture. You understand that the group is small, the tradition very old, and the culture great. This is why Quebec is not a province like the others.[5]

If English-speaking North America had not caused Laurendeau any undue anxiety thus far, that was probably because for the most part it had penetrated his world only surreptitiously, in the form of American material culture. Like everyone else he was attracted to the goods produced by American inventive genius—the phonograph, the automobile (or as he and his social set preferred, the 'machine')—which poured into Quebec in the consumer explosion of the 1920s. When he discussed Flaubert and Proust with his friends at the local student haunts, he ate hot dogs and drank pop. In fact, during one of his clandestine meetings with Ghislaine —which, thanks to the complicity of her brother Jacques Perrault, often took place after church or music lessons—André introduced her (with a worldly shrug no doubt) to the titillating decadence of Coca Cola. He was also addicted to aspects of American popular culture, especially radio broadcasts featuring music. He complained bitterly whenever his New York-based concert series or radio jazz sessions were interrupted by that latest Canadian cultural innovation, the Saturday Night hockey broadcast. Greta Garbo films at the Seville cinema and new American dance numbers were favourites of his as well. Archbishop Villeneuve may have forbidden Quebec City's youth to indulge in this sort of dancing,[6] but in Montreal André Laurendeau did the charleston. It wasn't until later in the 1930s that he began to write about American popular culture as a serious threat to French Canada's survival.

André's consciousness of the English-Canadian threat, by contrast, while far from acute was nevertheless established. His father's involvement in the Action Française movement of the 1920s meant that prominent nationalists of Arthur's generation—Groulx, Armand Lavergne, Edouard Montpetit, Olivar Asselin—came often to the Laurendeau home. While André conceded that his father had a strongly ideological viewpoint, he also claimed that this was more the product of enthusiasm than of a doctrinaire temperament, and that Arthur did not browbeat him into sharing the same perspective.[7] This comment appears somewhat ingenuous when one takes into account the susceptibility of a young boy to his father's 'enthusiasms', particularly when they were reiterated with such unremitting and unimaginative uniformity. But it is nonetheless true that, until his own nationalism had been aroused, the atmosphere of nationalist rhetoric and the daily rituals designed to hold the English language at bay were mostly background noise for him—persistent to be sure, but largely preconscious in their influence. They led him to youthful acts of defiance rather than an articulate anti-English prejudice. Most often these acts were aimed at the symbols of British imperialism in Canada. He recalled, for example, that at age fourteen he and a chum were visiting a nearby convent when the governor-general showed up. When they heard the fanfare for 'God Save the King', they raced to find a bench rather than stand at attention. On another occasion, more sharply etched in his memory, he was in Westmount when a solemn military entourage passed, on its way to honour the dead of the First World War. When the anthem started up this time, he kept his hat on. A middle-aged man with a cane touched him on the arm and motioned for him to remove it. Instead he pushed it farther down, almost to his eyes:

> It was, I remember, my first bowler hat after wearing a boy's cap and I rather liked it. We had the look of two defiant dogs, both very pale, getting ready, despite the difference in our ages, to go at each other. I confess that deep down I was afraid, he seemed like an old soldier; he was, however, too much of a gentleman to thrash me. We just stood there detesting each other, three feet apart, until the song ended, and of course that took forever. When . . . I estimated that my dignity was intact, I left. We didn't have to ask what our maternal languages were to know who we each had been dealing with. Later I told myself: this man was perhaps honouring his son killed in the War and I behaved like a boor. . . . [But] God Save the King . . . was an anthem that symbolized subjection to a foreigner; in the end one doesn't sing to the nation with the anthem of another country.

It wasn't until Laurendeau enrolled at the Université de Montreal and became a devoted follower of the historian Lionel Groulx that these sullen occasional acts of protest were transformed into allegiance to a full-fledged nationalist creed. Nor did he quite grasp that a contributing factor in this change was the externalizing focus provided by nationalism. Involvement in the cause offered relief from his personal problems, the way music had sometimes done, by fixing his attention outside himself. None of this was apparent, however, at the outset of his university career, which began with the same dismal prospects that had characterized his final days at Sainte-Marie. After graduating *cum laude* in 1931 he announced that he was relieved to be moving on to university. But the almost immediate return of his psychological depression and deteriorating health forced him to drop out that autumn. The same sequence recurred in 1932 when he left in November. On the latter occasion he wrote matter-of-factly in his journal: 'have to give up my year; Ghislaine is taking the news very well.' Finally, in September 1933 he enrolled in the *Lettres* degree program, where he stayed until his graduation in the spring of 1935. He chose *Lettres* over law, unlike the majority of his classical college friends, because he wanted the broadest possible intellectual exposure to help prepare him for his vaguely defined 'writing career'. The decision involved overcoming his aversion to parts of the curriculum, as well as negative recollections of Sainte-Marie: 'To drop literature, wouldn't that be half weakness on my part[?]. Wouldn't I be giving in, almost unconsciously, to the profound distaste that my Greek courses inspired?'

Unfortunately, his fears on this score were confirmed, and he considered dropping out again in November 1933 on the grounds that he found the majority of his courses unstimulating. As one of his less precocious friends would later observe, Laurendeau had arrived at university having already studied much of the curriculum's material, particularly where French literature and philosophy were concerned.[8] André was confident he could organize a better course of study on his own—which was, after all, what he had done the previous two years. He declared a fifteen-day 'retreat' during which he consulted with family and friends as to what he should do. Ghislaine supported him, writing in her diary on 21 November: 'He had a conversation yesterday with his parents, and he realized that he is wasting almost all his time at the university. Perhaps he could study on his own. I agree with him, and encourage him to do so.' His father, however, worried that he would not be adequately prepared for study in France, while M. Perrault suggested—likely through gritted teeth—that he should finish at least one thing he had started. In the end, André compromised, remaining enrolled but following his own plan of study. He attended only the classes he found interesting, which according to another friend were few and far between.[9] Nevertheless he was zealous in his attendance at the lectures of visiting French intellectuals like Jacques Maritain and Etienne Gilson. What he lost in structured learning he compensated for by eclecticism. As he put it: 'You understand that my plans are not precise . . . I look around me and I take whatever I can: interesting characters, slightly faded memories, beautiful landscapes, I try to capture it all.'

But by this time he had already fallen under the spell of Groulx, whose courses in Canadian history more than exceeded his expectations while nurturing in him a rising sense of outrage at the treatment of the French-Canadian minority throughout Canada's past. Until the autumn of 1932, when he and Ghislaine enrolled together in Groulx's course on the 'Union of the Two Canadas, 1841 to 1867', Laurendeau's familiarity with the nationalist interpretation of French Canada's history was sketchy at best. To that point his views had been based less on intensive reading than on his father's trenchant opinions. Thus when Ghislaine observed that she didn't think much of a recent, laudatory biography of Sir Wilfrid Laurier, he responded that her judgement was correct: '[Laurier] was a false great man, a clever politician who was unable to give any impetus to our politics, who was a disaster for French Canadians in the West, and who was responsible for our participation in the war. I got these views from father, and I think they are well founded.' Arthur Laurendeau, whose views were totally derivative, had undergone a conversion during the 1920s, away from Henri Bourassa's historical vision and towards Groulx's more aggressive viewpoint. As André recalled in 1963: 'My family were Bourassists of long-standing who later came under the influence of Lionel Groulx,' adding, 'I . . . followed Abbé Groulx's history courses and [was] marked by his thought far more than by Bourassa's.'[10]

This distinction is important, not only as an explanation for the militancy of Laurendeau's debut as a nationalist, but as a point of tension in his thinking about French Canada's past throughout his life. For those looking at Quebec from outside, the significance of nationalist theorists like Bourassa and Groulx can be difficult at first to appreciate. Intellectuals involved in explaining the meaning of the past to a minority people often have a much greater cachet among that minority's intelligentsia than is generally the case with those performing a similar function for majority peoples. Minority status is frequently the single most important issue in the present that requires explanation for the members of the group and, depending on the theory the latter adopt, everything from personal choices to political attitudes can be affected. At the same time, minority intellectuals often choose, or are forced, to play a more active role in the current affairs of their group. While Bourassa and Groulx were not as widely known among the French-Canadian masses, in the decades before the Second World War, as Sir Wilfrid Laurier, for example, their ideas became current among an important cross-section of the elite and were considered a starting point for discussions among nationalists. At various points in Laurendeau's long career, his views were closely associated with those of both Bourassa and Groulx, by himself as well as by others.[11] By the 1960s, moreover, his name came to be added to theirs as a third twentieth-century nationalist luminary. To fully comprehend his important role as theorist, then, the differences in historical perspective between Bourassa and Groulx must be considered.

Though he was not a historian, Bourassa had written extensively about French-Canadian history in his political pamphlets, in nationalist tracts, and in the pages of the newspaper he founded in 1910, *Le Devoir*.[12] His interpretation, like that of virtually all nationalist historians since F.X. Garneau in the 1840s, stressed the epic struggle of a conquered people to survive. But he did not attribute the success of this struggle solely to French Canada's vigilant defence of its identity. For Bourassa, survival also owed much to a series of hard-won compromises, based on enlightened respect, between Canada's two founding peoples.[13] Sustaining this mutually distinct but tolerant cultural duality was, in his view, the lesson of history and the best guarantee of French Canada's future. But the First World War and the crisis of conscription dealt hammer blows to this idealistic formula, just as they compromised the reputations of French-Canadian federalist politicians such as Laurier. Disillusioned nationalists turned during the 1920s to Abbé Groulx's more exclusive, them-or-us, confrontational theories. One of those who did so was Arthur Laurendeau. He had been Bourassa's devoted follower since 1910. But when in the early 1920s Bourassa published a pamphlet, *Patriotisme, nationalisme and impérialisme*, that openly condemned the nationalists of the Action Française movement, most notably Groulx, for their extreme anti-English program and separatist leanings, Arthur broke with him. 'For the first time in a political discussion,' he wrote Bourassa in December 1923, 'you have shown a lack of intellectual probity.' No longer believing that Bourassa had credible answers for French Canadians, he not only switched his allegiance to Groulx but became a close personal friend of the latter. Thus even before becoming a student of Groulx, André heard his father's reverent drum beating out a steady stream of tributes to Groulx's nationalist thought.

While Groulx's historical framework was also based on the *survivance* theme, he was able to infuse it with a fresh sense of urgency because he was far more interested in the present than the past. He began his career as a teacher at the Valleyfield Seminary near Montreal in 1901. By the time he left in 1915 to become professor of history at the Université de Montréal, a position he held for the next thirty-three years, he was convinced that French Canada's unique identity was in mortal danger and could be saved only by a renewed effort to recapture its essence: the French language, the Catholic humanizing mission, agrarian morality. For Groulx, an admirer of extreme right-wing Catholic nationalists in France like Charles Maurras, French Canada was more than a unique society; it was a 'nation' (he sometimes used the word 'race') that could go on surviving only by accentuating its differences from English Canada.[14] His histories—including *Notre maître, le passé* and *La Naissance d'une race*—were written, therefore, to reacquaint French Canadians with those differences and to remind them that the struggles of the past were the best guide for dealing with the challenges of the present:

> It is the sovereign authority of History, the ceaseless transfusion of the souls of the fathers into the souls of the sons, that maintains the unvarying essence of a race. For a small people like ours, unsure of its destiny, subject to doubts about its future, it is History, the vigilant and collective consciousness of a society proud of itself, that determines the supreme loyalties . . . It is also History . . . that maintains, in spite of distance, the essential brotherhood.[15]

During the 1920s, a time of relative prosperity in Quebec, Groulx was a fierce though frustrated polemicist against the twin dangers of creeping cultural assimilation and economic imperialism: both products of American and English-Canadian *laissez-faire* capitalism. Since he deeply distrusted politicians and rejected the state as an acceptable instrument for regaining control of the culture and economy, he could turn only to the people—who, alas, were largely indifferent. Groulx therefore committed himself to educating a new nationalist elite that in its turn would fight the deadly passivity of the French-Canadian masses. But the closing in 1928 of *L'Action française*,[16] his main propaganda tool among the professional classes, under the combined impact of Pope Pius XI's condemnation of the extremist Action Française movement in France and severe financial difficulties, left him with his historical writing and his teaching position at the university as the only tools remaining to mould the new elite. On the other hand, the onslaught of the Depression gave his critique of foreign capitalism in Quebec a new credibility, especially for those young notables who sat before him in class and whose professional aspirations were placed in doubt by the economic collapse.

While André Laurendeau was not nearly as concerned as his friends in the faculty of law about future career prospects, he found in Groulx an inspiring influence who offered a way out of his debilitating psychological depression by calling on him to play a heroic role in defending the beleaguered French-Canadian nation. It was an answer to his idealistic yearnings, one that he could throw himself into with zeal. In a spirit not far from grateful thraldom, he wrote to Groulx in 1933: 'I have met a true master, . . . more, much more than a teacher. . . . Moreover, you guided me through a difficult moment in my life. You saved me from despair.' Not all of his enthusiasm, it should be noted, was traceable to Groulx's history courses. The 'master' had also taken a hand in resolving Laurendeau's romantic crisis. When Antonio Perrault had learned that his daughter was attending Groulx's 1932 course with André, he asked Groulx to forbid it. The abbé temporized while extolling André's better characteristics, the existence of which had thus far escaped Perrault. He also hired Ghislaine as a proof-reader, presumably to indicate that he had an eye on things, and in the end gained Perrault's consent to act as her spiritual adviser in preparation for marriage. For Laurendeau this qualified as divine intervention, and he bent over backwards to show his appreciation. In July 1933, for instance, he transcribed and broadcast the abbé's turgid novel *Cap Blomidon* on CKCA radio. But in the final analysis it was Groulx's historical vision that had the deepest effect on him. It supplemented his scattered cultural impressions and feelings about his French-Canadian identity with an interpretive framework and factual account of its past. It constituted, in other words, the final chapter of his formation in the traditional nationalism that, though it would be challenged, eroded, and modified over the rest of his life, he would never entirely abandon.

Not surprisingly, Abbé Groulx also played a pivotal role in the gestation of the youth group known as Jeune-Canada.[17] One of many such groups that sprang up in Quebec during the 1930s, as the demographic cohort born in the period of the First World War rebelled against the status-quo mentality of their elders and sought more aggressive solutions to the woes of the Depression, Jeune-Canada would focus its attention on the problems of the French-Canadian nation. Its original members came from the same literary club, the Cercle Crémazie, that had functioned as a snobbish clique at the Collège Sainte-Marie.[18] Pierre Dansereau, the natty, urbane man-about-town who, along with Laurendeau, had been instrumental in founding the club, was also attending the Université de Montréal, and, with his admiration for things American, decided to create a fraternity which he called Club X.[19] The club rented a large room on rue Berri, to which the members brought furniture, pictures, and records and where they came and went at all times. As one of them later recalled: 'We got together there to argue, to talk, to criticize society, and above all to work on literature and theatre.' Thus the emphasis at this early stage was on culture; as Dansereau conceded: 'We were elitists . . . we were raised in that spirit.'[20] Laurendeau was only an occasional presence, particularly as he was enrolled in just one course, Groulx's, and worked for the most part at home. But the situation changed dramatically in December 1932, as a result of the blundering insensitivity towards French Canadians of R.B. Bennett's Conservative government in Ottawa.

The Conservatives had long been regarded in Quebec as a bastion of belligerent anti-French interests. They were remembered as the party that had hanged Louis Riel in the 1880s and that spearheaded the drive to conscription in the First World War. They were also seen by nationalists as the political front for the Montreal-Toronto capitalist interests whose economic expansionism was steamrollering French Canada's identity. Thus when the Conservatives returned to power in 1930 after a long period in the political wilderness, nationalists expected the worse. Bennett provided them with a *cause célèbre* in July 1932, when the Imperial Economic Conference was held at Ottawa. Coming so soon after the Statute of Westminster of 1931, which had finally given Canada control over its foreign affairs, the event had a special symbolic importance. For French-Canadian nationalists especially, who had always pushed for greater Canadian autonomy from Britain, it was an international event that would focus attention on Canada's dualistic identity. How galling, therefore, that of sixty-four federal civil servants named to the Canadian delegation, not one was a French Canadian. It was only after *Le Devoir* and other Quebec newspapers raised a clamour that the federal government condescended to name one middle-ranking French-Canadian official—a cure that merely underlined the nature of the disease.[21]

Although this issue dominated the fraternity's meeting of 19 November 1932, it was a second incident, somewhat closer to home, that finally provoked them to act. On 2 December Bennett's government appointed a unilingual English Canadian, Arthur Lang, as chief customs officer of the Port of Montreal—a traditional French-Canadian patronage post. According to Dansereau, André appeared at the club in a white-faced rage and urged his friends to organize 'an energetic and immediate reaction'.[22] After some talk, they decided on a bold plan. On the following Friday they would proceed to Windsor Station; they would seize two French-Canadian ministers in Bennett's cabinet arriving from Ottawa; and they would rough them up, douse them with ink, and send them packing.[23] As André observed years later:

> . . . the reaction was one of wounded pride. We felt humiliated, and we rebelled at the fact of our non-existence. It was a brand of nationalism that

is at one and the same time very emotional and very formalist, therefore very profound, for what is at stake is the sense of personal dignity.[24]

All the same, they were young men from notable families in whom respect for authority was deeply ingrained. And as devout Catholics they were used to consulting their priests on temporal as well as spiritual matters. So a delegation of four club members, including Dansereau and Laurendeau, visited Abbé Groulx to seek his opinion of their plan. Above all, they wished to know whether he thought their action would arouse public opinion against the Conservative government. As Dansereau wrote years later: 'Politics, that was the enemy! It was our hobby-horse, our *bête noire*.'[25] Groulx discouraged them, pointing out that they would be called young fools and would end up in prison. He urged them instead to call a public meeting, write a manifesto, and recruit other young people to their cause.[26] They didn't have to deliberate long before agreeing—especially Laurendeau, who detested all forms of violence. In the days that followed they decided to convert Club X into a nationalist movement and, at the suggestion of fellow member Robert Choquette, they called it Jeune-Canada (after Jeune-France, an obscure group of young literati and idealists involved in France's 1830 revolution).

Jeune-Canada never had more than thirty members, though there were several resignations and new additions during its three to four years of intense activity. This exclusivity was partly by design. As Gérard Filion, who joined in 1933, observed: 'We constitute[d] . . . an extremely closed group, a brotherhood, a clan. Not just anyone could get in. Applications [were] put under a microscope: no known sympathies for any political party, a pure nationalist mind, and irreproachable conduct.'[27] Dansereau was elected first president, though even he acknowledged in later years that Laurendeau was 'more profoundly convinced; much more truly nationalistic'. He explained this apparent anomaly by noting that Laurendeau, an only child, was not yet socially adroit.[28] Filion, on the other hand, pointed out that André was the one with the most time to invest in the movement: 'André Laurendeau [was] already André Laurendeau, distinguished, delicate, refined, subtle. He attend[ed] the university as a dilettante . . . which [left] him the time to think, to write, to organize meetings.'[29] Content to work from a secondary position, Laurendeau rapidly became the organization's indispensable person. He was, wrote one historian of Jeune-Canada, 'in a way the soul of the group, an often unobtrusive thinker, but how very present'.[30] Young men, particularly those who consider themselves intellectuals, love to talk and the discussions at the rue Berri headquarters were interminable. Meetings were held Saturday afternoons and very few initiatives were undertaken without everyone's having voiced an opinion. It was at this early stage that Laurendeau began to establish his life-long reputation as an intense, considerate, and infinitely patient listener.

The members of Jeune-Canada were amazed at the publicity generated by their first rally. *Le Devoir* published the manifesto and soon Laurendeau was in great demand as a speaker. Carried along by the momentum, he organized several more rallies in Montreal, Quebec, Chicoutimi, and Hull and opened Jeune-Canada branches in smaller cities. Before long 75,000 people had signed the manifesto, and André demanded, unsuccessfully as it turned out, a meeting with Prime Minister Bennett to present it to him in person. Since the movement had been launched with a call to action, its members felt obliged to try all avenues in spreading their message. They wrote letters to the editor and contributed articles to the Université de Montréal's student newspaper, *Le Quartier Latin*; they held fund-raising dances; they even opened a summer camp at St Michel de Wentworth. Laurendeau, bursting with energy after years of languor, gave virtually all of his time; Ghislaine wrote in her journal: 'these are sacrifices that we make for Jeune-Canada, for our country. We are going to do great things.' Taking advantage of his broadcasting experience, André made spot announcements on stations CKAC and CHRC in Montreal; the group also had a half-hour monthly show. In fact, he was a pioneer in Quebec in the use of radio for political causes and in the future would have occasion to benefit from what he learned now. Together with the support given by publications like *Le Devoir*, *L'Action catholique* and, after its debut in 1933, *L'Action nationale*, this exposure made Jeune-Canada appear a larger and better organized group than was really the case. Its members were also emboldened during these early days by private messages of support from sympathetic politicians and nationalist-leaning ecclesiastics such as Archbishop, soon to be Cardinal, Villeneuve, who wrote Abbé Groulx asking him to congratulate 'young Laurendeau' and 'the fervent and thoughtful young people'.[31]

Yet in the midst of their hectic activity, the members of Jeune-Canada were considerably more ardent than reflective. As Dansereau recalled, they often relied on eloquence when coherent doctrine was lacking. 'We were surprised to be taken so seriously. We were between 18 and 21 years old. But even though we were very young, we still spoke better than anyone else, thanks to our classical education.'[32] Their spur-of-the-moment way of dealing with current issues soon led them into troubled waters. On 20 April 1933, they held a public rally on the subject 'Politicians and Jews'. This meeting was their response to an assembly held earlier that month by the Montreal Jewish community at the Mount Royal Arena to protest Nazism in Germany. Prominent French-Canadian politicians including Senator Raoul Dandurand, a past president of the League of Nations, and Fernand Rinfret, Montreal's new mayor, had attended the Mount Royal rally. Jeune-Canada condemned them, claiming that the same politicians showed much less concern for defending their own minority. And this was only a first salvo in a barrage of anti-Semitic speeches. Among Jeune-Canada's statements were the following:

Even though they can be, and often are, peaceful citizens, Jews nevertheless represent an unreal and dangerous dream that must at all costs be suppressed, and that is the dream of a Messianic mission. Everyone knows that Israelites aspire to dominate the world, eagerly awaiting the day when this at last becomes possible. . . . Everywhere, through the power which money gives them, they control politics until a day will come when the people of a country will rise violently to despoil them and be rid of them.

* * *

The enormous hue and cry over Hitler's 'oppression'—and once again, none of it is absolutely proven- -and the sight of these multiple fireworks of protest lighting up the skies of so many civilized countries show us how unified are their troops, for, scattered at one command, they reunite at a single dictate from the same central will when the moment is ripe.[33]

Senator Dandurand wrote an open letter to *Le Devoir* bitterly condemning Jeune-Canada· 'To call a meeting to protest against the expression of sympathies for the oppressed [was] the most cruel act I've ever heard of.'[34] It was Laurendeau who responded with more attacks on Quebec's Jewish minority. He argued that because the Jewish community, which had been growing since 1901, assimilated almost exclusively into the English-Canadian majority, it was a serious threat to linguistic balance. He also accused the Jews—in a classic illustration of 1930s anti-Semitic contradiction—of being susceptible to international communism and in the vanguard of exploitative capitalists. He did not, of course, allude to the traditional religious intolerance of Quebec Catholicism *vis-à vis* the Jews or to the fact, often cited in studies of French-Canadian anti-Semitism, that the Jews in Quebec were hated by the French-speaking middle class not as exploiters but as face-to-face competitors in the small business and professional fields. It was Gérard Filion who, reflecting on these events, pointed out that Montreal's Jews were located on either side of boulevard St Laurent: 'they constituted a buffer between the French east and the English west.'[35] For Jeune-Canada this made them a constant and visible reminder of immigration's evils and of the more historically entrenched anglophone elite.

In later life André Laurendeau looked back with shame at his and Jeune-Canada's anti-Semitic excesses. Although he may not have recalled how frequently anti-Jewish remarks, passing for witticisms, entered into his friends' and families' correspondence in later years as well, he remembered that evening in April 1933 as a sin to be expiated:

I can remember down to the last detail how we got the idea for each of our political meetings, except for that one in particular, which we baptised 'Politicians and Jews'. I wonder to this day who or what inspired it. But we held it just the same, because a cloud of anti-Semitism had polluted the atmosphere. It was Depression time, everyone was hurt, and everyone was looking for a scapegoat.

I was one of the speakers at that meeting, and I spoke a great deal about politicians and just a little about Jews. But it was still too much. For our speeches were dreadful. One of us went so far as to proclaim: 'You can't tramp on a tail of that bitch Jewry in Germany without hearing it yap in Canada.'

'Forgive them, Lord, they know not what they do.' And, really, we didn't know. The speeches of twenty-year-old youths reflect ideas that are current in their milieu. And the ideas that were floating around then weren't always very lucid or beautiful.

But that's exactly the frightening part. Take my four friends, the speakers that night. They were nice guys, all of them. None, as far as I know, has turned bandit or Jew-baiter. They were sincere and ardent.

At the very time that Hitler was getting ready to kill 6,000,000 Jews, they could speak very sincerely about 'alleged persecution' and 'so-called persecution' in Germany, which they contrasted to the bad treatment, 'very real —by contrast', which French Canadians were subjected to here. I can still see myself and hear myself braying with the best of them at that meeting, while in another part of the world a German Jew, by accepting exile, was snatching his family from death. . . .

How many things are there today that we refuse to believe and yet are true? Six million victims haven't rooted out anti-Semitism. There are days when the progress of the human race seems dismally slow.[36]

The issue of French-Canadian anti-Semitism would come up again during the Second World War, but by that time André had been to France and had seen the perils of racism up close.

In the autumn of 1933 Laurendeau found himself in another controversy, this time with the premier of the province, Alexandre Taschereau. Jeune-Canada had directed its most withering attacks thus far at federal politicians, but as the Depression deepened in Quebec it was inevitable that the aging Liberal regime at Quebec City would come in for its share of condemnation. Since no one in Jeune-Canada had a grasp of economics, its members fell back on nationalist clichés and a mixed bag of ideas that had been put forward by *L'Action française* during the 1920s. The emphasis was not on specific economic reforms but on the issue of foreign control of the economy. As Laurendeau described this period:

What was the next step? Our recognition of the economic inferiority of French Canadians. . . . How could it be cured? For the most part we of Jeune-Canada were not much interested in economic problems, and yet we were drawn by our nationalistic fervour into this area where we were notoriously incompetent. The group accepted, almost without examination, ideas that were in the air at the time . . . the nationalization of 'big trusts', a vague word which directed our revolt against large companies financed by foreign capital which were exploiting the natural resources of Quebec. [We] got ourselves called 'revolutionaries' by Premier Taschereau.[37]

Laurendeau gave a speech in which he claimed that 'the trust is ruler in Ottawa. It is ruler in Quebec City.' He heaped scorn on the Taschereau government's open-door policy towards the great American and English-Canadian resource trusts, and he maintained that the political corruption linked to this policy was the major reason why Taschereau had been able to remain in power for sixteen years. 'Taschereauism', he later recalled, 'was in our view the mark of a conservative government, and of big capital, . . . whose influence extended everywhere, thanks to patronage; which succeeded in getting itself re-elected thanks to an . . . electoral machine in which the provincial police played a scandalous role.'[38] Taschereau fought back. On 16 December 1933, in a speech to the Young Liberals of Quebec, he described the Jeune-Canada group as seditious and warned the Jesuits that it was unwise to allow their facilities to be used by such extremists. While this did result in the relocation of some Jeune-Canada rallies, it did not stop Laurendeau. In an address to 1,500 people at the Palais Montcalm in Quebec City he taunted Taschereau: 'If our speeches are of that sort that disturb the peace, if we resort to sedition, let the Attorney-General arrest us [and] bring us before the courts. . . .' This was followed by a lengthy polemical battle in *Le Devoir* between the premier and André.[39] For a twenty-one-year-old university student, writing on behalf of a marginal nationalist cadre, there was a David-and-Goliath excitement about the entire episode. Perhaps it was Taschereau's own belated recognition of this, not to mention the publicity he was giving Jeune-Canada, that led him to finally break off the debate.

But by this time Laurendeau was also ready to take a step back. In less than a year he had gone from organizing a protest group that intended to throw ink at a few politicians to confronting several of Quebec's leading political figures over controversial issues. He was aware, moreover, that neither he nor Jeune-Canada was equipped to go beyond attacking those in power to propose effective solutions of their own. They were even less well prepared to turn their small group into a political movement, as many of their supporters were urging. As André explained in a letter to Groulx:

> We are not ready yet to launch such a movement. We have neither the experience nor the competence that such an action would require. For the moment, it would be enough to study the national problems from [our] point of view and to press on, without revealing our ambitions right away. We are very young; this is our strength and our weakness. If time does not break up our union or our ideal—and I have great confidence in some of my friends—we will reach our goal.

For Laurendeau, who was always uncomfortable when he felt his actions were in advance of his thinking, the time had clearly come for the members of Jeune-Canada to concentrate on formulating their nationalist doctrine. He proposed that they do this while reducing their public activities for the next five years. The idea created divisions, as he and Ghislaine observed in their joint diary entry of November 1933: 'Two different tendencies are evident in the group: those who envision immediate action and more outward show and those who want to conquer and form the mind first.' Although at least one member did leave at this time to join a more politically active group, Laurendeau's proposal was accepted, and over the next two years, until his departure for France in the summer of 1935, he worked indefatigably to elaborate a comprehensive nationalist theory.

For Laurendeau this transition was natural. As he explained to a friend at the time, 'you know that for me, the idea counts for 3/4.' The prospect of studying nationalism and writing about it in intellectual terms was at least as exciting to him as participating in public demonstrations. Still very much in the thrall of Abbé Groulx, he agreed with the latter's premise that the French-Canadian masses were not ready to accept nationalism and needed therefore to be educated. In 1934 Laurendeau published a pamphlet, entitled *L'Education nationale* that leaned heavily on Groulx's thinking. Looking back in 1963, he summed up this new orientation as follows:

> Forced to conclude that there was no sign of a Saviour on the horizon (otherwise we would have been easily seduced by the mystique of a leader . . . and what a pity Abbé Lionel Groulx was strapped into a cassock!), and disgusted by the mediocrity of our contemporaries, we sank all our hopes in education. What would save Quebec? 'Education,' was our reply. But by that we meant nationalist education. We reproached the public schools with being too neutral or lukewarm in patriotic matters. We wanted them intensely nationalistic, as if it was a foregone conclusion that nationalism was the final answer to all the problems that besieged the French-Canadian milieu.[40]

Beginning in the fall of 1934, Jeune-Canada published a series of tracts summarizing its views on various nationalist themes. The work was divided up and everyone discussed the results at length, but it was Laurendeau who co-ordinated the effort. He also did much of the research and wrote the most important and complete statement produced by the group, *Notre nationalisme*.[41] A synthesis of conservative nationalist thought in the early 1930s, this 56-page tract represented the beginning point for Laurendeau's impressive collection of writings on nationalism over the next three decades. While it contained many references to intellectuals, some of whom he was reading for the first time as he wrote, it was essentially a polemic that sought to justify the traditional hierarchy of French-Canadian values as the basis of nationhood: 'God, the family, the nation and the State.'

For Laurendeau, in this first phase of his nationalist theorizing, the most elementary defining characteristic of French Canada was its Catholicism. Although he would develop grave doubts about the precise nature of this connection in the near future, at this point he was convinced that 'French Canadian' and 'Catholic' were inseparable. He also insisted in

Notre nationalisme that the Pope's condemnation of right-wing Catholic nationalists in France was not an outright rejection of nationalism itself; it was the intolerance of the extremists that had offended the Holy See, and French-Canadian nationalism was not intolerant. On the contrary, it was respectful of other nations and even minority groups within the nation. 'A French Canadian from Quebec', Laurendeau wrote, 'is not exactly a Franco-Ontarian, still less an Acadian. Our nationalism respects individuality.' Although it would have been difficult to convince Montreal's Jews of this, Laurendeau was obviously intent on allaying the concerns aroused by Jeune-Canada's earlier excesses by portraying its doctrine as more in tune with a humanistic Catholic tradition. He also brushed aside the argument that nationalism sought to trample individual aspirations under the heel of the collectivity. The individual, he asserted, should always be free to develop himself, but it was vital to recall that the individual could not survive without the nation, for it alone provided each person with his or her cultural identity. The individual therefore had a primary duty to protect and expand the nation's cultural life. Here Laurendeau touched on a fundamental issue –individual versus collective rights—that would return again and again to complicate, though never to change, his nationalist loyalties; but in 1935 he was untroubled by doubt. 'The nationalist phenomenon,' he maintained, 'is essentially one of culture, not one of individual or collective free will.'

Notre nationalisme also addressed the thorny issue of the relationship between the 'nation' and the state. Laurendeau pointed out this was especially important for French Canada, where the two were not synonymous. He emphasized elsewhere that a state—for instance, the Canadian one—had an obligation in such cases to fully respect the national entities within it; otherwise they would be free to create their own states:

> The State is nothing but the final outcome of a series of elements (territory, language, religion, history, common traditions, shared joys and sorrows, expressed in the will for a common and independent life, in a collective wish to live together, strong enough to translate into the creation of an autonomous government) having as their essential characteristic political authority, the right to make final decisions, therefore independence, sovereignty.[42]

Put in these terms, and joined with Jeune-Canada's frequent claims that the Canadian state had trampled repeatedly on the rights of French Canadians, Laurendeau's argument inevitably led to the question of separatism. Jeune-Canada is often described as one of Quebec's most outspoken separatist organization of the 1930s. Certainly its members anticipated the imminent break-up of Confederation. For them the Depression conditions made what had always been a likelihood into a certainty. They speculated, too, about establishing an independent state, which they called 'Laurentie'. In August 1934, for example, André wrote to Ghislaine: 'Concerning the French state: Paul S[imard], in his letter, calls it: La Laurentie. We had already talked about the name, I believe. Do you like it? Given the importance of the Laurentians in this country, and the love that I feel for these old Mountains, the name is all right with me.'

Looking back on this period from the early 1960s, when he was opposed to the next generation of separatists chiefly because they were young extremists who did not base their ideology on realistic arguments, he saw many of the same negative characteristics in his own separatist period:

> I became a separatist, as a young man, when I became conscious of this fact: the nation to which I belonged, whose history I read and loved, whose future is linked with mine, this nation was, inside Canada, in a state of inferiority. During the days of R.B. Bennett, this became plain, not because the Prime Minister was so much worse than his predecessors, but because he did not know the way to handle French Canada, and he had the bad habit of speaking his mind. It was during the depression; and as everyone suffered from the economic crisis, every one was sensitive and emotional.
>
> Here is the way my generation discovered the situation as it was. First, the 'rights of the French language' were recognized nowhere in Canada, except in Quebec and in the Federal Parliament: in a supposedly bilingual Country, you could find eight English Provinces, and a bilingual one. This was particularly true in the Federal Civil Service, where French-Canadians were few, and without prestige. We did not seriously influence Canada's policies. And as a nation we were poor, left aside by big industry and finance. Outside Quebec, we met indifference or hostility.
>
> This situation had alienated an important part of our people from itself. In Quebec, our politicians were collaborationists; they had given away most of our natural resources. We were dominated by foreign trusts which exploited the population as well as the wealth of the Province. So, we were a colony inside a colony.
>
> English-speaking Canadians made us feel we were foreign, as French Canadians, everywhere outside Quebec: then, there was one thing to do: accept the fact, break a 'pact' which had never been fulfilled, and make ourselves completely at home in Quebec. Then, the new State would be a powerful tool in our hands, and we could liberate ourselves, at least partly, from the economic and political pressure that were [exerted] against us; and our culture could become creative at last.[43]

Most of Jeune-Canada's discussions about 'Laurentie' were superficial. Like all French-Canadian nationalists since the late nineteenth century who based their concept of the nation on religion and culture, they had difficulty visualizing a separate state that would include all of their countrymen presently living outside of Quebec. This was painfully apparent in the one page Laurendeau devoted to the subject in *Notre nationalisme*:

> Our true homeland is French Canada, which, following the example of others, we call Laurentie.

What are the geographical boundaries of Laurentie? This is exactly the point at which we cross into unknown territory; this is an entirely new question which must be solved by our own generation. Laurentie: an undefined country centred upon the present province of Quebec but stretching further, into northern Ontario, New Brunswick, and New England. Its focal point is the Saint Lawrence, which is its main axis, its principal artery, almost, one might say, its respiratory system. It is a territory upon which French-speaking people are impregnably established. . . . [44]

Thus while Jeune-Canada set forth a theoretical case for separatism, it never progressed beyond Abbé Groulx's utopian but vague image of a 'French state in America' and they did nothing concrete to hasten its appearance. As Gérard Filion conceded: '. . . we favoured the formation of a State. But we ended up with separatism, for which none of us really had any desire at that time.'[45] In Laurendeau's retrospective analysis it was 'a distant and hazy ideal which evaporated little by little as our movement developed'.[46]

Long before *Notre nationalisme* was published in 1935, Jeune-Canada showed signs of disintegration. Laurendeau's determination to avoid further political involvement was put to the test in 1934 by the appearance of a new, nationalist-inspired political party in Quebec, l'Action Libérale Nationale.[47] This party was led by Paul Gouin, the nephew of a former Liberal premier, who sought at first to reform the Taschereau government from within and, having failed, set out to topple it. As its name suggested, the new party took many of its ideas, such as its opposition to the resource trusts, from nationalist writ. It appealed to some Jeune-Canada members because of its youthful, untainted-by-power idealism. But Laurendeau and the majority thought otherwise. As he noted much later: 'We viewed the ALN with suspicion. Its reformist politicians weren't pure enough for our taste. . . .'[48] Evoking the traditional nationalist opposition to viewing the state as a primary mechanism for change, Laurendeau rejected an affiliation. Jeune-Canada delegates were authorized to attend the ALN's founding convention in 1934, though only to observe and report back.

But when in 1935 the ALN moved to unite with the provincial Conservatives under Maurice Duplessis to form the Union Nationale party, in a combined effort to oust Taschereau in elections that year, Laurendeau came under more pressure. For instance, Dr Phillippe Hamel, a maverick nationalist MLA at Quebec who had spent his career fighting the electricity trusts and who had supported Jeune-Canada from its beginnings, wrote Laurendeau to question his hesitation. 'When is Jeune-Canada going to plunge into the fray? . . . I beg you not to remain mere spectators in the battle.' Some of Laurendeau's colleagues in Jeune-Canada voiced similar misgivings, and one or two threatened to leave to join the ALN. Refusing to budge, Laurendeau nevertheless expressed his doubts to Abbé Groulx: 'But . . . how will my friends take the lack of action, the long obscurity? . . . Won't they feel they're wasting their time? . . . Ah! I am not giving up. So far, it has been too easy to be Jeune-Canada: now we will find out who the real workers are. . . .' It mattered little at the moment that he would be proven right in his stand. A blow had been struck at Jeune-Canada's unity and enthusiasm.

A more serious personal blow arose from opposition within Catholic youth organizations to the Jeune-Canada group. Laurendeau, it must be recalled, not only regarded Catholicism as ineluctably tied to French-Canadian nationalism but at this point in his life considered it to be the indispensable spiritual foundation of his personal philosophy. As late as 1935, he listed his priorities as follows: 'My function will not be to write books, to see other countries, to study philosophy or become a great politician. . . . My function will be that of all human beings: to seek God.' He had been active in various Catholic youth groups since early adolescence, and in 1934 he had jumped at the opportunity to become editor of *Le Semeur*, the magazine of the Association Catholique de la Jeunesse Canadienne-française (ACJC)[49]. It was only natural, therefore, that when he embraced nationalism and joined Jeune-Canada he would endeavour also to raise the nationalist consciousness of Catholic organizations. Indeed, in 1934 he travelled to New Brunswick to present his pamphlet *L'Education nationale* to the central committee of that organization, hoping that they might even assume the costs of its publication. But there were many in the ACJC who were hostile to nationalism, taking their cue once again from the Pope's 1926 condemnation. They forced at least three Jeune-Canada members, including their own president, to choose between the two groups, and they sponsored motions to expel others.[50]

Nor was it merely young lay Catholics who disapproved of Jeune-Canada. The extreme views put forward by Laurendeau and other members in 1933 now came back to haunt them. It became dangerous for some clerics to be seen associating publicly with them. Although Father Georges-Henri Lévesque, a young Dominican who was destined to play a key role in Quebec's future, corresponded with André, he would only sneak into a Jeune-Canada rally. As Ghislaine described the occasion: 'Father Lévesque came to the meeting, but incognito, hiding under his black coat, at the back of the room. Later he spoke to us, congratulated J.C. . . .' In the spring of 1935 the Jesuit Order sponsored a series of lectures by the aging tribune Henri Bourassa at the Palestre Nationale in Montreal. Bourassa strongly condemned the kind of nationalism that was based on racial antipathy and separatist yearnings, and singled out Jeune-Canada as a particularly misguided movement. His attack was clearly aimed as well at the influence of Abbé Groulx's theories on young nationalists like Laurendeau. André, who attended the final lecture, was fit to be tied. Father Lévesque too had warned him that Groulx was an unsuitable figure to hold up as a great leader, and he was well aware that Pierre

Dansereau, his closest friend in Jeune-Canada, resented Groulx's behind-the-scenes manipulations. Groulx, it seems clear, was a scheming politician in the covert tradition of the Catholic church; he would have prospered in the narrow passageways and whispered deal-making atmosphere of the Vatican. While exploiting his clerical collar in an elaborate ritual of self-effacement, he was not above using idealistic but inexperienced youths to build up his personal cult and advance his ideological goals. Dansereau, more worldly than the others, and devoted to his science-oriented mentor at the Université de Montréal, Brother Marie-Victorin, was caustic in later life when recalling Groulx's hold on Jeune-Canada. According to him, Groulx reviewed everything they wrote; to take one example, when Dansereau lavished praise on 'these magnificent revolutionaries' in Bolshevik Russia, Groulx made a slight alteration, so that it read 'these poor revolutionaries'.[51] Laurendeau nevertheless remained fiercely loyal to Groulx, although he went along with the decision recorded in Ghislaine's journal: 'Jeune Canada decided for the moment not to reply to Bourassa.'

By the summer of 1935 many of Jeune-Canada's members had drifted away. As Gérard Filion observed, the movement didn't die: 'it evaporated into thin air.'[52] Dansereau had moved to Oka, Quebec, in 1933 to pursue his scientific studies and participated sporadically thereafter; others either graduated and turned their energies to starting their careers, getting married, and having children—all risky undertakings in the mid-thirties—or left the country to study abroad. In other words, they proved themselves to be what Laurendeau disdainfully called 'apprentice reformers'. He had predicted as much to Groulx, while drawing a more steadfast portrait of himself:

> What should happen; that we be so involved in Jeune-Canada, that our personal interest be so associated with the national interest, that the failure of the movement threatens to mean the failure of our careers. For my part, this is not a problem: I was moulded with those ideas: to build my life outside them would be a torment—unfortunately, this is not the case for all my companions.

But the bloom was off the rose for Laurendeau as well. With his graduation that spring from university and his marriage to Ghislaine on 4 June, he too was poised to move on. And the public criticism he had suffered for his nationalist beliefs was also taking its toll. The fact that most of the criticism came not only from within the community he claimed to be speaking for, but to no small degree from the ecclesiastic ranks he had always deeply respected, caused him great anxiety. 'How confused my mind is, Ghislaine,' he complained. 'The more I think, the more I see the intellectual chaos I am living in, . . .' It was typical of him that after these years of frenetic action he would look to philosophy and his studies in France to find some answers. As he confided to Groulx, 'I realize that my mind is in chaos. As for my thoughts . . . until last year, I took them as they came. My hope lies in philosophy, through which I will try to put my knowledge and ideas in order.' As for Jeune-Canada, perhaps he wasn't quite as pre-pared as he had at one time boasted to sacrifice his personal prospects for the cause.

And yet, looked at from the perspective of his entire career, these years of nationalist action added immeasurably to the foundations of Lauren-deau's thought and long-term influence. His enthusiastic adoption of the nationalist cause—the result in part of Abbé Groulx's inspirational influ-ence, in part of his and his student friends' frustrations over the mis-treatment of French Canadians by the federal government—not only eased his psychological torments but confirmed the nationalist thrust of his traditional upbringing and education. Though he would never again feel the certainty of conviction he felt in this period—indeed, the long process of questioning, revision, and reformulation was about to begin—his nationalism formed the continuous thread in a public career that would have numerous twists and turns. The Jeune-Canada group had also made him a figure in Quebec linked to the nationalist cause, and while this hardly meant that he was a household name, his identity was established. As he himself observed when comparing the radical nationalism of the mid-1930s to that of the early 1960s: 'the ideas that were current then were . . . more dependent . . . on particular men and circumstances.'[53] He might have added that the French-Canadian elites were much smaller then, more hierarchical and inward-looking, so that a political neophyte like himself could gain a modest niche as one of those 'particular men'.

In personal terms, Laurendeau's leadership role in Jeune-Canada also made him more assertive and confident of his talents while forcing him to push his thinking about the French-Canadian nation beyond feelings and images towards a theoretical and historical framework. *Notre nationalisme*, though he would distance himself from it within a year, was nonetheless an impressive undertaking for someone in his early twenties. Despite its loose ends, its economic and social naïveté, and its occasional lapses into sophomoric philosophizing, it showed a keen and perceptive mind at work. If this stage in his life began with what he later characterized as the impetuous errors of an over-zealous youth, temporarily eclipsing his more humanistic inclinations, he soon found a much more typical focus in the determined effort to acquire more knowledge and to ground his activity in solid theory. It was this intellectual scrupulousness that would distinguish his later career as a nationalist and a journalist. More imme-diately, it led him to France and to discoveries that would convince him that the ideas of French-Canadian nationalists were too narrow, too cler-ical, and too bourgeois.

3

Personalism, 1935-1937

I met some new men and some new groups, from Catholic teachers to Marxist writers. At least this helps to broaden my perspective. I am trying to open myself to all the influences that appear to be good, even though there may be some risk involved ... the more I look around me, the more I realize our lack of intellectual daring.

André Laurendeau to Abbé Groulx, 1936

The crowd waiting outside the Palais de la Mutualité was excited and bois-terous, but in a good-natured, fraternal sense. Peddlers circulated shout-ing 'Read l'*Avant garde*! Read l'*Humanité*! Read *Regards*!', while a bellowing organizer cried, 'Over here ... journalists! Over here ... delegations!' A young man, engulfed in the throng blocking the entrance way, bought one of the newspapers and surprised himself by responding to the peddler's friendly greeting with the words 'Thank-you comrade'. Standing near him was a grey-haired, fiftyish man with impressive Slavic features who looked crest-fallen when an official yelled, 'It's useless to wait ... only those with tickets will be allowed in.' But after reflecting for a moment on the obvious success of the occasion he turned to the younger man, who did have a ticket, and said, 'There are no more places, but I'm content all the same.' Taking advantage of the openings created when those without tickets turned to leave, the young man pushed his way inside and found an empty seat. By the time the hall filled up there were five thousand people, several hundred of whom were standing. Soon the speeches began, interrupted again and again by colourful delegations of workers who stood, fists raised in the air, now singing, now chanting the words to the Internationale.[1]

This was Paris. It was February 1936 and André Laurendeau was wit-nessing first-hand the enthusiasm and confidence of the ideological left in France, which within weeks would carry the Popular Front of communists, socialists, and independents under Léon Blum to a historic political triumph. Blum was at the rally, sponsored by the communists, and Laurendeau was struck by his 'sobriety, eloquence and calm demeanour'. Not long before, the young man had visited a communist bookstore and, while reading the famous party monthly *Vendredi*, noticed a poster announcing the rally. He was entranced by the prospect of seeing luminaries including the writers André Gide and André Malraux, as well as politicians like Blum and the legendary Michel Cachin, the French communist leader whose name was linked to such great figures from the Russian revolutionary period as Maxim Gorky. Now as he watched Gide presiding, looking a little lost among so many 'devouring wolves', he was thankful that he and his friends from the Sorbonne had obtained their tickets beforehand. One speaker, chest heaving, 'hurled his insults at the bourgeois world' and a German novelist, whose name escaped André but who had the honour of having been expelled by Hitler, received a triple ovation. True, most of the speeches were short and artificial, but as André explained, it was 'the crowd that interested us more. Spontaneous, alive the way a French crowd can be, joyous, warmer than the speakers and very generous.' As they rose to sing and shout it was 'rather than a manifestation of hatred, . . . a sign of rallying, almost a sign of love'. When he got up to leave after three hours the crowd around him seemed surprised he was departing so soon. Here, he sensed, was a genuine atmosphere of hope, of 'profound and virtuous aspiration'.[2]

When Laurendeau reached his left-bank apartment he was deeply troubled by the same thoughts that had disturbed him time and again during the months since he began his studies in France. And they would assail him once more the next day at a performance of a play by the famous Catholic dramatist Henri Ghéon, where the theatre-goers were both staid and well-to-do. What a contrast! 'I thought I was on my way to a celebration of the people,' he observed, 'I ended up in bourgeois society.' The cause of his discontent had been articulated the day before by his student friend Emile Baäs, a Belgian who also attended the leftist rally: 'When we reflect on the great problems, we are inevitably drawn to the left; the rightists being unthinking.' André had to admit that it was true. 'Don't forget,' he wrote to his astonished father, 'that the (extreme) left offers mysticism, a strong doctrinal position, great things already achieved.' He added that in France the only credible alternative to the status quo was not the conservative ideology of Charles Maurras, the Action Française, and the Catholic right, so long admired in Quebec and held up as the example for him to follow since his earliest recollection, but rather the revolutionary Catholic left. It was this movement, he stated—itself largely a product of the 1930s—which despised conservative Catholicism even more than the communists did, and was known as 'personalism',[3] that increasingly occupied his thoughts.

Indeed, while he was only partly aware of it at the time, Laurendeau was on the brink of the most significant intellectual catharsis of his life. He was about to become a convert to personalism. And that in turn laid the groundwork for the transformation of his vision of French Canada along lines that would ensure his place at the centre of the nationalist debate there for the next three decades. It was a conversion, in other words, that —despite old friends' cries of treachery—would make him one of the few nationalists of his era who could deal not only with Quebec's past and present but with the profound changes that lay ahead. Long after his sojourn in France, he wrote about its importance: 'The two years I spent in Paris had been a prodigious adventure. I had thrown myself into it completely but, despite that, hadn't ever lost my sense of belonging wholly to French Canada. After explorations in several directions, I finally found myself in the Christian left . . . .'[4]

As this remark suggests, Laurendeau's intellectual conversion did not take place in a day. Nor did it begin at once, with setting foot on French soil. Like any French-Canadian notable, during his first months in Paris he revelled in the cultural feast he had dreamed about for so long. He and Ghislaine arrived on 24 September 1935, several weeks before his classes were scheduled to start at the Institut Catholique. They rented an apartment at 24[bis] rue Tonnenfort, just fifteen minutes from the Institut and about the same distance from the Sorbonne—as he remarked happily, 'a nice stroll' across the Jardin du Luxembourg. It is difficult today, in the age of rapid air travel and the 'global village' technology that can make the most exotic places seem familiar, to imagine the excitement of this moment. For André it wasn't just an idyllic end to a long sea voyage, or relief at escaping the tide of criticism levelled at Jeune-Canada. It wasn't only the sense, at last, of fulfilling his long-cherished dream of the European 'grand tour'—it was Paris! Gérard Pelletier has alluded to the special significance of France for the young intellectuals of that era:

> How can one say in a few words what an obsessive desire we had, almost all of us, from our very childhood onward, to leave Quebec, to leave Canada, to leave America itself. To leave! For us, there was not the slightest hesitation as to where to go. We knew New York, some of us had pressed on as far as South America or at least to Mexico, but our intellectual pole was located across the Atlantic, in France.
>
> I have often wondered about the reason for the strange power of this attraction. Were we giving in to a kind of sentimental nostalgia, or a blind atavistic instinct? Was it the real France that fascinated us, or merely a dream country secreted during the confinement of the thirties within the barbed wire of the depression or the war?[5]

Of course André had been too young in 1919-20, when he visited Paris with his mother, to have formed any lasting impressions, but Ghislaine had spent years studying there (at least in part to be kept an ocean away from him) and was therefore able to serve as an expert guide. Thanks to his parents' generosity—they paid for the lion's share of his stay—and periodic money transfusions from M. Perrault, they were reasonably comfortable. André felt guilty, given the Depression, about his parents' sacrifice. 'You have no right,' he wrote, '(it would be immoral) to deprive yourselves unnecessarily while we're floating in banknotes.' They were able to attend concerts, to visit galleries, and, above all, to take in numerous plays. André discovered the works of Ibsen and Musset, both of which would have a profound impact on his own theatrical style. Naturally he sought out performances of classics such as Corneille's *Le Cid*, although—in what can be viewed as a mild foreshadowing of insights to come—he observed that the classics in all fields were less popular than the moderns. Otherwise, during this brief idyllic period, perhaps the happiest of his life, only one thing troubled him: 'the lack of intimacy with others.'

As so often occurs with travellers in the time before they make new contacts, Laurendeau's attention was drawn back to the situation at home. He corresponded with members of Jeune-Canada and anxiously awaited copies of *Notre nationalisme*, which had been published only after his departure. Requesting extra copies in the hope that he might use them to propagandize for the nationalist cause in Paris, he also reasoned that he could offer the tract as an impressive personal introduction to French intellectuals. No wonder his friend and fellow Jeune-Canada member Robert Charbonneau wrote him to say that there was a little too much of 'I' and 'me' in it to suit him. When Arthur Laurendeau wrote in November to complain that the struggle to make Catholic organizations more nationalistic was going badly, his son immediately sought an interview with Cardinal Villeneuve, who was in Paris. The interview was so encouraging that André recommended to his father that a copy of it be read to nationalist groups, to hearten them. Other contacts with French Canada continued through a series of articles he had agreed to write for *Le Devoir* and *L'Action nationale* under the title 'Pilgrimage in the Real France'. While they would eventually become a journalistic Trojan horse for introducing his views on personalism into Quebec, his original intent had been to use them for commentaries on French-Canada's traditional cultural ties to France. His preoccupation with home at this early stage even extended to reassuring Abbé Groulx that his heart was still there: 'I miss . . . St Gabriel —and Montreal! . . . Suddenly, in the midst of working or having a conversation, I will have a dizzying [vision] of the country. I don't know what internal mechanism causes this. I see it all again, in detail, the colours, the distinctive light, even the smell.'

But it didn't take long for doubts about the quality of French Canada's cultural and intellectual life to arise. It is not unusual, of course, for a North American arriving in a great European city to feel an initial cultural cringe. But everywhere Laurendeau went he encountered Frenchmen with a general cultural literacy that he did not possess. After seeing

Ibsen's *Hedda Gabler* performed for the first time, for example, he wrote home to complain: 'We are taken so far. How is it that Ibsen's name is hardly known back home?' As time passed he made the same point about philosophers like Nietzsche, Hegel, and Bergson, not to mention Marx, as well as classical writers like Dante. In one instance he reported how embarrassed he was when in the course of a conversation comparisons were made to the latter: 'Not having read a single line by Dante, I know absolutely nothing about him.' Nor did it help his confidence when he had some difficulty with the Parisian accent—he who had spoken so arrogantly back home about the importance of linguistic purity—or when he caught educated Frenchmen staring down their noses at his 'colonial' turns of phrase. One professor at the Sorbonne, upon learning that he played the piano, asked if he might come along some weekend to his summer home to sing a few quaint French-Canadian folksongs. Otherwise, though, the French seemed hugely uninterested in French Canada: 'Generally speaking, the French people don't know much about us, and show no desire to get to know us. One has to understand that if they're not interested in us, it's because we're . . . not interesting.'

During his first few months at the Institut Catholique and the Sorbonne his embarrassment turned into a full-blown feeling of intellectual inferiority. It wasn't strictly the excellence of the French students: 'I don't feel that they're more intelligent, but truly more cultured (and they have a sharper wit).' He was simply overwhelmed by the variety and dynamism of intellectual life: 'I find myself in . . . a very diverse world, with subjects that are beyond me . . . and this awareness of my intellectual incompetence.' To this point Laurendeau's conception of the great and wise intellectual had been epitomized by Abbé Groulx, an aloof repository of traditional knowledge sitting above the fray passing along advice. But here intellectuals and their followers seized upon new ideas and fought for their theories in conversation, in journals and newspapers, and, if necessary, in the streets. He found himself speaking forcefully, in sheer self-defence, about books he had never read and ideological positions he barely understood. When he tentatively offered his *Notre nationalisme* to a few new acquaintances they were brutally critical, branding it as narrow, out-of-date, and one-dimensional. He quietly abandoned any notion of using it to introduce himself to his professors.

Laurendeau also criticized the conformity of the intellectual environment he had left behind in Quebec: 'Dear parents . . . I am more and more aware of our intellectual poverty. We are going to have to make a tremendous effort . . . I realize my own shortcomings.' When he summoned the courage to point out, during an interview for *Le Devoir* with the French historian Pierre Forrestier, that French intellectuals tended to undervalue French-Canadian achievements, Forrestier responded with a question he could not answer: 'What can you give us, what can you actually offer us now . . .

other than your survival[?]' By February of 1936, André felt the need to write an 'explanation' for *L'Action nationale* of his assertions in *Notre nationalisme* regarding the desirability of breaking Quebec's colonial ties to France. He now emphasized his people's desperate need for new ideas from outside: 'In this country [French Canada] we lack a serious, profound culture, and we are almost entirely without intellectual traditions. . . . Only an idiot would think that French Canadians can be intellectually self-sufficient. An ailing nation, we cannot do without a blood transfusion.'[6]

More than a quarter century later Laurendeau summed up both the culture shock and excitement of these first few months in Paris:

> In highly civilized cities . . . your first reaction is to feel small and provincial. Expectations and standards are different. Thrown a little off balance, you take stock of your own education.
>
> Inevitably, you encounter a lot of mediocrity. There's no shortage of that anywhere. I was even very surprised to have some mediocre professors. Their mediocrity was, however, if I may say so, more competent and more demanding than the usual variety. And then there are also the real masters. They are irreplaceable. Around you there is an abundant intellectual and artistic life. There are creative people who are no better than our artists but who are more numerous, which creates an atmosphere which is not easy to explain to people who have never known it and who suspiciously ward off such explanations when you get back. In these privileged places one's spirit expands, becomes more alert, more comparative. It can also become drunk on all this, but it's a stage one has to pass through, and the milieu provides its own antidotes. All the instruments of culture are ready to hand.
>
> Suddenly one day you realize that you too have entered this more intense kind of life. Intellectually you are participating in a society which is so much better structured and so much richer than your own, a society where thousands of intellects collaborate and compete with one another to make up one vast and endless movement of mind which is beginning to carry you on its tide. . . . [a young man] also remembers this or that faculty in one of our Canadian universities, our theatre, our reviews that scarcely exist yet, everything that in our country remains hastily improvised and not always very happily so, intellectual 'achievements' that are too quickly crowned or too soon discarded.
>
> Intellectual ferment isn't everything. Perhaps it isn't even the essential. But he experiences or at least gets a taste of what a great adventure it is. It is a heady wine. He finds it very strong. His defences buckle on every side. He tries in vain to restructure his thoughts into a new synthesis. He gives it up as a bad job. He starts over again. He grows.[7]

Determined, therefore, to plunge ahead despite his feelings of inferiority, Laurendeau threw himself into the pulsating intellectual life of Paris— a life that in the mid-1930s was even more dynamic than usual.[8] He was helped in this by a new spiritual mentor, the last in a series of priests he cast in this role. A Dominican, Father Pierre Doncoeur was founder of the

Cadets de France, a Catholic youth movement with a school on the out-skirts of Paris. André had encountered him for the first time at Montreal in 1934, when Doncoeur gave a lecture on 'Christian Youth and the World Crisis' and later dined with several members of Jeune-Canada. Now André visited the Cadet school regularly and Doncoeur encouraged him to be more open in his views, to seek out new knowledge rather than waste his time defending memorized positions. Laurendeau's letters home con-tained more and more terms like 'objectivity', 'tolerance' and 'research'. On 'the fruits of [Father] Doncoeur's influence,' he wrote, 'no doubt my con-ception is too individualistic, and man is less of a closed system than I seem to think.' Doncoeur may have provided only a nudge in the direction he was heading in anyway, but from this time forward Laurendeau's approach to virtually every issue was to keep an open mind, to continually seek out the opinions of others, and to emphasize his own inner spiritual and intel-lectual growth above action. He also began to develop the commitment to exhaustive investigation that was to become such an unmistakable char acteristic of his journalism and involvement with issues such as Canadian bilingualism. As he confessed trenchantly, 'I generalize too much. . . .' It was, in fact, this new investigative spirit that had led him to attend the com munist rally at the Mutualité in February 1936.

Nevertheless, he was already coming rapidly to the view that only the ideological left held any uplifting hope for the future. His professors, some of whom were priests, had urged him to study Marx, Engels, and Trotsky. The same André Laurendeau who in November 1932 had participated in a Jeune-Canada meeting devoted solely to communist-bashing was now struggling to integrate Marx and Lenin into his thinking. 'To use the lan-guage here,' he wrote home a little sheepishly, 'I feel myself slipping more and more towards the left. . . . Sometimes this worries me a little. . . .' Fortunately for his family relations, if not his own peace of mind, he stopped short of embracing socialism or communism. Instead he encoun-tered the Catholic left intellectuals and their doctrine of personalism. His arrival in Paris coincided with the early stages of an effort by these intel-lectuals to spearhead a revolution in Catholic social thought. Sharing the widespread view that Western civilization was at a crisis point and that the Depression signalled the collapse of the liberal-bourgeois order,[9] they rejected the communist and fascist extremes that were emerging in the wake of this collapse; however, they admired the populist, revolutionary spirit of the communists and yearned to bring about a Christian renais-sance that might exert a similar appeal in placing primary emphasis on the spiritual liberation of the individual:

> [Personalism] can be defined as a statement of concern for the human person, the human being considered in all his dimensions. . . . It can also be less charitably defined as a 'flotilla of abstractions, a fleet of capital letters'

... among which 'Person' and 'Community' were the most recurrent. But the assertion of the 'absolute value of the human person' was not simply an abstract affirmation of human dignity but rather a movement of defence against two antithetical threats. . . . It mirrored the desperate effort of intellectuals in the early nineteen-thirties to navigate a 'third way' between capitalism and communism.[10]

It is frequently noted that this 'personalist' movement never enjoyed the high profile of the other philosophy that emerged from the mid-thirties Parisian environment: existentialism. 'It did not stimulate safaris into the misty realm of Being and Nothingness,' intones one commentator, 'or provide the catch-phrases for beatniks unravelling the absurdities of the universe.'[11] But it was equally important in bringing about what the French historian Jacques Ellul called a 'major shift' in French intellectual life.[12] The thinkers most responsible for the elaboration of personalist ideas were the philosopher Emmanuel Mounier, founder of the review *Esprit*, the movement's major organ; Jacques Maritain, author of the book *Integral Humanism*, a theoretical touchstone of personalist ideas; and Nicholas Berdyaeff, a Russian emigré, social theorist, and convert to Catholicism. The historian Henri Daniel-Rops played a prominent role, and the writers Charles Péguy and Paul Claudel were said to have evoked the 'purity' and spirit of this new Catholic renaissance. Laurendeau became a devoted admirer of them all. In their works, he wrote, 'you have the climate of an entire generation and the tradition of thought to which I belong.'[13] Nor was it just his generation that was sharply influenced by personalist idealism. Younger French-Canadian intellectuals like Gérard Pelletier and Pierre Elliott Trudeau, who would be active in the liberalizing prelude to Québec's Quite Revolution, were also affected.[14] Over the ensuing decades the names of the personalists and titles of their books were invisible footnotes at the bottom of virtually every page that Laurendeau wrote.

André had become aware of individual personalists while still in Canada. He recalled his first encounter in a 1962 article entitled 'The Origins of My Social Catholicism':

When I was twenty, a friend lent me a pamphlet he had been given by a former teacher who had become a bishop. . . . It was a Russian Philosophical essay by Nicholas Berdiaef [sic], 'The Worthiness of Christianity and the Unworthiness of Christians'. It was the first time we had ever found the problem approached in such a real, fundamental way. I admit that it was a formative experience.[15]

In Montreal in 1932 he had attended a series of lectures given by Jacques Maritain, who was a guest professor for a term that year at the University of Toronto; his lectures on this occasion were based on the ideas in *Integral Humanism*. Laurendeau met him briefly afterwards and many years later summed up his contribution to personalism:

From reading Maritain we retain the idea that even in the political or social spheres, Christianity is leavening. Loyalty to the Church and its dogmas need not entail stagnation. We see, too, that this Christian leavening, which has been acting on humanity for the past two thousand years, is still potent, still able to inspire new civilizations. Consequently, we refuse to oppose automatically anything that is modern. Quite the reverse, we consider anti-modern prejudices in Christians as a sterile lack of hope; lacking its leavening, their Christianity will be like granite-hard dough, inedible, undigestible. The kind of Christianity Maritain so often describes does not exhibit itself brashly on the social or political level, yet it provides a profound inspiration for projects in these fields. He contrasts it with what he calls 'decorative' Christianity, an artificial superstructure, showy in appearance, but without any deeper influence upon either institutions or customs.[16]

But despite these preliminary contacts with personalist ideas, their impact on André had been marginal during his Jeune-Canada days. It was not until he reached Paris and began to read the works of Charles Péguy more extensively than he had done in Montreal that he fully appreciated the revolutionary spirit of the Catholic left. In this regard at least he was following in his father's footsteps, for Arthur Laurendeau had also fallen under Péguy's spell in Paris in 1908. Besides paving the way to the personalist philosophers, Péguy's works would have a long-term influence on André's theatrical and creative writing. It was an influence he cherished: 'As to Péguy, I shall not be so rash as to summarize my memories of him in a few words. Those memories are too intimately linked with some special images and emotions; yet without any doubt they are the ones whose roots plunge deepest in my mind.'[17] When he found a new Péguy he would rush home with it so that he and Ghislaine could read passages aloud to each other. He experienced a feeling of 'profound liberation' from all considerations of money, politics and mediocrity when he read Daniel-Rops's stirring biography of his hero, and was outraged by Péguy's 'real-istic' portrayal of the morally degrading effects of capitalism. His rapturous praise even inspired old Father Mignault, his former mentor at the Collège Sainte-Marie, to include a few of Peguy's works in his courses, predictably scandalizing his conservative colleagues.

Laurendeau's enthusiasm for personalism also led him to restructure his formal studies in Paris. 'After a good deal of trial and error,' he explained in December 1935, 'I believe that I have found a decent study formula. . . . I am specializing (somewhat) in social sciences and I do the metaphysical work at home.' This choice of specialization was clearly a response to the Catholic left's preoccupation with the 'social question', and the books he devoured at home by Berdyaeff, Mounier, and Daniel-Rops made him increasingly impatient with those of his professors who were, to use his phrase, 'too historical'. His love of the classics, though by no means extinguished, began to pale in comparison to the excitement of a struggle that was here and now. The students at the Sorbonne were concerned with things modern. He pointed out that the vast majority were either communists or personalists: 'I got into the young French intellectuals' current of thought. There is something intoxicating about it. What an ambience! What riches, what tension, how learned, and yet how personal!' He persuaded his father, who was then editor of *L'Action nationale*, to publish a series of articles based on interviews he intended to conduct with the leading personalists. They would be short and hence somewhat superficial, but at least these important contemporary voices would be heard in Quebec. During 1936 and early 1937 he interviewed Daniel-Rops, Berdyaeff, Maritain, and Mounier, among others.

His session with Emmanuel Mounier was the most memorable. They met at Mounier's office at the review *Esprit* in the Faubourg St Denis. Although Mournier was deaf in one ear, owlish, and a little timid, Laurendeau soon felt that he had found in him the person who best embodied the union of Catholic and revolutionary ideals. The son of a Grenoble pharmacist, Mounier had rejected his middle-class upbringing and preferred to identify with the purer spirituality of his peasant ancestors. After abandoning his pre-medical studies in favour of theology he became a student of Jacques Chevalier, a philosopher who was opposed to the rigid orthodoxies of conservative Catholicism, and searched instead for a modern philosophy of the individual within the Catholic community.[18] Mounier took up the search. Entering the École Normale Supérieure in Paris, he passed the formidable *agrégation* in Philosophy despite his narrow provincial background, and ranked second in the same year Jean-Paul Sartre failed.[19] By the 1930s he had forged strong intellectual ties with others who opposed communism, fascism, and liberal democracy, but who despised complacent middle-class Catholicism most of all. As Mounier had once explained in a letter to his sister:

> You see, my dear Madeleine . . . we all have one or several conversions to make. And the passage from a traditionalist and bourgeois pietism to a truly Christian life . . . is at least as difficult as that from atheism to faith. Because those who believe in nothing and are searching have a hundred times more value than those who are sleeping in exterior practise . . . the bourgeois of the faith must be brought back from the dead.[20]

For Laurendeau, Mounier was a living example of a Catholic who had developed a rich and full interior life, who exemplified the very essence of individuality in his radical spiritual viewpoint and yet was selflessly devoted to the community. Mounier seemed to confirm that the individual and the collectivity could be united—and in a far more exhilarating way than André had suggested in *Notre nationalisme*. It is easier, of course, to become a convert when one is young. The cautionary layers of scepticism that build up with age regarding the possibility of any one all-satisfying philosophy do not need to be penetrated. His interview with Mounier completed Laurendeau's conversion to personalism. Not long after it, he attended a lecture in which Mounier fleshed out his conception of humanism. 'I was beside Berdiaf [sic],' he explained proudly, '. . . almost facing Mounier (who recognized and greeted me). I take a childish pleasure in being physically close to these men.' Many years later he could still write with zest of the forward-looking enthusiasm that Mounier always inspired in him: 'Mounier's philosophy is a living one, flexible and yet profound. His revolutionary zeal is tempered, or rather purified, by his charity. Rarely will you find in Mounier's works phrases designed to set your mind at rest, or lull you into peaceful somnolence. Nothing in his writing is fixed, or dead. . . .'[21]

It was inevitable that Laurendeau's identification with the Catholic left in France would lead him to criticize the conservative Catholicism of French-Canadian nationalists. The contrasts were overwhelming. Mounier had expressed the same view as all of the other personalists he interviewed—namely, that Quebec was a bastion of 'clericalism'—and had left no doubt in his writings what he meant by that term:

> These crooked beings who go forward in life only sidelong with downcast eyes, these ungainly souls, these weighers-up of virtues, these dominical victims, these pious cowards, these lymphatic heroes, these colourless virgins, these vessels of ennui, these bags of syllogisms, these shadows of shadows, are they the vanguard of Daniel marching against the Beast?[22]

André had visited the *Action française* offices in Paris, partly out of loyalty to his father and Abbé Groulx, but he found the people there virulent and unthinking: 'Truly, I find them a little alien!' Their views sounded too much like the narrow-minded, warped religious instruction he had received in school: 'St Thomas,' he remarked, 'would hardly be a Thomist according to the understanding of the term in Quebec. . . .' Recalling how he had often rushed to his confessor to find out if a book he wished to read had been placed on the Index, he inveighed against the church's attempt to control thought: 'What disturbed me was that almost all the important works in philosophy of the last four centuries . . . have been placed on the Index—and that [Christians] are no longer aware of history. . . .' Laurendeau made it clear that the days were past when he would base his nationalist views on the pronouncements of Quebec's ecclesiastical establishment.

He announced his intention instead to restructure his nationalism around the tenets of social Catholicism. He conceded that French readers were correct in criticizing *Notre nationalisme* for its near-total absence of social thought. And how could its perspective have been otherwise, when the Catholic church in Quebec, his guiding light at the time, was so hypocritically tied to the exploitative, industrial bourgeoisie? 'It is scandalous to think that even the Jesuits were gambling on the stock exchange, that our female communities were as miserly as they were rich . . . that our Canadian Sulpicians owned the streetcars in Philadelphia or some other American city.' He recalled the remark of a communist he had interviewed in Paris, that nowhere had the church ever been ahead of the socialists in drawing attention to social problems. The time had come, André asserted, to see the poor not as a class, or as potential converts, but as a target for social reform.

In this he was drawing heavily on Nicolas Berdyaeff, the emigré Russian whose book *The New Middle Ages*, published in 1927, had established him as the most advanced social critic among the personalists. 'From the social point of view, my ideas are becoming more radical . . . ,' André wrote at one point, 'I have been immersed for a month in reading Berdiaff [*sic*] . . . . I find in it substantial and thrilling food for thought.' In an interview with André in August 1936, Berdyaeff insisted that a Christian had no right to accept harsh social realities with a deterministic allusion to God's punishment or to divine testing. It was his or her duty to change the realities. For Berdyaeff, the Christian had a responsibility to carry forward God's creative enterprise by intervening to reshape the material world so that it might better serve the spiritual cause. He urged Laurendeau to become involved in this effort. Describing a lecture in which Berdyaeff had debated the merits of his brand of socialism with an orthodox Marxist, Laurendeau reported: 'Then the big fellow was transformed into the great philosopher, the thinker perfectly in control of his thought, even though he was speaking a foreign language'. According to André, Berdyaeff disposed of his opponent like an adult lecturing a child. How much more aggressive and courageous an approach this was, compared with that of his old mentors, whom he now described as 'too academic'. Laurendeau would carry Berdyaeff's message back to Quebec and, in seeking to transform French-Canadian nationalism into a more active social force, he would use these same forceful arguments to denounce the old elitist view that the misery of the masses was to be endured rather than changed. In the long term, this issue would play an important part in his complete loss of religious faith.

Nevertheless, as important as the personalists were to the development of Laurendeau's intellect and nationalist conceptions during these critical two years, they were not alone. André Siegfried came a very close second. A professor of sociology at the Sorbonne, Siegfried had visited and written books about many countries, including Canada, and was a proponent of the theory that international 'macro' forces shape national cultures. Following his travels in Canada in 1904, he published a book called *The Race Question in Canada* (1907).[23] In it he developed the thesis that while the major preoccupation of Canadians at the level of politics and ideology was the English-French cultural conflict arising from history, the country was in the midst of an industrial transformation, and the social and economic forces that this was releasing were potentially more problematic, yet barely understood. Siegfried's current lectures were based on a new book about Canada, entitled *Le Canada: Puissance Internationale*,[24] to be published in 1937, which developed many of the earlier work's themes. Although Laurendeau had not read either study when he enrolled in Siegfried's course beginning in January 1936, it seems that he chose the course because he wanted to hear what a Frenchman had to say on Canada, a country about which so few Frenchmen appeared to care. He was also hoping to learn something about English Canadians, having been embarrassed several times already by how little he knew on that subject when acquaintances in Paris asked him questions. But Siegfried's course turned out to be much more than home study from abroad. It uncovered forces at work upon French Canada that Laurendeau had never seriously considered, and it broadened his international perspective in a way that altered many of his most cherished political beliefs.

Siegfried's detached, objective approach impressed André from the outset. This was scientific history, especially when compared with the *a priori* assumptions, based on Thomistic philosophy and cultural tradition, that he had been raised on. The papal encyclicals that had stood in for social analysis in his early education mattered little here. Siegfried began with Canada's geography, noting the contrast between its 'natural' North-American features and its less natural cultural and historical ties to Europe. He then ranged through demography, immigration, social psychology and economics to build a picture of Canada that had nothing to do with God and precious little to do with the conscious efforts of individual men and women. For Laurendeau it was an analysis that revealed to what a decisive degree French Canada had been shaped by influences beyond its control. For instance, he became aware for the first time of the extent to which the urbanization linked to North American industrialism had permanently changed Quebec society; in this light, the agricultural mystique preached by the nationalists was an exercise in nostalgia. Although he did not accept all of Siegfried's theories, even stopping by his office at the end of the course to challenge him on some of them, he could not deny Siegfried's 'brutal' conclusion that, assessed by any reasonable comparative standards, French Canada had failed to progress adequately in economic terms. To the personalist charge of intellectual and social stagnation in French Canada was now added that of material backwardness.

Even more stunning for André was Siegfried's claim that the greatest threat to French-Canadian survival was not English Canada but the United States. Laurendeau, who to this point in his life had paid scant attention to the Americans, summarized Siegfried's view this way: 'the Canadian life is inseparable from American life, and each province has more ties with the corresponding region in the US than with the neighbouring province. Here again is Siegfried's great idea: the predominance of North-South influence.' In conversation Siegfried went so far as to state that the end of Confederation would lead to the absorption of all provinces except Quebec into the United States, and that Quebec itself would be severely damaged in economic terms. Reflecting on this view, Laurendeau began to question himself: 'I asked myself if distance has developed or brought out in me a pan-Canadian sentiment. . . .' The nationalism of Henri Bourassa, who had always seen the need to co-operate with English Canada, made more sense to him now. Writing to a friend, he observed: 'I can't deny it, the courses I took with Siegfried have influenced me. . . . I wonder if there isn't a good Confederation to be established.' As late as 1963 he singled this out as the moment when he turned away from separatism:

> In the summer of 1935, I was writing a pamphlet on our nationalism, that is, of Jeune-Canada, which I concluded with a logical adhesion to separatism. After that, I left Canada to study in Paris for two years. It was there, the following year, that I lost my faith in separatism, and I have never regained it since.

There were other factors influencing this decision—the personalist insistence that the problems of humanity could be understood only in an international perspective; the violent and reactionary character of European separatist movements, like the one he saw at first hand during a short visit to Brittany; and, in fascist Europe especially, what he called 'the ravages of the Nation-State'. But Siegfried's teachings were decisive because they focused on French Canada itself.

By the middle of 1936, when the full impact of his new intellectual discoveries had hit home, Laurendeau's personality too was undergoing a subtle change. Earlier feelings of inferiority melted away, thanks in part to the heady excitement of his interviews with leading French artists and philosophers. His letters homes took on the tone of a man who had now outdistanced his old mentors. He was not arrogant, but neither was he above lecturing his friends, his father, and even Abbé Groulx. It was more than just enthusiasm for the cosmic insights he felt he had gained. It had something to do as well with the tendency among young expatriate French Canadians to adopt more radical and critical attitudes away from home. (Decades later, in the early 1960s, he would remember this particular face of intellectual snobbery when his oldest daughter, motor-scootering around Europe, freely passed judgement on what she saw as the closed, stifling ideological life of Quebec.) The fact that by now André and Ghislaine had many French friends also made them feel still more Parisian in their outlook. At the same time, the Europe beyond Paris was beginning to open up for them.

To this point, Laurendeau had shown little interest in European politics.

Not long after arriving in Paris he reported that Hitler's name was on everyone's lips, but confessed that he and Ghislaine rarely discussed such matters. He was content to reassure his parents that if war broke out they would return home at once. The intrepid journalist of later years was buried, for now, under the searching intellectual who had all that he could handle with the intellectual debates on the left bank. But this indifference didn't last long. His new friends were the first to pull the blinkers from his eyes. Father Doncoeur gently chided him to get his nose out of his books long enough to look around. The Belgian Emile Baäs came often to his apartment to talk feverishly about events in Germany, Spain, and Italy. The personalists he interviewed dwelt on the same subjects, emphasizing the immediate dangers to and the contemporary nature of the revolution they were striving to achieve. In addition there were the refugees, particularly Jews from Germany, whom he met at the Sorbonne and the Collège de France. Notably, early in 1936 he encountered a young German Jew named Heinz who told a story of persecution that nearly made him swallow his anti-Semitism whole. Determined that other French Canadians would learn of these things, he invited Heinz to write an article for *L'Action nationale*,[25] paid him in advance, and translated the articles himself. When Heinz turned out to be a fast-talking charlatan, André insisted that 'the value of the witness is nil, not that of the testimony.' To his father, who squirmed at the notion of publishing a Jew in *L'Action nationale*, he maintained that the details of Heinz's story were true for too many others to be dismissed.

Laurendeau's growing political sophistication was not solely the result of what he learned in Paris. It stemmed as well from his travels during 1936 and 1937, especially his trips to Alsace, Belgium, and Italy. In April 1936, when Emile Baäs invited the Laurendeaus to visit him for three weeks in the small Alsatian industrial city of Gruebwiller, André saw it as an opportunity to study a cultural and linguistic minority within France. Like so many other experiences in this period, however, it also changed some of his views on French Canada. He was surprised first of all to discover that virtually everyone spoke Alsatian, a German dialect; the older people could not speak ten words of French. The years of French rule had had little effect on the people's allegiances. It was clear to Laurendeau that the majority, including the government deputies he interviewed, disliked the French and were strongly autonomist. 'The problem of Alsace', he wrote on 6 April, 'is not as simple as one might think. . . . The French are annoying, centralizing, and above all unsympathetic. The problem of the languages is very complex, and sometimes reminds me of ours.' But what struck him palpably was that, although discontented, the Alsatians were not separatists. 'Politically they are on France's side, but not culturally. . . .' He could see in this case that cultural solidarity and a large measure of autonomy were vital for a minority's survival, but that these were not necessarily incompatible with political ties to a central government. His as yet nascent commitment to the idea of autonomy rather than separatism for Quebec was being shaped in part by foreign examples.

A second, more complex example came to light during his eighteen-day visit to Belgium in February 1937. Although he used Brussels as his headquarters, he visited other cities as well, including Bruges, Liège, and Kain. He had several interviews with members of the French-speaking Walloon majority, which had dominated the country since 1830, but he was primarily interested in the Flemish minority. His journalistic skills improving with experience, he cast a wider net than he had in Alsace by focusing on opinion-makers such as priests, writers, politicians, and union leaders. The impact of personalism was also more apparent now in his preoccupation with the 'social question' and economics. Indeed, he became convinced that the Walloon domination was more economic than cultural, and that this was the underlying cause of Flemish separatism. He also drew attention to the nefarious role of clericalism and the incomprehension of the Catholic establishment as to the reasons why the workers were being driven to socialism. Here too he was most impressed by those socially conscious *Flamands* who favoured autonomy over either strong federalism or separatism.

Convinced that no one could unravel the complexities of the Belgian situation in such a short visit, Laurendeau was certain nonetheless that it offered invaluable comparative insights. As he noted in a letter from Brussels in February 1937, whereas previously he had looked for differences in people, now he paid attention to similarities. And later he observed that 'the example of Flanders is not unique; there is also the case of Alsace, of Poland, Ireland, the Central European nations, and of ourselves.' It so happened that his trip to Belgium closely followed Queen Astrid's death as the result of a car accident. He was amazed that the Belgians, divided in so many ways, could set their differences aside to rejoice in their new monarch, Leopold III, and his young wife. It became clear to him that a constitutional monarchy, even reduced to powerlessness, could have more meaning for a people than an elected chief of state. 'A Royal family can represent the living traditions of a people . . . very, very curious. . . . But it does explain the British to me.' It was this sort of insight that made his travels such a broadening experience, and the many notes he took in Belgium were filled with similar comparisons to the situation in Canada and Quebec.

Laurendeau's final visit was to Italy, on the way home to Montreal in the spring of 1937. Ghislaine had given birth to their first child, Francine, the previous year, and so their travels around Italy were done separately for the most part. Whichever parent was charged for the moment with babysitting remained at a Franciscan convent in Assisi. As good Catholics, the Laurendeaus almost certainly did not practise any form of artificial

birth control; indeed, André was scandalized when in Florence he encountered some Canadian Franciscan priests who expressed grave doubts
about the church's doctrine on this issue because they were forced to
deal with so many large families living in terrible poverty.[26] Certainly the
birth of a child, while celebrated joyously after the fact, had not been
anticipated, and there are indications, especially in André's private journal
entries during this period, that he had some difficulty adjusting mentally
to this new responsibility. He had grown up, it is worth recalling, in an
adult environment without having to adjust to or compromise with siblings; when he wished to pursue a project, read a book or listen to music,
he had been free to do so. And Ghislaine had been his close companion in
all of these activities for a good many years, before and after their marriage. A deeply intelligent woman with a quiet, rather formal demeanour
—in later years, people from outside the Laurendeaus' circle would find
her somewhat cold and intimidating—she functioned as the level-headed,
practical force in the marriage. Now Ghislaine was constantly involved
with Francine, and he was forced to adjust. Their letters back and forth in
Italy, though devoted as always, give some indication that this new development aroused worries about the future intensity of their own relations.

While he could not have foreseen that family obligations would limit his
foreign travels to this one experience, he did worry about their effect on his
immediate projects, most particularly on the formidable task that awaited
him in Canada with respect to changing nationalist theory. This was one
reason why he endeavoured to do more in Italy than just see the sights.
Italy had always been a compulsory stop on the traditional 'grand tour' of
Europe for a French-Canadian nationalist. Besides the artistic and historical treasures cities like Venice, Florence and Rome, all three of which
André visited, there was a powerful religious incentive; as he put it, he was
going 'to see the Rome of the Popes [as well as] that of the Caesars.' But
his other motive was to 'engage on the spot . . . in a little investigation into
fascism and state corporatism.'

He had arrived in France not long after Mussolini's invasion of Ethiopia
and in conversations then took a rather detached view of the episode. As
he looked back on it later:

> When Fascist Italy pounced on Ethiopia (because, as a latecomer, this was the
> only colonial bone she could find to gnaw on), I shared the opinion of those
> Frenchmen who condemned the war as odious. But when those same
> Frenchmen approvingly held up the example of that England of clergymen
> and pacifists who wanted to see Mussolini's Italy ostracized by all civilized
> nations, the memory of the recent history of Ireland, and of London's harsh-
> ness towards India, and, above all, of the history of my own people, came
> back to me too vividly for me to be taken in by such pious nonsense.[27]

But if in his eyes one imperialist was much like another, his opinions on fascism hardened during his stay in Europe. He took a sceptical, even hostile view of most of the fascist officials he interviewed in Italy, including the Ministers of Propaganda, National Education and Agriculture. He was also deeply frustrated by the language barrier, which prevented him from gaining a broad insight into how the common people viewed fascism: 'I'm not as comfortable as I was in Belgium. Maybe because the contacts with the natives haven't started yet.' His most illuminating conversations appear to have been with fellow travellers staying in the convent at Assisi. But he learned enough to confirm his opinion that Italian fascism was a dangerous model for French-Canadian nationalists to emulate. It was an indication of how far he had drifted from the views of Abbé Groulx that he felt the need to warn his former mentor on this score:

> Mussolini has accomplished marvels thanks to his nationalist mystique. All right. But at what price? There is the serious question: should one accept any kind of a success for the simple reason that it is one?
> Do I have the right to forget that Italian nationalism is a . . . threat to world peace? That it ignores international justice? Should I forget that in this nationalism, in principle, freedom of the individual scarcely exists any more? That . . . the workers' movement is being diverted, and thus some dearly won advantages of history are being lost for a long period of time? Do I have the right to forget that Catholic-fascist friendship constitutes a formidable danger for the future of the Church?

Another upshot of Laurendeau's travels in Europe was the emergence of a new, critical attitude on his part towards the French. The starry-eyed fascination of his first months in Paris—when he claimed to be 'not sure what people mean when they talk about "the decadence of France"'—had given way to the sort of remark he made near the end of his Belgian excursion: 'This is the right place to see France and its shortcomings.' He was disconcerted by the insularity of the French, including the cultural and political elites; by their failure to see and condemn the injustices of German and Spanish fascism. 'You write that "the French elites are the best in the world",' he replied sarcastically to his father. 'Me too; I've said that a hundred times—but one question, do you know any others?' He observed that all aspects of French life turned towards and flowed from Paris, and that the Parisians neither knew or cared about anyone else. The city that had once been the 'light of the world' was thoroughly mired in a foolish isolation. True, one could buy a translation of Hitler's *Mein Kampf* in a bookstore, but only because it attacked the French and because Hitler held power in Germany. The French had paid no attention to the Nazis' insidious racial theories, which to him were more dangerous than communism. Who in France was responding to the Rosenberg thesis? he asked rhetorically, in reference to the main pseudo-scientific theory behind national-socialist racism.

Laurendeau was just as appalled by the failure of Léon Blum's Popular Front government to take the side of the republicans in the Spanish Civil War.[28] Its non-interventionist stand was in his opinion both short-sighted and immoral. For the personalists, as for Ernest Hemingway, John Dos Passos, George Orwell, André Malraux, and many others, the conflict in Spain represented a line in the sand beyond which further intellectualizing and fine points of theory were irrelevant. It was time to act against fascism. In a several articles written for *Le Devoir* and *L'Action nationale* Laurendeau condemned the Spanish fascists as defenders of feudalism and of the most exploitative capitalist elements in Spain. Their claims to be a bulwark against communism he rejected as nothing more than a camouflage for their own oppressive, anti-democratic alliance with the entrenched elites. Prominent among those elites, he pointedly remarked in a letter to Groulx, was the Catholic church: 'The horrors of the Bolshevists and anarchists appal me, like everyone else, but I wonder if the Catholics' laziness, the opposition to social progress of the religious communities especially, the conniving traditionalism of the clergy, did not create, in reaction to them, a revolutionary climate, and then precipitate events . . .' He was horrified by the reaction of those in French Canada who sided with the fascists in the naïve belief that they were defending the church; from what he could tell in Paris, the French-Canadian press was almost united in this view. But, he protested, 'God is not the bourgeois police responsible for defending the great properties of the nobles and of some religious communities, and the shameful exploitation of the poor by big capitalism.' He served notice that he would denounce this idea, and the nationalists who espoused it, in France and in Quebec.

Writing many years later, Laurendeau acknowledged that his vehemence over this issue was the last straw for many of his friends in Quebec who were alarmed by his minted-in-Paris, left-leaning views:

> When the Spanish Civil War broke out my sympathies weren't pro-Franco. . . . I was growing more and more opposed to fascism, particularly to the Nazi brand, for I was discovering the challenges and grandeur of the idea of democracy purged of its capitalist poisons. In those days my stand on the Spanish War estranged me somewhat from my fellow French Canadians. . . .[29]

It was true that André came very close during these years to abandoning the nationalist cause entirely—for perhaps the one and only time in his career. His doubts had begun during his first weeks abroad: 'When I arrived in Paris, I called myself a nationalist: I soon stopped: it was arousing both sympathies and antipathies of which I don't understand a thing.' He soon learned that 'here nationalism is truly synonymous with egoism' and therefore was viewed by many as a dead end. The majority of the friends he made in Paris, especially among the intellectual left, were anti-nationalist—and he could see why. Wasn't nationalism, he asked, always allied with the anti-democratic, executive branch of government? Was it not always opposed to finding international solutions to problems like the abuses of capitalism? And were not the fascist regimes a perfect illustration of the ill uses to which nationalist sentiments could be put? Laurendeau was still weighing these questions as late as December 1936 when he wrote: 'Back to the question of nationalism. I'm often preoccupied with it.' In the end, however, he concluded that the Catholic left, more specifically personalism itself, had furnished him with a set of principles that could help to purge French-Canadian nationalism of its reactionary tendencies while making it more creative, progressive, and socially relevant: 'Socialism is oriented towards Progress . . . and justice. Nationalism glorifies tradition, culture and power. If that is the case, I am a socialist-nationalist.'

By 23 June 1937, when Laurendeau and his family boarded the ship *Vulcania* at Trieste for the voyage to New York, en route to Montreal, he was somewhat amazed himself at the changes these two years had wrought in his outlook. Although he had expressed a belief months before in the 'near-impossibility of communicating experience', he spent the three months in Italy trying to make sense of his own in letters to and conversations with Ghislaine. He concluded that he needed time to absorb all that had happened in an atmosphere free of daily bombardment by new ideas and images. Looking back at this time in 1963, he wrote that 'it took me years to clarify my own thinking and give it some kind of unity.'[30] But he had nevertheless reached a point, without quite realizing it fully, where the fundamental tenets of his personal philosophy were in place. From now on he would be less impressionable—less likely to embrace impetuously the theories of those he admired at the moment. At twenty-five, the foundations of his intellect were established and from here he would become a more mature, intensely rational weigher and balancer of ideas and alternatives. How often, in the years ahead, would those in conversation with him notice that wary smile as he considered his answer to a question, as though all the fault-lines of his own argument were already apparent to him? Like so many of the intellectuals who would contribute to Quebec's post-war transformation, he had reached this point only after leaving Quebec. By experiencing other cultures, more worldly attitudes, and more expansive viewpoints he had come to see himself and his people in a new light. Though he would never again leave for so long, neither would he lose this international perspective—or his social nationalism.

4

L'Action nationale, 1937-1939

There are opposite notions that, if pushed too far, would be harmful to one
another, like the order-justice pair, or the authority-freedom pair. If we give
too much room to one of these notions, say, authority, the results would be
monstrous. To let these notions counter-balance each other would be a
happy but ineffective medium. We have to live both of them in a continuous
state of inner tension. This, I thought, was a perfect analogy for French
Canada within Canada. This unease is part of our life.

André Laurendeau, 1937

When André Laurendeau arrived back in Canada in the summer of 1937,
he was in a highly agitated state. He had set off two years before as a brash
but rather narrow French-Canadian nationalist, proud of the pamphlet,
Notre nationalisme, he had written concerning his people's fight for dignity,
but searching too for intellectual enrichment in philosophy and in the cultural life of Europe. He returned utterly transformed by the experience
and, while still a nationalist, wondering how he could possibly adjust his
thinking to what he now regarded as a backward, conformist society. As
he explained near the end of his life to the young generation of radicals in
the 1960s, he understood why they were impatient and hostile towards
their own Quebec environment, for he had experienced similar feelings in
1937: '. . . on my return from Europe, I was at one and the same time
strongly nationalist, anti-clerical and tending towards socialism. . . .'[1]
During the 1960s, moreover, he could reflect with greater detachment on
the combination of enthusiasm and anxiety that a person in his position
must inevitably feel at such a time:

> He thinks of everything there will be to do on his return, of all the discoveries
> there are to share, of the enthusiasm burning inside him that he is going to
> try to communicate to others. But at the same time he is aware that he
> won't always find people ready to share his discoveries. He can foresee the
> resistance he will encounter. And he anticipates his own solitude.[2]

He estimated that it took him four or five years to finally make the 'home from abroad' adjustment, and traces of his French experience were evident long after that.

Laurendeau had practical concerns as well. Up to this point in his life he had always been a student, though not necessarily one interested in piling up degrees. His recently completed studies in France, for example, had not resulted in an advanced graduate degree, and while he certainly was an intellectual—one whom Abbé Groulx considered a good prospect to succeed him at the Université de Montréal[3]—he was not really qualified to pursue an academic career. There weren't many other job descriptions in Quebec during the 1930s containing the word 'intellectual', and he had not yet clarified what sort of writer he planned to be—'writing' being the rather vague career he had ostensibly been preparing for. True, he had written articles in France for *Le Devoir* and some highly specialized French-Canadian periodicals, but that hardly qualified him as a seasoned journalist. With no end to the Depression in sight, prospects were bleak in all fields. Journalism would not become his main livelihood until another decade had passed. In the meantime he had not only a child but, in his traditional view of a woman's proper place, a wife to provide for. He could live with parents and in-laws, but at twenty-five he couldn't expect them to support him. Fortunately, it had been Abbé Groulx's and his father's plan all along to turn the editorship of the monthly nationalist journal *L'Action nationale* over to him upon his return.[4] His father had been editing it for the previous three years and his mother did a good deal of the secretarial work. It was another family enterprise, like music, and while it paid him only $100 a month, plus twenty per cent of the profits every six months,[5] one could get by on that in the 1930s. If the job meant that his role would be confined for the immediate future to nationalist circles—a narrow environment for someone bursting with reformist ideas and concerned about Quebec's overall ideological climate—it would at least provide the opportunity to play a significant part in reshaping nationalist doctrine. From this one could hope for a wider impact. Thus for the next two years Laurendeau was immersed in the problems of nationalist theory and the cause of intellectual reform.

What is an intellectual journal? In contemporary society it is a rarefied, upper-atmosphere phenomenon that even the intelligentsia may encounter only during university days, after some fumbling in the library's periodicals section. Its 'intellectual' content often seems to be deliberately obscure, as if to draw a line in the sky between the philosophic minds and the goings-on down below. But no one on either side of the line really imagines that such a journal could play an immediate role in societal change or in sparking an ideological revolution. In this respect we are very far from Laurendeau's vision in September 1937, when he officially became director of *L'Action nationale*. His models were the French journals *Esprit* and *Sept*, whose personalist philosophy he had come to enthusiastically endorse during his two years in Paris. He had visited the offices of *Esprit* many times just to imbibe the enthusiasm and idealism of the young intellectuals who worked there. 'Esprit', he explained in *L'Action nationale* while he was still in France, 'is an international journal founded in October, 1932 by a group of young men whose aim was to explore spiritual values in some depth, and search together for ways of translating these into necessary changes on the temporal level.'[6] It was not, therefore, solely a vehicle for ivory-tower musings but one deeply involved in the issues of the day, and determined to inspire change in the outlook of France's elites. There was no such journal in Quebec, and as André frequently lamented, *Esprit* itself had only three subscriptions there—including, presumably, the one his mother took out for him at Christmas 1936. His friend Robert Charbonneau had helped establish *La Relève* as a journal of personalist inspiration, but it failed to satisfy André's other side — the nationalist one. French Canada needed a review that would fuse personalism with nationalism and thus transform nationalist theory.

Laurendeau's high hopes for the future role of *L'Action nationale* were not entirely unrealistic in French-speaking Quebec during the late 1930s. The society was still strongly influenced ideologically, if much less so in its day-to-day material life, by a small petty-bourgeois elite whose control of the major socializing mechanisms had not yet been seriously challenged by business and bureaucratic elites. Voices of protest against the ideological 'blockage' imposed by this traditional elite were more numerous now, to be sure, but it would take the painfully obvious socio-economic realities produced during the Second World War to permanently rout the notables' ideology. Meanwhile it was possible for a publication with a small circulation—in the case of *L'Action nationale*, about 3,000 subscriptions[7]—among professionals and the clergy to have considerable influence, especially if its *raison d'être* lay in the volatile sphere of nationalism. *L'Action française*, the forerunner of *L'Action nationale* in the 1920s, was said to have had an inordinate impact on nationalist thought during a relatively unpropitious period for nationalism itself.[8] How much better, then, were the prospects in the late 1930s. The Depression had by now created a widespread conviction that industrial capitalism, at least in the *laissez-faire* form it had always taken in North America, was finished. Nationalists, who had always condemned its abuses while searching for utopian alternatives, felt vindicated and were buoyed by the notion that they were in the vanguard of some soon-to-be-defined new order. A more negative factor favouring Laurendeau's doctrinal orientation was the sheer helplessness felt by nationalists in the political sphere following the ignominious demise of the Action Libérale Nationale party at the hands of Maurice Duplessis not long after the Union Nationale was formed in 1935. Those nationalists who had believed, when Paul Gouin's ALN and Duplessis's Conservative party joined to form the UN, that a truly viable nationalist political option was finally at hand, were shocked when Gouin suddenly left the alliance on the grounds—which turned out to be true—that Duplessis was merely using the ALN to defeat Premier Taschereau's Liberals in the election of 1936.[9] The realm of ideas seemed to many nationalists the only place left to turn, and it was as a young man with fresh ideas from France that *L'Action nationale* introduced André to its readership:

> It is at Paris, close to the masters of Catholic and French thought, that he has been devoting himself to . . . beneficial labour. This stage has not only permitted M. Laurendeau to perfect his knowledge, but to make contact with significant figures, to penetrate important groups and even to pursue an instructive humanistic inquiry in different European countries.[10]

André had complained almost from *L'Action nationale*'s inception in 1933 that it fell far short of his expectations. The fact that Abbé Groulx and Esdras Minville, the president of the Ligue de l'Action Nationale, eventually chose him to become the journal's director did not mollify him or change his view that it wasn't combative enough. During his first few weeks in Paris in 1935 he had criticized recent issues and urged his father to remember, in the spirit of Jeune-Canada, that 'behind the little review is Laurentie'. Soon, however, his enthusiasm for personalism altered the tenor of his critique: 'Your October issue . . . is lacking in something,' he wrote Arthur; 'It lacks an article on theory. . . . It seems to have a rather narrow outlook on the world . . . because it doesn't exploit all the possibilities.' He urged his father to be less polemical in his approach to Catholicism and to include more about 'the Laurentian social reality . . . strive more in the direction of the actual people of Laurentie; the habitant, the worker. . . .' In a foreshadowing of his own intention to open nationalist theory to outside influences, he complained about turgid, platitudinous articles written by uninspired local writers and was miffed that his father had accepted a piece from Abbé Groulx's latest protégé, Guy Frégault, who was only eighteen. It was enough to make a twenty-three-year-old wonder, and with unfilial arrogance he advised Arthur 'to have an eye open for the great French books, reviews and movements but also from elsewhere. This in order that one can sense fresh currents in the air perpetually.' In his own introductory editorial in October 1937, entitled 'Requirements of a Movement', he called for vigorous spirit of dialogue.[11]

But this new spirit was not easy to generate. In the first place, *L'Action nationale*'s readers were conservative and traditional, about forty per cent being parish priests.[12] They liked the old nationalist tunes best and never tired of hearing them repeated. Innovative ideas from France they seldom thought worth listening to, and then only with arms folded across the chest and eyes slowly closing—one had one's beliefs, after all! They greeted André's breathless initiatives with stony silence. He later remarked that he rarely heard from anyone during the first three years of his editorship. Perhaps they detected between the lines of his carefully worded articles the same impatience that led him to scribble in his diary that summer, 'there is something ridiculous in certain conservative pretentions.' He was well aware himself of the gulf that separated his ideas from those of the majority of Quebec's nationalists. As he informed a friend in 1939, 'The reader . . . of the Action Nationale would be astonished to learn that, for two or three months, his sympathetic and devoted editor has been indulging himself daily with . . . Flaubert and Jules Romains.'

It was the same gulf that had long since alienated his Jeune-Canada friends. 'Pierre [Dansereau],' he wrote in 1937, 'didn't like my articles [from Paris] in Le Devoir . . . like almost all my friends.' At one time the Jeune-Canada group had planned to add ten to twelve pages of their own writings to each issue of *L'Action nationale*. But early in 1937 Thuribe Belzile, the group's president, wrote to André,

> to judge by the articles you've published since you've been in Paris . . . I have reason to fear that by the month of September you will hardly be capable of giving us the journal I have in mind. . . . The brutal truth is this: your state of mind is rapidly leading you away from the correct line of thought on French-Canadian nationalism as we in Jeune Canada . . . and you along with us conceived of it . . . before you left.

Laurendeau did make a perfunctory effort to publish articles from his old Jeune-Canada comrades, but his heart wasn't in it. In fact, they were among the strongest critics of his editorial leadership. He worried about the arrogant impression he was making:

> When I was very young, I knew a lot of people who had come 'back from abroad' . . . I was struck by the ridiculous figure they cut. As a general rule, they seemed to me to be insupportable, never satisfied with what they found back here, unjust and hypercritical, always ready to make odious comparisons. Or else they were simply maladjusted, having lost all sense of the possibilities of life here. Or else they just made a mess of things and clammed up, their only preoccupation being to return to Europe, in dreams if not in reality.[13]

The hardest part for him was that the personalist enthusiasm and spirit of inquiry he had brought back from France were not accepted by his closest associates at *L'Action nationale* as a certain formula for nationalist renewal. Even family members tip-toed around him as though he had caught a fever overseas that would leave him in good time.

The routine involved in editing the journal and in writing about the issues confronting nationalists in 1937-38 brought Laurendeau out of his despondency by plunging him back into the French-Canadian milieu. He wrote short editorials to lead off each issue as well as longer 'chronicles' on specific topics, and contributed to a new feature called 'Actualité', which he began in order to capture a wider range of intellectual opinion. His initial contributions drove home his strong commitment to the ideas of the Catholic left. He went out of his way, for example, to take on the extreme right-wing nationalists who had emerged in Quebec during the Depression and who were attempting to exploit what he described as a 'pre-fascist' mentality among French Canadians. He had already fired the opening shots in this confrontation while in Paris, both in articles written for *Le Devoir* and *L'Action nationale* and privately, in his correspondence with his father and Groulx. He cautioned the latter against showing any sympathy for the opinions expressed in Paul Bouchard's extremist publication *La Nation*: 'I read *La Nation* regularly. First with enthusiasm and full sympathy. Then with a good deal of reserve. Now, with the certainty that we'll soon have to fight it as an enemy.' He acknowledged that this might lead Groulx to suspect that his studies in France were leading him away from nationalism *per se*, but he insisted that wasn't the case: '. . . I remain a nationalist and I am even becoming more of one. But this nationalism has nothing in common with that of M. Mussolini. . . . Many of *La Nation*'s positions are the same as ours. . . . But they take their inspiration, often without knowing it, from ideologies that we reject.' To his father, who found *La Nation* quite to his liking, he condemned its violent, 'crazy' rhetoric and its penchant for fulminating in left-right, communist-fascist dialectics, as though Quebec were the same as France. 'Why import diseases,' he asked, 'don't we have enough of our own?'

In the autumn 1937 issues of *L'Action nationale* he carried these arguments to his readers. 'French Canadians are always quicker to applaud when the extreme left is condemned rather than the extreme right,' he noted in one article. 'Too often we find ourselves amongst those who believe . . . that God belongs to the Right.' He condemned the fascists in Europe repeatedly. His brief note introducing a refutation of the Rosenberg racial theories written by the Belgian Emile Baäs contended that 'to demolish the national-socialist doctrine, we need only remember that according to modern ethnology there is no longer any pure race in this world. . . . We are confronted with a pseudo-scientific fantasy, but one whose dynamic appeal we should not underestimate.' Two months later he referred to Pope Pius XI's recent encyclical on the Holy Rosary, which condemned both communism and pagan racist theories, inquiring ironically as to why it had not received anything like the publicity in Quebec that normally accompanied Papal utterances. Was the reason, he wondered pointedly, that it condemned the pernicious Hitlerian doctrines that so many French Canadians seemed to think represented law and order as well as a bulwark against communism? He himself opposed communism, 'but . . . in the name of Christianity, its message and its philosophy, not through blind obedience to fascist prejudice, and not through an exalted idea of the value of order.'[14] He maintained, however, that there was no serious communist threat in Quebec and thus no reason for anyone to adopt fascist arguments. For him a centrist ideological and political position was best for French Canada: 'The formula for the future seems to me a sort of social-nationalism based on personalism, or if one prefers, a strong and dynamic centre.'[15]

All the same, by January 1938 Laurendeau was less concerned with the interpretation of European ideologies in Quebec than with the way those ideologies were being exploited by unscrupulous provincial politicians. He wrote scathing denunciations of both the governing Union Nationale party and the opposition Liberals: the former for using the communist scare to justify its own social inaction and introduction of repressive measures, and the latter for its shrill but phoney anti-fascist response. He found it ludicrous that Adélard Godbout, the Liberal leader, should use the word 'fascist' to describe the Duplessis government while conveniently forgetting that the Union Nationale were simply carrying on the policies of the former Taschereau regime:

Mr Godbout's anti-fascism takes the form of protecting an odious past and present against some doubtful enemy. (Such anti-fascism would soon throw me into the arms of fascism!) He fights dictatorship in the name of a liberal notion of freedom. He is disgusted by a regime which destroys the freedom and dignity of a human being. All very well. But we remember certain things. Once upon a time there was a Liberal government in Quebec, Mr. Godbout's. In those days, we had freedom of speech, in the same way as under Liberal economic policies workers have the freedom to die of hunger. Once upon a time there was a Liberal government . . . it was indeed a period of freedom for high finance. . . . And what about the dignity of workmen or farm labourers forced to beg for patronage, of civil servants effectively muzzled, of Members of the Assembly entirely bound by party discipline? Heretical dogmas were censored and banned. . . . Once upon a time there was a Liberal government.[16]

He accused both old-line parties of being 'fathers' of separatism in Quebec because they had totally negated the spirit of Confederation through political patronage, corruption, and electoral fraud. They had allowed Quebec's democracy to be perverted by 'the secret dictatorship of high finance'. Employing an argument that he would use with more telling effect in the next decade, he attributed the province's social backwardness, in part at least, to the fact that 'in Quebec, rights granted by the federal power were never used.' But despite the severity of these criticisms, Laurendeau cautioned once more against resorting to extreme political options: 'we must not abandon government to the whims of fanatic nationalists. We lack a fully developed sense of social justice. . . . French Canadians must become more conscious of their own identity through their political education and through the many elements which contribute to the making of a nation.'[17]

With this last argument Laurendeau was evoking his own and the nationalist movement's traditional anti-statism.[18] He had learned to distrust politicians and the state as a disciple of Abbé Groulx and a member of Jeune-Canada. In the early 1930s he had resisted repeated calls for the latter to enter the political arena or to support the nationalist Action Libérale Nationale led by Gouin. During his early days in Paris, moreover, he had warned his father not to put politics high on the *Action nationale*'s agenda; 'all this excitement about Gouin has a panicky air.' When Gouin joined with Duplessis and the provincial Conservative party to form the Union Nationale, he remained sceptical in spite of widespread nationalist enthusiasm: 'I continue to dislike the Duplessy[*sic*]-Gouin union [since] Gouin's role must necessarily be on a smaller scale.' Yet it was also true that his conversion to personalism began to act as a check on his anti-statism. He adopted the personalist view that society's immediate problems, which were more socio-economic than cultural, demanded a degree of political involvement. While democracy was admittedly in a sad state throughout the Western world, it was still worth preserving as superior to any of its authoritarian alternatives—if only it could be purged of its many abuses. Thus he confessed to having some initial feelings of joy when he received news of the Union Nationale's electoral victory in 1936. But he continued to profess that the 'necessary revolution' in Quebec politics would only be brought about by his generation or perhaps the one after. He was anything but shocked, therefore, when word reached France that Duplessis had betrayed Gouin and the nationalists.

By the time he returned and began editing *L'Action nationale*, enthusiasm for a nationalist political movement had all but evaporated. As he explained years later:

> When I came back to Canada in the fall of 1937 . . . Duplessis had been in power for a year. The province was already disillusioned, and my friends saw him as a chief agent in the miscarriage of the nationalist reform movement of 1935-36. They calculated that chances for the revolution we had all dreamt of had been set back a full generation.[19]

The fact that his budding political consciousness proved too weak to stand up against this pessimism was just one example of how French-Canadian realities modified his progressive views during this period. It would require the crisis atmosphere and even grimmer realities of the Second World War to impel him towards politics. Meanwhile André used his first editorial to inform his readers that *L'Action nationale* would continue to emphasize nationalist education over political action. 'We never promised to throw ourselves into the political mêlée, and it's an adventure we will carefully guard against; . . . for the nation to concentrate all its energies there would be a disgrace.' True to his word, Laurendeau carried on a spirited private debate during these years with conservative nationalists who wanted *L'Action nationale* to support the Créditiste movement. Describing social-credit monetary theory as 'abracadabra' economics, he further alienated traditionalists by dismissing the movement itself as a rural-funda-mentalist throwback, the wave of the past.

Still, Laurendeau's political scepticism did not prevent him from taking up the cause of provincial autonomy with renewed vigour. His experiences in France, as we have seen, had snuffed out his earlier separatist speculations. The teachings of André Siegfried with respect to Quebec's peripheral role on the edge of the great geo-industrial forces shaping North American life had convinced him that a viable independent 'Laurentie' was a fantasy. Then too, his new commitment to internationalism, together with the admiration he felt for the minorities struggling for autonomy in Alsace and Belgium, had rekindled his belief in the potential of the federalist system. Yet he returned to find the federal government still attempting to upset that system's balance by invading provincial jurisdictions. There was nothing new, of course, in this nationalist complaint; it was nearly as old as Canada itself. But when the Depression's stubborn persistence finally provoked the essentially *laissez-faire* Bennett administration in Ottawa to do an about-face and introduce its own New Deal social legislation in 1935, the implications for provincial rights were obvious. Laurendeau, then still with Jeune-Canada, wrote to a number of French-Canadian intellectuals sounding the alarm and seeking their support. One of them, Georges-Henri Lévesque, the Dominican priest who was in the early stages of a brilliant career dedicated to modernizing French Canada's social and economic thought,[20] wrote back in March 1935 with a response that revealed how concerned even non-nationalists were about Ottawa's threat to Quebec's autonomy. Lévesque pointed out that extensive social and economic development had made it imperative that social measures be centralist in character. But centralism at the federal level was a danger to French Canada. In his view Quebec could not remain in Confederation and refuse such centralist policies, for to reject the necessary legislation would be to deny the other two-thirds of Canada's population the reforms they so badly needed. On the other hand, Quebec could not accept centralization. The answer seemed to be to leave Confederation and organize a separate reform program in Quebec. Recognizing that this position was quite radical, Lévesque pointed out that it was the product of long, often sad reflection.[21]

While at the time Laurendeau took Lévesque's remarks as a further justification for the culturally-based Laurentian separatism he then espoused with Jeune-Canada, they also summarized cogently the difficult choices he would face in the federal-provincial field from 1937 on. Aware now that social progress was crucial—though not yet convinced that the state, any state, should be the wheelhorse for such progress—he could nonetheless accept only provincial initiatives in the social sphere as constitutionally legitimate. The defence of Quebec's autonomy, as an antidote to either an omnipotent central government or an inadvisable separatism, was to be his central focus for decades to come. Hence he was one of the first nationalists to sound the alarm when Mackenzie King's government appointed the Rowell-Sirois Commission in 1938 to investigate dominion-provincial relations. Well aware of King's reputation for political manoeuvring, André viewed the establishment of the Commission as an effort to set the stage for the subversion of federalism at the expense of the provinces. Although the Commission did not submit its full report until 1940,[22] its very existence, not to mention the centralist tenor of its interim musings on federal-provincial relations, raised Laurendeau's hackles. Rowell-Sirois became a permanent *bête noire* for him and served to crystallize his initial arguments in what was to become a long and exhausting campaign for provincial autonomy.

While the spill-over effect of European ideological conflicts, the political climate in Quebec, and Canadian constitutional issues were important subjects for Laurendeau in his first years as director of *L'Action nationale*, they did not provide a great deal of scope for generating the dynamic nationalist renewal he was aiming at. Having returned to Quebec with a transforming vision rooted in a revolutionary Catholic social consciousness, he felt thwarted by the narrow-minded nationalist preoccupations that continuously entangled him in defensive responses. Disenchanted too with the general climate of 'negativism', he had to remind himself in his personal journal to try and keep 'my interior life . . . in a peaceful perpetual motion.' His sense of 'Catholic mission' kept tormenting him like an insomniac superego—all the more after the spiritual revival he had experienced in Italy. Rome's daunting Christian monuments had played a part in this, but it was at the convent in Assisi that he felt a real fervour— for perhaps the final time in his life—which inspired him to write a short biography of St Francis of Assisi soon after his return to Quebec.[23] The spirit of personal sacrifice and devotion to the down-trodden that he associated with St Francis also gave an added boost to his personalist social concerns. When Ghislaine teased that he had become almost a Dominican in this regard, he replied, 'No, I'm not a Dominican. Or, if you prefer, I am a Jesuit in education, Dominican in preoccupation (philosophy, social problems etc.) but Franciscan in my deepest sympathies.' It was natural, therefore, that he should look for allies among Quebec's Catholic intellectuals. Two who helped fill this role, Father Lévesque and the eminent botanist Brother Marie-Victorin, were intensely disliked by most nationalists for their reform-minded views.

Laurendeau's relationship with Lévesque, Quebec's most radical Catholic social thinker of that time and a man widely regarded as the intellectual oracle of the Quiet Revolution, revealed both the strengths and the limitations of his own reformist mentality in the years before the Second

World War. Despite the reservations of some older directors of *L'Action nationale*, he wrote Lévesque in the autumn of 1937 requesting that he contribute to the journal. Lévesque readily agreed, and was sufficiently impressed with André's personalist viewpoint to consider him a fellow toiler in 'our cause' of social reform. He pointed out too that he had been profoundly influenced by Emmanuel Mounier, and that he had been present at the 1932 meeting in Paris when *Esprit* was founded. Lévesque sent André the prospectus for the new School of Social Sciences he was starting up at Laval in 1938;[24] this school would eventually produce a corps of influential graduates who became severe critics of the *survivance* ideology as well as the defensive nationalism espoused by politicians like Maurice Duplessis. Lévesque also kept Laurendeau informed about the efforts of those politicians and his conservative Catholic superiors in Rome and Quebec City to have the school closed: and while 'very few things are happening publicly . . . it is clear that they want my poor head: it is always dangerous to be too genuinely social.' But when Laurendeau wrote about the school in *L'Action nationale* he tempered his praise for its efforts to develop a more realistic form of social awareness in Quebec with the observation that its program should reflect Thomistic philosophy and Catholic social doctrine. The fact that the journal also repledged its support for the conservative interpretation of that doctrine represented in the Jesuits' 1933 'Program for Social Restoration'—a status quo-oriented and clichéd version of Papal encyclicals relating to industrial society— only underlined the tentative nature of Laurendeau's public support for radical theorizing. He was discovering that while his Parisian personalism made him a risqué thinker in nationalist circles, there were intellectuals in Quebec who were prepared to go much farther.

The same timid, one-step-forward-half-a-step-back approach characterized his dealings with Brother Marie-Victorin. André was familiar with the latter's work as an internationally recognized professor of science at the Université de Montréal from his days as a student there. His closest friend and fellow Jeune-Canada member Pierre Dansereau had studied with Marie-Victorin and would himself become a world-class botanist. Dansereau, in fact, had always preferred his mentor's outward-looking pure scientific vision to Abbé Groulx's exclusivist form of nationalism.[25] Largely responsible for establishing Montreal's botanical gardens as a symbol of scientific achievement in Quebec, Marie-Victorin was a fierce advocate of pure research. In the 1930s he condemned the nationalist perception of science as subservient to chauvinist ends, and he criticized Quebec's education system for giving scientific instruction such a low priority. Laurendeau took issue with his central premise:

> The idea that science must replace national feeling seems to me the primary idea: it's like saying that the discovery of aspirin will drive love

out of the human heart . . . I doubt that Marie-Victorin adheres to such a simplistic opinion. That the scientist searches for the truth and not the nation is clear: he is nonetheless bound by it, supported, nourished by it (to a certain extent). . . .

But he did invite Marie-Victorin to engage in dialogue with nationalists like himself. In accepting, Marie-Victorin observed that 'you and I are searching for a formula that is not unilateral. We will undoubtedly achieve a degree of unity in our ideas.' In December 1938 Laurendeau came full circle and defended the scientist against the rage of his fellow nationalists when, in a speech at Trois-Rivières, Marie-Victorin carried his criticism of the educational system to new lengths and charged that only the Catholic church, because it controlled education in Quebec, could bring about desperately needed changes. André insisted that Marie-Victorin was not opposed to a classical humanist education, but was merely emphasizing how vital science was for solving the social, economic, and political problems in modern society: 'he called on us, in the name of national dignity and our own interest, to work towards victory through science.' And yet his attempt to deflect the anti-nationalist critique that permeated Marie-Victorin's thought was not very convincing to his colleagues at L'Action nationale or even, perhaps, to himself. It was becoming increasingly clear that French-Canadian nationalism was regarded by at least some progressive intellectuals in Quebec as part of the problem, not the solution.

The contradictions within Laurendeau's struggle for nationalist renewal were also apparent in the vital sphere of economics. Economic theory had always been the weakest link in his intellectual formation and the Achilles heel of French-Canadian nationalism itself. He returned from Europe still critical of laissez-faire capitalism, but unlike the damn-them-all fusillades he had launched from within the Jeune-Canada movement, his remarks were now focused on the abuses of capitalism, most notably its monopolistic, anti-social character. In his criticism of extremist ideologies, for example, he wrote:

> Communism, fascism . . . yet what if there was a third thief? A very respectable-looking gentleman, full of concern for parliamentary democracy, always talking about liberty, and all the time lining his own pockets? . . . And who is this menacing figure? He is called liberal capitalism or more specifically, the abuses of capitalism. A Punch and Judy show is staged before our eyes; the rustics assemble to gape, while backstage money still calls the tune and pulls the strings.[26]

But even if he could still work up a fiery rhetorical edge on the subject, he recognized that industrial capitalism had come to Quebec to stay, Depression or no Depression, and he could barely conceal his disdain for the pie-in-the-sky economic ideas of older, right-wing nationalists. Some of them, including his father and his old mentor Esdras Minville, had

Corporatism

fallen in love with the theory of corporatism—the reigning economic
dogma in fascist countries. They argued that French Canadians could
avoid the odious aspects of fascist economics by developing a form of corporatism that would be free of state domination.

But André had seen corporatism close-up in Italy and, while he agreed
to devote a special issue of *L'Action nationale* to studying all aspects of the
theory, he did so without any enthusiasm. He found it easier to write positively about Quebec's co-operative movement—corporatism's sibling in
the closely knit family of nationalist tools for economic 'reconquest'. Co-
operatives were, after all, a well-entrenched feature of agricultural life in
Quebec, and it was not entirely utopian to imagine them as a force for collective French-Canadian economic strength in that sector. On the whole,
though, Laurendeau considered all of these theories pitifully inadequate
for a society that was becoming primarily industrial. They were no more
likely to help French Canadians regain control of Quebec's economy from
English Canadians and foreigners than were the *'achat chez nous'* cam-
paigns that usually accompanied them. He knew they were based on a
flawed, petty-bourgeois conception of French Canada's industrial reality.
But since he had no concrete alternatives to offer himself, being totally
ignorant of economic theory and the business world, he concentrated his
efforts on supporting the trade-union movement.

Prior to this time Laurendeau had never paid a great deal of attention to
the working class. As a privileged 'notable' he had directed whatever
thoughts he had for the masses to the virtuous qualities of the rural
peasant. What he knew of the grisly conditions in Montreal's east-end
ghetto was gained mostly from hearsay; he seldom ventured there. His
concern for the worker's plight was usually couched in muted praise for
the confessional trade unions—which, being Quebec-based, Catholic in
character, and only occasionally militant, conformed to the nationalist
ideals of respect for order and spiritual over material aspirations. Like other
nationalists he seemed to believe that the workers' plight would be substantially improved only if a way could be found to make French Canadians the owners of industry. But in France he had learned how important a
militant trade-union movement could be for fighting capitalist abuses and
demanding social reform. Writing from Paris in 1936, he took issue with
those nationalists in Quebec who opposed international unions. 'It is good
to see compatriots escape from the demagogic and demoralizing interna-
tionals,' he allowed. 'But don't forget what capitalism is. It is international. To have a group of nationalist syndicates ranged against such an
omnipotent enemy: they would be extremely weak. . . . The workers'
action must remain international.' Back in Quebec with the conservative
old-guard all around him, he retreated and described the confessional
unions as still the best alternative, but only if they achieved palpable
results for the workers. As if to underline this point, he used one of his first

articles in *L'Action nationale* to deal with the explosive textile strike in Montreal during the summer and autumn of 1937. Supporting the workers, he condemned both the Dominion Textile Company and the Duplessis government for their anti-labour collusion. He also commented negatively on the confessional union's activities and he criticized Cardinal Villeneuve for intervening against the strikers. This, he contended, was proof that a sense of moral justice had not yet developed among Catholics in Quebec. Clearly, then, Laurendeau was anxious to steer the nationalist cause towards a healthier awareness of Quebec's social and economic realities, even if at this stage he himself was unclear as to how far it should go or which solutions were best. But this did not mean that he ignored the traditional nationalist concern for the survival of French Canada's culture. In fact, the cultural field provided a comfort zone where he could share common cause with traditionalists like Abbé Groulx and thus plaster over, temporarily at least, the cracks developing between them on other issues. Here too, however, his views showed signs of internal strain and revealed contradictory tendencies. He considered it both ironic and amusing that his voyage to Europe—something he had anticipated since his idealistic school days as the transforming experience that would lift him out of the tawdry cultural world of North America—had in fact inspired him to want to learn more about the United States and English Canada.

In the American case his reason for doing so was entirely negative. André Siegfried had convinced him that America was a far greater threat to French Canada's culture than the traditional foreign enemy, England. 'We may be apprehensive about the English influence,' he wrote in October 1937, 'but it acts at a distance and, as far as civilisation is concerned, it is less hostile to our own. Yet we pit the best part of our energy against it, while largely ignoring the dangers of American influence.'[27] Recalling Siegfried's assertion that 'American civilisation is based on quantity', he described American materialism as an insidious danger:

> Whether one considers their elite impressive or not . . . [the] United States sits beside us, with its ebullient interests and ambitions, its technical mastery, and its mass production, which springs from the very nature of its life and genius and which is likely to submerge us; with its faults as well, of course, and these are the very aspects we tend to imitate . . . spiritual poverty, with which they inoculate us and which we are in a poor position to resist; and a vast desire to conquer the material world, . . . which appears to me like those feverish spasms and epileptic fits which presage the sleep of death. . . . We are bewitched by this hyper-capitalist view of life. . . . As a result, spiritualism loses its effect on men, the New Testament is sometimes explained on a natural level, and ideas lose their propelling force, their power to motivate; they become watered down and engulfed by comfort and luxury—not necessarily along millionaire lines. The American way of life is to prefer a cigar, a radio and a couch. . . .[28]

Perhaps recalling his own youthful infatuation with American jazz and cinema, he argued that French Canada would have to develop its own popular culture, 'an original style of living to counter the alien one'.[29] But his advice on how to do this was contradictory and elitist. What did he really know, after all, about popular culture? What he did seem certain about was that creativity demanded openness to outside stimuli. It was mandatory, he claimed, to abandon the culture of 'passive virtues, those which made good slaves'.[30] He placed little hope in perpetuating a rural mystique or trying to be creative behind sealed walls:

> For a long period, French Canada was a closed society, and necessarily so. The situation was imposed by geographical as well as historical conditions, and the economy of the times allowed a certain isolation. From this fact, which became an obsession, sprang an entire defence system which was appropriate at the time but is increasingly losing its rationale and its vitality. The problem is no longer to conserve, but to conquer anew. We are surrounded. Our problem is no longer to survive but to live.[31]

Yet the only initiative he could suggest along these lines was to send out a questionnaire to intellectuals and members of Quebec's artistic elite to ascertain the current strength and future potential of French-Canadian culture. A few of the respondents drew attention to the fact that a vibrant and creative high culture might be of no interest to the urban masses, and would therefore do little to blunt the invasion of American popular culture. Others observed that Quebec's high culture itself was still largely mired in the world of *Maria Chapdelaine*—the novel by the Frenchman Louis Hémon that was often cited, both positively and negatively, to symbolize the dominance of *survivance* themes in French Canada's arts.[32] Dr Phillippe Panneton, whose 1937 novel *Thirty Acres* (published under the pseudonym Ringuet) raised a furore among traditionalists because of its grimly realistic portrayal of the declining viability of the family farm and the moral world it represented, answered Laurendeau by observing that French-Canadian culture was too embryonic and therefore too fragile to be seen as serving some broader purpose. It was 'self-mockery' to believe otherwise: 'That reminds me of exultant parents who bend over the cradle already discussing whether their son will be a general or a notary.' Although responses to Laurendeau's inquiry were published in *L'Action nationale* well into the war years, it was apparent from the beginning that the transformation of Quebec's traditional society during the late nineteenth and early twentieth centuries had brought about a delayed crisis in its high culture and a sense of uncertainty as to whether something distinctive and fresh would now emerge.

While Laurendeau shared this uncertainty, he had no doubt whatsoever that the prospects for a cultural rebirth were inextricably linked to the fate of the French language in Quebec. One of his major concerns during this period was the decline of French and the corresponding proliferation of English in Quebec. André, it is worth recalling, had always been opposed to bilingualism. His father tried to shield him from exposure to English at an early age, partly out of fear that learning two languages would damage his intellectual development—a prejudice that was not uncommon in those days. Whatever English André learned during his year in England, when he was seven, soon wore off and from that point on the English phrases he picked up, from the radio or elsewhere, were threaded into his conversation as jibes and quips. He became convinced during his student days, moreover, that the French language and culture were superior to those of the English. When he became a nationalist in the 1930s, he acquired additional, historical reasons for opposing English; the language itself was considered to be the thin edge of the wedge in the ongoing English-Canadian campaign to assimilate French Canada. No wonder he announced, soon after arriving at Paris, the centre of all learning: 'I don't wish to learn English.' Not even personalism, with its strong internationalist spirit, could change his mind, though it did raise troubling questions: '. . . I have doubts about that [learning English], but not for immediately practical reasons. I wonder if this sort of separatism would be realistic and . . . in the spirit of openness.' On the other hand, his trips to Alsace and Belgium had provided strong evidence that bilingualism led inevitably to the undermining of a minority's language and, eventually, to the reduction of its culture to an oddity of folklore.

His return to Quebec in 1937 coincided with the Second International Congress of the French Language, held in Montreal, where Abbé Groulx among others called for a vigorous program of *'refrancisation'*. Laurendeau joined the campaign, condemning those French-Canadian leaders who were preaching the virtues of bilingualism. Studies documenting the decline of French were only beginning to appear at this time, and the sophisticated quantitative compilations available more recently from Quebec's Gendron Commission (1969-73) and, of course, from Laurendeau's own federal commission on Bilingualism and Biculturalism (1963-71) could not have been imagined then. But he didn't need them to feel alarm at the way bilingualism was increasingly regarded by urban French Canadians as the best route to material success. The Catholic Council of Instruction in Montreal was recommending that English should be taught from grade three on. One only needed to walk through the city to see the conquering march of English in every form of advertising. It was clear to him that bilingualism was simply a method for getting the French to learn English. 'When all French Canadians have become bilingual,' he contended, '. . . they will all speak English . . . and French itself will soon be useless.'[33]

There were other dangers too. With urban families becoming smaller, and a decline in the French proportion of the population in Quebec therefore likely, would the masses strive to keep up their French? It was fine, he argued, for those who loved languages and wanted to learn five or six to extol the virtues of bilingualism; 'but the average man will not force himself for very long to learn a language whose practical value has become debatable.'[34] To paint a picture of the future in a bilingual Canada, he pointed to the federal civil service, where French was hardly spoken, and the federal parliament, where only one speech in fifty was in French —because by and large, only the French-speaking members of parliament were bilingual. The unequal size of the two language groups could only lead to the slow asphyxiation of French.

> On the one hand, then, you would have a solidly entrenched language spoken by seven and a half million Canadians and understood by three and a half million Canadians, formerly French, and on the other, a now useless dialect, still spoken for a time in the churches and families, and slowly disappearing. No doubt the death stroke would be a long time coming, as witness some of our minorities who have kept their maternal speech in the face of a hostile environment right up to the present. However, French life, popular culture, and soon the thinking rooted in that language and culture would begin their final agony.[35]

In light of these views on language, it might seem contradictory for Laurendeau to recommend that French-Canadian nationalists should seek to improve their relations with and knowledge of English Canada. But that was precisely the example he endeavoured to set in 1938-39. It was the first of three such deliberate efforts in his life, the other two coming in 1955, when he made an extensive tour of western Canada, and from 1963 to 1968, during his tenure as co-chairman of the Royal Commission on Bilingualism and Biculturalism. Yet prior to this time he had never expressed the slightest interest in learning about English Canada, not even Quebec's English-speaking minority. As he observed to a member of that community in 1939, 'I had lived more than 20 years beside you without my curiosity having been awakened about you.' The impetus for this new attitude arose—as in so many other instances—from his experiences in France:

> In France I was always humiliated whenever anybody asked me a question about English Canada because of my almost total ignorance of the subject. I had gleaned the better part of my meagre information at the Collège de France from a course given by André Siegfried. So here was a young French Canadian replying to questions about his own country with answers that had been slipped to him by a French intellectual. It was a pitiful situation. I resolved to seek some kind of dialogue with English Canada as soon as I got back.[36]

Siegfried, we have seen, had also convinced him that English Canada could be a vital ally against American economic and cultural domination. At the same time, André was hopeful that he might find English-Canadian partners willing to compromise in a policy of neutrality *vis-à-vis*

British imperialism, just in case the looming war clouds in Europe became a real storm.

Since his major intellectual quest during this period involved broadening his knowledge of social philosophy, he calculated that he might kill two birds with one stone by enrolling in sociology courses at McGill University. What a curious feeling he must have had as he made his way through the pretentious arch and up the green-flanked sidewalk towards the horseshoe of buildings that formed the heart of McGill's campus. He had spent his whole life in close proximity to it, looking down from Mount Royal in the course of his wanderings between the Université de Montréal and Outremont, or passing by on his way to the city centre and the eastern francophone districts. But it had always been a physical affront to him. McGill symbolized the smug superiority and arrogant indifference of Quebec's English minority. It looked down on the city from its position at the base of Mount Royal, just as its Anglo-Scots founders and supporters with names like Robertson, Molson, and Redpath had looked down on the city's French-speaking minority. McGill's colonial-minded administrators would rather ape British forms and curricula than make even a token adjustment to Quebec's French character. They preferred African students (especially the polite, well-turned-out, British-accented ones) to young French Canadians—even if the latter were bilingual. Along with Westmount, Eaton's, the Stock Exchange, and the *Gazette*, McGill was one of the names that, far more often than English symbols from outside Quebec, reminded Laurendeau why he was a nationalist. It was a worthy test of his tolerance and new spirit of dialogue for him to enrol in what he had always regarded as the spawning ground of the oppressive English-speaking business class.

Imagine his surprise, therefore, when the English-Canadian professors and students he met and befriended turned out to be socially progressive and sympathetic: 'belonging to the political left for the most part—and some of them, as I learned later, to the extreme left—their opinions coincided quite closely with those of a nationalist fresh from Paris.'[37] Two of those he met were Professor F.R. Scott, the Canadian poet and socialist who played a key role during these years in the Co-operative Commonwealth Federation,[38] and Neil Morrison, both of whom would later work with him on the Bilingualism and Biculturalism commission. He also came to know Ken Woodsworth, nephew of the CCF's founder J.S. Woodsworth, and Secretary-General of the Canadian Youth Congress. These connections provided Laurendeau with access to English-Canadian organizations and further personal contacts. Scott, for example, invited him in 1939 to the Canadian Institute of International Affairs at McGill to discuss French and English attitudes to Canadian foreign policy.[39] Next a working group was organized that met several times to try and work out a common approach in the event of a European war. Laurendeau was gratified to discover English Canadians who seemed to favour neutrality. He also received invitations to speak at Sir George Williams University in Montreal and at the Assembly of Canadian Students in Ottawa on 'The Philosophy of Education and the French-Canadian Mind'. By 1939 he was resolved to translate these fraternal relations with English Canadians into a more ambitious culture-to-culture effort.

André joined forces with Neil Morrison, whom he persuaded to contribute to *L'Action nationale*, to read a dialogue on English-French relations for CBC radio on 3 June. Their script, entitled 'Canada: a Country of Two Cultures' was stilted and amateurish even for those times, but Laurendeau pulled no punches in getting across the French-Canadian nationalist viewpoint. Arguing that English-Canadian treatment of the French minorities in the other provinces produced a kind of separatist thinking in Quebec, he called this 'moral separatism' and went on to point out:

> The school situation, for instance, in all the provinces where we are the minority, remains unjust from our point of view. . . . When it is a question of the nomination of federal civil servants, of bilingual stamps or money, how many idle, mean discussions we have to suffer! . . . As a result many among us have said to themselves: 'so be it, let us accept the *fait accompli*. In practice they push us aside, as *French-Canadians*, in other parts of Canada. We are truly at home only in Quebec: then let us be completely at home there.' Moral separatism—once and for all I tell you that organized political separatism scarcely exists in Quebec—moral separatism . . . leads us to isolate ourselves. That is why, almost voluntarily, I completely ignored English Canada.

The success of this show led André to propose a regular series of similar dialogues to the Director of Talks for the CBC. 'You know', he explained, 'to what degree the world of the English language and that of the French language are isolated from one another'; here was an opportunity to break down the walls of ignorance. He made a similar proposal to Augustin Frignon, Director General of Radio-Canada, a man with whom he would have much less pleasant dealings in the years ahead. So began a long association between André and the government broadcaster.

Perhaps the most intriguing activity that André engaged in as part of this effort to construct a cross-cultural *entente* with English Canada involved the Canadian Youth Congress. As we have seen, he had been involved in French-Canadian youth groups from a very early age and at this time was president of the Conseil des Jeunesses Canadiennes. (The leadership of this organization was a breeding ground for future French-Canadian leaders; to take just two examples, both Daniel Johnson, the vice-president, and Jean-Jacques Bertrand would become premiers of Quebec in the 1960s.) Delegates from the council were invited to attend the Canadian Youth Congress meetings at Winnipeg in June 1939 and André, who was excited over the prospect of making his first visit to the Canadian west, made a point of inviting the Quebec nationalist politician René Chaloult. Not sharing Laurendeau's enthusiasm for English-French exchanges, Chaloult indignantly declined. Nevertheless, an effort was made at the Congress to accommodate both cultural groups. One-third of the delegates were French-Canadian, bilingualism was practised, and a seventy-five per cent vote was required to pass a resolution. This gave Laurendeau initial grounds for hope that his delegates might secure support for recognition of Canada's dualistic cultural character and the principle of respect for provincial autonomy; it would not be the last time he travelled to Winnipeg seeking approval for these two measures. He was further buoyed by the defeat of a motion of censure against Quebec's Union Nationale government for passing the Padlock Act in 1937, a piece of anti-labour legislation that gave the provincial police the right to close any union hall suspected of communist activities. His position was embarrassing, however, given his pro-union stand at home and his own condemnations of the Duplessis government's communist-bashing. Now, in a foreshadowing of the contradictions to be forced upon him in the future, he defended the Union Nationale in order to support the principle of provincial autonomy. And on other major issues, such as foreign policy and federal social legislation, there was no agreement.[40] Laurendeau returned to Montreal pleased with his participation in such a large-scale co-operative enterprise, but with some residual forebodings of the damage that a foreign-policy crisis could inflict on such efforts.

He was also frustrated by the limitations of his small circle of nationalists. He wanted to get beyond what he called 'the reserved group' at the Ligue de l'Action Nationale to bring the message of social nationalism to a wider French-Canadian audience. Even though he published an uncritical biography of Abbé Groulx in 1939, he regarded the conservative old-guard of the Ligue as complacent. When he was in France, his father had written to tell him that L'Action nationale had $6,000 in its war chest, leaving him with the impression that he would have the resources to perform wonders in the years ahead. But in 1939 it proved a major victory just to free up $350 from the Ligue's directors to pay a few contributors in advance for articles that he badly wanted. They seemed to think that even non-nationalists should contribute their work for free, out of patriotic feeling; or perhaps their parsimony was a way of showing Laurendeau that they disapproved of his editorial strategies. In any case, in his report to the directors of November 1939 he advanced a number of proposals for the financing of a new weekly journal. Not only would it reach a much larger audience through an initial circulation of up to 5,000 copies but, as he explained to a friend, it would allow him to syphon off the tiresome, repetitive material from L'Action nationale in favour of fresh ideas. The start of the Second World War gave the directors an excuse to postpone these ambitious plans.

That Laurendeau's anxieties reflected much more than mere differences of opinion with the directors over the operations of L'Action nationale was evident from his dealings with other reform-minded publications. It had been relatively easy for him to kill any attempt by the conservatives to strike up ties with the extreme right-wing movement centred on the journal La Nation, but they in turn had vetoed his suggestion for co-operation with Robert Charbonneau's La Relève. Charbonneau, lamenting the sudden closing in France of the journal Sept, had proposed to André that their two publications issue a joint declaration in favour of the Catholic left's principles. When André informed him of the Ligue's decision not to do so, Charbonneau claimed Laurendeau was abandoning his principles and betraying the Catholic left. Here in truth was the root of André's growing frustration. Coming back from Paris determined to overhaul the nationalist doctrine along liberal lines, he knew there were a number of intellectuals in Quebec who were also opposed to the prevailing ideology and could therefore be a help to him—Lévesque, Marie-Victorin, Charbonneau. These men, who would be the true intellectual precursors of Quebec's Quiet Revolution of the 1960s, had clearly passed him by. Why? Was it just because of his efforts to placate the old guard, or was Charbonneau right: was he losing some of the reformer's zeal that he had carried back from Paris?

While Laurendeau's filial ties to what one scholar has called the 'double paternity' of Arthur Laurendeau and Lionel Groulx[41] did indeed compromise his reform efforts, he was also held back by the internal contradictions of his own nationalist thought. For example, he loved Quebec's traditional culture, but found it backward as well and unlikely to flourish when confronted by the more dynamic and modern English-Canadian and American cultures. How, then, could French Canada's culture open its doors to life-giving outside stimuli and at the same time hold them closed enough to resist being overwhelmed? Similarly, to acknowledge that Quebec had become an urban and industrial society, and therefore required a corresponding set of institutions and ideologies, did not answer the question of how to resist external capitalist and cultural domination. To defend provincial autonomy only to reap social stagnation and political demagoguery in Quebec City left him yet another circle to try and square. The tension in André's thoughts was underlined by a short note in his personal journal of March 1938, where he mused about writing a book on the human spirit that would bring together (surely for the first time) St Francis, St Ignatius Loyola, and Lenin. This idea also pointed to another of his shortcomings: he was still too much the man of theory. Personalism's philosophic speculations had indeed helped to direct his intellect and spiritual life down progressive paths, but here in late-Depression Quebec he was entirely lacking in concrete knowledge of the grass-roots social and economic problems about which he professed such aching concern. When he felt the need for answers in this area, he would sooner reach for a book—almost always a volume of French philosophy at that—than walk into Montreal's east-end ghetto. The libraries of Outremont were not going to yield all the answers he required. In the years immediately ahead, monumental international events would have the double effect of overshadowing, if not entirely suspending, these theoretical questions while thrusting him into the tangible world of Quebec's politics and working people.

5
War and Conscription, 1939-1942

> ... the conscription crisis underlined once again the fact that Canadians are
> two nations. The evidence was made unmistakably clear at the time of the
> Riel affair, then again over certain school problems, then in 1917 at the time
> of the first conscription. It is only when two nations confront each other with
> intense feeling that one can measure to what degree they really exist.
>
> André Laurendeau, *The Conscription Crisis*, 1963[1]

André Laurendeau was in the countryside on 5 August 1940, when word
reached him about Camillien Houde. The mayor of Montreal and a former
leader of the provincial Conservative party, Houde was a flamboyant
politician with a keen sense for the wind's direction and an allegiance that
was just as changeable. With a heavy drinker's bulbous nose and a body
that was gathering itself for a formidable obesity, he was a man of huge
appetites and strong passions. On 2 August passion had got the better of
him. At a news conference in Montreal he denounced the federal government's new mobilization law, which ordered all Canadian men and
women between the ages of fourteen and sixty to register later that month
for military service. Houde promised to defy the law, and he urged his
fellow French Canadians to do the same. Never mind that France had
fallen earlier that summer before the Nazi blitzkrieg, along with Denmark,
Holland, Belgium, and Norway. Never mind either that Britain now stood
alone and in dire need of help against Hitler. And most particularly never
mind that Prime Minister Mackenzie King, flanked by his French-Canadian ministers, had solemnly promised that registration did not mean conscription for overseas service. Houde had heard such promises before. To
him and to French-Canadian nationalists generally, registration was
simply the next step in a well-orchestrated plan to bring in conscription
and, in so doing, to humiliate French Canada. He underlined his defiance
by distributing a communiqué whose contents were soon plastered across
the front page of Montreal's English-language newspapers. On 5 August,

as he left the city hall still wearing his robes of office, Houde was arrested by the RCMP and whisked away to an internment camp at Petawawa, Ontario. He would be held for four years, returning to a hero's welcome at Montreal's Windsor Station in August 1944, whereupon his fellow citizens showed their defiance by re-electing him mayor.[2]

Laurendeau regarded Houde's gesture as 'logical' and even heroic in its opposition to the Canadian government's inexorable march towards conscription, but also futile. In the first place, he considered Houde to be a tarnished standard-bearer. 'My faith in him had dwindled considerably—he had changed tack too fast, too often.'[3] As for the nationalists among André's friends who wanted to follow Houde by writing and signing a letter that would surely get them interned, what good would it do when so many prominent French Canadians were supporting the federal government? Among the latter he included not only those he regarded as toadies in King's cabinet and the spineless politicians at Quebec City, but even Maxime Raymond, a respected nationalist in Canada's parliament who had accepted registration precisely because it was limited to the defence of Canada. And there was also Cardinal Villeneuve, a significant voice in Catholic Quebec. Laurendeau was personally appalled by his pusillanimity: 'I am more scandalized,' he wrote to Abbé Groulx, 'at Cardinal Villeneuve's foolishness . . . than at our federal deputation's vote for participation. . . . The Cardinal is voracious. He likes to accumulate mistakes. He accuses those who don't blindly accept English propaganda of being small-minded and unnatural.' And what did the people think? While Laurendeau was certain that they would never accept conscription for service abroad, he had to admit they were in shock over France's swift defeat. He conceded that 'to choose the moment of France's greatest distress to refuse to collaborate in policies that were intended to avenge her had . . . something repugnant about it.' In such circumstances individual acts of rebellion seemed fruitless. 'What finally influenced me,' he wrote, 'was . . . the feeling of impotence. . . . If a resistance movement had existed, I think I would have joined it.' Instead he went to the registration office near Saint-Gabriel, answered all of the official's questions, signed his name, and left feeling 'that I had just contradicted and perhaps betrayed myself'.[4]

Laurendeau had seen the war coming since 1937. Before leaving Europe in the spring of that year, he had come face to face with the belligerent spirit of fascism in Italy, and he foresaw that Franco's successes in Spain would embolden his German backers to enter upon new adventures. He had written soon after his return to Canada: 'Since they are such an extreme phenomenon, Hitler's policies seem unlikely to spread like wildfire; yet many of their elements are exportable and are in fact exported.'[5] He warned that the danger of confrontation emanating from this corner was far greater than that presented by the spread of communism, Quebec's traditional *bête noire*. In 1938, when the Sudetenland had become the main issue, Laurendeau argued that neither justice, nor the law, nor their own best interests called French Canadians to the defence of the Czechs. He went so far as to picture the Germans of the Sudetenland as a beleaguered minority, tyrannized by the central government in Prague. He had changed considerably, in other words, since the time in Paris when he strongly opposed fascist belligerence during the Spanish Civil War. Now he endorsed the more familiar French-Canadian nationalist view that European conflicts were not worth getting involved in and were quite as dangerous for Canadian unity as the ever-lurking threat of British impe- rialism. Although he was still much less extreme than his ultra-conserv- ative colleagues at *L'Action nationale*, neither was he as remote from their influence as his later writings on the subject suggest. Thus he applauded the settlement at Munich just as vigorously as they did, but he remained sceptical of Mackenzie King's judgement, after meeting Hitler, that the Nazi leader did not seem like a man who wanted war. He regarded the visit of the King and Queen to Canada in the spring of 1939 as a clear signal that war was inevitable, and he bitterly condemned their tour as an insulting piece of imperialist propaganda. He was so incensed, in fact, that he declared himself a republican: 'Nowhere near so much out of love for republicanism as out of resentment for this ambiguous allegiance, used in an emotional way to drag us into adventures that are primarily British.'

Laurendeau and his fellow nationalists had also been keeping a wary eye on Canada's national political scene and were alerted to the intentions of the Liberal government in Ottawa by the sudden escalation—a seventy per cent increase—in the defence budget of 1937.[6] Despite assurances that this was only a precautionary measure, necessary for Canada's defensive readiness, Laurendeau saw it as a sharp break with Mackenzie King's long-standing policy of non-intervention in foreign squabbles. King was of course too shifty to be pegged as an out-and-out isolationist, and too politically shrewd to be identified as a committed neutralist where the British tie was concerned, but since the 1931 passage of the Statute of West- minster he had given many speeches declaring that Canada would not be drawn automatically into British imperial conflicts and that Canada's interests must come first. *L'Action nationale* sponsored a celebration in 1939 to emphasize the importance of the Statute and to underline that now, more than ever, King's policy of enlightened neutrality was wisest. But as Laurendeau later noted, the interpretation of that policy had always depended on the audience:

> Liberals and nationalists alike acclaimed such statements, but they sounded somewhat different to French-Canadian ears than they did to English- Canadian ears. For the former they meant a policy of almost total neutral- ity. For the latter they signified the freedom to stand outside any minor conflict that Great Britain might become involved in to protect her interests, but at the same time the freedom to fly to the aid of the mother country if

her life were threatened in a major war. King knew how to juggle such equivocal attitudes admirably, and his Quebec lieutenants gave his pronouncements—which were nearly always ambiguous—the interpretation that best suited their constituents.[7]

In any case, by the late summer of 1939 any form of Canadian neutrality looked more and more like a lost cause.

For French-Canadian nationalists, however, conscription was the all-important issue. Their other complaints were intended to forestall any possibility of its eventually being imposed. The reason was not merely that conscription would be disastrous for Canada—that was a secondary concern for them—but that it would mean the isolation and humiliation of French Canada: the crushing of the minority's will and historic sensibilities under the brutal heel of the majority. André had grown up hearing stories about similar humiliations in the past, and during his early twenties Abbé Groulx had put the flesh and sinew of historical fact into those stories in his courses at the Université de Montréal. Laurendeau himself had felt the sting of English Canada's insensitivity in the early thirties, so sharply indeed that he had helped to organize Jeune-Canada. Now all of the familiar signs were once again at hand; with the memory of conscription during the First World War still fresh, it was not difficult to recognize them. And wasn't it the purest irony that the federal Liberal party was most responsible for never allowing French Canadians to forget that crisis? André could remember as far back as 1930, when he was a student on summer vacation, not at all interested in politics, being dragged by friends to a political meeting where the Liberal candidate, all but ignoring the start of the Depression and sundry other issues, based his pitch to the voters solely on reminding them about Sir Robert Borden, Arthur Meighen, the Conservative Party, and the conscription crisis of 1917. For decades the Liberals had successfully nurtured the myth that they were blameless in that crisis, though Laurendeau was well aware that English-Canadian Liberals had abandoned Laurier and his Quebec rump to join the drive to conscription. In fact, Laurier himself had contributed mightily to his own downfall by compromising too often with the British imperial sentiments of English Canadians.

For Laurendeau, it was Henri Bourassa who had led the French-Canadian fight against conscription in those times. It was Bourassa who possessed the integrity and foresight to resign his seat at Ottawa in 1899 over the precedent-setting compromise that Laurier had forged with respect to Canadian participation in the Boer War. It was Bourassa too who had seen clearly what Canada's naval armaments policy during the early 1900s would bring in the way of involvement in Britain's wars. And when the war came in 1914, it was again Bourassa who urged limits on participation that he believed would show respect for both sides of the Canadian duality:

But though Bourassa proclaimed his message from coast to coast, French Canadians were about the only ones to hear it. Blood is thicker than water. Anglo-Canadians were too near to their British origins, too tied to strong, fresh memories, too intimately involved in the Empire, too deeply convinced that to defend 'Mother England' was to defend the most precious and noble part of themselves, to hear such a call for liberation.

French Canadians, on the contrary, were extremely sensitive to the least appeal to their desire for autonomy, to the point that some of them became deaf to all else. They have often been called cowards; the accusation is not only unjust, I think it is ridiculous. It required more courage to refuse to go along with the rest than to conform, even though conforming meant going against one's personal convictions. Individual cowardice is, of course, often masked by patriotic attitudes, and fear is an incentive common to all people. But fear wasn't the basic motive. The French Canadian of 1917 felt that he possessed only one country, the little bit of land that belonged to him. It was a poor man's reaction, if you will—the attitude of an agricultural people, somewhat closed in upon themselves, who know their own weaknesses and know that they must husband their strength, for there is no one else in the world to help them. Even though his religious and political leaders preached loyalty to him, he could see the cold hard facts of his situation; his sense of loyalty didn't stretch that far. He had no love for England; he didn't like the English. . . . They [French Canadians] wanted to be left alone. Peaceable by nature, they could get angry on occasion. In 1917 they got angry, and they never forgot that they had been forced . . . no one ever gave them a chance to forget it.[8]

This assessment of conscription in 1917 held important lessons for Laurendeau and his fellow nationalists in 1939. Bourassa's struggle had proven that to give an inch in the battle against British imperialism or, worse still, to concur in half measures designed to placate English Canada, as Laurier had, was to assure the eventual degradation of French Canada.

Consequently, when Hitler's armies stormed into Poland on 1 September 1939, beginning the war in Europe, Laurendeau returned at once from Saint-Gabriel to Montreal to help organize demonstrations against Canadian participation. 'I was', he admitted, 'a militant anti-participationist.'[9] With the War Measures Act already in effect and the National Defence Regulations about to be applied on 3 September, nationalists were under no illusions as to the federal government's intention to issue its own declaration of war. To them the parliamentary debate in Ottawa was simply a superficial attempt to give credibility to King's oft-repeated promise that 'Parliament will decide'. Nevertheless, the battle for public opinion in Quebec was engaged, and the nationalists were determined to win: 'The job cut out for them', as Laurendeau put it, 'was, in the space of a week, to show, prove and even more, make French Canadians feel in their bones, that in the modern world participation and compulsory military service go hand in hand, that one inevitably follows the other.'[10] Looking back on this moment from the perspective of later years, Laurendeau saw these nationalist efforts as terribly ineffectual: 'one is always confined to the same futile acts: preparing manifestos, issuing communiqués to the press, holding meetings—and all that, in our case, without the least organisation.'[11] At the time, however, he was full of purpose, and he took part in the rallies held at Montreal.

On the evening of 4 September, for example, he went to the Maisonneuve market in Montreal where Paul Gouin, who had recently revived the Action Libérale Nationale party, spoke strongly against Canadian participation and other speakers talked of fighting tyranny in the streets of Montreal rather than in Europe. As always in times when English-French tensions ran high, there were calls for the end of Confederation. The next night several Quebec-based labour organizations held another anti-participation rally at the Monument National where a large crowd that was, in Laurendeau's words, both 'sombre' and 'tense' shouted 'We won't go' every quarter hour—a slogan that became a symbolic chant in the months ahead. There were more rallies, all technically illegal under wartime provisions, through which nationalists hoped to apply enough pressure on King's government to prevent it from adopting more aggressive policies such as the immediate dispatch of an expeditionary force to England. But Laurendeau sensed that the crowds were not as agitated as their leaders: 'It seemed to me that what we were witnessing was a surface reaction, not a ground swell . . . a lot of smoke but there wasn't much fire.'[12]

Laurendeau paid little heed to the speeches in Parliament that were intended to secure French Canadians' co-operation in the war effort. For one thing he had heard versions of them before, in December 1937, when the nationalists had mounted an electoral challenge to the Liberals during a federal by-election in Quebec's Lotbinière riding. The virulent nationalist Paul Bouchard, editor of *La Nation*, ran against the Liberal J.N. Francoeur and lost. He did manage, however, to worry the government enough to draw federal cabinet ministers like P.J.A. Cardin and Ernest Lapointe, Mackenzie King's Quebec lieutenant, into the fray. They made strong statements affirming their intention to defend French Canada's pro-neutrality and anti-conscription sentiments in Ottawa.[13] It was therefore no great surprise when Lapointe made his historic promise in the House of Commons during the debate over Canada's declaration of war:

> The whole Province of Quebec—and I speak with all the solemnity I can give to my words—will never accept compulsory service or conscription outside Canada. I will go further than that. When I say the whole Province of Quebec, I mean personally I agree with them. I am authorized by my colleagues in the cabinet from the Province of Quebec . . . to say that we will never agree to conscription.[14]

Laurendeau naturally had no way of foreseeing how often he would have occasion to quote this passage by heart in the future. He simply did not consider the promises of federal politicians worth his time: 'We were convinced we were being handsomely deceived, and we always felt that the official explanations masked the true ones . . . we judged those who swallowed them without question as naive indeed.'[15] The ghost of Laurier hovered in the consciousness of nationalists.

One of Laurendeau's greatest disappointments during this period was the discovery that his carefully nurtured personal ties with English Canadians were fated to be among the war's earliest victims. Understanding that the protests that nationalists held in 1939 against Canadian participation would be far more credible if English Canadians joined in, he invited some of those he had met during the previous two years to attend. They included F.R. Scott, Neil Morrison, and the Canadian socialist and writer George Laxton. When they had all been part of a study group in 1938 39 to help broaden the basis of support for neutrality, they had come along willingly.[16] Although the subsequent discussions underlined important differences in their historical and constitutional viewpoints, personal bonds had developed and they were even capable of being 'gently ironic' with each other. In their joint CBC radio broadcasts of 1939, Laurendeau was able to get across to Morrison that French Canadians did not have the same attachment to France that English Canadians had to Britain, and for good historical reasons:

> . . . we tend to believe ourselves [to be] the only true and authentic Canadians. We have been here for centuries . . . yes, we have 150 or sometimes 200 years advantage over most of you. Thus while many of the descendants of English, Scotch and Irish have their loyalty divided between the country of their origin and Canada, we have only one native land: Canada, and we consider ourselves exclusively American. That does not prevent a tender sympathy for France, and a loyalty to the British crown. . . . But this means that we feel ourselves rooted on this continent. We have made our choice, or rather, it was made for us centuries ago. Irrevocably Canadians![17]

At a meeting on 6 April 1939 the group had worked towards a joint program that both English- and French-speaking members could live with. Laurendeau and the other French Canadians accepted a compromise in favour of a neutrality that was friendly to Britain and France—a policy much like the one the United States would adopt in the early years of the war. The group had agreed to meet in the fall to produce a final document, but the outbreak of war came first. Now, one by one, the English-speaking members refused to support neutrality openly. Several maintained that they could not risk being branded as traitors or worse by their own people. 'That day,' Laurendeau recalled, 'I felt an indignation and a bitterness that was difficult to surmount. Despite all our patient efforts, the bridges we had tried to throw across from one nation to the other had been swept away like rubbish.'[18] If he had been naïve in the first place to believe that these left-of-centre contacts with the English community were in any way representative of mainstream English-Canadian thinking, he now learned that in times of crisis even they were not prepared to break ethnic ranks by backing words with deeds.

In the first weeks following Canada's declaration of war on 9 September Laurendeau felt more and more isolated from his own people as well. Within his close circle of hardened nationalists there was, of course, near-unanimity. They were certain that Canada was the only American hemispheric nation (the United States had all at once become an example worth emulating) to enter the war strictly because of British imperial sentiments among English Canadians. As Laurendeau wrote in 1940, all other explanations were designed to appeal to French Canada's ethnic and religious sensibilities. How, for example, could one take seriously the argument that 'the defence of England and France . . . coincides with the defence of civilization and of Christendom'? In later years he would revise this monocausal assessment of English-Canadian motivation, acknowledging that those who supported the war did so for several interrelated motives:

> The religion of war sinks deep roots in the hearts of men. It is related to a powerful and complex network of feelings and interests. Democracy, civilization, Mother England, British supremacy, the struggle against racism, cultural solidarity—all of these were mixed together and unanimously, though with varying degrees of intensity, loved, respected and pinnacled as absolutes.[19]

But what did French Canadians think in September 1939? 'The war had fallen on them like an act of God,' Laurendeau wrote; '. . . the nationalists were active . . . and were passionate enough to soon reach extremist attitudes. But perhaps in this respect they out-distanced the French-Canadian nation. . . . The people remained closed in upon themselves, unmoved and unmoving.'[20]

Within weeks, however, an unexpected opportunity arose to gauge the political mood of Quebec's people. Maurice Duplessis dissolved the legislative assembly and called a provincial election for 25 October, one of the earliest possible dates. He explained this action, coming one and a half years before the end of his mandate, by maintaining that the federal government's invasion of provincial jurisdiction was already making it impossible to govern effectively, and that the problem would surely grow worse in wartime; hence he needed a strong political mandate to resist any new incursions. Some nationalists speculated that Duplessis, realizing the war would create severe difficulties for whoever was premier of Quebec, was hoping to lose in order to let the Liberal leader, Adélard Godbout, take the blame. Laurendeau considered this notion far-fetched. He reasoned that Duplessis, as head of the provincial Conservative party for many years, had been forced to struggle helplessly against that party's image in Quebec on account of conscription in the First World War; now that the federal Liberals, by declaring war, had made the same sort of error, he hoped to capitalize on it at the provincial level. Besides, at the time Laurendeau believed the strategy was politically shrewd: 'I can remember writing myself that the election would be a kind of plebiscite on participation and that we knew in advance what Quebec's reply would be.'[21]

But this did not mean that André supported Duplessis. In addition to his general distrust of politicians, there was the still poignant memory of the Union Nationale leader's betrayal of Paul Gouin and the Action Libérale Nationale in 1936. In fact, Gouin and the ALN were running a slate of candidates against Duplessis in 1939. To André they were 'the only logical alternative', but he had no faith that the 'disorganized' ALN would have an electoral impact [22] Thus he did little more than observe from the sidelines as the nationalist vote fragmented. Even the independent nationalist politicians like René Chaloult, Dr Philippe Hamel, and Camillien Houde sought support through a variety of party affiliations. The absence of nationalist political unity was especially harmful, in Laurendeau's view, because Duplessis ran an uninspired, lacklustre campaign. Seeing the Union Nationale leader in action, he was surprised by his lack of vigour. He also observed that the Union Nationale had failed to anticipate how Quebec's moneyed interests would flock to Godbout's Liberals in hopes of securing war contracts.

But for Laurendeau, as indeed for most political historians, the decisive element in the 1939 election involved the hijacking of the provincial Liberals' campaign by Mackenzie King's Quebec ministers under the leadership of Ernest Lapointe.[23] Laurendeau saw this intervention as a blatant example of political blackmail. Lapointe made it clear that the French-Canadian members of King's cabinet would interpret a defeat for Godbout as a rebuff of their position on the war, forcing them to resign. This, he underlined forcefully, would have the consequence of removing the only real barrier in Ottawa to the introduction of conscription. It was a bare-faced threat to go along with the carrot of Lapointe's earlier promise never to remain in a government that brought in conscription. According to Laurendeau, King's Quebec lieutenant was very effective. The election, he contended, 'was dominated by one man from Ottawa: Ernest Lapointe. For the provincial Liberals he was . . . the only strategist and the only leader. Adélard Godbout was completely overshadowed by him. Lapointe charged his adversaries head on, but at the same time he enveloped and smothered them. I remember following his campaign, cursing him and secretly admiring him.'[24] On one occasion Laurendeau slipped into the Montreal Forum to observe how the Liberal campaign was going. Lapointe was surrounded by a huge contingent of Montreal police expecting anti-war protests. But before long the 'debonaire giant'— to use André's words—with the rich Lower St Lawrence accent had the crowd eating out of his hand: 'who wouldn't have believed him when he declared . . . "Between conscription and you, we are the barrier, we are the rampart"?'[25] On election day the Liberals won 69 seats, the Union Nationale 14, and the ALN none.

The result was a depressing blow to all nationalists including those, like Laurendeau, who were anti-statist and had few illusions about the efficacy of political action. There was no denying that the participation issue had been front and centre and that the anti-participationists had lost badly: 'People who thought the way I did found themselves pinned to the ground. . . . We thought of ourselves as outcasts.'[26] The nationalists would have another opportunity during the federal election of June 1940, but Mackenzie King's lopsided victory on that occasion was not unexpected, nor was it as devastating. They could interpret Quebec's support for the Liberals at the federal level as a classic illustration of voting for 'the lesser evil'. What were the options, after all? The Conservatives under the improbable leadership of R.J. Manion, a Catholic with some sympathy for Quebec, were nonetheless still the party of jingoism, the British tie, and 'ready, aye, ready'. As for the CCF, it was possible to admire its pacifist leader J.S. Woodsworth without supporting the party's socialist-centralist program. Laurendeau's own yearning for a more advanced 'social nationalism' was inspired by his personalist philosophy based on French and Catholic theoretical models, and had little in common with the CCF's state-centred Fabian socialism. And in any case, such considerations came a distant second to the conscription issue. André's pronouncement on the 1940 election result was short and trenchant: 'The democratic machine is distorted to the point that three million citizens could not express their opinion and thus have an influence on the future of their country.' But it was also inescapably true that during the 'Phoney War', that eery period between Hitler's invasion of Poland and the unleashing of his armies against Western Europe in April 1940, French-Canadian nationalists could find nothing on the domestic political front to suggest that the people supported their stand.

Laurendeau was left to preach Canadian neutrality in an atmosphere of isolation at the offices of *L'Action nationale*:

> We continued to run our little monthly war against the powerful government and its policies. . . . Our readers began to subscribe again but correspondence was practically nil and we were left wondering whether they really shared our ideas. . . . The French-Canadian bourgeoisie whose representatives I met from time to time, accepted the war effort and the idea of collaboration. At least they seemed to. The rest were silent.[27]

Nor was André free to editorialize as he saw fit. Censorship was in force under the Defence of Canada Regulations of 3 September 1939. He was boiling with rage at this restriction when he prepared the September issue, and before long he was hauled up on the carpet. The government censors in Montreal responsible for reading publications like *L'Action nationale* were Fulgence Charpentier and W. Eggerton.[28] When André recognized Charpentier as a man he both knew and admired he felt a momentary relief:

> But the man I found myself sitting opposite was no friend. . . . He didn't let me speak for myself, he threatened me, and I left his office with the distinct impression of having been the victim of attempted intimidation. That kind of behaviour doesn't convince; it inspires either fear or obstinacy. I realized bitterly that the fight for liberty had begun for us with the death of our liberties.[29]

From then on, Laurendeau's fighting tactics with respect to censorship had more to do with artful dodging than direct confrontation. He had to keep in mind that *L'Action nationale* was published by *Le Devoir*, and that the newspaper's publisher, Georges Pelletier, was consequently also at risk. André became very adept at condemning federal politicians out of their own mouths by quoting from their old speeches to demonstrate their hypocrisy. Moreover, he prefaced each issue with a reference to the fact that it was subject to censorship—in effect inviting his subscribers to read between the lines. 'Censorship drove us', he recalled, 'to perform veritable mental gymnastics. . . . As for those of our opinions that were totally unpublishable, we chewed them over amongst ourselves.'[30]

The fall of France in the summer of 1940 was a major blow for Laurendeau personally and for his stand against Canadian participation in the war. He was at Saint-Gabriel—as he seemed fated to be whenever there were bad tidings during the war years. A French couple he had known in Paris were visiting him that summer, and they took turns monitoring the news; someone was always glued to the radio. When they heard that Marshall Pétain, a military hero from the First World War and the future leader of Vichy France, had replaced the French civilian leaders, they knew a formal surrender was not far off:

> For my family and myself, Paris meant more than the Eiffel Tower and the Folies-Bergère. My father had lived there. My wife and I had lived for two years in the Latin Quarter, and our first child had been born there. France wasn't just a prestigious but distant intellectual symbol: I had French friends and memories . . . what had happened to Emmanuel Mounier and Father Paul Doncoeur, our concierge, our classmates, and the vegetable woman in la rue Mouffetard? Where would the Daniel-Rops, André Siegfried, and Emile Baäs go now, and all those young families who had welcomed us when we felt alone in Paris?[31]

His anguish was even greater because in 1939 he had received letters from Madeleine and Emile Baäs reporting that they had been separated by the war situation, that she was pregnant and he was in the army. They added that Father Doncoeur was most likely a French army chaplain, and made a point of insisting that it was a 'just war'. He admitted to becoming choked up every time he heard the nostalgic American popular song 'The Last Time I Saw Paris'. He was struck, furthermore, when he returned to Montreal, by the look of 'dull pain' on the faces of the people. Although Quebec's links to France over the previous century and a half had been chiefly cultural and for the most part elitist, an atmosphere of mourning persisted for weeks. No wonder there was so little public reaction to the King government's full mobilization plans and so little anger when Camillien Houde was spirited away. In the gloomy atmosphere of that time, had he not hung his own head and registered for service?

During the difficult months that followed, André was emotionally and ideologically torn between his abhorrence of the Nazi onslaught in Europe and his fear that conscription was coming nearer in Canada:

> ... in those days I would shut my eyes and think of the misfortunes of men on the battlefields and [the people] in the bombed cities of Europe. I felt incapable of helping them. . . . The comfort of our life sickened me. . . . But I detested physical violence; I felt a premonitary horror of certain types of liberation; and I didn't believe in crusades.[32]

He was sick off and on for weeks. The horrible migraine headaches that had been one of the symptoms of his depression in the early 1930s returned as contradictory questions stampeded through his mind. Had he not been among the first people in Quebec to see what fascism really was and to warn French Canadians against it? Had he not striven, in the years since his return from Paris, to redirect French-Canadian nationalist thought away from its xenophobic, clericalist bias towards a more open, internationalist perspective? Did it not follow therefore that his first priority, the 'higher good', should be the defeat of Hitler and the liberation of France at whatever cost, as so many of his friends in Europe and Quebec insisted? And could one really close one's eyes and harden one's heart—no matter how intense the objection to British imperialism—to the sheer pluck of the overmatched English? All of Quebec was stirred by the moving broadcasts of Louis Francoeur from the fire-bombed cities of the British Isles and by the unshakeable defiance of the British people.

But when his thoughts returned to Canada, André faced other questions. Wasn't this just the sort of crisis that led English Canada to ride roughshod over French-Canadian rights during the First World War? Wasn't it always a crisis in Europe, which really meant a crisis for Britain, that was used to justify turning French Canadians—here in the true homeland they were prepared to die for—into second-class citizens? And weren't the sleazy politicians in Ottawa once again systematically breaking one promise after another in the name of a distant 'higher good'?

> The Liberals had gradually dragged us from neutrality to participation, then from participation that was mainly economic to war policies that were much more intense. General mobilisation was yet another stage that neither King nor Lapointe had let us anticipate. From now on, all they would have to do was strike out three little words from the text of the law—'for overseas service'—and all the promises would be violated, and we would be back starting 1917 all over again.[33]

Laurendeau never did resolve these contradictions satisfactorily. For the time being, at least, he turned away from them to concentrate on a more clear-cut issue: the defence of provincial autonomy. He had been worried about the federal government's growing appetite for constitutional power since the late 1930s, particularly in view of the Bennett New Deal and what he regarded as the blatantly centralist findings of the Rowell-Sirois Commission (finally completed in 1940). The exigencies of Canada's war effort now offered Ottawa a fresh opportunity to push forward its claims, and in Quebec City there was no one to offer resistance but Adélard Godbout—who owed his electoral victory to the federal Liberals. Although Laurendeau came in later times to admire some of the Godbout government's achievements—the extension to women of the right to vote in provincial elections; the nationalization of the Montreal Light, Heat and Power Company, and the creation of Quebec Hydro; education reforms[34]—he saw it in 1940-41 as utterly dependent on federal initiative and unwilling to defend Quebec's constitutional position: 'Instead of keeping its distance, it collaborated for all it was worth.'[35] Not only did Godbout agree, after the federal-provincial conference in 1941, to permit Ottawa access to provincial taxation fields in the area of personal and corporate income for the duration of the war, but in 1940 he had accepted Ottawa's intrusion into the social-assistance arena through the Federal Unemployment Insurance program. André warned that 'the province of Quebec at the moment is like a derelict house. It could almost have a sign on it saying "Premises for sale to the highest bidder".... Quebec administers, it does not govern. ... A provincial state? No, merely a county council.'[36]

Happy to have seized on an issue that had some potential for rallying his fellow nationalists, if not the population as a whole, Laurendeau developed his views on Quebec's autonomy in an article of November 1940 entitled 'A Warning to French Canadians'. Noting that there had always been 'fanatics' in English Canada who wished to see the French totally assimilated, he claimed that the war had now given them a pretext to employ 'the strategy of strangling us softly, surreptitiously.'[37] He used dramatic language to portray the Quebec state, which he now claimed was the major instrument of French Canada's survival and the only real force for French-Canadian political influence in Ottawa, as a fortress under siege:

> We are now beleaguered within our stronghold. Our supplies have been cut off by the assailant. We must starve, unless we make a vigorous sortie to replenish them. Yet we are afraid to venture out of our entrenchment. Panic is almost upon us. At this point the besieger appears to relent. Here is bread, he offers generously, on one condition only: take down your fortifications, fill in your moat, and we promise to let you prosper. In other words, Ottawa offers us shiny gold pieces in exchange for our rights.[38]

Laurendeau termed the federal government's strategy 'fascism . . . the thing itself'[39] and called for a vigorous defence of Quebec's autonomy. While he was not yet at the point of contemplating direct political action by nationalists to fill the lamentable void at Ottawa, he was clearly abandoning the anti-statist position he had held throughout the Depression years. The Quebec government's potential for defending as well as enhancing the lives of French Canadians was beginning to loom large in his nationalist thought. And the rush of mail that arrived at the *Action nationale*'s office in response to the November issue confirmed that he had struck a chord: 'it was the first sign in our immediate circle of a resurgence of public spirit.'[40]

Thus by the spring of 1941 Laurendeau had recovered his emotional equilibrium—in part, at least, by suppressing thoughts of the grim struggle in Europe as though it were a secondary theatre of action where others would decide the outcome—and he was able to use this period of public lethargy to resume his intellectual quest for a nationalist theoretical synthesis. He continued, for instance, to invite a wide variety of thinkers to write for *L'Action nationale* on subjects that were far removed from either war or autonomy, such as the future of Quebec's literary culture. He had no way of knowing that this was merely the brief calm before the storm, or that the shoals immediately ahead would be more dangerous for him than the ones he had so far navigated. It was only with the benefit of hindsight that he could picture these months as the end of the war's first and, in comparison to what followed, quiet phase:

> We had already gone through some difficult times. Canada's two nations were not functioning at the same rhythm. But appearances had been saved, for neither group followed its own ideas, traditions, or will to their ultimate consequences. English Canada accepted a minimum of discipline. French Canada didn't seriously think of rebelling. Under these conditions a group of politicians . . . had succeeded in maintaining a semblance of unity.[41]

But in the dramatic days ahead, during which he would play a leading public role, many Canadians came to despise and loathe each other; English and French became in his words, 'mutually intolerable'.[42] The issue that precipitated and would continue to dominate this second phase was the introduction of conscription 'for overseas service'.

To Laurendeau the death of Ernest Lapointe in November 1941 was the symbolic beginning of the conscription crisis: 'His death struck the popular imagination. . . . Wasn't it a sign that the rampart was beginning to crumble?'[43] Lapointe had guaranteed the King government's promise of 'NO CONSCRIPTION' with his personal honour; could his death mean that the promise was off as well? Historians of the Second World War, on the other hand, generally focus on international developments in the last half of 1941 as the primary cause of Canada's 'overseas' conscription crisis.[44] They refer in particular to events like Hitler's invasion of Russia in June 1941 and Japan's attack on Pearl Harbour in December of that year, as the chief factors that contributed to the broadening of the war into a world-wide conflict and in turn gave credibility to those in Canada who called for a policy of 'total war'. With the United States now fully involved, the latter argued, with the new threat of an attack by Japan on Canada's west coast, and with close allies like England and the United States committed to conscription, it was criminal to tie the hands of Canada's military; besides, unrestricted conscription was the least one could do for the morale of troops already serving overseas. There were many French-Canadian leaders who agreed, as did a powerful element in Mackenzie King's cabinet. And goading them on was the Conservative leader Arthur Meighen, who had replaced Manion following the party's election defeat of 1940. Meighen was arguably the most hated English Canadian in French-speaking Quebec, because of his uncompromising pro-conscription stand during First World War and because he was seen as the spokesman for Toronto's Committee of Two Hundred, a collection of Protestant clergymen and business leaders who were portrayed by nationalists like Laurendeau as foaming-at-the-mouth francophobes. Next to their tirades, the pro-conscription rhetoric of Ontario premier Mitchell Hepburn and opposition leader George Drew seemed almost mild.

Ironically, Laurendeau and his nationalist colleagues were now forced to regard Mackenzie King as their last beacon of hope in English Canada. Would he resist the pressure building for conscription? While André had little genuine faith in King, he was shocked nevertheless when the prime minister gave his answer on 22 January 1942 in the Speech from the Throne. The government would hold a national plebiscite on 27 April to seek support for (as the question was eventually worded) 'releasing the government from any past commitments restricting the methods of raising men for military service'. Though King reserved the final decision to implement overseas conscription for Parliament, Laurendeau could smell the all too-familiar odour of gradualism: 'In short, the anti-conscription promise had had its little hour of utility; it had facilitated Canada's entry into the War and the conduct of the country's war effort.'[45] Now it had lost its usefulness. Despite the promise made specifically to tranquillize the people of Quebec, a national plebiscite was being held to secure a certain 'yes' vote. French-Canadian nationalists, André wrote, were 'opposed to the very principle of the plebiscite'. In the January issue of *L'Action nationale* he heaped scorn on all those French Canadians who had been willing to compromise for the sake of unity while claiming that those, like himself, who had seen conscription coming from the outset were fully vindicated.

However deep his cynicism about the purpose and form of the plebiscite, Laurendeau set about obtaining a 'no' vote in Quebec with renewed energy and purpose. The 'resistance movement', as he called it, was up against difficult odds:

> French Canadians had to organise their resistance from the meagre means at their disposal and had to feel their way almost by touch, for the official representatives of the nation in Ottawa, in Quebec, and in the highest echelons of the Church . . . all preached submission to the inevitable. Popular feelings that were to defy loyalty, political organisation, financial power . . . and develop to a high pitch in less than two months, had to be passionate, universal and desperate.[46]

But it was also important to control the passions of the more radical elements, so that random acts of nationalist violence could not be exploited in the propaganda of the 'yes' campaign. It was vital, therefore, to have an organization that could co-ordinate and unite the 'no' forces. In early February André attended a meeting at the home of Paul Gouin during which the Ligue pour la Défense du Canada was formed.[47] Representatives from the Catholic trade unions, the St Jean Baptiste Society, and youth organizations also attended, along with veteran nationalist politicians and, in the background, the inevitable Abbé Groulx; Jean Drapeau, the equally ubiquitous future mayor of Montreal, was one of the enthusiastic younger voices. J.B. Prince, an eloquent veteran Bourassa nationalist, was chosen president. André became secretary and chief executive officer—titles that in almost any organization mean 'the real work horse'.[48]

The Ligue pour la Défense du Canada 'was born', according to Laurendeau, 'from the divorce between official opinion and popular feeling. . . .'[49] From its modest kitchen-table origins it became the principle organization working for a 'no' vote and quickly gained the support of many French Canadians who, although not ardent nationalists, felt that their support for the war effort had been betrayed. Under the leadership of Prince, Georges Pelletier, Maxime Raymond, and Laurendeau, the Ligue even held its doors open to English Canadians who opposed conscription for whatever reason. In addition, some of the arguments advanced in its manifesto were designed to appeal to other ethnic minorities who had objections to the concept of 'total war':

> A small country of 11,000,000 inhabitants cannot be, as it is claimed, the arsenal of the democracies and the allied nations, and at the same time an

inexhaustible reservoir of fighting men. Because Canada has already achieved and even surpassed the limit of its military effort, and because we do not wish to find ourselves in a situation where we will be worse off than defeated nations; because relatively speaking we have already done at least as much as any of the major belligerents—Canada has no right, let alone obligation, to sabotage itself.[50]

While it might as well have spared itself the effort where English Canada was concerned, and while few if any of its members really cared what was happening to the west-coast Japanese or to German and Italian Canadians, the Ligue's singleness of purpose over so short a time-frame did help it to achieve uncommon unity among its own adherents.

Laurendeau, who had very limited experience in such matters, was faced with organizing a province-wide campaign from nothing: 'We were a headquarters without troops.'[51] They were also short of funds, with the bulk of their support coming from one-dollar donations; he estimated that the major organizations supporting the Ligue never raised $1,000 among them. But before long the group had branches in fifty provincial centres. From their cramped office (rented in a building owned by the Royal Bank) on rue Ste Catherine in Montreal, Ligue workers wrote to Chambers of Commerce, union offices, and 1,600 municipal councils, and received hundreds of supportive resolutions in reply.[52] André took personal charge of the radio campaign, broadcasting the Ligue's message in short segments on private stations like CHRC in Quebec and CKVL and CKAC in Montreal. But he was frustrated at every turn in his efforts to gain access to Radio-Canada's extensive facilities. His correspondence with Augustin Frignon, Radio-Canada's director, became increasingly shrill as he pleaded for fairness towards the Ligue's legitimate requests in what was, after all, a 'yes or no' plebiscite, not an election in which formal parties alone could be accredited. And after each rejection he castigated the public broadcaster for yielding to government pressure in adopting fascist propaganda tactics.

On 22 April, five days before the plebiscite, the authorities informed André that just two more days of broadcasting would be allowed. Determined to have the last word even if it was on only one private station, he waited until 11:45 p.m. on 24 April to give his final speech on CKAC. After he had finished, however, the announcer calmly read a statement by Mackenzie King in a solemn, approving tone. Though Laurendeau was a man with a reputation for never losing his temper, he lost it that night. It was the final episode in a long list of harassments. Transit workers and police had ripped down the Ligue's posters as fast as they were put up. The Royal Bank refused to renew its office rental arrangement, having found out who the renters were. The operators of the Montreal Forum cancelled an agreement with André just hours before the Ligue's final rally. He learned the hard way that plebiscite politics was no different from party politics in Quebec—a dirty game at the best of times. He also discovered in the course of the 'no' campaign that politics could be violent.

With censorship in force and the public radio waves reserved for the 'yes men', as Laurendeau liked to call them, political assemblies were the most effective tool remaining for stirring up public opinion. According to him, the rallies he participated in during the 1930s with Jeune-Canada and in the 1940s with the Ligue had a distinctive character of their own: 'Public meetings in those days were quite different. . . . They were heavily attended. There was electricity in the air. The crowd was partisan, participant, and full of life, often to excess.' While there were few rousing speakers, that didn't matter because the theme of the occasion itself 'excited the masses.'[53] At the Ligue's first assembly, held in east-end Montreal's Saint-Jacques market on 11 February, the 'masses' caused a small riot. The scheduled speakers were J.B. Prince, Maxime Raymond, Gérard Filion, Jean Drapeau, and the venerable Henri Bourassa, who came out of retirement for the occasion. The ever-innovative Drapeau brought along a new-fangled record-making device, no doubt so that his own words could be preserved in close association with Bourassa's. Drapeau's biographers have set the scene well:

> By 7 p.m. it was clear that a big crowd was on its way. From all over the city the people came: men who made battle tanks on the assembly line at the Angus Shops arriving on streetcars with charwomen who worked in the big houses of Outremont and Westmount; farmers in snow-encrusted pick-up trucks from South Shore villages like St-Denis; travelling salesmen, small-time lawyers, insurance brokers, city councillors. The students came, wave upon wave of them, hanging out of streetcars yelling slogans, marching in a phalanx up St. Denis Street from the university waving banners and placards. They had the most to lose by the draft. The *Gazette* and *Star* sent reporters, but mostly the English stayed away.
> The hall filled quickly and soon the crowd was backed up by the thousands, out through the market stalls and onto the street. They stood bundled up and stomping their feet on the hard-packed snow. Their breath came in puffs of white, like the sight of muskets discharging. Rally organizers had seen to it that a loudspeaker system was strung along the rafters outside. Every nationalist group in the province was represented.[54]

The crowd was about 10,000 strong by the time the speeches began. But the loudspeakers were faulty, and much of the fiery oratory was drowned out by the passing tramway cars. To make matters worse, Bourassa, always conscious of his career-long commitment to a pan-Canadian duality, chose to rebuke the crestfallen Drapeau for excessive zeal in declaring that French Canadians were the only true Canadians. This threatened to end the evening on a sombre note, but as part of the crowd turned to leave they decided to take out their disappointment on the English-owned tramway cars by hurling bricks through the windows.

Before long other groups were running through the streets looking for people to beat up. They invaded one of Montreal's best-known brothels and ransacked a tavern—giving rise to the observation that 'it was a mob with a presbyterian heart'—and went on to smash whatever was breakable up and down St Lawrence Boulevard: 'It was a night of crystal.'[55] The next day Laurendeau, as secretary of the Ligue, was called before a desk-thumping, apoplectic Chief of Police. The bellowing was so loud that André—the reedy intellectual and pacifist—couldn't get a word in edgewise: 'I was jerked out of my books, my lectures, my editorship. This time I felt I had been well and truly precipitated into a life of action.'[56]

In the weeks that followed he worked eighteen hours a day. Soon one activity began to merge into another, but he had good reason never to forget the Ligne's youth rally, held on 24 March at Montreal's Jean Talon market. It was one occasion when an English Canadian addressed the anti-conscription crowds. A Toronto-based union representative named London Ladd, whom Laurendeau never saw again, gave an impassioned speech in English. With his rich tenor's voice he got the crowd stirred up by shouting slogans like 'Down with the Toronto Two Hundred'. Then someone yelled 'Down with the Jews!' Ladd stopped short, eyed the man for a moment and then, with what André later described as surpassing courage, said:

> No, my brothers, no. Don't say 'Down with Jewish finance.' Don't say 'Down with the Jews.' The Jews are our brothers, too, and they have been slandered often enough. The question we are asked today has nothing to do with Jews or Christians. Some people in here are trying to use us. You don't like the Toronto Two Hundred, eh? You don't care for them? . . . Well, take a look at who they are. Look at their names one after another. They're all Christians, my brothers, all Christians. . . . My enemy is not the Jew or the Christian but anyone, whatever his race or creed, who wants to conscript our youth but doesn't want his own wealth conscripted . . .[57]

The people roared their approval. But later, as André left the rally and attempted to edge his car through the crowd, he encountered another group who were looking for Jews. While he acknowledged in later years that there was always 'a vague anti-Semitism' in these French-Canadian assemblies, he felt this group was too well organized to be accounted for in that way; he suspected they were from Adrian Arcand's fascist party and were using the occasion for their own purposes. While that may have been so, it is also true that Laurendeau was too quick, during this period, to play down French-Canadian anti-Semitism. To do otherwise would have forced him to admit that his father, Abbé Groulx, and many of his personal friends were not free of it.

As 27 April and the plebiscite approached, André worked himself and his team to the point of exhaustion. 'How can one recreate for one who did not live through them an accurate impression of those times?' he asked rhetorically years later. 'Feelings that had long been suppressed at last found an outlet. They burned to the point of incandescence.' He had no time for his family, for new intellectual projects, or for those creative activities that had always been his refuge. Secure in the belief that a 'no' vote would restore a measure of pride to French Canadians—and at the same time prove that he and his colleagues were not alone in their convictions—he was determined to leave no stone unturned. Nor would it be going too far to state that at this juncture in his life he despised the English: 'the Anglo-Canadians thought we were traitors who hadn't the courage to fight. We saw in them the horrible embodiment of "might makes right".'[58] Though he scarcely dared to believe it, there were many last-minute indications that the government in Ottawa had totally botched the campaign in Quebec. They hardly dared to hold a rally except by invitation, and the vaunted Liberal party machine was nowhere to be seen. Or perhaps it was just that having spent the previous twenty-five years reminding French Canadians of what a terrible thing conscription was, the machine wouldn't work in reverse. By the night of the Ligue's final rally before an up-beat crowd of 20,000 at the Atwater market in downtown Montreal it was no longer a question of whether the 'no's' would win, but by how much.

The answer, to use Laurendeau's jubilant term: by an 'avalanche'. While the national vote was 63.7 per cent 'yes' and 36.3 per cent 'no', in Quebec it was 72.1 per cent 'no' and only 27.9 per cent 'yes'. Nor was this the complete story. While the anglophone population of Quebec was accounted for as a solid phalanx of 'yes' votes, between 80 and 90 per cent of French-speaking Quebec had voted 'no'. And in provinces like Ontario and New Brunswick, French-Canadian voters constituted the lion's share of 'no's'. Laurendeau called it a 'vote by race' for this reason and because, within Quebec, the 'no' vote had cut across geographic, class, and political lines. Neither the dire warnings of political and ecclesiastical leaders nor the more practical consideration that most French Canadians had a relative or friend serving in the volunteer forces had prevailed:

> . . . we had, after all, despite provincial and sociological frontiers, lived together an experience of unanimity which we had rarely known in our history. And this experience, thanks to the plebiscite, was recorded in official statistics. On the other side, English Canada had also manifested its unity with, as its rallying point, a total war effort. But French Canada had refused to be pushed around.[59]

If the joy of celebration was somewhat tainted by the certainty that the federal government would use the nation-wide result to justify bringing in conscription, this outcome had been taken for granted from the start. 'In the end,' wrote Laurendeau, 'it was all a question of feeling. But one of man's feelings is his sense of self-respect. . . .'[60]

On 8 May 1942 Mackenzie King introduced Bill 80 in the Parliament of Canada; revoking article 3 of the Mobilization Act, it made conscription for overseas service legal at last. Cardin had the decency to resign from cabinet, as did Maxime Raymond from the Liberal party. But on 10 June King delivered his remarkable—if characteristically contorted—speech promising 'conscription if necessary, but not necessarily conscription'. He explained that while the government had considered it prudent to remove the restriction on overseas service, it still believed in the superiority of the voluntary principle and would impose this type of conscription only if the military situation absolutely demanded it. For Laurendeau, this was simply more of King's underhanded hair-splitting:

It should be well understood that as far as we were concerned Mackenzie King had known since the start of the war where he was leading us. We were convinced of his bad faith vis-à-vis French Canadians, but we feared his shrewdness, for he knew how to scramble a problem and manipulate the right psychological levers. Thus, you could never believe the first sense of what he said; you had to look for the hidden meaning that he would ingeniously find there later on. Maybe his skill was admirable, but in the long run it inspired something closer to disgust. With him a problem was always devious. It was impossible to tackle it straightforwardly. The idea that the plebiscite had nothing to do with conscription, but was merely concerned with giving the government its freedom, for all its ingenuity, was treated as a joke; its malice was too transparent; it cut no ice.[61]

But in later years Laurendeau's judgement of King was tempered with more respect. Without King, he conceded, there would surely have been violence. Nor could one ignore the many contending demands that the prime minister was forced to balance. In the end he saw King as a 'diligent tailor' who spent each night of the war frantically darning the holes made that day in the national fabric, and whose patience somehow held the tattered garment together.

He also credited King with holding off conscription for overseas service until 1944; moreover, the 2,463 National Resources Mobilization Act troops posted to the First Canadian Army in Europe was a relatively small number[62]—although he cited the massive 'no' vote from Quebec in the 1942 plebiscite as a contributing factor in the federal government's restraint. Laurendeau's anger was fierce, however, when instances of coercion and brutality in the enforcement of conscription, especially on the part of the RCMP, came to light. One such case occurred in May 1944, when a conscript named Georges Guénette was shot dead fleeing from the RCMP. To André it was an out-and-out case of murder. He wrote several articles and gave at least ten speeches on the topic, pointing out that

Guénette was no different from any other French Canadian who made the mistake of believing the politicians. He had been conscripted for a four-month term but found himself committed for the duration of the war.

> ... the parents of conscripts, who are already obliged to inform on their children, have the right to know whether, through some escapade or other, their sons risk being shot at close range.
>
> In the past we have seen the province terrorized to the point of being reduced to silence. Those were the days when, right out on the street, as though he were a common malefactor, they arrested the Mayor of the City of Montreal. Those were the times when certain newspapers were specialized as informers and got the Minister of Justice and his Gestapo to do the dirty work dreamt up by the hatred, spite, or envy of their scribes. Those days are over. And those who are responsible for them have got to pay.[63]

André was further outraged when René Chaloult, who had spoken defiantly at a Ligue rally to protest Bill 80, was arrested and charged with seditious libel. Such incidents, coming after the people had made their democratic views so overwhelmingly clear in the plebiscite, struck him as practices typical of a foreign occupation.

Laurendeau speculated occasionally, in later years, about the long-term psychological impact of these events on French Canadians. In his view, the abuses of the War Measures Act, the arbitrary arrests of prominent dissidents, and the use of censorship weakened French Canadians' ties to the central government and estranged them from federal institutions. The government in Ottawa, the RCMP, and the concept of a sea-to-sea nation state came to be regarded more and more as part of English Canada's identity, with decreasing relevance for French Canada. There were long periods, of course, when the conscription crisis was banished to the cellars of French Canada's collective memory. But whenever a new crisis arose between English and French the episode was hauled up for re-examination, to be viewed as yet another item in a negative legacy of oppression and insensitivity. This was doubly the case for nationalists like André since, as he pointed out, from the beginning 'our heroes were the conscript, the nay sayer, the rebel'.[64] The conscription crisis, in which he played such a partisan and high-profile role, would always remain in Laurendeau's consciousness as a manifestation both of how far English-French relations could degenerate and of how helpless the French minority could be, without strong safeguards in the form of entrenched powers and political strength. English-French co-operation was always preferable, but it wasn't much use in a crisis. Concrete steps had to be taken to protect Quebec's autonomy and to promote its socio-cultural integrity: that was the crucial lesson for nationalists. And, after so many setbacks and days of doubt, they could look to the plebiscite result as proof that the people were behind them at last.

For Laurendeau personally the conscription crisis brought his years of intellectual nationalism to a sharp, if temporary, halt. He was catapulted to the centre of events, into the tumultuous world of political action, and he would never again be allowed to retreat so far into his ivory tower of theory. Furthermore, he had proven himself to be a capable political organizer who inspired loyalty among those he directed. No one worked harder, nor—as his increasingly hollow-eyed, cigarette-stained appearance readily testified—did anyone else agonize so over details. The experience also hardened him. He had learned to weather the blusterer's storm and to feel an adrenalin-pumping, visceral dislike for his opponents. Seeds of doubt about the church's role in French-Canadian nationalism had also been planted in his thoughts, not as the consequence of some new philosophic doctrine, but because of the hierarchy's practical collaboration with the forces of conscription. Feeling closer to the people as a result of his stand on that issue, he realized that a strong will was just as important to advance their cause as a long-term policy or a sound idea: 'Perhaps to refuse so doggedly one had to be blind and deafen oneself. I sometimes have felt to the point of suffocation the bitter solitude of my own people in the world.'[65]

6

The Bloc Populaire, 1942-1947

Twenty years ago I was stumping the province as secretary of a new political party. My travels were usually uneventful but for someone who until then
had led the life of an intellectual and who was rather intimidated by the
prospect of a life of action, they were not without certain hazards.

André Laurendeau, *The Churchwarden*, 1964[1]

Intellectuals who enter politics are often required as an initiation rite to
digest a stomachful of their own unsavoury remarks about politicians. It
was true for Pierre Trudeau, who did such a thorough job of pillorying
federal Liberals from Quebec during the 1950s and early '60s, only to
become one himself in 1965.[2] It was also true for André Laurendeau in 1942.
After more than a decade of denouncing French-Canadian politicians of
whatever party affiliation, he became a founding member of a new nationalist party: the Bloc Populaire Canadien. Early in 1944 he was chosen
provincial leader of the Bloc and that same year was elected to Quebec's
Legislative Assembly. From the party's launching in September 1942 until
his controversial resignation in 1947, he lived a day-to-day existence of
party work and practical issues and was obliged to deal with men, such as
Adélard Godbout and Maurice Duplessis, whom he had often attacked as
either mediocre or corrupt. Such a turnaround required an explanation,
especially for those devoted anti-statist nationalists who had been listening to or reading his negative political rhetoric since his Jeune-Canada
days. His refusal, back then, to let the nationalist youth movement plunge
into an alliance with Paul Gouin's Action Libérale Nationale party had
been vindicated by events, as Duplessis exposed Gouin's political ingen-
uousness and gobbled up his party.[3] André wrote at that time that there
was no sign among nationalists of 'a great politician', and that at best 'men
in their forties like Paul Gouin can only serve as means of transition'. But
in 1941, during the conscription crisis and as a result of what he saw as a
massive federal assault on provincial autonomy, he began to abandon

112

that view. The momentum of the successful plebiscite campaign completed the process.

To have some understanding of how significant such a change was for Laurendeau, it is important to recall that he had lived his whole life to this point vacillating between two attitudes towards political life. During his early years, before he became a nationalist, he looked down his nose at what seemed a sordid, unworthy realm for French Canadians of any culture to try and make their mark in. He was one of the few young middle-class men in his circle, for instance, who showed no interest in a law career, the normal stepping-stone to politics. His aim instead had always been to make a contribution to French-Canadian culture—in music, in letters, or perhaps in the sphere of ideas. Consequently he ignored Quebec's political history and the active politics of the day. It was when he became a nationalist in 1932 that he began to take closer note, but then only to criticize politicians for their various failures towards French Canada. Federal politicians, seen to be acting always in the interests of the English-Canadian majority, naturally had the worst reputation. But provincial leaders—except for a few heroic independent-minded exceptions—were also given low marks. That such an attitude was deliberately encouraged by the conservative clerical interpreters of French Canada's national destiny in order to denigrate the state in relation to the church goes almost without saying. In André's case, it was part of his nationalist viewpoint until this critical juncture.

In an April 1941 article entitled 'The "Impossible" Third Party', Laurendeau admitted that 'a third party . . . would be an unknown phenomenon, an aberration in our solar system.' But he went on to speculate that the time for such an option was perhaps at hand:

> no party has ever truly represented the ideas and genuine interests of French Canadians. These ideas and interests have not even been fully outlined by any group—not even the nationalists—or, where they have, only by a minority of intellectuals, and in such abstract terms that people could not recognize them. But they exist. When the tragic misunderstanding which presently separates people from their natural interpreters has been bridged, when the mass of people are given a few hard and clear formulas in which they can recognize policies in accordance with their deepest instincts, their vital needs and desires, then they will rise in an irresistible movement. The role of a third party is precisely to be that intermediary. Each one of us, even those who oppose the idea, or those who apathetically declare themselves indifferent to politics, each one secretly desires the emergence of such an intermediary.[4]

Beyond 'secret desires' and his reading of the desperate political situation, Laurendeau thought he saw a sign of maturity in the remarkable unity of the Ligue pour la Défense du Canada, which had come together rapidly and effectively to fight against conscription. Nationalist politicians who were notorious for their fierce independence and single-minded devotion to pet issues, like Dr Phillippe Hamel in his dogged campaign to nationalize Quebec's privately owned hydro-electric companies, had been able to co-operate in a broad movement and achieve a landslide victory. There were signs as well that if an equally unified new political movement with a credible nationalist doctrine could be organized quickly, it might capitalize on a wave of post-plebiscite voter enthusiasm.

One such sign, which greatly impressed Laurendeau, was the public reaction to the arrest and trial of René Chaloult during the summer following the plebiscite. The Ligue had held a rally on 19 May 1942, at Montreal's Saint-Jacques market to protest the King government's Bill 80, which amended the National Resources Mobilization Act to include 'overseas service'. Chaloult, the MLA for Lotbinière, gave a fiery speech blasting British imperialism, the allied fiasco at Hong Kong, the Western powers' alliance with 'communist' Russia, 'so-called' national unity, and, once he was warmed up, just about everything that had ever irked him. It is difficult to know which of his remarks most offended the tender sensibilities of the RCMP; nevertheless, urged on by Montreal's anglophone press, they seized Chaloult and charged him with seditious libel. The trial, which dragged into July, was a bizarre affair with conflicting accounts of who said what and how strongly. Chaloult was acquitted, but not without a dash of sarcasm from the judge who observed that, as a politician, the member from Lotbinière had undoubtedly been exaggerating in a manner common to the species.[5] Meanwhile the nationalists, led by Laurendeau, did everything possible to focus attention on the trial. They mounted a fund-raising campaign to help pay Chaloult's legal costs and followed that up with a sold-out banquet to celebrate his release. Armed with favourable Gallup Polls (which they soon learned were the only useful kind), they felt confident that their public support was sustainable beyond the conscription crisis. 'What a headache, what a lousy meal,' André recalled, 'but what a new day seemed to be breaking. . . . That August evening at the Atwater Market we all . . . felt in our bones that a new party was about to be born.'[6]

Actually, it was a new 'movement' that was about to be born. Those who worked feverishly during its embryonic stage in July and August could not quite bring themselves to tarnish their idealism with the word 'party'. Instead they chose the name Bloc Populaire Canadien to convey the sense of a unified movement of ideas 'rather than a replica of the excessively partisan old-line parties'.[7] This was particularly important for those older conservative nationalists who retained a lingering allegiance to traditional anti-statism and who participated in politics while feigning, at least, to hold their noses. But Laurendeau, whose own anti-statism gave way rapidly during these years as he acknowledged the need for governments to deal with serious urban-industrial and resource-sector problems, represented a younger group of nationalists who maintained that in this area 'our hands are clean because we have no hands'. He therefore played a vigorous part in efforts to pull together French-Canadian nationalist politicians in Ottawa who had deserted the King government over conscription and old-guard provincial nationalists from Quebec City, led by Gouin, Hamel, and Chaloult, along with his own group from Montreal, including Jean Drapeau. Most were still active in the Ligue pour la Défense du Canada. 'Indeed, without the participation of the League . . . ,' writes one authority, 'the Bloc . . . would never have attracted the younger more liberal-minded generation of French-Canadian nationalists who provided the movement with the bulk of its organizational personnel and its reformist zeal.'[8]

The difficulty—as is so often the case with new parties—was in finding a leader with political experience and a record of electoral success. Laurendeau was part of a broad consensus that favoured Maxime Raymond, the federal parliamentarian who had been first elected in Beauharnois-Laprairie in 1925 and who it was thought (wrongly, as it turned out) could bring most or all of the eleven other anti-conscription federal MPs with him. Raymond considered himself too old, at fifty-nine, and too ill to lead a new party. Time would prove him right, but in that summer of '42 he was persuaded to accept the leadership during several long discussions with Abbé Groulx, who had himself been put up to the task by Gouin, Chaloult, and Hamel.[9] Despite Groulx's 'no-I-couldn't-possibly' protestations against involving himself in active politics, there were few nationalist backrooms he hadn't been in, and he plunged into the Bloc's affairs with unpriestly abandon. He even wrote André to instruct him on the type of ovation Raymond should receive when the new party was publicly announced at a meeting in September.

By that point it was widely anticipated that Laurendeau would be the Bloc's 'secretary-general'—a rather imposing title for such a small party. He had obvious qualifications for the post. Though still only thirty, he had established impressive credentials, dating back to his active role in Jeune-Canada and, more recently, his intellectual stewardship at L'Action nationale. He was also regarded in nationalist circles—though due allowance must be made here for the inflationary zeal of the moment—as the organizational 'genius' behind the Ligue's successful plebescite campaign.[10] Add his reputation for hard work, his experience with both the printed media and radio, and, perhaps most important, his freedom from association with past political failures or the peevish cliques they had spawned, and his suitability was clear. But André took some time to weigh the Bloc's offer. For one thing, there were practical considerations. He was a family man with two children, Jean having joined Francine in 1938. Without the extended family support network that swirled around the Laurendeau house in Outremont, it would not have been possible to indulge himself in yet another high-risk, low-paying nationalist adventure. Editing *L'Action nationale* had been one such activity, but he was thirty now and had never enjoyed a well-paid position. Though a man of few material ambitions beyond owning enough books and records, he along with Ghislaine would nevertheless have enjoyed freedom from financial worry. That day would not arrive until at least the 1950s, and even then they never owned expensive things or travelled: they spent winters in Montreal and summers in Saint-Gabriel, just as he had as a child. In 1942, however, he insisted that, if he joined the Bloc, he be paid the equivalent of his combined salaries at *L'Action nationale* and the Ligue pour la Défense du Canada—about $2,000 per year.[11]

André also had doubts about the withering daily routine of political life, of which he had received more than a taste during the 'no' campaign, and whether it would be compatible with his continued intellectual growth. A related question was whether or not he could hope to carry forward his pre-war advances in nationalist ideology while at the same time managing a political movement. On the other hand, there was his nationalist duty to consider. He had become part of a team. Could he turn his back on it, with his own rhetoric of crisis and urgency echoing in everyone's ears, to return suddenly to his books? Was this not, moreover, a glorious opportunity to test his ideas, especially his social nationalism, against the practical realities of life in Quebec? It was this last notion that seems to have won him over. In his letter of acceptance to Raymond on 24 December he explained:

> The way I first understood my position as Secretary of the party, it would involve a break with the work that I've been doing for the last ten years or so: for you know my life has been oriented toward intellectual pursuits rather than immediate political action. If I had agreed to be an 'odd-job man', it would have been a total waste, with no real benefit to the movement, and to the detriment of my own personal work. At thirty, one is still far from mature, the stock of intellectual knowledge is still incomplete, the age when one gives without hoarding has not yet come.
>
> But, defined as it is, the role of secretary general not only allows for study, research, and reflection, it presupposes them. It minimizes routine work.

It wouldn't take long for André to realize that this job description was utopian and that Raymond's fragile health, the lack of financial resources, and the incompatibility of some of his Bloc colleagues would severely limit his time for 'study, research, and reflection'. As one analyst of the Bloc's inner workings at the time observed: 'André Laurendeau is playing a key role at the side of Maxime Raymond and often in his place.'[12]

As the Bloc's key operative Laurendeau was involved, almost from the party's first days, in tiring and tangled diplomatic efforts to preserve unity. All studies of the Bloc Populaire's short history underscore the fact that it never boasted the co-operative spirit of its predecessor, the

THE BLOC POPULAIRE, 1942-1947 / 117

Ligue.[13] There were serious rifts, involving shifting alliances and various personalities, that mortally wounded every one of its electoral efforts. The major schism, from which the movement never would fully recover, involved the Quebec City branch and began early on. Maxime Raymond was both a friend and a supporter of Edouard Lacroix, a long-time nationalist voice in the Quebec legislature and, not incidentally, a wealthy businessman. Like Raymond, Lacroix provided a great deal of the money required to get the Bloc established. Indeed, together the two seem to have been the party's major source of funds in the early years. In return for his generosity, Lacroix assumed himself to be, in fact if not in name, Raymond's chief lieutenant at Quebec City.[14] This did not sit well with the Quebec Three—to use Laurendeau's term—of Chaloult, Gouin, and Hamel. Though often at odds with one another, each believing himself best suited to take the lead at Quebec, their differences were lovers' quarrels compared with their collective loathing for Lacroix. This animosity, which they never bothered to hide and which Lacroix fully reciprocated, extended beyond ego considerations and jurisdictional rivalries to the fact that in their eyes Lacroix's business-oriented ideals were incompatible with an anti-establishment party hostile to Quebec's elite and seeking profound social and economic change. Raymond, with Laurendeau's help, spent a good part of his first months as leader trying to pacify both sides.[15] For instance, he decided not to appoint lieutenants but to rely instead on a Supreme Council (the Bloc apparently had a weakness for grandiose titles) where he hoped to dilute antagonisms. It is difficult to know whether Laurendeau was referring to the Bloc's Quebec leaders or its supporters when he wrote later on that 'after the idealists, malcontents made up the bulk of our natural clientele'.[16]

The Bloc was able to put on a show of unity for its inaugural rally at Montreal's Saint-Jacques market on 27 January 1943—Laurendeau having done his best the night before on CHLP radio to create a crisis atmosphere by declaring that the Bloc had been formed 'because [French Canada] has never ceased to be threatened'. But the internal tensions had an impact on a number of important party decisions. Some members saw the Bloc's future exclusively as a federal party that would, in Bourassa's pan-Canadian tradition, fight for nationalist issues in Ottawa. This would leave the Union Nationale to carry on the struggle for autonomy at the provincial level while its solid grass-roots organization would be available to the Bloc for federal elections. Maxime Raymond was one who saw this plan as practical, financially, and beneficial to both parties. But there were others, including the Quebec Three, who still despised Duplessis for his treachery towards the ALN in 1936 and who dreamed of electoral revenge. For them the Bloc had to be a two-tiered party with a strong provincial wing—which, of course, they saw themselves dominating. Laurendeau agreed with them, chiefly because he was convinced that Duplessis, should he win the next election and replace Premier Godbout, would never use greater autonomy for Quebec to initiate social and economic reforms. Autonomy, André always maintained, was only a key: 'once we have the key, we must boldly enter the house, drive out the parasites, restore order, arrange things to our own liking . . . in a word, become masters of our own domain.'[17] Raymond, fearing that Chaloult, Hamel, and Gouin might form a separate provincial party themselves and anxious not to lose the reformist zeal of younger nationalists like Laurendeau, went along with the two-tiered idea. It was a fateful decision, as we will see, both for the Bloc's and for Laurendeau's political fortunes.

André's role in formulating the Bloc's official program was quite limited, in spite of the hopes he expressed in his letter confirming his acceptance of the secretary-general's post. He wasn't exactly forced out of the process, but his other duties at this stage were overwhelming, and the more experienced, fractious politicians in the party had too much at stake to leave 'doctrine' in the hands of a relative newcomer. The task of drawing up a statement of principles fell instead to Marie-Louis Beaulieu, a law professor at Laval with strong links to the Quebec City faction.[18] He was also entrusted with drawing up the official program that was adopted in draft form at a meeting in Montreal on 1 May 1943, which neither Raymond nor Laurendeau attended. That meeting struck a small committee to produce a final document for the approval of the Party Congress, and it was argued that Laurendeau was too busy to take part in it. His activity was confined to introducing subtle nuances of interpretation, in his role as the party's chief radio propagandist, and to developing some of the official program's main planks in articles he wrote for *Le Devoir* and the monthly party journal *Le Bloc*. He would have to wait until he became provincial leader to have a more direct influence on the party's political philosophy.

This is not to say, however, that he disagreed fundamentally with the bulk of Beaulieu's formulations. They contained all the 'politically correct' ideas for a French-Canadian nationalist, especially at the federal level. Beaulieu issued the usual tirade against British imperialism, with proposals for abolishment of appeals to the Privy Council, a Canadian Governor-General, a distinctive Canadian flag, and new emphasis on pan-American linkages. His program also stressed the old grievances concerning the lack of bilingualism in the federal bureaucracy and the failure to extend bilingual services to the French minorities outside Quebec.[19] There was much more besides, for nationalists were nothing if not critical of practically everything the government and institutions in Ottawa represented. But the most important and innovative theme, for Laurendeau in particular, was Beaulieu's emphasis on a stricter adherence to federalism, particularly in the political sphere. Here one could observe the strong influence of the Quebec City faction who, like André, were deeply alarmed by what they saw as the federal government's wartime assault on Quebec's autonomy. As one astute student of the Bloc's program has argued: 'the Bloc Populaire's strong critique of centralization foreshadowed the federal-provincial constitutional wrangles of the postwar era. It was the first nationalist movement to launch an offensive against the emerging Canadian social welfare state and the increased centralization which such a state entailed.'[20] Laurendeau feared that Godbout's passivity with respect to federal incursions into the provincial fiscal domain in order to finance the war effort had in three years wiped out all that Quebec had gained since 1867. It also meant that new state-initiated social programs, properly the responsibility of the provinces, could be undertaken only by the federal government. Hadn't this been the case with unemployment insurance in 1940? The Bloc was determined to get those fiscal powers back. The issue was one that as provincial leader Laurendeau would seize upon and make his own.

In the Bloc's early days, however, André was more preoccupied with getting the organization in place to fight elections. Without power, programs meant little. He believed the ALN's failure in this important area had been a major factor in its downfall, and he warned as early as 1941 that hard work and planning were crucial: 'the . . . organisation cannot be set up in a few days, and conviction by itself is no substitute. There is a technique to electioneering. Specialists in the art do not spring up overnight . . . for the invention of adequate rituals.'[21] He was given an opportunity to gain experience himself before leaving the Ligue for the Bloc, during the Outremont federal by-election called by Mackenzie King for 30 November 1942.[22] This would turn out to be one of the most spectacular by-elections in Quebec's political history. In calling it, King had initially hoped to regain some prestige and credibility for the Liberals after the shattering defeat in the Quebec sector of the April plebiscite. He was furious, apparently, with his French-Canadian advisers over that débâcle, and with no Ernest Lapointe to depend on, he felt obliged to take a hand himself in the Quebec political theatre. A parallel by-election in Charlevoix was a lost cause, but in Outremont King had every reason to expect success. The riding has an Anglo-Jewish majority and had voted sixty per cent 'yes' in the plebiscite. King chose his Associate Defence Minister, Major-General Léo Laflèche, as the Liberal candidate: a decorated war hero whose visible wounds would make a favourable contrast to the healthy young bodies of the anti-war nationalists. Prospects were that much better when the Conservatives and the newly-formed Bloc decided not to run candidates—the former because they did not want to split the pro-conscription vote and the latter because they were not yet ready. There must have been some chuckling over the ouija-board as King contemplated the pleasure of sticking it to the nationalists right in the petty-bourgeois heartland of so many of their leaders.

The situation was embarrassing for the Bloc and for Laurendeau personally. Not to run a candidate in either Charlevoix or Outremont was sensible but frustrating, given that the party had been formed partly to exploit the still strong anti-conscription feeling. To run in Outremont, however, where André lived and where his nationalist sentiment had first taken wing, would inevitably start off the Bloc's political life with a thorough whipping. King had chosen well. But the young nationalists in André's Montreal circle were not prepared to let Laflèche win without some sort of fight. Jean Drapeau, ambitious but still hurting from Bourassa's public dressing-down months before, saw the opportunity to sacrifice himself in a way that might earn him considerable gratitude and political IOUs for the future. He became the 'candidate of the con-scripts' and worked like a fanatic from the first day towards the inglorious goal of not losing his deposit.[23] At thirty Laurendeau was not only four years older than Jean Drapeau but also the oldest member of his campaign team. This enthusiastic young group concentrated all their efforts on a working-class French district called Jean-de-la-Croix, a name that nicely reflected the candidate's own martyrdom every time it was mentioned in a speech. Before long they managed to turn the campaign into an intense and vicious replay of the plebiscite.

Laurendeau admitted later that his colleagues were as bellicose and intemperate as their opponents were devious. Drapeau's campaign manager, Marc Carrière, received his conscription call-up during this time and, noting the 'coincidence', declared publicly that he would ignore it. The RCMP scooped him up and began harassing all the others, including André. Carrière was replaced by Michel Chartrand, a former monk, a future radical union leader, and a man who never used a moderate word when a ferocious one was available. 'In his virulent style and with a caustic violence that left us all breathless,' Laurendeau commented, 'he mustered every historical grievance we had ever held against Mother England.'[24] Chartrand would remain a life-long friend, one recalled by André's relatives as a booming presence in the otherwise quiet Lauren-deau home. He was a person it took some courage to acknowledge as a friend. Later in the campaign, at a rally where Laflèche appeared with his French Legion of Honour and British Distinguished Service Order, one of the hecklers in the back of the hall was another young Outremont resident, Pierre Elliott Trudeau.[25] Like Drapeau, Trudeau was a law student at the Université de Montréal and, while no nationalist, he volunteered his ser-vices out of disgust for the Liberals' undemocratic and cynical fear-mon-gering. He was careful, however, to picture Drapeau as someone who would be unqualified to win even if it was a one-horse race. 'Don't vote for Drapeau', he is reported to have said, 'vote against Laflèche. Even if the general's opponent was mediocre, as long as he was honest, one would have to vote against Laflèche.'[26] It is unclear whether Laurendeau encountered Trudeau during these events, but he employed the same sort of incisive wit in conducting Drapeau's radio campaign. He had long since learned how to drop his intellectualism and, without resorting to Chartrand's histrionics, to rouse an audience. Opinion is mixed about his impact on a political crowd, but one observer who witnessed his oratorical efforts with the Bloc said that he was very effective: '. . . Laurendeau had a personal radiance, a sort of magnetism and, without being a tribune, he was a remarkable orator, able to connect with crowds and stir them.'[27]

As election day neared Laurendeau saw living proof that, important and inspiring as strong feelings could be, they would not replace sound tactics and good people on the ground:

> We closed ranks. . . . But could one really speak of an organisation? Jean Drapeau had extraordinary energy, a sense of propaganda, and the ability to lead his troops at the double. Did he ever sleep? He ate only one meal a day, at Goby's on rue Laurier where we met every evening. My own home became one of our committee rooms, much to the astonishment of my young children.[28]

Drapeau was given a last-minute boost when Henri Bourassa, now a creaky-voiced seventy-five, gave him a glowing tribute before an overflow crowd at the Jean-de-la-Croix auditorium. But Laflèche won by more than 13,000 votes and the Liberal party gloated long and hard. All the same, Drapeau did more than just save his deposit. He won the Jean-de-la-Croix district by more than 4,000 votes and all fifty-one polls where French Canadians were the majority.[29] Nationalists proceeded to do what they always do on such occasions: they claimed a resounding moral victory. To Laurendeau, however, it was a good indication of what the Bloc was up against. Moral victories were for losers and he was not about to throw away the Ligue's hard-won momentum or become a key figure with the Bloc merely for that—something he could as easily have achieved while remaining an editor. Regarding Outremont as a dose of reality, he set about at once to be better prepared for the next time.

The opportunity came sooner than expected. The Bloc made its official electoral debut in August 1943, with two more federal by-elections in Stanstead and Cartier. Both ridings held pluses and minuses for the nationalists. Stanstead, near Quebec City, had a strong English-speaking minority, and its 'no' vote in the plebiscite was a relatively low sixty-three per cent. On the other hand, the Bloc's leader Raymond was well respected among the textile workers in the middling large urban centre of Magog. Cartier was an urban Montreal riding of mixed ethnic elements that had voted seventy per cent 'yes' in the plebiscite. The Bloc had a multilingual and energetic candidate there in Paul Massé, but for him to win, the vote would have to split among several candidates including a communist, Fred Rose. Laurendeau was in charge and 'from the central office in Montreal I directed our propaganda and the deployment of our militants.'[30]

Believing that Stanstead offered the best hope, he spent the bulk of his time there. But too much of that time was consumed in shuttling back and forth between the Quebec Three and Edouard Lacroix to try and cover, if not mend, their deteriorating relations. Gouin, Hamel, and Chaloult refused to help in the elections and were threatening to resign from the party. 'We're facing a triple resignation,' he scribbled hastily to Ghislaine on 31 May. 'When will I come back? It's a matter of life—Can't give up right away.' A week later he reported: 'No solution in sight for now. I feel quite pessimistic.' Raymond was prepared to accept their resignations, but the idea only depressed Laurendeau more: 'Internal disunity . . . this is what nationalism amounts to.'

With Raymond sick again, Laurendeau and Drapeau did much of the campaign work in Stanstead. André travelled to Magog numerous times and from his main base in Quebec City he ventured into rural towns he had never heard of before to meet the voters one on one. As he remarked much later, '. . . I pampered Stanstead.'[31] His letters home apologized for not being able to see the family, for missing the children's special days, and for constantly complaining. But many of the party's workers and sympathizers had simply taken off on their holidays. 'We have a lot of work at the moment,' he reported on 15 July, 'documentation, writing, talks, organization. . . .' By now he was too tired to care about rumours that the Quebec Three, far from staying quietly on the sidelines as they had agreed, were actually conspiring against the Bloc. And he took it as a positive sign when he and Drapeau drew nearly 900 people to a rally in a town near Magog, when the CCF had attracted just 70 that same afternoon. On election day the Bloc took Stanstead and lost by only 150 votes in Cartier to Fred Rose.

Overall Laurendeau was pleased, but he blamed himself for having given Cartier up for lost while spending too much time in Stanstead. Looking ahead, furthermore, he warned that volunteer helpers were simply not reliable enough. This would prove crippling in a provincial fight, when the UN workers who had helped out this time would be on the other side. In what was destined to become his most familiar refrain, he contended that everything hinged on solving the financial problem. Elections were just too expensive to depend on a few loyal backers who could withdraw their support, as the Quebec Three had done, at any time. Although he remained civil to Gouin, Hamel, and Chaloult, from this point on André had no faith or respect for them. When they carried out their threat to resign from the Bloc he considered it good riddance, while recognizing that their departure would hamstring all future efforts in the Quebec City region. For himself, André had learned that he didn't like the sacrifices involved in political life. Where was the time to think, to write? The bickering, small-minded grudges, and petty tasks had left him exhausted. The main benefit was in meeting the people face-to-face and learning something of their day-to-day hardships and concerns. This he would not forget, and the experience had the effect of modifying his high-sounding principles in favour of concrete proposals.

Many years later Laurendeau related one of the insights he gained while campaigning for the Bloc in this period—an experience that he described as opening his eyes to the suffocating atmosphere created by Quebec's religious conformity. It seems that one evening he found himself in a small town, sitting in a tavern and wondering where to get a bed for the night. A respectable-looking professional man, whom he called the churchwarden, offered to put him up and, after talking and drinking for several hours, the man suddenly confessed that he had lost his faith long before. Because such a thing was regarded as a sin in itself, he had been forced to live a double life. Though intelligent and well read, he had hidden his learning: 'What struck me most in . . . books were the objections raised against faith. I think there are people who are born atheists. There must be a lot of them in the province. But everyone lives in his own hole. Like rats!' Laurendeau was both saddened and disturbed by the religious intolerance that had forced the man 'to piece together his own philosophy, but in the worst possible circumstances—without ever expressing it openly, without airing it, without having it shaped by discussion and exchange of views, without ever going down as deep as he could in himself' He could only imagine what such an existence must be like:

> At the time he gave me the impression of a man buried alive. Alcohol helped a little to dull the pain of his spoiled life. The man must have possessed considerable vigour just to be able to keep up appearances when he was such a mess inside. Watching him I had a sense of terrible loss, of an impoverishment of himself and the society he lived in, of a stupid and useless sacrifice. And I wondered how many 'rats' like him there were in our French-Canadian society, each buried in his own separate hole.

A new day dawned, the Bloc's affairs took over again, and André moved on, 'but I have never been able to look at this society in the same way since.'[32]

When Laurendeau wrote this account in 1964, it had a deeper meaning than his readers perhaps realized. For, as he revealed privately, it was during the Bloc Populaire years that he lost his own faith. The church-warden was surely voicing some of the same private agonies that he himself had suffered over a long period. Writing to his son Jean in July 1964 he referred to the moment itself and the reasons why he kept his silence about it thereafter:

> So I lost my faith and if I could put a date on this event, it's thanks to you. . . . You celebrated your first communion on May 19, 1945. As usual, at this ceremony, parents also take communion: I had done it for Francine two years earlier. But I had just vowed that I could no longer do it. As a result,

I played sick, and I spent the day in my bed—furious at having to play this game. I believed myself forced to: I was the provincial leader of an officially Catholic party, I sat as deputy opposite Duplessis. . . . I was thirty-three years old. I had been fighting 'against doubt' for at least 7 years, maybe [for] 10 . . . , maybe all my life: it seemed to me that I had always oscillated from unbelief to fanaticism (religious). But in that year 1945, it was necessary that I bring myself, that I admit to myself: there is nothing left, it's over.[33]

It is difficult to imagine the anguish this secret caused Laurendeau as he moved within his Catholic circles, but it was clearly a factor contributing to the less spiritually idealistic and more pragmatic approach to social issues that he began to adopt during the war. And it was an anguish that would grow.

Late in 1943, an ailing and dispirited Maxime Raymond turned to Laurendeau to lead the provincial Bloc in the election that Premier Godbout would have to call in 1944. The decision was ratified at a party congress of about 800 people, but Laurendeau understood that it was a decision forced by circumstance: 'With Hamel, Gouin and Chaloult gone, and Lacroix powerful but unacceptable, they had to fall back on me.'[34] The Congress itself was far more interested in the scandal over the resignations than in discussing the new leader. Nor did André have any illusions about his abilities to manoeuvre and manipulate. Even his close friends agreed that it was his intelligence, integrity, and dedication that would make him a great leader, and not a wily political sense. As was observed in a later study of the Bloc: 'One could hardly imagine him concocting electoral strategies where . . . cunning play[s] a major role. Laurendeau manipulates ideas, electoral organizers count on patronage and a clientele mentality.'[35] He accepted largely out of his sense of duty and perhaps partly because he reckoned on being better able to translate his ideas into action from a place in Quebec's legislative assembly than in the role of party secretary-general. By late July he was still amazed at this personal twist of fate. In a letter to Ghislaine he wrote, 'I wouldn't mind philosophizing on the strange turn of events. . . .' By then, however, there was no time, since Godbout had called the long-anticipated election for 8 August.

As leader André's overriding concern in the election campaign was to adopt a strategy that would permit the Bloc to pick up a substantial portion of the protest vote—which his travels and analysis indicated would be substantial. The people, he believed, didn't trust Godbout and still resented his acquiescent role in Mackenzie King's war policies. Sure that the premier would fail in his apparently desperate last-minute attempt to appease nationalist sentiments by introducing a bill to nationalize Montreal's Light, Heat and Power Company, Laurendeau attacked the legislation as a belated half-measure that left the biggest power companies, like Shawinigan Light, Heat and Power, still entrenched while doing nothing to bring down Quebec's high power rates.[36] But if Godbout was politically vulnerable, it was important for the Bloc to make sure that Duplessis and the Union Nationale did not reap all the benefits. The shrewd UN chief was trying to hog all the anti-conscription and pro-autonomy ground for himself. Thus Laurendeau concentrated on Duplessis's past deceptions in these areas, reminding the voters over and over that *le chef* had been a last-minute convert to the anti-conscription movement and that his so-called nationalism had been exposed as pure pragmatism during his years in power from 1936 to 1939.

At the same time Laurendeau understood that voters were also deeply fearful of a post-war return to depression conditions and might be open to radical social and economic proposals. This was a field, moreover, where the conservative, do-nothing Union Nationale was bereft of ideas. Actually, Laurendeau had been striving to identify the Bloc with social reform and strong opposition to the powerful economic interests who supported the old parties since his acceptance speech at the party congress in February:

> The kind of government we have had from those old parties entirely lacking in feeling for their own country has been deplorable. They have let themselves be dragged along passively behind a great power, and have gradually eroded the sovereignty of the provinces. Theirs has been an odious kind of government, which allowed the unemployed to stagnate in their misery during the depression because the jobless are unable to go on any kind of strike except a hunger strike, and of this the government has no fear. They gave us miserable governments which tolerated slums instead of reclaiming them, which despised the family instead of supporting it, because neither slums nor families can go on strike, and the government knows it. They gave us hypocritical governments which taught the proletariat much more effectively than any Marxist that the only way to triumph over a liberal capitalist state is through revolution. Only when the poverty-stricken masses threaten to adopt the red flag does the government finally stir itself to relieve their suffering.[37]

In this regard it was mandatory to pay close attention to the CCF, which targeted the same unhappy constituency. True, the CCF had never been a factor in Quebec political life, but in the uncertain economic atmosphere of the times it had achieved some shocking successes, including the defeat of Arthur Meighen in Toronto's York South federal by-election at the height of the conscription debate in 1942.[38] Laurendeau was not above employing 'red scare' rhetoric against the CCF and he dwelt heavily as well on its record of state centralization. Even though he was moving steadily in that direction himself, with the Bloc listing a tidy number of industries and resource sectors that were potentially open to nationalization by the provincial government, he chose to accentuate the differences between the judicious social nationalism of the Catholic left and outright 'socialism'. A mid-election Gallup Poll gave him cause to believe that this strategy was sound. It showed the UN with 25 per cent, the Liberals with 37 per cent, the Bloc with 22 per cent, and the CCF nowhere in sight.[39]

With the Bloc's financial and human resources still threadbare, Laurendeau's tactical approach was to try and push innovation and energy to the limit. His campaign opened on 12 July at Montreal's Jean Talon market, the scene of earlier anti-conscription rallies, before a crowd estimated at 30,000; he and Raymond rode in a jaunty open-car parade trailed by chanting young people waving placards with slogans such as 'Let's break the chains with André Laurendeau.'[40] Hoping initially to have candidates in ninety-one ridings, but settling for eighty, he pressed his friends to run even in hopeless circumstances: thus Michel Chartrand cheerfully lost his deposit in Chambly-Rouville. Though women could now vote, the Bloc's old conservative guard was not interested in making them candidates, using them more often for the Quebec version of the political coffee meeting. Given the party's dependence on small private donations and volunteers, every form of local meeting was needed to reach the voters. For the same reason André allocated as many of the Bloc's slim resources as possible to get around the lack of newspaper exposure by buying radio time. When election day arrived there was good and bad news. The Bloc polled almost 200,000 votes, or just over 15 per cent.[41] Laurendeau, thanks to his irrepressible campaign manager Jean Drapeau, won by 670 votes in Montreal-Laurier—a riding that, although its Liberal name was hardly appropriate, would eventually become the stronghold of another third-party leader, René Lévesque.[42] However, the Bloc elected only three others, and two-thirds of its candidates lost their deposits. The Union Nationale, with 47 seats to the Liberals' 37, formed a majority government. The CCF was elected in only one seat and gained a mere 2.5 per cent of the vote, but, as André had feared, its protest vote hurt the Bloc in several ridings.[43]

In his immediate post-election analysis Laurendeau found room for cautious optimism. As he wrote privately to a friend:

> Once the initial surprise was over, I must admit I was not really disappointed by the election result. In fact, we've only worked for about a year and a half, and in extremely difficult circumstances where a lot of our time was wasted on petty quarrels and disagreements. We had little organization and almost no money; that, in such circumstances, roughly 200,000 French Canadians should vote for us I think is a promising start.

But as the weeks passed and the reality of the Bloc's having only four seats in the Legislative Assembly took hold, he became discouraged about the prospects for making any impact at all. He had no parliamentary experience and would be up against veterans like Godbout, now opposition leader, and the dreaded Duplessis, whose home was parliament and who had a reputation for devouring weak opponents like a wolf among sheep. The Bloc's meagre resources—a monotonous theme that was beginning to wear him down—also meant that he could not hire adequate staff, but would have to rely for expert advice on relatives like lawyers Jacques and

Antonio Perrault and friends like the economist François-Albert Angers. Nor were his spirits buoyed when, in the days following the legislative session's opening on 7 February 1945, he was interrupted by the speaker again and again for improper procedures. Recalling this period, he wrote:

> . . . when, at the outset of 1945, I entered the Legislative Assembly as a provincial deputy and leader . . . it was absolutely the first time I set foot there: unless I'm mistaken, such was also the case for my . . . Bloc companions. . . . We had looked through the manual of parliamentary procedures, but our knowledge was recent and not confident. We felt surrounded by adversaries. . . . We never became adept at procedures, but we managed to say more or less what we had to say.

When he gave his maiden speech in a 'weak and hesitant voice', with Ghislaine looking on from the gallery, some Union Nationale ministers got up to leave and some talked to each other, while Duplessis pointedly read his newspaper.[44] Nevertheless, as the session neared its end he was able to offer a mixed review. 'To sum up my impressions to date,' he wrote on 25 July, 'It seems to me that I rather enjoy parliamentary life — and that I would like it even more if our opponents stopped their petty politics and we had a stronger team.'

Despite his rocky start Laurendeau succeeded during this first session in establishing the Bloc's priorities for the next four years. While the party's official program contained all the important themes, it was also a contradictory soup in which tired clichés left over from the ALN's heyday and a social philosophy burdened by conservative Jesuit thinking were combined with other, very progressive electoral, social, and economic ideas — the best morsels had to be carefully fished out. In practice, Laurendeau 'had more to do than anyone . . . with elaborating the provincial programme. His causeries and conferences and his definition of issues in the legislature, really defined the program.'[45] He made it clear first of all that the Bloc, puny though its parliamentary influence might be, would take the high ground and vote solely on the quality of the measures placed before it. He was true to his word, according to at least one account, which reported that during the first session the Bloc voted thirteen times with the government, and twenty-four times against, abstaining once.[46] He had used his ostentatiously ignored maiden speech to make the defence of provincial autonomy the Bloc's top priority. But throughout the rest of his leadership he was primarily and genuinely concerned with utilizing the provincial state to deal with the problems of Quebec's workers and farmers in the context of their material and family life. He studied, proposed, intervened, and debated tenaciously over issues such as housing, industrial working conditions, medical insurance, rural education, and family assistance. It was during these years, in fact, that he finally came down from the clouds of his social theorizing to confront social problems on the ground and, in the process, moved out in front of the majority of his nationalist colleagues in recognizing the extent to which, during the war, Quebec had been transformed by urban-industrial forces. Though obliged by the political company he was keeping to mutter old formulae as well, he favoured new approaches. As he had maintained in his inaugural speech as provincial leader: 'The people have a vague desire for a policy that, without being chauvinist, would respect the provinces' autonomy; a policy that, without being socialist, would be boldly social, in short, a policy that, without being anti-British, would prove to be Canadian.'

But if 1945 was the beginning of a new direct-action phase of Laurendeau's social nationalism, it was also the beginning of the end for the Bloc. Confronted with yet another election, this time at the federal level, the party had no fight left in it. The disintegration in morale that followed the poor results of the provincial election was everywhere apparent. Laurendeau always considered it a 'piece of bad luck . . . that in Quebec a provincial election preceded the federal one. The Bloc was engaged on both fronts. It faced its first test of strength on the one where it was the least well armed and most divided.'[47] In addition to the usual problems—money, a shortage of good candidates, lack of publicity—it had a different atmosphere to contend with in 1945. The people were no longer worried about conscription and were not in a mood to punish Mackenzie King as they had Adélard Godbout a year earlier. In André's words: '. . . public opinion identified [the Bloc] with the crisis which had given it birth. Once the war was over the Bloc was unable to survive.' In these circumstances an ill-advised attempt to form a vote-getting alliance with the mercurial Camillien Houde did more harm than good.[48] The Bloc, in its last campaign, captured just eight per cent of the federal vote in Quebec and elected only two members, one of whom was the 'great survivor' Raymond. As André remembered this dispiriting time:

> We had felt defeat coming. I remember an enthusiastic rally held for Roger Duhamel in the Saint-Jacques Market. Jean Drapeau had gone down to inspect the crowd, both inside the hall and out. He wanted to study their reactions. Coming back to the platform he gave them a dirty look and, turning to me, said: 'You see those people out there? It's really going to break their hearts to vote against us.'
>
> Unless I am mistaken that meant: They think the way we do, we're telling them what they want to hear, but what they want doesn't seem possible any more. They don't believe we stand a chance, they think we're licked. Sum it up this way: With Quebec you can do what you like; with Ottawa you do what you can.[49]

Laurendeau returned for the fall session of Quebec's legislature with a heavy heart and an empty war-chest. 'The more I think about it,' he wrote, 'the less keen I am to start a winter in these present conditions.'

And well he might worry, for Duplessis had smelled the odour of impending death and set about trying to demolish what was left of the Bloc: as André remarked, 'Duplessis was as unpleasant as possible, especially towards me.' He learned indirectly from a Union Nationale official that Duplessis's strategy was to take every chance to humiliate him in order to discourage the Bloc's constituency-level supporters and leave them ripe for the plucking. The Liberals, he noticed, were trying for much the same result, only with oily kindness. The worst part of feeling like his opponents' next meal was 'the sense that there is no movement behind you. The Bloc is crossing a desert.' Not equipped by training or temperament to return Duplessis's snide personal attacks, Laurendeau continued instead to offer his carefully rational analysis of each legislative issue. But he never forgot the Union Nationale leader's guttersnipe bullying, and it was during this time that he developed a personal enmity that in the 1950s would feed into his political and ideological repugnance and make Duplessis a living symbol for him of all that was wrong with Quebec.

What made the immediate situation even more difficult was the bone-numbing fatigue he experienced as a result of having to shoulder almost all of the Bloc's work himself: 'I should work harder, but I'm tired and inert, so no excessive efforts.' By 1946 the party had only three permanent staff members and he was forced to research and present positions on subjects, such as the plight of Quebec's miners, that he knew nothing about. Although he tried at party congresses that year and in 1947 to confront the Bloc's financial and other problems head on, frankly warning that its future was at stake, none of the ambitious salvation plans that were hatched bore any fruit. His correspondence contained ever more pessimistic statements: 'I am physically weak (. . . and mentally!). . . . The Assembly is creating a real phobia in me!' To Ghislaine he confessed his private doubts about the wisdom of having gone into politics at all. 'Life is very strange: we spend our lives wishing. And the more we wish, the less happy we are.'

Given the depressing political scenario and his personal state of mind, it was perhaps inevitable that Laurendeau began to consider resigning. During the spring and summer of 1947 two rationales for doing so, running more or less in tandem, presented themselves and became a source of bitter controversy within the party. On the one hand André was approached in early April by Gérard Filion—an old friend who had just become director of *Le Devoir* following the death of Georges Pelletier— who invited him to become an associate editor.[50] But there was a hitch: because of *Le Devoir*'s long tradition of political independence, Laurendeau could not be affiliated with any party. It was at this time, according to a furious Maxime Raymond, that Laurendeau began manoeuvring to find a less selfish-looking, more political reason for leaving. Thus at a Bloc council meeting on 10 May André informed Raymond privately that he might accept the offer for family and financial considerations, but said nothing to the Bloc's executive or to the congress when it met in late June. Finally, on 8 July he wrote to Raymond resigning on the grounds of differences in principle that reflected badly on the federal leader and many others in the Bloc as well. Raymond answered with a long letter essentially accusing him of duplicity. Now it was Laurendeau's turn to be offended. He admitted to considering *Le Devoir*'s offer from approximately April onward, but he did not believe his personal affairs were a concern for the party. He resigned, he insisted, because on 10 May the Bloc's executive had voted to suppress the provincial wing, thus denying it any chance to contest another election and reducing his own previous efforts to naught. Worst of all, this move would cede the struggle for autonomy to the 'anti-social' Duplessis:

> Even though I don't see myself as a supporter of the status quo, I believe that eliminating the provincial wing of the Bloc would be the wrong solution; because it would necessarily mean taking away the very identity of the party and leaving it to the direct influence of M. Duplessis. In other words, it would give the Union Nationale the federal party it wants but seems unable to get.

Proving he was not wedded to the status quo, he had proposed turning the Bloc into a political movement instead of a party at both levels if it was the majority's feeling that seeking office was just too costly. The majority, however, had supported Raymond: thus 'I did not think about leaving the Bloc because another job was offered me. But I'm accepting this job because . . . I feel I should leave the Bloc.'

Whatever had truly been uppermost in his mind (and there were convincing arguments on both sides), his resignation made him a participant in those same internecine conflicts that had plagued the Bloc since its inception and that he had so deeply hoped would not be the ruin of yet another nationalist political movement. When he returned to the legislature to sit as an independent, old friends shunned him and he joked that he had to look in the gallery to find smiling faces. Perhaps more disconcerting was the fact that Duplessis didn't think there was enough of Laurendeau left to bother attacking; on one occasion, when André gave what he himself regarded as his best speech in parliament, the old fox even put an arm around him and called him 'a brilliant young man'. But if Duplessis was angling for some friendly editorials in future editions of *Le Devoir*, time would prove him overly sanguine. With the pressure off, André was even able to smile at the parliamentary practices that had formerly appalled him. When he tried, for instance, to get three housing bills through as a final testament to his efforts at Quebec and found himself thwarted for weeks by mindless delaying tactics focused on a milk bill, he wrote, 'we are swimming in milk.' He summed up his situation in a letter to a friend dated 11 February 1948:

> Since the movement was evolving in a direction I found repugnant, I quit and I am now sitting as an independent member. But the Bloc is not really active. . . . One could sum things up in these terms: the ideas which were incarnated in the Bloc were strong enough to inspire a vigorous movement, but were not widespread enough to sustain a party. The enterprise seems to have redefined itself into a movement, or something less, for the moment. However, you couldn't call it a political factor. . . .

In February of 1948 he actually considered carefully a request from Drapeau and a few others to run again that year in Laurier as an independent nationalist. Filion agreed that he could continue to do his *Le Devoir* job while holding a seat. But after a meeting with about forty loyalists in the riding he commented, 'I recognized among the militants not enthusiasm, but good will and loyalty.' He noted that many of his former conservative nationalist friends would now be working against him, and he posed a question that revealed a lesson well learned: where would the money come from? Deciding against another try, he asked Ghislaine to bring the children for a last look at their father in the legislature. His son Jean, just nine, has recalled the occasion: 'Once—just this one time—I saw the member for Laurier stand, facing Duplessis, and say something or other about sugar beets.'[51] André wondered whether, on passing the government buildings in future, 'I would regret not being among those who have a "seat" in the chamber. . . . But I am more and more convinced that it is not up to me to be a deputy for the second time.'

As time passed, Laurendeau's opinion of politics and politicians, while not quite descending to pre-war levels, became cynical enough to prevent him from ever reconsidering his decision. For other nationalists the logic of turning to the provincial state as the main instrument of French-Canadian progress implied a corresponding duty to participate in the political process, but he would always have the memory of his Bloc experience to put such thoughts to rest. He used the term 'morally liberated' to express his relief in 1948, and henceforth he preferred the higher ground of a 'fourth estate' political commentator to that of political activist. Moreover, he believed that the legislature was only the clearing house for broader political conceptions, and that to generate the latter, thinkers were required as much as political leaders. Looking back on his legislative experience from 1963, he drew a clear picture of why he had since chosen the former role:

> My colleagues, mostly divided on issues, all had one sentiment in common: boredom. Brief battles would sometimes awaken the fighting spirit: but almost everyone would gradually sink again into the awful monotony of never-ending speeches. Imagine having to put up with them for three, six,

even eight hours a day, that they are rarely substantial or amusing, that the speakers are always the same men: in the chamber, an intelligent back-bencher soon runs the risk of turning into an object.[52]

As for the Bloc itself, the fact that Laurendeau wrote very little about it in later years suggests it was one memory he wanted to forget. When he did decide to write a book about his wartime experiences in 1963, *La Crise de la conscription*, he stopped his account at the plebiscite, offering just a few per-functory remarks on what followed. It was as if he'd been stricken with the old weariness and could only bring himself to say that, if he was to write a book about the Bloc, it would begin with the subject of internal quarrels; 'it was a weird group that claimed to unite French Canadians and couldn't remain united itself, a cracked block, inexplicably divided. . . .'[53] More recently scholars have claimed (as they usually do) that, in spite of its fail-ures and very marginal political impact at the time, the Bloc had great long-term significance. A few have even spied virtually the whole program of Quebec's Quiet Revolution of the 1960s in the doctrines and public pro-nouncements of the Bloc. Another positive but more restrained assessment sees the Bloc's impact rather in terms of an emerging nationalist ideolog-ical split that would become permanent:

> . . . during the Bloc's short life-span, 1942-8, there was a growing divergence between nationalists who favoured the preservation of traditional cultural and socio-economic values and institutions and a small but significant minority of younger generation nationalists who had come to perceive the need for extensive and thorough socio-economic reforms. These reforms required a significant growth in the role of the Quebec state. In a very real sense then, the Bloc . . . was both an expression of traditional nationalist aspi-rations as well as a harbinger of neo-nationalist aspirations to be more clearly defined in the post-war era.[54]

Laurendeau was one of those moving inexorably away from traditional postulates and, in the process, at last abandoning those conservative nationalists with whom he had been trying to reconcile his views ever since returning from France, and whom he would henceforth treat with studied politeness. Here no doubt was his real 'liberation'.

After six years of exhausting and passionate political activity André was about to return full-time to his first love, writing. These years had given him a far more realistic perspective on what needed to be done not only to guarantee French Canada's place in Canada as a distinctive cultural and political entity, but to make Quebec a more progressive place to live for the working class as well as for the notables, whose values and concerns, he now realized, had played too large a role in his thinking. At *Le Devoir* he anticipated a far greater opportunity to 'break the chains' by shaping public opinion than had ever been a realistic possibility with the Bloc. The person who made this new role possible, Gérard Filion, perhaps summed up Laurendeau's personal transition best in his own memoirs:

In fact, the 'Bloc populaire' adventure was the wrong course for Laurendeau to take. His turn of mind, his intellectual inclinations, his physical constitution, everything about him marked him out as suited for tasks other than electoral debate. He was not made for political action, but for intellectual inquiry. Instead of a writing career, he chose journalism, which at the time was the only way to earn a living with his pen.[55]

7

Le Devoir, 1947-1954

We have not been able to find the elements of an indispensable synthesis, one of men who, while evidently accepting the conditions of a highly industrialized and technical civilization . . . , intend nevertheless to preserve and diffuse spiritual values and a conception of life in which they are both heirs and artisans . . . we have revealed ourselves thus far to be incapable of passing from the stage of survival, to that of a full, bursting and radiant life.

André Laurendeau, 1953[1]

In 1947 rue Notre-Dame in Montreal's old town was still dominated by its austere, stone-faced basilica. Unsuited for the post-war bustle of people and modern vehicles, its venerable charm scarred here and there by tawdry echoes of the nearby waterfront, the street seemed to trudge along under a heavy burden of history. The building, at 430 Notre-Dame, that housed *Le Devoir* was itself a kind of basilica for the local rat population and, in the opinion of people who worked there, should have been condemned for its smells alone. At the newspaper offices and at the Imprimerie Populaire, where the technical work and printing were done, the odours emanated from machinery dating back to the turn of the century. The workers in the shops, many of more ancient vintage than the machines, creaked along too and accepted scandalously low wages—out of loyalty, according to their bosses, but more likely out of pensionless fear.[2] When visitors dropped by to look over this curious half-European, half-rural newspaper operation, they found the ramshackle conditions depressing.[3] But Henri Bourassa, who founded *Le Devoir* in 1910, considered them fittingly 'virtuous' for a nationalist publication dedicated to French Canada's survival. As for André Laurendeau, who joined the paper in September 1947 as associate editor-in-chief and remained there until 1963,[4] the surroundings were as comfortable as an old sweater. And they were a marked improvement over Quebec's legislature, where the rats were bigger and much meaner.

Laurendeau's transition from politics to journalism would be complete only in 1948, when he decided not to run again in the provincial election of that year. In the meantime he shuttled back and forth between Montreal and Quebec City, sometimes jotting down notes for his *Le Devoir* editorials en route. He could not have been aware then that his choice of journalism would turn out to be his most momentous career decision. At thirty-five, with a growing family, his chief concern in abandoning political life was to find a position that would allow him to support a modest lifestyle while continuing his close ties to the nationalist movement. Journalism, he soon discovered, offered this and more. What a relief to be in one place, Montreal, enjoying the regular domestic routine that had not been possible since he joined the Ligue pour la Défense du Canada in 1942. Editors did not have to go and get the stories, and from this day forward Laurendeau would resist leaving home for any length of time. Journalism also meant resuming his *métier* as a writer—the vocation he had been pursuing indirectly ever since giving up on music as a career in late adolescence. It would permit him to remain in touch with the issues on a day-to-day basis, but with more time to investigate and think about them. Furthermore, at *Le Devoir* he could remain true to his nationalist principles, for its long tradition as an independent nationalist paper would require fewer intellectual compromises than would have been the case with virtually any other French-Canadian daily. Then too, had he not, since 1936, been moving away from Abbé Groulx's nationalist ideology and towards Henri Bourassa's?

Laurendeau joined *Le Devoir* at a critical moment in its ideological and financial history. His hiring was a condition imposed by Gérard Filion when the latter joined the paper as director in April 1947 as part of a concerted effort to prevent it from falling into the outstretched arms of the Union Nationale.[5] Henri Bourassa had insisted that *Le Devoir*, while free to support political options as it chose, should always remain independent of party affiliations. His successor Georges Pelletier, who was director from 1932 to 1947, had remained true to this ideal while strongly supporting the Bloc Populaire in 1942-43. But in the latter year Pelletier fell seriously ill and the paper lacked strong leadership. Some of its editorial staff began to edge *Le Devoir*'s political line towards the Union Nationale, particularly after Duplessis's victory in the 1944 election. A group of directors led by Laurendeau's brother-in-law Jacques Perrault moved to stop them. By hiring Filion—a successful and business-smart union leader from the agricultural sector—well before Pelletier's death, they effectively forestalled any further drift.[6] Filion had no use for the Union Nationale and he knew that Laurendeau's anti-Duplessis credentials, so recently evident in the Bloc Populaire's internal disputes, would ensure the newspaper's independence. He also had first-hand knowledge of Laurendeau's intelligence, writing ability, and strength of character from their days together in Jeune-Canada, the Ligue pour la Défense du Canada, and the Bloc. Although he hired Laurendeau to share the editor-in-chief's job with Omer Héroux, this was largely a respectful gesture towards Héroux, who was one of the numerous old-timers hanging on at *Le Devoir*. Laurendeau gradually took charge of editorial policy both before and after his appointment as sole editor-in-chief in 1957.[7]

There was a second ideological issue, stemming in part from the first, that threatened the paper's independence in the late forties and early fifties. During the complicated legal manoeuvring that helped the anti-Duplessis faction secure first Filion's and then Laurendeau's appointment, Georges Pelletier was persuaded to sign over his controlling shares in *Le Devoir* to Joseph Charbonneau, Archbishop of Montreal.[8] While the arrangement was considered an act of trust involving a liberal-minded and trustworthy ecclesiastic, it raised questions in many minds as to whether *Le Devoir* had succeeded in maintaining its political independence at the price of abandoning its traditional arm's-length relationship with Quebec's Catholic hierarchy. Although the paper had always been reflective of Catholic thought and was at times slavishly uncritical of the church's role in Quebec society, it had consciously striven to keep the clerical establishment at a distance, and thus could not be compared with the many Catholic publications in Quebec that merely echoed the church's line. As Laurendeau emphasized in a 1952 editorial:

> M. Bourassa had reflected upon the experiences of the Catholic press in Europe during the nineteenth century. He came to the conclusion that the paper should maintain a lay character—the meaning of which soon became clear.
>
> Bourassa's paper would be directed and edited by lay Catholics; but it would not have an official nor an effective church role. Catholic in inspiration, it would not involve itself beyond that. This tradition was maintained by Georges Pelletier; it remains alive under Gérard Filion, who has re-affirmed it several times.

Filion did indeed uphold the tradition, but not without incident. While Archbishop Charbonneau disagreed sharply at times with the liberal-minded direction adopted by the Filion-Laurendeau team at *Le Devoir*, he never attempted to exploit his legal advantage. But his successor, Paul-Emile (later Cardinal) Léger, did seek to exert a direct influence on the paper, and at one critical point Filion was required to travel across Canada to Victoria, BC, to secure a promise from Charbonneau—who had been transferred there in 1950 largely because of his own liberal tendencies—not to transfer his control to Léger. Charbonneau agreed and held the shares until his death in 1958, when they passed to Filion.[9]

This issue of clerical interference was far more important to André in 1947 than would have been the case in his early twenties. Since then his experiences in France had made him a severe critic of clericalism. Having been converted to a left-of-centre Catholicism, he frequently criticized the conservative mentality of Quebec's church leaders in the social field, while never openly breaking with them. In the late 1930s his aim was to encourage a compromise so that the strongly Catholic nationalists could experience, as he had, the enriching, more contemporary ideas of personalism. But the war and his political career had thrown cold water on these prospects. What he regarded as cynical and blind loyalty to the Canadian government's war policies by the Catholic hierarchy had left him with painful questions about the church's respect for the democratic voice of French Canada. His travels and down-to-earth political activities had shown him as well that the clerics were deficient in their awareness of the people's material needs, often mouthing empty clichés from a doctrine that no longer had any real relevance for the church's beloved farmer, let alone the industrial or resource worker. He had even begun to question privately, as he would more and more openly in the years ahead, whether the church's close alliance with the business and political elites didn't actually serve to stifle progressive thinking, thus placing it on the side of the reactionary forces in Quebec. While his concerns on this score would take time to coalesce with those of other postwar critics both inside and outside the church, Laurendeau began to signal his doubts over issues like education not long after joining *Le Devoir*. Filion, who worked with him every day, observed that André Laurendeau in 1947 was not the religious 'mystic' who had joined him fifteen years before in the Notre Dame basilica to pray for the success of the Jeune Canada movement. Now he seemed more like a 'sceptic', though one who could still function within *Le Devoir*'s vague mandate as a paper of 'Catholic inspiration'.[10]

But Filion didn't know the half of it. If Laurendeau's critique of the church was based primarily on his assessment of its failures in the temporal sphere, it was undoubtedly influenced as well by his own religious crisis. Just how significantly is difficult to measure, but we do know that he was not the sort of person who could build high partitions between the chambers of his mind and then deal with each one separately. A Pierre Trudeau might logically argue a devastating case against the church's long-term influence in Quebec, while remaining personally devout; but for André the spiritual, emotional, and logical dimensions were like psychic pools connected by subconscious currents that flowed back and forth at the deepest levels of mental activity. When one of them dried up, the equilibrium of the others would surely be affected—particularly in the case of a man who was committed to intellectual integrity and yet for other reasons felt obliged to keep this monumental change a secret and to live a lie.

In 1964 he wrote openly to his son Jean about the frustration his concealed agnosticism caused him during those early years with *Le Devoir*.

He pointed out that his loss of faith was never a full-blown atheistic catharsis—a definitive unbelief—but rather 'an emptiness' or 'even . . . an infirmity' that provided no exultation of release. 'I didn't have a triumphant agnosticism, but a shameful one.' In 1953 he had wanted badly to confess this to his children, Francine, who was then seventeen, and Jean, fifteen. 'I felt like an impostor with you; should I tell you?' After consulting Ghislaine, he decided to seek advice from a third party, a priest. It was a reversion to the habits of his youth. But the priest didn't take his agnosticism seriously, equating it instead with neurosis. Thus the church had failed him once again:

> As a result I said nothing. Besides, I was afraid of youthful indiscretion [on the children's part] and, socially, I needed secrecy, because I was a journalist with a Catholic daily.
>
> This posed a problem for me. I would say to myself: do I have the right? The reader takes me for something I'm not. . . . It's still the same: secrecy is still necessary to me socially, and I find it shameful. . . .[11]

Later in the 1950s, André would create characters in some of his dramatic works, such as *Deux femmes terribles*, and in his novel *Une vie d'enfer*, who were darkly evocative of the chasm between appearances and reality. Some analysts have speculated that they also echoed the psychological price he payed for keeping quiet in order to remain a voice that was listened to in Quebec, rather than taking the more courageous route of defiance and inevitable ostracism.[12] His critique of the church was more muted than that of other radical reformers of the 1950s and it was only in the following decade, when he came to grips with his inner conflict, that he felt free to bring his full analytical abilities to bear upon the issue.

Meanwhile, *Le Devoir*'s relative independence from political and clerical interests came at a high cost. The paper had always been on a financial shoestring, the more so because it had also been traditionally opposed to advertising as yet another form of unwelcome control. Laurendeau knew that there would be a perpetual struggle to stretch meagre resources, but felt that the independence this permitted was worthwhile. In his many observations on modern journalism over the next two decades, he complained bitterly that the age of political control of newspapers had given way to business domination, and that in both cases the public was deprived of a vital independent democratic voice:

> A newspaper, especially a large modern paper, is an enterprise, a business, where money has the last word. A man, a family, a group of entrepreneurs can always say: 'I'm the boss because I'm the owner. I risk my money, I'm responsible for deficits and surpluses, so it's only normal that I exercise authority.'
>
> Rarely do North Americans or Europeans contest the validity of this reasoning, whose strength is its extreme simplicity.
>
> One can ask nevertheless if the rules that apply to those who make jam are

equally valid for those who make newspapers—that is, for institutions presiding over the dissemination of news and ideas.[13]

Because *Le Devoir* stood apart from this system, however, it was heavily dependent on its loyal subscribers and on-street sales. But after experiencing a brief upward trend in both areas as a result of its 'no' stand during the conscription crisis and its follow-up support for the Bloc Populaire during that movement's heady first days of enthusiasm, its readership declined sharply.[14]

The disarray during Pelletier's long illness from 1943 to 1947, competition from six other Montreal dailies, and the newspaper industry's postwar accent on mass-appeal journalism all combined to leave *Le Devoir* behind. When Filion and Laurendeau arrived there were roughly 1,000 names on the subscriber list, most of them loyalists from the fast-disappearing older generation of notables and conservative country clerics. Alarmingly few young people bothered to pick up one of the 14,000 copies sold in stores and on street corners. The paper's rickety physical plant and the average age of its employees (about sixty) told the rest of the story. 'From the technical standpoint,' wrote Filion, 'the Imprimerie Populaire showed all of the signs of an enterprise that was dying.'[15]

When he arrived, *Le Devoir* was losing $150 to $200 per day, a massive haemorrhage in 1947 terms. Wielding a large broom, Filion changed everything from the front-page type size to the average age of the employees (down to Laurendeau's comparatively youthful thirty-five). Filion used more photographs, accepted a wide array of advertising, and bumped the street price from three to five cents. But his most daring and significant change came into effect on 27 November 1953, when he took advantage of *Le Canada*'s long-anticipated demise to make *Le Devoir* a morning paper. It was a punishing move financially; in fact, the operation nearly went bankrupt in 1955 and was saved only through the establishment of a fund called 'Friends of *Le Devoir*', into which anonymous donors would pour some $400,000 by 1960. But it increased daily circulation to about 27,000 per day.[16] Instrumental too was *Le Devoir*'s new editorial line, which, while still intensely nationalist, abandoned the old conservative finger-wagging about the need to preserve traditions in favour of an increasingly militant stance on behalf of Quebec's working class. Many of those who now began to buy the paper were union and co-operative members who were anxious to read André Laurendeau's incisive, carefully reasoned but deeply critical social and political commentaries.

Although he came to *Le Devoir* with no experience as a newspaper editor, Laurendeau quickly established a distinctive regime that was memorable for all those who worked with and for him. Claude Ryan, who succeeded André and regarded him as a mentor, described him as a low-key and reserved editor who inspired a desire in others to emulate his intelligent inner passion.[17] He had nothing in common, in other words, with the classic image of the post-war newspaper editor: that loud, hard-bitten former police-court journalist who handed out assignments with a glower and who would often grab the copy from an inexperienced reporter to 'show-ya-how-it's-done' on the nearest typewriter. For one thing, Laurendeau rarely used a typewriter, preferring to write out his own material and edit others' in a tight, often illegible script that must have puzzled his staff (and is even harder on biographers). He readily acknowledged, moreover, that apart from a few interviews in France, Belgium, and Italy during the mid-thirties, he had no background as a field journalist and was therefore obliged to learn along with his team. His task was made easier in one way because Filion, both to cut costs and to force change, brought in eager young people like Pierre Laporte, Jean-Pierre Houle, and Gérard Pelletier—journalists who would develop in close association with Laurendeau over the years.[18] To them André gradually imparted his ideal conception of a journalist. His own model was a man named Lamberti whom he had first encountered a decade earlier in Belgium: 'he had a very sympathetic quality, I think it was his intelligent curiosity: but he also knew how to listen, how to question, and he was genuinely interested in the other person. . . .' These were precisely the qualities he brought to his editorship. He would listen attentively, according to one colleague's account, for thirty, forty, even sixty minutes to a journalist's latest brain-child, interrupting only to draw out ancillary possibilities. He would then send the person off to work on the idea, checking occasionally but never oppressively to see how it was coming and, when the time came for editing and correction, he made suggestions with 'that indefinable discretion which characterized him'.[19]

Nevertheless, Laurendeau's major impact on *Le Devoir* came from his own writing. Because of the tight financial situation and the very small staff, he did a great deal of it. In addition to the three-or-four-per-week flow of editorials, which he admitted were often written late into the night because of 'mental constipation' or because 'as always I put off to the last possible minute beginning to write', he often wrote *Bloc-notes* providing background information or trenchant fragmentary insights. Under the pseudonym 'Candide' he also wrote regularly on off-beat subjects or cultural topics, articles in which he frequently made use of devastating sarcasm. 'And what a sense of humour', recalled one journalist, 'what a splendid ability to mock himself and others in all those notes signed Candide.'[20] As Gérard Pelletier observed, Laurendeau's 'special calling was the journalism of opinion.'[21] For this he did most of his work surrounded by books either at his *Le Devoir* office or at home:

. . . the editor-in-chief of Le Devoir in that epoch was never a reporter. [Laurendeau's] entire career in journalism was devoted to the editorial, the column, the critique and the short note. From time to time he would make use of what he called a poll, but it had nothing in common with Mr Gallup's invention. For him the word signified an exercise that amounted to several long conversations, either on the telephone or in person, with a sampling of his friends and acquaintances from whom he would gather facts, impressions and opinions to nourish his next day's article.[22]

Laurendeau rarely if ever wasted an editorial on a trivial subject, for he still considered his role to be closely tied to the serious business of nationalist education. Although obliged by considerations of space and readership to save his most probing intellectual commentaries for *L'Action nationale*, which he again edited from 1948 to 1954, he was determined that *Le Devoir* would inform the wider public about the implications for French Canada of socio-economic and political issues in an on-going framework of consistent, detailed, and rational analysis. He considered the fourth estate to be a far better platform for this purpose than politics, even if it was not quite the sort of writing he liked best. In the words of one historian: 'André Laurendeau joined *Le Devoir* in order to adapt French-Canadian nationalism to the new post-war situation.'[23]

Between 1947 and 1960 the Filion Laurendeau team gave *Le Devoir* a new identity as a nationalist voice seeking social reform and greater political democracy in Quebec. As a result, the paper later came to be seen as one of several reformist forces that helped to bring about Quebec's Quiet Revolution of the 1960s. Laurendeau was the one most responsible for sustaining this liberal-nationalist line:

> In marked contrast to Filion, André Laurendeau was a man of almost Florentine delicacy. Putting active politics behind him, he wrote sensitive, finely nuanced, carefully crafted editorials that often had a hint of disenchantment, as if he regretted that the world was not as perfect as he would have wished it to be. Intellectually, he seemed incapable of committing himself to a firm position on an issue, whether in politics or any other worldly domain. But, true to his origins, he did clearly adhere to the Henri Bourassa school of nationalism.[24]

Filion's chief contributions—important ones to be sure—were in finance, in administration, and in protecting his staff from outside pressures. Though he wrote a good deal too, his writing was most effective when dealing with down-to-earth issues—as, for example, in *Le Devoir*'s trailblazing investigations into police corruption and municipal influence-peddling in Montreal during the 1950s. While Laurendeau was pleased to leave the business affairs to the director, it seems he never thought enough of Filion's intellect to discuss philosophic or cultural subjects with him.[25] For his part Filion conceded that Laurendeau was the one, with his intellectual background and remarkable range of interests, to take the ideological helm. Pointing out that 'I never changed a comma of his; he censored me sometimes, with good cause,' he went on to paint this picture of their partnership:

> We were separated . . . by our cultural backgrounds. Mine had its roots on the banks of the Vase River; his in the macadam of rue Notre-Dame and to a lesser extent in the slopes of the Laurentians. . . . He had been a student of the Jesuits and it showed. I came from a small college in the country and that showed too. He took pleasure in abstractions, philosophic speculations. Me, I argued about concrete things, real situations.
>
> How did we manage to get on together? That's simple: we were pursuing the same end by different ways and means.[26]

Laurendeau made it clear in his first editorial in September 1947, entitled 'In order to Continue the Struggle', that he intended to accentuate the reformist theme in Bourassa's nationalist tradition. At the same time, his recent political experiences had convinced him that grass-roots socioeconomic issues were the most important aspect of post-war life in Quebec, as well as the area where nationalism was most seriously deficient: '. . . in the present circumstances, our nationalism will only be fully effective, fully just and true to the extent that it addresses the endless problems of our social life . . . in which it will rejuvenate itself.'[27] If his own long theoretical struggle to reconcile social progress with the traditional, backward-gazing cultural values of French-Canadian nationalism had made him an avant-garde thinker in the late 1930s, he had since learned that his own ideas about Quebec's social reality were only slightly less *a priori* than those of his conservative colleagues. Who could dispute, moreover, that the war had brought about the recovery of capitalism and the further transformation of Quebec society along industrial and urban lines? In these new conditions, traditional nationalist shibboleths seemed even more hoary and passé, but so too did the vague and faintly patronizing personalist formulae he had been fond of repeating before the war. The time was surely at hand to come to grips with the industrial economic system that, no matter how repugnant its abuses, was in Quebec to stay. To Laurendeau it had become pointless to treat urban life as something fundamentally alien to an ideal type of *canadien* existence. Years later he described the lingering effect of the 'agrarian mystique' on the thinking of his generation of nationalists:

> Young men of my generation came under its sway in the cities. In my experience, 'agriculturalism' consisted . . . [of] the myth of the land and the infinite moral superiority of rural living over modes of life in the cities, the big city especially. . . . According to this theory, our people had drawn their strength and their moral superiority from their agricultural way of life. To abandon this would be to leave the path of history and invite the worst possible disasters. From this point of view the city appeared as sin personified, or at the very least as an error which one hoped would only be temporary. The people would return to the country and would once again learn to

admire tracts of untamed wilderness. In this way they would regain their sense of vitality and truth.

We students spent hours dreaming of this and imagining bucolic lives for ourselves in which we would have a significant role to play. Consequently, our real plans for the future seemed to be morally flawed, because in the back of our minds we knew that we would go on living in the city just the same. The only result of subscribing to this mother-earth mythology was that it gave us a guilty conscience and led us to view various land settlement schemes with an obstinate optimism never justified by the facts. In this way we were lured away from real tasks and spent our time living imaginary romances.[28]

In Laurendeau's view the French-Canadian worker should no longer be regarded as either a displaced *habitant* or some new species of modern Catholic ready to breathe the bracing air of a new urban humanism. He was simply a proletarian, with all the problems of a proletarian, living within—even embracing—a fully revived North American capitalism. This proletarian needed to be served by nationalism in terms of his actual existence; otherwise he risked being exploited mercilessly by the powers-that-be—English-speaking capitalists, French-speaking petty bourgeois politicians, and Catholic reactionaries. That was what trudging the streets for the Bloc Populaire had made manifest to him and that was the cause he intended to serve. He began by launching an 'Inquiry on the Proletariat' in *L'Action nationale* and by devoting a good portion of *Le Devoir*'s editorial page to the plight of Quebec's workers and farmers. While the first initiative was based on a genuine recognition that nationalists, including himself, needed to know more about the working class, the second was geared to immediate action on three fronts: an ongoing critique of the negative effects of large-scale capitalism, especially in the natural-resource sector; support for Quebec's militant post-war labour movement and co-operatives; and the need for the state centred in Quebec City to initiate solutions to social problems.

Laurendeau had always been a severe critic of capitalism, and his denunciations of foreign and English-Canadian capitalist domination of Quebec's economy in the early 1930s had been visceral. But this was an impoverished facet of his nationalist theoretical formation. His major concerns had been cultural, and he had simply repeated economic formulas from the 1920s. In France, at the height of the Depression, he adopted the Catholic left's view that capitalism need not in itself be pernicious if its abuses could be curbed. During the war he maintained this outlook while focusing on the practical problems created by capitalist growth, thus putting the Bloc Populaire in a more natural position to compete with anti-capitalist parties like the CCF than with the pro-business mainstream parties. Having never been involved in business himself, and with few friends who were, he would always be an intellectual critic of the bourgeois class. In the immediate post-war years, however, he was more concerned with making certain that nationalism did not lose the support of the lower classes.

But there were significant differences from his earlier approach. First, he now accepted that the industrial-urban surge launched by the war and leading to a consumer society was permanent. Alternative systems such as communism or utopian corporatism could not be taken seriously, whether they were bandied about by the government to create fear or by conservative nationalists whose thinking was mired in the past. Laurendeau was determined to make post-war nationalists understand this. He used facts and figures to show how completely industrial capitalism had changed Quebec's society. Second, he underlined how vital it was for nationalists to abandon their professional middle-class vision and see life from the workers' and farmers' perspectives. For example, he summed up the many submissions to his 'Inquiry on the Proletariat' as follows:

> We must admit that many nationalist circles have been content to remain within narrow traditionalist bounds and make all the usual demands. In so many sectors, nationalism is still linked exclusively with questions of language, schools, bilingualism, and a proper share in the civil service. While it includes all these questions, of course, it should never be reduced exclusively to them.
>
> The danger in this is not only in letting the movement become exclusively middle-class—we know that workers are not fanatically interested in such questions!—but also in allowing the development of purely 'negative' attitudes. . . .
>
> Nationalists have too often been content to preach, from their academic pulpit, to people who, understanding nothing of what was said, found it all rather boring. Through a kind of intellectual laziness, we have been satisfied with approximations, content to repeat facile, syrupy slogans.[29]

But however advanced his outlook on industrial capitalism had become, Laurendeau continued his strong condemnation of foreign exploitation in the natural-resource sector. He complained repeatedly in *Le Devoir* about the secret deals struck between Duplessis's Union Nationale government and private American and Canadian industries. 'The big companies treat publicity with disdain because it would reveal their abuses to everyone. Do they feel safest in their own closed environment? Do they think that discussion would somehow taint their dignity as Grand-Dukes of capitalism?' He was outraged in 1948 when the provincial government, after being re-elected, made a deal with Hollinger mines (later the Iron Ore Company of Canada) for the iron ore resources of the vast Ungava region. This deal, which called for a royalty of one cent per ton of ore extracted on a $6,000 per year lease, in the years to follow would become symbolic of Quebec's colonial economic status. André asked why at least some manufacturing jobs were not guaranteed for Quebec. In a 1954 editorial he pointed out just how this sort of enterprise perpetuated Quebec's inferiority:

> The Ungava enterprise may be a technical success. It will be useful for American industry, which needs iron. But Quebec will get very little or nothing from it. As far as the province is concerned, this undertaking began as an economic fiasco, and appears to be turning into a social one.
>
> The people who exploit the mineral wealth of Ungava are powerful magnates. They brought with them considerable capital, and both federal and provincial governments treated them as though they were coming to perform humanitarian works.
>
> For a fixed fee, Quebec gave them extraordinary privileges. They are like despots exercising their authority over a small kingdom. The province, of course, was acting in the dark, since the value of the mineral deposits granted was only known through the company itself. Under pressure of public opinion, the concession, which had originally been planned for a century, was reduced to twenty years with, of course, obvious possibilities for infinite renewal.
>
> What prospects remain for us, then? We can at least provide the manpower required.
>
> It appears, however, that we stand on the lowest rungs of the manpower ladder. A journalist who visited the site claims that he did not meet a single French Canadian in its administration or technical management, with the exception of a few research workers. We are not, it seems, allowed to go any higher than foreman or junior accountant.
>
> Moreover, the work force there is, it seems, very badly paid.[30]

He demanded that the state develop an iron and steel industry itself on the north shore if a better deal than this one could not be worked out.

By the same token, Laurendeau's editorials in *Le Devoir* had a strong pro-union flavour. The post-war industrial boom resulted in a rapid rise in average annual wage increases, estimated at 90 per cent for the 1947-54 period,[31] and this fuelled greater expectations among workers anxious to make up for the hardships of the recent past. Unions experienced a corresponding boom in membership. In December 1947 Laurendeau put the membership of the nationalist, Catholic unions that composed the Confédération des Travailleurs Catholiques du Canada (CTCC) at 70,000, with 40,000 each for the American Federation of Labour and the Canadian Congress of Labor-Congress of Industrial Organizations; out of approximately 800,000 Quebec workers, 150,000 were union members. He strongly endorsed the CTCC's new leadership, especially its director Gérard Picard, who was turning away from moral and respect-for-authority values—so often the key concerns of confessional unions in the past—towards militant economic demands. Although he would have preferred an improved and more rapid arbitration process to settle disputes, Laurendeau gave editorial support to strikers in the meat-packing, textile, and mining industries, among others, during 1947-48. He also pushed hard for a new provincial labour code that would amend the one introduced by the Godbout government during the war in ways more favourable to labour. In an editorial on 27 December 1947, entitled 'The Labour Politics of the CTCC', he argued that in its demands for a new code the union 'was expressing the will of a long neglected class, which has found some organization and some leaders, which has thought about its condition and which has made its views known with firmness and dignity. It would be wise to listen while there is still time.' He rejected with contempt the old knee-jerk argument that whenever there was a strike the communists were behind it: 'Communists are quick to exploit such situations but they rarely create them.' What did create them, he insisted, were poor working conditions, unfair compensation, and 'social retardation'.

The dispute that came to symbolize the new militancy of Quebec labour in these years occurred in the town of Asbestos in 1949. Thanks to an unusual amount of publicity at the time and a number of subsequent accounts,[32] the Asbestos strike has often been seen as a unifying experience among intellectuals, reformers, and labour against all the reactionary forces holding Quebec back from full modernization. On the one side were the workers in one of Quebec's many notoriously exploitative single-industry towns, along with their CTCC union representatives, intellectual supporters like Pierre Trudeau, and liberal clerics like Archbishop Charbonneau. On the other side were the foreign-owned trust, Duplessis's Union Nationale government, armed 'scabs', and the provincial police. Laurendeau had already established *Le Devoir*'s position on the issue of working conditions in these industries a year earlier, in backing the sensational revelations of Berton Le Doux, in the review *Relations*, concerning silicosis deaths at St Rémi d'Amherst; now he came out swinging on behalf of the Asbestos workers. In an editorial on 2 May 1949 he noted that negotiations had broken down and that 'the government and Johns-Manville are at fault'. Claiming that the union had made reasonable concessions, he went on to argue:

> The fact that neither the government nor the company was willing to accept [these concessions] is a sign that they are not satisfied with simply bringing the workers to their knees; they want to smash and grind them to dust. They believed that the workers had reached the limits of hardship and were now without any further recourse. They thought they had them in their hands at last. . . .
> We support the asbestos unions, not only because they are Catholic unions but because they are in the right.
> [An] industry which takes risks with the health and even the life of its employees is seeking to defend itself with lies and false accusations. The government is supporting it whole-heartedly, siding with the foreign capital against its own labour force here in Quebec.[33]

In subsequent editorials he charged that the provincial police were responsible for the violence at Asbestos and that they were being paid by the company. He asked rhetorically, 'Is the province in the midst of a transformation? Is it following the example of some notorious predecessors and becoming a police state? Is Mr Duplessis drunk with power to that extent?' As the strike dragged on, *Le Devoir* received regular articles from Gérard Pelletier, its labour reporter, who had asked to go to Asbestos and was obliged to hitch a ride because the newspaper could not afford to send him.[34] Together, he and Laurendeau assured *Le Devoir* a place in the mystique that would develop around the Asbestos strike later, during the Quiet Revolution.

It should be acknowledged nevertheless that Laurendeau's efforts to link French-Canadian nationalism with the cause of labour were not without contradictions. In the first instance, he was guilty of backsliding when the issue came too close to home with a typographers' strike at *Le Devoir*. Pointing out that the paper was losing money and the typographers were its best-paid technicians, he opposed the strike. He also took a stand against a CTCC-sponsored strike on behalf of Montreal's poorly paid teachers. Although he agreed that the teachers were much worse off than their counterparts in English Canada, and urged the government to raise their salaries, he was opposed to a strike in such a vital public-sector area. What these examples underline is that Laurendeau still acknowledged limits on the extent to which he would modify his traditional nationalist ideals to accommodate material values. This was also evident in his summation to the 'Inquiry on the Proletariat' in *L'Action nationale*, where he made it clear how important spiritual and cultural values still were:

> A man who lives in a state of destitution, we are told, cannot surmount his immediate problems, nor rise above his daily quest for bread and shelter. Any form of culture appears to him as an uninteresting luxury; he cannot feel anything for it but indifference, ignorance, or complete disdain. His material poverty, in fact, is nothing compared with his spiritual poverty.
>
> If this analysis is accurate, the workers' passive resistance to national values is an example of the way an industrial, capitalist society paralyses its victims (that is to say everyone, but especially its automatons), rendering them incapable of rising to spiritual values. . . . We are fully aware of the gulf between national and religious values. We know that they are not to be put on a common footing. . . . Equally, however, we know that to recognize the communal values of a culture requires a transcending of self and of purely material qualities; in a certain sense, it is indeed a rising to spiritual things.[35]

A further limitation on Laurendeau's labour radicalism was imposed by his commitment to provincial autonomy. Just as he favoured the CTCC, whether or not it was the union movement seeking the most for the workers, because it was Quebec-based, so too he opposed the federal labour code, Bill 195, introduced in 1948, because, as he put it, 'though constitutional in its legality, it is assuredly centralizing in its inspiration. . . .' Thus he was repeatedly trapped into defending the provincial government's jurisdiction in the labour field even though the Duplessis government was an enemy of labour in everything that it did.

He ran up against precisely the same paradox in his advocacy of state initiatives in the housing and social-security spheres. Inadequate housing was one of the most serious social problems facing Quebec in the post-war period. Studies throughout North America have shown how the phenomena of urban sprawl and suburban home ownership sprang not only from urbanization and industrial growth, but from the pressures caused by returning soldiers and the post-war baby boom. It was driven as well by a desire on the part of those who had survived Depression and war, including immigrants, to possess the symbol of security that a paid-off home represented. But, as Laurendeau observed in a long series of articles devoted to the issue, only 3.5 per cent of Quebec's workers owned their homes, and as many as 87 per cent in Montreal lived in overcrowded housing. Here, then, was a crisis that could only be solved by massive government intervention. 'A part of the problem,' he commented, 'arose from the inaction of the provincial government during the Depression; it is a heritage of indifference and of cowardice which still weighs us down now.'[36] But neither the federal nor the provincial government seemed prepared to remedy the situation with aggressive programs for urban renewal and urban housing credits. During his days in the legislature Laurendeau had witnessed Duplessis's empty-handed rejection of sweeping reforms in housing as dangerously 'socialist', and it seemed that no matter now bad the situation became, the Union Nationale would not change its stand.

Laurendeau considered the dilemma in the social-security field to be even more serious for the long term. As one of those who had led nationalism out of the dark age of anti-statism during the war towards a more progressive appreciation of what the Quebec state could accomplish through social programs ranging from unemployment insurance to pensions, he was appalled by the Union Nationale's socially retrograde philosophy. During the war the federal government, unhindered by the complacent Godbout regime, had got a running start in the field of modern social legislation. André had understood the implications of the Marsh Report (based on the Beveridge Report in England), which outlined the King government's intention to use the fiscal powers acquired during the war to create a network of social-assistance schemes after 1945.[37] If Quebec allowed this to happen, a government dominated by English Canadians in Ottawa would impose its social-policy priorities on French Canadians. This was already the case with unemployment insurance and the family allowance, which according to Laurendeau clearly did not meet Quebec's special needs, particularly where the large family unit was concerned. But while Duplessis was much more prepared to fight for autonomy than Godbout had been, and while he made certain to beat the anti-Ottawa drum before every election, his government did little or nothing to provide desperately needed social assistance. What was most frustrating for Laurendeau was Duplessis's grotesque masquerade as a champion of nationalism. 'I believe,' he wrote in 1948,

> that nationalism in our province took on its conservative aspect from the moment it was used by a party in power. The Union Nationale supports some of the ideas (that is, provincial autonomy, the flag, etc.) which have traditionally been nationalist ones. At the same time, it adopts social attitudes which are generally very conservative. That represents a very serious threat to the future of the nationalist movement, and consequently those nationalists who are aware of the danger have an even greater responsibility to maintain their independence.[38]

One area in which Laurendeau and *Le Devoir* strove to maintain their independence was education. Expansion and reform in this sphere became a major issue after the war as more and more French Canadians came to view education as the linchpin of social progress and upward mobility. As one analyst has written, 'French-Canadian society was at a crossroads. It could choose to perpetuate an inefficient, anachronistic educational system and continue to survive merely as a quaint folkloric pre-industrial community' or it could modernize education and 'in the process, become a francophone-inspired and directed modern industrial system'.[39] This latter concern was vital to Laurendeau, for his nationalist bias led him to emphasize educational reform as a vehicle for French-Canadian advancement and control almost as much as for modernization. For nationalists during the 1950s, education had the same attraction with respect to francophone power that language legislation would have in the 1970s and '80s. If anything, however, their nationalism kept them lagging behind other progressive groups in society who were urging educational reform during the late 1940s and early '50s. Laurendeau, for example, opposed more direct government intervention in the educational sphere in 1948, fearing that it would become merely a new patronage pot for the Union Nationale. While he advocated sweeping change in primary education, favouring proposals for compulsory education to the age of sixteen, increased government spending, better wages for teachers, and overhaul of the curriculum to accent 'modern' subjects like science and mathematics, he was reluctant to endorse massive government financing because it would compromise the autonomy of local boards and thus politicize the educational hierarchy. Though reasonable and based on democratic concerns, this outlook did not address the backwardness of Quebec's primary-school system with sufficient vigour.

Another area in which this tension between nationalist and modernizing tendencies became apparent was secondary education, most notably the classical college system. In the late 1930s Laurendeau, a product of this

secondary education

system, became critical almost to the point of contempt about the outdated aspects of the college curriculum. His studies in France had revealed this clearly, but so too had the isolated yet intelligent complaints levied by Quebec's small francophone scientific community prior to the war. During the early forties he had been largely preoccupied with other issues, but now he focused once more on the way French Canadians were held back from full participation in modern society and the well-paying technical fields by the crippling inadequacy of their secondary and university education. To his mind this was a major, if not the principal, cause of French Canadians' economic inferiority in their own province. It was an indicator, in fact, of how far the pendulum was swinging in his nationalist thinking, from a preoccupation with external threats to the nation to a focus on the internal barriers against progress. Elitist, dominated by clerical instructors and administrators (and thus discouraging to the emergence of a strong lay teaching profession), with a curriculum still emphasizing Catholic humanism, the colleges simply didn't graduate enough students ready to enter the modern economy. From an early stage, therefore, Laurendeau began to favour the development of a more pluralistic secondary-school system, even though at many points, as we will see, this would bring him into direct conflict with the church authorities. It also brought him into conflict once again with Maurice Duplessis and the Union Nationale government, who were reluctant in this period to do more than tinker with the church's control of the classical college system and who were definitely not interested in facilitating advancement for working-class French Canadians to the higher levels of education, since that would only increase business costs. It was becoming more apparent to Laurendeau with each passing year that in Quebec progress on a great many fronts—including those, such as primary and secondary education, where the issues of provincial autonomy were not directly involved—was dependent on surmounting the terrible social backwardness of the Duplessis government.

In Laurendeau's view, this task and the broader aim of public education towards a more open and enlightened society also depended on breaking down the barriers that isolated French Canada from the outside world. His own educational experience abroad during the 1930s had awakened him to the xenophobic nature of French-Canadian thought, and while the war had, by its international character, helped to lower some of the barriers, it had also given rise to political crises, such as the one over conscription, that had the short-term effect of heightening the siege mentality. This had certainly been the case for him personally, but he had never been deluded into thinking that 'opening doors and windows' wasn't important. He had tried in small ways, at *L'Action nationale* especially, to keep alive an outward-looking nationalist perspective, and now with *Le Devoir* he pushed himself to do much more. His most important activity in this respect was to write regularly about international events and Canada's role in the world. Laurendeau was one of the first post-war nationalist *International* writers to trace the development of the Cold War and to define its impli-cations for those, like himself, who were lifelong enemies of imperialism. He realized early on that Britain was in rapid decline, both as an imperial force and as a future threat to French Canada's identity. The world had become polarized by the ideological struggle between two imperialist powers: the Soviet Union, with its international communist vision, and the United States, which, as the war's biggest winner, had abandoned its tra-ditional isolationism and—in the name of freedom—was expanding its influence everywhere. Laurendeau argued that in these circumstances neutrality was the best policy for Canada, just as it had been when Britain was the omnipresent imperialist threat.

Between 1947 and 1954 Laurendeau took issue again and again with the Canadian government's close foreign-policy alignment with the United States. He had recognized American influence as a serious threat to French Canada's as well as Canada's survival after returning from France in the late 1930s. He now saw that influence as even more ominous, threatening to draw Canada, along with the rest of the world, into a post-Hiroshima atomic confrontation. Neither the government of Mackenzie King nor that of his successor Louis St Laurent seemed willing to align itself with other middle powers and small nations to offer a balancing third voice between the two great powers. Laurendeau opposed Canada's entry into the North Atlantic Treaty Organization in 1949 because it meant a loss of peace-and-war decision-making power, even more than had been the case in the war just finished: Canada would automatically go to war on the side of the United States. Rejecting the principle of collective security, but equally adamant that isolationism was out of the question, he urged Canada's more active participation in international organizations like the United Nations and the Organization of American States. He had long admired Mahatma Gandhi's pacifist, civil-disobedience form of resistance to imperialism, and he held up India as a worthy example of a non-aligned nation that pursued an enlightened third path in international affairs:

> We are betraying our international duty as a small nation, a status that should align us with the peacemaking politics of Nehru. Instead of being among the states that attempt to stand between the two great rivals, we link ourselves more closely to war. . . . A middle-sized country, by nature an adversary of all imperialisms, Canada should find itself, when a crisis breaks out, on the side of the peace-loving smaller countries. . . . For here is the dilemma . . . : communist expansionism and the policy of Mr Truman are in the process of imprisoning the world; the people have a choice between sovietization and war. . . . The Indians point to a third way. The Indians stub-bornly strive to be mediators. . . . Nehru's India, which in these matters, remains the India of Gandhi, has shown a moderation in the face of Russian cunning and American severity from which many of the Western states could have taken inspiration.[40]

Perhaps no single episode in this period illustrates Laurendeau's internationalist conceptions more clearly than the Korean War. He argued, first of all, that the threat in the Third World came less from communism than from Western economic imperialism. If the United States took as much trouble to help these areas develop as it did to arm them, the communist threat would be substantially reduced. Anyway, how could one assume that the US had more right to intervene in such a distant region than did the USSR or China? He condemned the St Laurent government in Ottawa not only for sanctioning the American anti-communist crusade but for dispatching Canadian troops in support. Here was an action, he contended, that was purportedly taken for greater world security but that actually contributed to destabilization and insecurity. It must be conceded that Laurendeau was always more attuned to those aspects of foreign involvement that could have a harmful impact on French Canada—especially those that could lead once more to the damaging internal conflicts always synonymous with Canadian participation in foreign wars. He was less sympathetic to the purely international dimensions that made those involvements necessary in the first place. In this sense his French-Canadian nationalism continued to dominate his own international perspective, but there is no question that he was a pioneer in awakening French-speaking Quebec to the stake it had in this area.

Another way in which Laurendeau played a key role in broadening the international perspectives of French Canadians was through his pioneering activity as a television broadcaster. As we have already seen, his broadcasting career began in radio as a piano recitalist and occasional lecturer on music during the early 1930s. Later, with Jeune-Canada, the Ligue pour la Défense du Canada, and the Bloc Populaire, he turned to political broadcasting, a function that pruned the intellectual sophistry from his presentation and no doubt helped to develop his lean and lucid journalistic style. During the Depression years he tried other radio projects as well, including the transcription and broadcast of Abbé Groulx's leaden novel and the series of CBC broadcasts with Neil Morrison in 1939, aimed at improving French and English Canadians' knowledge of each other. He was experienced and open-minded, therefore, when he was approached by the CBC's French-language service, Radio-Canada, during its first season of television programming.[41] It made sense for television in its early days to turn to the other media for talent, and Laurendeau had a well-established persona. Enough time had passed, moreover, for both sides to have forgotten their epic battles over radio air-time during the conscription crisis.

While the Radio-Canada executives could hardly have foreseen that Laurendeau would eventually make a name for himself in the field of television drama, they did believe that his interest in promoting international awareness made him a prime candidate for a show they had in mind about other countries and exotic foreign locales. Beginning in 1952, 'Pays et Mer-veilles' was expected to run for only a few weeks, but it stayed on the air until 1961 and made Laurendeau one of the best-known and most highly regarded television personalities in Quebec. 'Pays et Merveilles' was a Wednesday-evening window on the world, and Laurendeau, who was well aware of how revolutionary television could be in moulding a more informed and expansive public spirit, built up an extremely loyal audience. Like René Lévesque, whose Radio-Canada interview show 'Point de Mire' made him known throughout Quebec in the 1950s, Laurendeau benefitted from an image of honesty and intensity that would extend well beyond his years in television; also like Lévesque, he usually conducted his interviews with a cigarette burning somewhere nearby. But there the comparisons ended. He was self-effacing where Lévesque was aggressive; he concen-trated on quietly drawing out his guest where Lévesque pushed and prodded. With pictures of the foreign places in question appearing on the screen periodically, he would ask his questions in a nervous, level voice; the answer having been given, in order to clarify this or that he would say, 'Then, if I have understood you correctly . . .' after which he would repeat his guest's point. It was a plodding, low-key style that probably could only have succeeded in television's early, pre-videotape days, when it could sometimes take ten hours to get things right.[42]

Laurendeau joked privately that it was very odd to spend hours, some-times days, with individuals he had never met before and would never see again. It was amusing too to receive fan mail from total strangers who were keenly aware of his every physical characteristic and idiosyncrasy. One letter, complaining that he rarely smiled, commented:

> Permit me to be a mirror and send your image back to you, the way it appears on our screen Wednesday night! A wan, almost worried face, espe-cially when you say 'Bonsoir' to us in a curt and unsympathetic voice. Come on, make a little effort! Loosen up. Practise yoga, if necessary, but, since you are surely capable of it, smile pleasantly and speak to us warmly. Between us, you know how merciless the TV camera is: it practically reveals your subconscious to us. So give up this dreary, monotonous personality and bite into your role the way you'd bite into an apple. With pleasure, with joy, with satisfaction . . . with a smile! Let the screen light up with the inner fire that inspires you and then we really will feel that you are communicating with us, that you want to make contact, and in doing so you'll forget the cold eye trained on you, sense an audience that is altogether receptive and, in the end, perceive our applause.[43]

The novelist Gabrielle Roy also wrote him: 'I have admired you so much already as a journalist with a broad perspective who brings people together; I found this once more . . . with your television program which has done so much for us [French Canadians] to break down prejudices and to enlarge . . . our knowledge.'[44]

By 1954, however, Laurendeau had become painfully conscious of the huge gap that had opened between himself and others who called themselves nationalists in Quebec. In his efforts at *Le Devoir* and *L'Action nationale* and on television to develop a more progressive, outward-looking, working-class ideology, which he called social nationalism, he was fundamentally at odds with those who continued to take a conservative line and hide their socially backward, middle-class outlook behind a façade of nationalist rhetoric. He found his views on most issues to be more in harmony with those of the liberal-minded intellectuals, clerical leaders, and union representatives who were growing stronger each year. Pierre Elliott Trudeau, one of those intellectuals, drew attention to Laurendeau's progressive outlook in his book *La Grève de l'amiante* when he observed: 'From the moment M. André Laurendeau became director of the journal, at the end of 1937, the nationalism of *L'Action nationale* freed itself from all accusations of racism, dissociated itself from the doctrines of the extreme right, and sought to give a more social slant to the autonomist cause.'[45] But Trudeau and many other liberals also condemned nationalism as a reactionary and outdated ideal. While Laurendeau was not prepared to go that far in agreeing with liberal critics like Father Georges-Henri Lévesque, of the School of Social Sciences at Laval, or Trudeau, co-editor of the influential journal *Cité libre*, he admitted nonetheless that nationalism faced a crisis of conscience. In a long article devoted to that crisis he wrote:

> Having lived almost all my adult life among nationalists, I am still struck by their extraordinary diversity. There are nationalists in language, and their close neighbours, the nationalists of 'rights': I mean that, for them, nationalism must be seen first of all as a claim for minority rights, or as linguistic devotion. . . . There are economic nationalists who give real priority to problems of this nature, and there are social nationalists. Besides, there is cultural nationalism, political nationalism, not to mention pure and simple traditionalism when it takes itself for a doctrine.[46]

As he pointed out farther on in his analysis, the present crisis was rooted in the fact that this rich diversity of nationalists had become sharply divided into 'left' and 'right', and it did not appear the two could go on together:

> And so the already latent divisions between the nationalists have become more precise and accentuated. They did exist at other times . . . but now they are more bitter. We used to be in agreement on the essential matters when we were unaware of the world we were entering. The coming of awareness broke up all that was unreal in this unity, and we now see only the divisions. Nationalism does not say what one must think of family allowance, of the Louiseville strike, of health insurance, or of social and political institutions. A 'right' and a 'left' will continue to separate yet further, each one accusing the other of betraying the nation.[47]

While there was no doubt that Laurendeau would be found with the 'left' or social nationalists in the days ahead, it was less clear whether he could find an answer to the critical problem facing the left: namely, whether to go on supporting the provincial government of Maurice Duplessis in its struggle for greater provincial autonomy when by now it was obvious that he had no intention of using that autonomy to achieve social progress. André had been confronting this dilemma since Duplessis's re-election in 1944, and he had always placed the autonomist horse before the cart of social progress. During these years at *Le Devoir*, however, he had run up against the Union Nationale's intransigence on every important issue from labour legislation to housing and education. The state was such a potent force in modern society that to tolerate the smirking medievalism of a Duplessis was to undermine the whole point of the nationalist struggle. For Laurendeau, who had been seeking for nearly two decades to unite nationalism and social progress in one movement, the price was becoming intolerable.

André Laurendeau
the ballet student,
November 1921.

His parents,
Blanche Hardy and
Arthur Laurendeau,
April 1910.

Laurendeau and
Ghislaine Perrault,
May 1933.

With a friend in the countryside, September 1931.

At a Bloc Populaire rally with Maxime Raymond and Henri Bourassa.

En route to Europe, 1935.

Speaking for the Bloc Populaire at the Jean Talon market, Montreal, July 1944.

At the Cercle Juif de la Langue Française, May 1952.

Interviewing Abbé Pierre on 'Pays et Merveilles'.

The Royal Commission on Bilingualism and Biculturalism, June 1964, from left to right: Gertrude Laing, le Père Clément Cormier, Neil Morrison, Paul Lacoste, Paul Wyczynski, Jean-Louis Gagnon, André Laurendeau, Wilfrid Hamel, A. Davidson Dunton, Jaroslav B. Rudnyckyj, Royce Frith, and Frank R. Scott.

8

The War Against Duplessis, 1955-1959

Mr. Duplessis . . . considers power as his personal property. He does with it whatever he likes. His friends obtain preferential treatment. Counties which support him receive favourable treatment. Opposition members of the provincial Legislature, however, only deserve half-rights as far as he is concerned. He treats them as though they had not been elected as honestly as those in his own majority party.

Mr. Duplessis seems to think it right and fair to starve the Opposition. In matters of jobs, roads, schools, bridges, only his favourites are served. He has just applied the same principle to the press. An opponent, to his way of thinking, has no right to hear him speak. Choosing those newspapers he considers loyal to him, he is starting to exclude all the others.

Such an arbitrary exercise of power is against democracy and the parliamentary system.

André Laurendeau, 'Is Quebec Led by a "Negro King"?', 1958[1]

During the 1950s André Laurendeau lived in a haunted house. It was an older, two-storey brick building with numerous nooks and crannies on Stuart Street in Outremont. Two ghosts occupied the house with the Laurendeaus and their six children. One was the mysterious but welcome shade of someone who had never visited North America, much less Montreal, and who had died almost a half-century before; the other was the brooding shadow of a living legend whom André detested more than anyone he knew. Their names were Debussy and Duplessis, and the younger Laurendeau children can recall getting the two names hopelessly confused—until they were taught that Claude Debussy, the great modern French composer, represented light and Maurice Duplessis, the Premier of Quebec, darkness. At night, tucked in their beds, they could hear the rueful melodies of *Pelléas et Mélisande*, and they didn't have to see their father's face to know that at the corners of his mouth was a sad, world-weary smile and that his eyes had a far-away look.[2] Debussy meant he was travelling once more to that inner sanctum where no one else could follow. It had been that way since the first time he observed his own father's rapture at the sound of Debussy's music, as if this were a passion that ran in the blood-lines. He loved other composers too, of course, and was eager to play the new recordings that arrived every three or four weeks from New York and London, for him to review in his capacity as music critic for *Le Devoir*.[3] But none of them could match Debussy's magical ability to transport him to another realm.

At this point in his life Laurendeau's cultural concerns were stronger than ever. This was apparent in the atmosphere of the household on Stuart Street: one relative observed that, despite the presence of six children, the ambience was always more reflective of delicate chamber music than the crescendos of a full-blown orchestra. André's second son, Yves, has remarked that his father did not so much instruct the children in high cultural pursuits as provide an example of someone who lived each day as a dedicated humanist. He had a 'rare modesty' and tended to keep a certain distance between himself and others; he made it clear that cultural appreciation involved a personal relationship between the individual and the work of art. He also insisted that one had to truly listen to music, not treat it as a secondary activity.[4] Guests who came to the house often found themselves almost forced towards the dining room and away from the parlour with its records and associated paraphernalia; music quite clearly 'dominate[d] the place reserved for it, that is the best place'.[5] Those who were not aware of music's priority soon discovered it. Yves tells the story of a young foreign visitor, with doubtful connections to the Laurendeaus, who showed up at their door and quickly managed to communicate his interest in classical music. That was it—he could stay as long as he liked.[6]

But literature was also given an honoured place. Books were everywhere —in the bathrooms, on the staircase, piled on top of the radiators. While Laurendeau developed a keen interest in the human sciences during these years, for insights into character and circumstance he still looked first to the great literary masters. His faith in the superiority of these timeless sources would never weaken. When he reviewed the most profound intellectual influences on his thought at the time of his induction into the Royal Society of Canada in 1964, the names were almost exclusively those of French literary figures—Racine, Molière, Stendhal, Flaubert, Mauriac, Péguy.[7] Reading and discussing these authors was such a persistent ritual that not only the Laurendeau children but their cousins and friends too acquired a precocious learning almost by osmosis. Yet whereas his own father used to meditate for hours on a page of literature and then, in a loud voice, regale his son with his views, André was diffident and low-key, waiting until near the end of a conversation to summarize and synthesize his own impressions. With his mime-like pallour, darkly sensitive eyes, and Errol Flynn moustache, his intensity on these occasions struck at least one of his nieces as very romantic: 'with just enough hesitation in his bearing and remoteness in his eyes that beneath the traits of uncle journalist one suspected the secret identity of an exile from the world of the imagination'.[8] In 1957, as we will see, Laurendeau would finally realize his long-standing ambition to escape into this world more completely by taking a sabbatical from Le Devoir to write a variety of creative works.

But the ghost of Debussy and all that it stood for in the Laurendeau home was frequently pushed aside by that other 'supernatural' presence, Maurice Duplessis, who had rapidly come to represent everything André stood against. As one close relative commented, when the premier himself wasn't the topic of bitter condemnations, his Union Nationale government's sorry record was, particularly in those areas that Laurendeau considered vital for Quebec's future—social legislation, educational modernization, electoral reform, cultural growth. Whether it was a normal Sunday dinner with ten or twelve family members or a meeting with a journalist, union leader, or political activist, the conversation inevitably focused on Duplessis. As Chantal Perrault, Laurendeau's niece, recollected:

> Duplessis never set foot on rue Stuart, but he was there in all conversations. For a long time, I had the impression that the Laurendeaus' living room was the general neighbourhood for the soldiers of the left, where each came to pour out his heart and recover his strength.[9]

The evening often began with the host mixing cocktails of gin, grapefruit, and pineapple. He would then listen attentively to his guests, who were almost always as obsessed as he was with the Premier's failings. Offering his own thoughts initially as nuances and subtle digressions, he would then sum up what he took to be the essence of the discussion. The longer the night wore on, the more animated and expansive he became until that moment, usually well after midnight, when he sat down with black coffee and cigarettes to write. The next day, when the essentials of their critique would appear in Le Devoir, his guests would often realize why he jokingly described himself as 'a repetitive bore'.[10] In this way 'Duplessis himself . . . held [Laurendeau's] family and friends of the family to combat posts for more than 15 years.'[11]

Why did the 'war against Duplessis', as he so often called it, become Laurendeau's major preoccupation during the late 1950s, both in his role as a newspaper editor and as a French-Canadian nationalist? It is worth recalling, first, that his distrust of the former provincial Conservative party leader stretched back at least as far as 1935-36 and the Action Libérale Nationale fiasco. Not only had Duplessis's deception at the time of the Union Nationale party's formation discouraged an entire generation of young nationalists from further political action, but his policies as premier between 1936 and 1939 had offended Laurendeau's recently acquired personalist social conscience. When Duplessis attempted to

exploit French-Canadian misgivings over Canada's entry into the Second
World War by calling a snap election in the autumn of 1939, Laurendeau
was disgusted. And his disgust turned to disdain when the Union
Nationale leader, sniffing the political mood in every direction, waited
until the last minute to declare himself in favour of the 'no' side in the anti-
conscription campaign. Laurendeau was first humiliated and then patron-
ized by Duplessis in the Quebec Legislative Assembly during his stint as
leader of the Bloc Populaire, and he joined *Le Devoir* in 1947 as part of a
movement to prevent the Union Nationale from gaining control of the
paper. During the early 1950s, furthermore, he had been forced to
acknowledge the schism in the nationalist camp between the old, conservative traditionalists who saw Duplessis as their champion and the emerging group of younger, left-leaning social nationalists to which he belonged.
It was always difficult to break with older friends and nationalist comrades, but he was convinced by that time that Duplessis's leadership
style and impoverished conception of social policy were the chief imped-
iments to linking nationalism with the cause of progress. Laurendeau, in
short, had always seen Duplessis as an opponent.

But there was also something personal to his feelings of repugnance.
Although he didn't have the temperament to engage in diatribe—in fact,
his commitment to journalistic objectivity would oblige him to write a
rather balanced political obituary when Duplessis died in 1959[12]—there
was a festering anger inside him towards the premier that seemed to grow
year by year and that at times he could barely contain. It's not hard to see
why. Duplessis managed to combine all the traits he detested, not only in
a politician but in a human being. Admittedly the premier did possess a
shrewd political instinct (he had been re-elected with tidy majorities since
1944) and he was a master of the parliamentary game, but his intelligence
was limited to the domain of politics. His proud claim that he remained a
bachelor because he was betrothed to the province and had devoted his
life to it struck Laurendeau as a sign of narrowness, not dedication. In his
view Duplessis regarded political success as an end in itself rather than a
means to improve society. His style of leadership, in which he was the one
and only star, seemed a throwback to the nineteenth century or the politics of the American Deep South, where Big Daddy figures such as Huey
Long of Louisiana dominated their marginalized empires. Duplessis had
the same crude sense of humour, which regularly descended to punning
put-downs of friend and foe alike, and the same tendency to pander to the
lowest common denominator among the electorate. He dismissed intellectuals of all types as 'poets' and regarded culture as an exotic foreign
country that was probably not worth even a visit. With his starched shirts
and suits creased to a knife edge for the rural crowds to admire, he projected an image of French Canada that fitted the worst caricatures—outdated, authoritarian, and stupidly self-satisfied. While others might smile

or shrug at the premier's over-the-back-fence political persona, the refined and erudite Laurendeau felt tainted by it.

Beyond these personal considerations, however, Laurendeau opposed Duplessis because over time, and particularly in the changing circumstances of the 1950s, he had come to see Duplessism as the major obstacle to the liberation of the French-Canadian nation. The premier now outranked the federal government and foreign capitalists as the most immediate threat to progress. One of the changing circumstances responsible for this shift, according to Laurendeau, was the increasingly vital linkage between the state of Quebec and the fate of the nation. His own nationalist thinking had undergone a remarkable metamorphosis since the 1930s with respect to this issue. In those days he had taken his cue from traditional nationalists and equated the state with politics, for which he had little more than contempt. As the historian Michel Brunet and many others since have demonstrated, this anti-statism[13] was a fundamental tenet of French-Canadian nationalist ideology, and was promoted by the Catholic church in particular. It turned on the idea that throughout its history politicians had been much less effective than the church in defending and sustaining French Canada's national survival. The state was too easily corrupted and should therefore remain a less-than-equal partner within French-Canadian society. Laurendeau began to lose faith in this doctrine, without actually abandoning it, during the late 1930s, when his own critique of clericalism in Quebec took hold and his personalist philosophy led him to focus on social issues.

But it wasn't until the Second World War that, as a result of his practical experiences with the Bloc Populaire, he started to argue for more aggressive action by the Quebec state in promoting the welfare of French Canadians. Following the war, he lost confidence that the Catholic church could perform effectively the critical social and economic tasks required in a modern urban-industrial society. In fact he was moving towards a reversal of institutional roles, with the church secondary to the state in these areas. This was all the more necessary, he believed, because in the secular society that, despite the church's efforts, Quebec had already become, only a political authority such as the government in Quebec City could hope to defend the province's autonomy against the steady federal onslaught on provincial jurisdictions. His editorials in *Le Devoir* during these years dwelt heavily on the Quebec state's importance in all of the dominant social and economic spheres: 'Quebec is the heart of French Canada,' he wrote in April 1955, 'Quebec is the only province where French Canadians form the majority. Quebec is the only provincial state with its key in French-Canadian hands, the only one where they control the educational system, the natural resources, and a large part of the life of society.'[14] But it had also become grimly apparent to him in the early fifties that as long as Duplessis was in office the powers of the provincial state would never be used aggressively to modernize and improve conditions:

> Quebec is, wants to be and asserts itself as being different, because many French Canadians see the provincial state as their starting point for more effective participation in the life of Canada.
>
> This does not mean that the provincial state completely fulfils this role; it has almost always been in the hands of conservative groups that forever lag behind on the measures to be taken. The tasks leading to French Canada's renaissance and hence to the possibility of its full co-operation in the life of Canada are twofold: the rescue of the political instrument—the provincial state—and then its alignment with the needs of today.[15]

Now Laurendeau and Gérard Filion stepped up their attacks in *Le Devoir* against the Union Nationale's economic policies. They were particularly acerbic about the provincial government's willingness to sell off resources, even after the hue and cry raised over the cheap sale of the Ungava ore rights, on the grounds that it encouraged foreign capitalists to create jobs. Duplessis's cosy relationship with foreign and English-Canadian capitalists, combined with his tight-fisted educational policies, simply meant that the monopolists and trusts would continue to dominate the economy, and a French-Canadian entrepreneurial class would never develop fully. Although their concern on this score at least partially blinded them to the fact that elements of a business class, as well as a bureaucratic class, geared to modern large-scale enterprises—and in many cases acquiring expertise in managerial positions with large companies and agencies—were in fact already emerging, they were correct in their assumption that Duplessis was making little effort to nurture French-Canadian entrepreneurship.[16] At the same time, with each new example of the government's anti-labour legislation they pointed out that the Union Nationale valued a growing economy, in a climate favourable to any and all capitalists, far more than the material well-being of French-Canadian workers. For Laurendeau these were not new complaints—he had been making the same ones since the Taschereau days—and sometimes he wondered aloud if the situation would ever improve.

By the late 1950s, however, the provincial government's social policies, or rather its lack of them, came to assume even greater importance. Throughout the Western world, citizens had come to expect more and more social benefits from the state as a democratic right. In Canada the introduction of such programs as unemployment insurance and the family allowance in the 1940s were leading incrementally to the 1960s' vision of the welfare state and the cherished, if not quite realizable, dream of 'cradle to grave' social security. Laurendeau had consistently supported the Union Nationale's autonomist stand against federal government invasion of this provincial jurisdiction, whether directly, through federally initiated programs, or indirectly, through the complex shared-cost fiscal arrangements that gave Ottawa a controlling voice because of its grip on the purse-strings. But as time passed and tremendous new demands arose for such things as health insurance and university education, the Duplessis government's failure to match its strong opposition to the federal government with well-financed social programs of its own led to a further widening of the gap between Quebec and other, more progressive milieux with respect to services provided by the state. Duplessis's reluctance to offend the church by taking over its traditional but inadequately fulfilled responsibilities in these areas, his penchant for balancing the books while keeping taxes as low as possible, and his medieval mutterings against 'socialists' and 'communists' who advocated too much state intervention in spheres best handled by well-established private initiative—supported by direct state grants that he, of course, controlled—all contributed to a situation described by Laurendeau as 'social retardation'. As the decade wore on it became more difficult for nationalists to tolerate this situation and even more difficult to change it.[17]

But if Laurendeau had good reason to pour his energies into the fight against Duplessism because of its continuing failures in the critical economic and social spheres, he became still more angry and combative over the issue of political corruption. It wasn't as though he was just now discovering the failings of politicians and the political system in Quebec. He had been railing against electoral, parliamentary, and administrative skulduggery ever since the 1930s, when he cut his political teeth on the Taschereau Liberal machine. He was fully aware as well that patronage practices and winner-take-all political attitudes based on the spoils system were endemic in Quebec, a product of history, and were unlikely to end with a simple change in government. But the Duplessis regime, which he had despised for its undemocratic practices during his own brief political career as far back as the war, had been in power for so long that it had institutionalized corruption and made it seem normal. Worse still, in his opinion its supporters had come to regard the Union Nationale and the state, the leader's and the people's will, as virtually synonymous:

> The most pernicious thing about the Duplessis regime is precisely its constant tendency to resort to despotism, its determination to evade the general rules, its skill at using the impulses of the chief as means of government. Contracts without submissions, non-statutory concessions, reprisals against people. These are the daily symptoms to which despotism gives rise. When it allies itself with intolerance, everyone's freedom is in danger.[18]

During the middle years of the decade especially, Laurendeau and his *Le Devoir* team launched a crusade against political corruption in Quebec politics. Although this included trail-blazing investigations of municipal and police corruption in Montreal as well as regular commentaries on the

French-Canadian political delegation in Ottawa, the main target was Maurice Duplessis.[19] 'Le Devoir' wrote one observer, 'a magic word, a newspaper, to be sure, but first a battlefield where the war continued.'[20] Perhaps the key figure in this campaign, which aimed at nothing less than the total unmasking and ultimate defeat of the Union Nationale, was Pierre Laporte, who as *Le Devoir*'s Quebec City correspondent became one of the province's most famous investigative journalists.[21] Later he published a book entitled *The True Face of Duplessis* which cast the premier in the role of a vengeful and petty autocrat. In 1956 he wrote a devastating series of articles in *Le Devoir* documenting by chapter and verse the electoral fraud practised by the Union Nationale in the same year's election victory.[22] So angered was Duplessis by *Le Devoir*'s continuous criticism that he evicted another *Le Devoir* political reporter from his office press conferences indefinitely.[23]

As editor Laurendeau made it clear that he preferred an excess of journalistic agitation to the silence that had prevailed for so long. He set the tone in his editorials and, in consequence, earned Duplessis's undying enmity. As Gérard Pelletier observed: 'Without visiting political figures, without playing confessor to the top ranking ministers, he stirred things up by the sheer authority of his thought.'[24] But Laurendeau's attacks were not usually based on short-term political issues or individual acts of corruption. He aimed to demonstrate how a lack of democracy in Quebec weakened the province's institutional life. In the case of the civil service, for instance, he wrote extensively about its notorious politicization as a patronage pool for Union Nationale party faithful. He noted too that its

> technical poverty—apart from some brilliant exceptions—is directly related to its material poverty and its chaotic recruitment. The very structure and efficiency of the provincial state are endangered by the ... long-lasting criminal neglect, aggravated by a system of political favouritism which is equally long lasting and equally pernicious.[25]

He called for a complete overhaul, with the introduction of professional entrance standards, a modern merit system, better salaries, and promotions free of political interference—in other words, for what was accepted practice in other modern democracies.

In addition, Laurendeau held Quebec's English-speaking minority partly responsible for the low level of public life and participatory democracy. The minority's elite and its newspapers had been content to tolerate political abuses as long as they did not affect their interests. Overlooking for the moment his own contradictory attitude in the late 1930s, he pointed out that when Duplessis passed anti-democratic legislation such as the Padlock Act, with few exceptions the English remained silent and reaped the economic benefits of an easily-exploited labour environment. He likened Duplessis to the compliant 'Negro Kings' of Africa, who sold out their own people through oppressive dictatorial rule with the blessing of their 'freedom-loving' imperialist masters:

> The British possess sound political sense. Very rarely do they destroy the political institutions of countries they conquer. Instead, they control the native ruler, while allowing him a few illusions. On occasion they will let him cut off a few heads, since it is the country's custom. It would never enter their minds to expect this native monarch to conform to Britain's own high moral and political standards.
>
> What must above all be obtained from the native ruler is his collaboration with Britain, so that her interests are protected. Once this is ensured, the petty despot no longer matters. If he should violate the rules of democracy, well, can one really expect much more from these primitive people?
>
> I am not saying that this is what our English-speaking minority in Quebec is actually thinking. But it seems from what is happening that some of their leaders do in fact believe in applying the theory of the native ruler. Since Mr Duplessis is merely the ruler of the Quebec natives, they absolve behaviour in him which would never be tolerated in one of their own leaders.
>
> As a result, a blow has been struck at democracy and the parliamentary system; instead of these, we have the rule of arbitrary power, and a continuing collusion between Anglo-Quebec finance and the province's most corrupt political elements.[26]

Laurendeau's struggle for a more democratic Quebec extended well beyond the political field to the general atmosphere of fear and conformity in the province. He had become convinced that it was the repression of free thought by the entrenched elites in the professional bourgeoisie, the church, and the government, for which Duplessis was merely the chief spokesman, that was suffocating innovation and reform. In February 1957 he wrote an editorial entitled 'Is the Devil on the Left?'[27] in which he traced the long history of conservative repression in the province. At the centre of the repressive forces he placed the Catholic hierarchy, which had striven to suppress any and all left-wing or even liberal progressive movements. 'We must now bear the humiliation of realizing that in so many fields, socially-minded atheists are far ahead and have won the first stages of true freedom and equality, which their Christian counterparts, faithful to their vocation, did not cease to condemn as heresy.'[28] He went on to point out how the church defined virtually every new idea as heretical:

> Every time there seemed to be any possibility of a left wing emerging in French Canada, entire flocks of conformists went into a state of communal, patriotic, religious panic. Wishing to communicate their fright to the masses, they had recourse to a few magic formulas. The enemy, to start with, was a doctrinaire liberal. Then he was a Freemason. He tried to become a Jew, without success. He is always, of course, a communist.[29]

Even now, where he lived in Outremont, he had heard his own children mouthing anti-Semitic remarks against Jewish neighbours of several years.

He continued to take a strong stand against such intolerance, and was one of the first French Canadians to be invited to speak at the Cercle Juif de Langue Française, founded in 1950 by the Canadian Jewish Congress.[30] But he alone could hardly overturn the prejudices that flourished in such a narrow ideological climate. As he stated, 'My personal conviction is that here in French Canada, in 1957, we still lack a sufficiently structured and active left wing.'[31]

Laurendeau actively sought the co-operation of others in Quebec who were standing up to Duplessis and seeking a freer intellectual and ideological atmosphere. Most often they were the left-wing intellectuals that the premier detested. As he observed a few years later: 'When Duplessism was still in flower but had begun to lose some of its bloom, intellectuals in Quebec shone with a certain lustre.'[32] There were two groups with which he forged particularly strong links. The first consisted of the young academics at Université Laval, many of whom were associated with the School of Social Sciences that was established there in the 1930s by Georges-Henri Lévesque. Laurendeau had been involved with Lévesque and his school since its inception and he was well aware that Duplessis had endeavoured to use his control of university financing to have it closed. In this period, critics like Jean Charles Falardeau and Léon Dion (who was to become very close to André) were among the strongest advocates at Laval of institutional modernization and social reform. The second group were the liberal-minded intellectuals in Montreal who in 1950 began publishing a journal of opinion called *Cité libre*, and rapidly established themselves as a vital rallying point for democratic reform. Men like Pierre Trudeau and Gérard Pelletier were prominent *Cité libristes*, and in the 1950s Laurendeau met regularly with them, as well as the popular journalist René Lévesque, at Pelletier's house.[33]

While Laurendeau shared the general critique of these groups in so far as the need for change in Quebec was concerned, he always felt challenged by their more youthful, free-spirited outlook. They had not been as thoroughly reared as he in the traditional values of the interwar period and they were more prepared to dismiss the past as irrelevant. A good number of them, moreover, were opposed to all forms of nationalism, without distinguishing as he did between conservative and social or left-wing nationalism. He explained this difference a few years later:

> It happened to me with the Cité Libre group . . . and with the School of Social Sciences at Laval. While my classmates and I had believed in nationalism, the new wave signed its death warrant. It spoke in the name of individual liberty, social values, technical reforms. It rudely challenged 'monolithic' French-Canadian nationalism. It was vigorously critical of clericalism, and little by little reformulated the problems of education.[34]

Trudeau was a case in point. Laurendeau greatly admired his superb rationality, his incisive critique of French Canada's past failures, and his fearless approach to confronting his opponents. But he disagreed with Trudeau's blanket denunciation of nationalism as the force most responsible for warping French Canada's democratic outlook and promoting a xenophobic siege mentality in Quebec. When Trudeau published an introductory essay to his 1956 book on the Asbestos strike in which he described Quebec as a society crippled by nationalism and clericalism, André responded in Le Devoir with a strong critique of his own. In an article entitled 'One Hundred Pages by Pierre Elliott Trudeau' he maintained that Trudeau lacked the historical insight to appreciate the interplay of time and circumstance that made the past a good deal less black and white than he, as a polemicist, cared to acknowledge:

> M. Trudeau's work is based on a vast amount of reading; his attempts to synthesize it are noteworthy and often obtain remarkable results; his thought is clear and lucid, his analysis pointed, keen, and simplifying by nature. I only regret that when he was so well equipped he did not write a chapter of history for us. His pen, however, portrays everything in two dimension; his portrayal of men and doctrines sacrifices depth. Trudeau comes at them all like a partisan journalist attacking his adversaries sword in hand. Shock treatment seems to be the effect constantly sought after, to the detriment of an intelligent reading of real and fully explored events. Trudeau gives the impression that he has spontaneously chosen those elements which by today's standards seem the most absurd. One might say that from this point of view he has collected an anthology of idiocies.[35]

One fundamental issue that separated Laurendeau, with his social-nationalist perspective, from the Cité libristes and other anti-nationalist intellectuals was provincial autonomy. Even those Cité libristes who accepted the notion of a strong Quebec state in a truly federalist system could not bring themselves to support Duplessis when he attempted to hide his many faults by posing as the champion of autonomy. Their argument was that Duplessism had to be disposed of first; only then could a healthy, progressive reconsideration of federal-provincial relations take place. But Laurendeau was unable to sacrifice the principle of autonomy even if, on certain key issues, it meant supporting Duplessis's brand of laissez-faire politics. Since the 1930s, when he abandoned the separatist fold, he had seen the autonomist struggle as the most viable alternative to separatism as well as to a centralist form of federalism that would inevitably lead to the assimilation of French Canada. In the autumn of 1955 he toured Canada's western provinces at the request of Radio-Canada, and what he discovered with respect to English Canada's attitude towards French Canadians confirmed that a strong Quebec base was the key to French Canada's survival in a larger Canada. In his words, 'We can consider . . . an effective co-operation only if we are supported by a political structure, Quebec, that makes it possible for us to assemble and unify our forces.'[36] In response to Prime Minister St Laurent's famous observation that Quebec was 'a province like the others', he maintained that it was the homeland of one of Canada's two nations and not comparable to Prince Edward Island. In a long series of articles in Le Devoir he offered numerous penetrating insights into English-Canadian society and thinking gained during his western tour, but in the end the continuing isolation, one from the other, of the country's 'two solitudes' was his most lasting impression:

> French Canada remains a very remote reality for them. Many of our attitudes remain strange to them and those of us who act as informal ambassadors among them (and we are very rare) often reinforce the illusions they have about us. Except for a few researchers (specialists in French-Canadian affairs who often know as much or more about us than we do ourselves), they don't leave much room for French Canadians in their considerations. In general they are very consciously Canadian but they don't always realize that the Canada they dream of is an English Canada.[37]

Duplessis put a great deal of pressure on pro-autonomist, social nationalists such as Laurendeau when in February 1953 he appointed the Tremblay Commission—officially, the provincial Royal Commission of Inquiry on Constitutional Problems—as a counterpoise and justifying mechanism for his strong autonomist stand. Nationalists were obliged to show their true colours when the commission ended up, in many areas, justifying Duplessis's conception of conservative nationalism as well. Laurendeau and Le Devoir, however, seized upon the final, four-volume report, which they obtained early in 1956, to praise the strong case it presented for a decentralization of Confederation. It recommended a return of Quebec's lost powers and fiscal freedom amounting not just to a viable provincial autonomy, but to what would soon be referred to as 'special status' within Confederation for Quebec. For Laurendeau and Le Devoir, this central focus of the report superseded all other aspects, and if Duplessis could also use it to justify himself, that was a price worth paying.[38]

Besides distancing him somewhat from certain of his fellow liberal reformers at a time when unity among the anti-Duplessis forces was desperately needed, Laurendeau's autonomist stand led him to frustrating and contradictory positions. Like all nationalists in this period, he was vitally interested in educational reform; indeed, it had been a long-term priority for him. But whereas in the past the main concern had been primary and secondary education, attention now was focusing on the universities. The older generation of Depression and war veterans, along with new immigrants, saw a university degree as a chance for their children to have a better life, and the sheer size of the baby-boom generation meant that universities would have to expand tremendously to meet the demand. In Quebec the university system, especially for French-speaking citizens, was in a deplorable state. Elitist, backward, with a pathetically inadequate capacity, it required an immediate transfusion of funds. 'Soon', Laurendeau wrote, 'we shall have had forty years of provincial pettiness in dealing with universities'; the results were 'criminal':

> In order to survive in 1957, a university requires equipment and research which costs infinitely more to maintain than it used to. All universities are facing a state of crisis. Ours are just being established, just developing; we cannot say that they have yet asserted themselves. They are struggling to exist. Some of their faculties—the ones most important for a nation, in which research and invention take place—are only shadowy institutions where amateurs muddle through or innovators work themselves to death. Moreover, our universities continue to mistrust any line of thought that is too idiosyncratic, any research that is so original that it might shake old conformist ideas. They sometimes have little respect for what is called academic freedom, and they rarely foster enthusiastic research, both of which constitute the necessary conditions for discovery. Our university scene is a desolate one.[39]

In these circumstances it was the federal government that offered financial help, introducing a program of federal subsidies to the provinces during the 1950s that would facilitate the construction of universities and cover some of their operating costs. Duplessis rejected the grants on the grounds that they were a direct invasion of a clearly-established sphere of provincial authority, a violation of provincial autonomy. Instead he promised to use the revenues from a new provincial income tax to provide more money to Quebec's universities than the federal offer would have given them. Laurendeau was sceptical at best, but he felt bound to support Duplessis's stand. He recommended that the universities refuse the grants—otherwise they would surely lead to federal control of educational priorities in Quebec.[40] Considering the great need, he realized that this was a painful decision, one requiring a sacrifice that should have been unnecessary.

> These attitudes, and many others, give the provincial state—this state we persist in giving ourselves—the air of some old Model T Ford. Our people are deluded enough to take its dilapidated condition as a sign of increased dignity, and meanwhile this old jalopy turns provincial autonomy into a brake instead of the motor it should be.[41]

What Quebec needed was a political vehicle that would be both socially progressive and autonomist.

This quest for a political alternative gained momentum following the disastrous election of 1956 in which—despite the best efforts of *Le Devoir* and other anti-Duplessis elements—the Union Nationale won a landslide victory. Laurendeau had given his cautious support to the Liberals, led by Georges-Emile Lapalme, who boasted a new team that seemed to be in tune with the spirit of reform. But they failed utterly to connect with the electorate on the issue of autonomy and were steamrollered in the election. While he would have preferred them to the Union Nationale, it seemed to Laurendeau that traditional political options offered little hope. And yet a political solution was mandatory. From 1956 to 1959 a number of third-party initiatives appeared, as the anti-Duplessis forces thrashed about seeking a vehicle they could all unite behind. Laurendeau, still wary as a result of his Bloc Populaire experience, approached each one with a mixture of hope, even admiration, tempered by arm's-length scepticism. This was clearly the case, for example, with respect to the Parti Social Démocratique (PSD), the refurbished provincial version of the CCF party. He had strong personal reasons for backing it. His brother-in-law and colleague at Le Devoir, Jacques Perrault, was one of the party's co-leaders, along with Thérèse Casgrain, the remarkable women's-rights activist. During this period, moreover, his daughter Francine joined the party and the family crusade against Duplessis, participating in a three-month protest at Quebec City for greater freedom in the universities.[42] Then too, Laurendeau was attracted to the PSD's socially progressive, labour oriented platform.

In the long run, however, he could not see the left-liberal forces rallying behind the party. For one thing, nationalists of his stripe were still not convinced that the PSD, with its emphasis on issues of class, was sufficiently aware of the French-Canadian workers' distinctive cultural consciousness. Second, despite its credible French-Canadian leadership, the PSD was still the offspring of the national party and therefore committed to centralist policies. 'I feel a great deal of respect for those expressing their sincere support for the CCF', he explained, 'but I do not believe that the solution lies in this direction.'[43] Nor was he convinced that the 'new' third-party strategies had much hope of success. A number of the intellectuals at Cité libre sought his support in 1956 for the creation of a party called simply Le Rassemblement, whose founding convention took place in September of that year. Before the election, the bleak political scene had driven him to reconsider the possibility of the third party. Now, with his old Jeune-Canada friend Pierre Dansereau as president of the Rassemblement and Trudeau as vice-president, he had reason to believe that a serious alternative was at hand. He did join the movement, but it quickly developed the old third-party proclivity for internal dissension, and when it became apparent that, for all its reformist intellectual clout, it was not going to become a political machine capable of challenging Duplessis, he withdrew.[44] As he had feared, it was a replay of the Bloc Populaire, but this time at least his participation had not been total.

It was increasingly obvious to Laurendeau that the forces for political change in Quebec had too many differences, especially over the issue of nationalism, to remain united for long in a new third party. There would be other attempts to forge such an alliance, among them the Union des Forces Démocratiques founded in 1958, but by then André was more enthusiastic about the prospects for reformers to unite behind the revitalized Liberal party led by Jean Lesage. Following his leadership victory in May 1958, Lesage skilfully reached out to both liberal reformers and nationalists like Laurendeau in his attempt to unite all the dissident elements in the province.[45] Along with a platform favouring sweeping modernization and social reforms, he offered nationalists the expectation that he would match Duplessis and even go farther in the cause of political autonomy. Here at last was an opportunity for Laurendeau, as both a nationalist and a liberal reformer, to have his cake and eat it too. But these developments were still in the future in that dark year of 1957. For the moment, Laurendeau faced the discouraging prospect of several more years of Duplessism, with no real hope that his quest for an open, progressive, and constitutionally secure Quebec had any chance of succeeding.

Perhaps it was the weight of this discouragement that led Laurendeau, in 1957, to ask Filion for a sabbatical from his editorial duties at *Le Devoir* in order to devote himself completely to creative writing. The cultural world had always represented a rejuvenating escape for him, and, in his conscious thoughts at least,[46] it was the place where he belonged. He wrote the novelist Gabrielle Roy during this period to tell her how much he admired, without any hope of being able to emulate it, her determination to maintain her creative solitude. At the same time he was depressed by what he regarded as the short-term and comparatively superficial nature of journalistic writing. He complained frequently to friends and family about having to grind out several editorials a week, remarking on one occasion, 'this profession involves so much "talk" for nothing.'[47] Filion was often reminded of his dissatisfaction in this regard:

> For him, journalism was worth more than politics, but this was not exactly the goal towards which he was aspiring. Born 20 years later, he would have perhaps lived by his pen, as a novelist or a dramatist. He was aspiring to become, in the best sense of the word, an intellectual as well as an artist.[48]

Adding to his frustration was his recognition that, at forty-five, the benchmark of middle age, he had achieved nothing noteworthy, no singular triumph to satisfy his life-long ambition to make a cultural contribution that might stand in the shadows, at least, of the literary masters he so loved. At moments like this he did not see his life as the multi-dimensional voyage it was, but rather as a fragmented series of disconnected episodes. With his oldest children fast approaching that expensive phase when university and trips abroad have to be financed, this might be the last chance to focus his creative powers. As Filion put it: 'The writing demon was haunting him.'[49]

Over the next several months Laurendeau completed a number of creative projects he had been working on for some time as well as several new ones. In every case the focus was psychological, with themes involving interpersonal relations and aspects of the human condition; plot, setting, and circumstance were always secondary. The contrast between his earlier, more celebratory style of writing and his present preoccupation with the torments of the divided soul was starkly apparent in his two novels. The first, *Voyages au pays de l'enfance*, was actually a series of radio scripts that were first broadcast in 1953 as quarter-hour vignettes. Pulled together, polished, and refined into book form, they were published in 1960. In them Laurendeau reached back to his own childhood and drew from the still unfolding experiences of his children to recapture the wise innocence of the very young. It was more than an exercise in nostalgia: evoking the profound simplicity of his literary hero Péguy, he sought to explore the emotional and spiritual purity of childhood. His style was lean and mystical as he wandered back and forth along the frontier between prose and poetry.[50] He received a great deal of praise for this book, even if it did seem that several of his admirers were thinking less about his art than his other contributions. The novelist Hugh MacLennan, for example, wrote:

> This is an exquisitely tender book, most beautifully and truthfully written. I always sensed that tenderness in you, that love of children, that sensitivity to life. Your politics always seemed to be essentially chivalrous, inspired by a desire to protect what was both fragile and precious. That is the chief reason why I think you have done so much for your country, by which I also mean my country, for your vision of Canada has not been too different from mine. . . .[51]

It was a far different story with his second novel, written in the black period of his sabbatical. *Une vie d'enfer* is the complex study of the interior life of a journalist who dreams of recognition as a great writer. While it is always dangerous to draw too strong an autobiographical connection between a writer's own life and the characters in his or her creative works, there has been a good deal of speculation that in this novel and the other writing begun in 1957-58 Laurendeau was expressing the forbidden feelings and inner turmoils that he did not dare to reveal publicly as his own.[52] The book's despairing tone; its sombre exploration of the way life ravages youthful idealism; the secondary characters who, for the most part, represent domineering, jealous, or merely guilt-arousing female influences; the sub-themes of lost faith, the agony of repressed sexual yearnings, and alienation from one's self—all are ripe for the psychological voyeur. When André gave the book to Filion to read, the latter refused to let *Le Devoir* have anything to do with its publication on the grounds that the paper's readers would be offended. Although he denies it, there is some evidence to suggest that he threatened to fire Laurendeau. In his memoirs he described the book as 'black, black, black'.[53] Realizing that Filion's opinion was representative of Quebec's conformist and conservative mentality at the time, Laurendeau tried to have the book published in France. In his letter to Paul Flamand, literary director at Editions du Seuil in Paris, he explained:

> I have a short novel in manuscript: I first tried to have it come out in Canada. But it is—how to put it—a little 'free'—and even though they now publish much more scandalous books here, the fact still remains that I am the chief editor at the Devoir and that this accentuates the difficulties. My wife suggests that they would not be the same if the book were to appear in France.

But the publishers' readers in Paris were hard on the work and, despite a continuing correspondence regarding a potential revision, it wasn't published until 1965, and then in Montreal.[54]

In retrospect, Laurendeau's most significant contributions to French-Canadian culture were the television dramas that he wrote in the late 1950s, which were performed in a variety of formats into the 1960s. His interest in theatre dated from early childhood, when he would prowl around backstage at the Montreal theatre where his father mounted comic operas:

> If I trace back the roots of my love for the theatre to its beginnings, I find them in the backstage atmosphere I first absorbed at the age of five or six— before the first sudden revelation then, before the great discoveries, before the realization or the presumed realization that one knows what it is one loves and what one is looking for.
>
> The 'entrails' of my sacred monster were neither commodious nor grand. It was a little opera house in the east of Montreal soon to be transformed into a cinema. We used to arrive early, well before curtain time. Through the stage door trooped people I knew well, just ordinary everyday people already metamorphosed by stage fright. They would go down a dark little staircase to the basement dressing-rooms and temporarily disappear; you could hear them trying out their voices; there was a smell of powder and greasepaint. Then they would emerge, inhabitants of another age: Heroes, Scarlet Women, Bandits, the King of France and the Queen of England. . . . It only needed the stage lights to put the finishing touch on the transformation.
>
> It was a game, the very stuff of childhood ('I'll be a robber and then you'll come and try to get me and I'll kill you. . . .'), a game organized and played by adults, a serious game that required long preparation.[55]

Later on, at the Collège Sainte-Marie, he played piano for the theatricals regularly mounted by the Jesuits at the Gésu theatre: 'But this time the adventure was less pure—it was mixed with vanity and calculation, and the sense of lessons unlearnt and homework neglected.'[56] During the summers he and his friends converted a barn near Saint-Gabriel into a theatre and wrote their own plays. In time, of course, he realized how amateurish these efforts were; in fact, there really was no dynamic professional theatre life in Montreal until the Second World War.[57] It was in France, during the 1930s, that he discovered Ibsen, whose troubled, despairing characters influenced him profoundly.

The tragedy of the idealistic individual trapped in unsatisfying, often oppressive personal relationships and limited by society's conformist strait-jacket, who retreats to a world of fantasy or contemplates the morbid release of suicide, was a recurring theme in his television plays. Three appeared on Radio-Canada during his sabbatical of 1957-58: *La Vertu des chattes*, *Les Deux Valses*, and *Marie-Emma*. Very new in Quebec, television drama won instant acceptance, allowing the writer to reach an audience in the hundreds of thousands. With his experience in the medium Laurendeau had contacts well-placed to promote his work, and he found himself comfortable with the idea of adapting his dramatic form to reach the cold eye of a camera rather than a vast theatre audience. This is not to say that his work was greeted with universal applause—if anything his reviews ranged from bad to lukewarm—but such coolness reflected less his ability as a dramatist than the anger provoked by the sensitive themes he touched on. Quebec was only on the brink of the Quiet Revolution and though a tidal wave for change was building, there was still a large segment of society that had no tolerance for public expression of such disturbing themes as that of *La Vertu des chattes*: namely, that modern marriage is often based on social conformism and not true fidelity. Laurendeau received a good deal of critical mail based solely on moral outrage.[58]

Even more than his novels, his plays have given rise to speculation about the links between his characterizations and themes and certain aspects of his own life. A constantly recurring relationship in his work, for instance, is that of a jealous, oppressive, and suffocating mother with her self-destructive son. To what extent, in 1957, the year of his own mother's death, was Laurendeau consciously evoking their relations? Other frequent themes are the unhappy, passionless marriage and the terrible guilt of the idealistic man who engages in an affair only to find that his escape is a kind of prison in itself. It was about this time, apparently, that Laurendeau began his own eleven-year affair with Charlotte Boisjoli, an actress and later a short-story writer herself.[59] Whether or not he had known her before, he was thrilled with her performance in the lead role of Marie-Emma when it was performed on 21 January 1958. Ten days later he wrote to a friend, 'Mme Boisjoli especially was so perfect as Marie-Emma that I didn't know how to congratulate her.' He solved this problem, but it remains unclear to what extent the guilt-ridden men in his plays were expressions of his own feelings about his infidelity. It is also difficult to know how much emphasis should be placed on the theme of 'reality versus appearances' that is so often mentioned in relation to his creative writing during this period.[60] Certainly by this time in his life Laurendeau was hiding a good deal from the world he lived in. Together, his agnosticism and his affair must have weighed heavily on a man who functioned as a persistent voice of moral outrage against Duplessis from the high ground of Le Devoir's editorial page. In the closed society of Quebec he could not reveal who he truly was.

Laurendeau returned to his duties at Le Devoir in 1958-59 without having completely subdued his creative urges. He would try his hand at various other projects in the years just ahead, including an adaptation for radio of Dostoevsky's Brothers Karamazov and a play, Deux femmes terribles, produced by the Théâtre du Nouveau Monde.[61] But he needed time to assess the direction in which his writing career might lead him, and he had to decide whether his temperament could tolerate, without undue torments, the inevitable wounds inflicted by reviewers on those who expose their talents and themselves so publicly.

There were some hopeful signs, moreover, that Quebec might be emerging from the dark night of Duplessism. The premier's sudden death in Ungava in 1959 pointed to the prospect of renewal, at last, within the government itself. When Paul Sauvé, a young and socially conscious politician, became the new premier, the glacier began to crack and thaw. Jean Lesage, furthermore, had effectively pieced together the broad coalition of 'unhappy ones' and gave every indication that he might displace the Union Nationale. Laurendeau's political scepticism, we know, ran deep; he would wait to see if the promise offered by either Sauvé or Lesage was in fact realized. But there could be no doubt that the building pressure for change outside of politics was causing the fortress doors to be opened. Perhaps, just perhaps, the great siege machines with which Quebec had imprisoned itself would at last be dismantled.

9

The Quiet Revolution, 1960-1963

Many of us are passionately involved in our adventure; we are less poor, less helpless; we are beginning to accomplish things; our more ambitious projects don't frighten us off any more; we are ready to discuss in public problems which only yesterday we scrupulously hid from one another. This new ferment constantly goes beyond politics but never ceases to have political repercussions. It is just the euphoria that follows the demise of Duplessis? Many of us feel that is has become possible to be creative again. And that the only sure prescription for survival is to start to live

André Laurendeau, *Le Magazine Maclean*, 1961[1]

In the spring of 1963 North Americans were shocked to discover that there was a revolution under way in Quebec—that 'quaint' but rarely-heard-from Canadian province of high church steeples and red-sashed folk dancers. English Canadians first became aware of this revolution the same way they became aware of most national and international events in the 1960s: on the evening television news. From the comfort of their own living rooms they watched explosives experts in Montreal cautiously approach Westmount mail boxes in hopes of ferreting out crudely wired terrorist bombs. One night they watched in horror as a policeman was blown up, catching glimpses of burned flesh and throbbing wounds as he was carried away on a stretcher. And there were other pictures too, of bombed churches and mutilated statues of British military heroes. These images seemed distinctly un-Canadian. The viewers were told, and there were graffiti everywhere to support the contention, that a terrorist organization called the Front de Libération du Québec was (in a curious phrase that would have a long life) 'claiming responsibility'. But when the terrorists were finally captured and turned out to be mostly adventure-some students, Quebec faded rapidly from the news in favour of spec-tacular upheavals elsewhere. It is doubtful, in fact, that English Canadians would recall these events with anything like the vividness associated with that other bloody incident, later in 1963, in Dallas, Texas. But just as the words 'grassy knoll' would automatically conjure up powerful memories in the years that followed, so too would the initials FLQ. And this terrorist nightmare would return in the October crisis of 1970. In the meantime those who sought an explanation for the violence in French Canada were sometimes puzzled when informed by 'Quebec experts' that what they were witnessing was a *Quiet* Revolution.

The Quiet Revolution that began in 1960 was a turning-point for French Canada, second in historical importance only to the British Conquest two centuries earlier, and its long-term impact, like that of the Conquest, has still not been fully realized. What was the Revolution about? Alas, the graveyard of the 'Quebec experts' is crowded with tombstones bearing that question as epitaph. Those still bravely searching for an answer offer occasional 'on the one hand . . . on the other hand' musings about class struggle, self-determination, neo-nationalist yearnings, cultural renaissance, and so forth. But perhaps the wisest are those who echo the wisdom of the late Chinese communist leader Zhou En-lai who, when asked to assess the historical importance of French Revolution of 1789, is reported to have answered: 'It's too soon to tell.'[2] There is nevertheless some agreement about the Quiet Revolution's overall character. It is usually described as an ideological revolution marked by the conversion of Quebec society, at long last, to an urban-industrial value system. According to this view it was around 1960 that Quebec's French-speaking elites, along with a growing majority of the general public, were converted to the cause of the institutional and socio-economic modernization for which reform-minded intellectuals and opinion leaders had been clamouring during the 1950s.[3] The death in 1959 of Maurice Duplessis—the individual who had come to symbolize Quebec's traditional, conservative ideology—was the specific event that finally released this pent-up momentum in favour of change. Duplessis's successor Paul Sauvé was the first to signal the dawn of a new political era, but his sudden death after only three months in office left the task of fully initiating it to Jean Lesage, the Liberal leader elected in 1960. In spite of the FLQ, it was not a revolution of barricades and molotov cocktails; nor was there a Fidel Castro storming down from the Laurentians. Instead it was a rapid catching-up, or *rattrapage*, that got noisier over time, but of which even French Canadians were only partially conscious in 1960.

André Laurendeau, however, was aware of the revolution's potential from its earliest days. As we have seen, he was one of those reformers who yearned for the end of Duplessism. The barrier to progress personified by the old Union Nationale chief had become an obsession for him, and the removal of that barrier was, to his mind, the inescapable precondition for a true renaissance in virtually every sphere. This was especially true because he had become convinced over time that in a modern society the state must function as the main engine for equitable reform. Thus when

Paul Sauvé outlined plans for sweeping changes in politics, education, social programs, and culture, Laurendeau hailed them in *Le Devoir* as proof of a long overdue rebirth. He did so despite his suspicion of politicians, particularly Union Nationale politicians, who had falsely promised a great deal in 1936, at the outset of Duplessis's long tenure. And he did so while knowing full well that, in its bowels, this was still the party of Duplessis. For Laurendeau it was the reforms themselves that mattered. But he was also conscious that a reformist juggernaut, should it start rolling, could pose a serious threat to French-Canadian nationalism. There were those among his fellow reformers, the young intellectuals of *Cité libre* for example, who equated French-Canadian nationalism with Duplessism, clericalism, and tribalism. To them, therefore, the Quiet Revolution was in essence a rejection of nationalism. It was these same intellectuals, Laurendeau explained, who had made him realize during the 1950s that he was no longer a spokesman for the younger generation, that he had been 'promoted' without his consent into the ranks of the 'old fogeys'.[4] But while he might be considered passé, nationalism was not. It could not be turned out the way a bad government could:

> . . . it is in our vocabulary. It is not easily defined, for there are all kinds of nationalists. We find three ideas common to every one of them however. A keen love of nationality, a sharp awareness of the way national values have been threatened, and the conviction that the state has an important part to play in protecting and especially in projecting these values [5]

Having battled since 1937 to create a progressive social nationalism in Quebec, he considered it a vital element in the process of *rattrapage*. Indeed, one of the most significant developments of the Quiet Revolution involved the emergence of a dynamic neo-nationalism in the post-1960 years.[6] The task ahead, as these nationalists saw it, was to build a more modern and open society, of course, but also to defend Quebec's culture and autonomy.

But this was not a challenge that Laurendeau looked forward to taking on himself. He had been drained by almost three decades of nationalist commitment. In addition to grappling with day-to-day issues affecting virtually every aspect of French-Canadian life, he had striven to maintain a measure of the detachment and independent intellectual growth that are critical to sound theorizing. The late-night telephone conversations that lasted for hours, the tyranny of the editorial deadline, the sacrifice of sleep to read from an ever-growing pile of books, not to mention the seemingly endless requests to speak, attend, and assist, which could not be refused —all had taken their toll. There was never enough time to do a thing well, let alone to indulge in the higher cultural pleasures he so enjoyed. He was beginning to acquire the weary look of someone who had to consciously rally his enthusiasm if it was to break through to his face. Years of fatigue were forming webs around eyes that were ever more deeply set in their racoon circles. In brief, Laurendeau had earned the status he was beginning to acquire as the third name, after Bourassa and Groulx, in a triumvirate of twentieth-century nationalist gurus. Younger journalists confided in him as their mentor and intellectuals from a variety of viewpoints came to hone their newest ideas on the hardened edges of his experience. At forty-eight he didn't qualify as an elder statesman, but he was ready to play the role of counsellor to a younger generation of nationalists. Let them wrestle with the 1960s, while he used his space in *Le Devoir* and the monthly article he had agreed to write for *Le Magazine Maclean*[7] to delve more deeply into the human condition.

There was also the family to consider. The house on Stuart Street was still brimming with children, but not all of the six were still of the age to be rounded up for bed before he retired to his study: most were either young adults or that new category, teenagers, with the normal range of insurmountable problems. Francine, the eldest, was twenty-four in 1960. An intelligent young woman of strong opinions, she had already gone to live in France, where she would stay for years, honouring for yet another generation the ritual of the sojourn abroad. Laurendeau's mother was dead and his father near death. Ghislaine of the red pyjamas was well into that period so delicately described as *un certain âge*. Had the time not at long last come to get on with creative writing? His *Voyages au pays de l'enfance* had recently been published. (His son Yves commented much later that it was strange to see his childhood experiences translated magically into print: 'I can't believe my parents went about having their children with the specific goal of one day providing my father with the opportunity to write Voyages.'[8]) The television plays he had written during his sabbatical had received mixed reviews, but enough good ones to suggest a modestly promising debut. And though his novel *Une vie d'enfer* had been a little too unconventional for the 1950s, it might be just right for the new decade. This, after all, was the 'unfinished business' of his life, and while he was resigned to the fact that he would never attain the freedom of the purely creative writer, it was surely a good moment to shed some of the nationalist responsibilities he had been shouldering since 1932.

But it was not to be. In truth, Laurendeau was on the threshold of the most stressful and exhausting period of his career as a nationalist—so stressful and exhausting, in the opinion of many intimates, that it killed him. The changes brought about by the Quiet Revolution drew him inexorably into the debate about nationalism's future and this led him in turn, by 1963, to play a central role in new efforts to shape Quebec's future in Canada. As 'one of those who contributed most to preparing the ideological groundwork for the reforms brought about by the Quiet Revolution,'[9] Laurendeau found it impossible in the post-Duplessis era to remain aloof when such issues as education, democratic political reform, the state's role in society, or federal-provincial relations were discussed. If for no other reason, he believed his role as editor of *Le Devoir* carried with it an obligation to scrutinize the Lesage government's actions with a 'sceptical vigilance' to make sure it did not betray the cause of reform—as so many previous regimes had done—and that French Canada's legitimate interests were not ignored. He wrote a great deal about the watchdog role of journalists during these years, and he intended to practise what he preached.

He was also worried that the rising generation of nationalists were too inexperienced and too extreme to be entrusted with the responsibility he had hoped to pass on. They disturbed him even more than the smart set at *Cité libre* whom he at least understood and, in some cases, admired: 'History never moves in straight lines. Not so long ago I was baffled by a younger generation that seemed to be turning away from nationalism. Today that same generation is taken aback by the breed of young wolves who are making nationalism their career.'[10] It became apparent that Laurendeau was one of the few men of stature in Quebec who had a sound perspective on the various ideological factions seeking to capture the headwaters of the Quiet Revolution. Between 1960 and 1963, his editorials were required reading for anyone trying to understand the remarkable changes in Quebec as they unfolded.

He was particularly astute, unlike the general run of French-Canadian journalists, at enumerating the ways in which Quebec was influenced by international trends. He dismissed as pure 'egoism' the idea that the Quiet Revolution was an exclusively internal affair. Ever since his return from Paris in 1937 he had been urging a wider perspective both for nationalists and for French Canadians generally, emphasizing again and again that Quebec could not ensure its unique culture's survival by sticking its head in the sand. In the 1950s, on television and at *Le Devoir*, he acquired a reputation for opening Quebec's eyes to the outside world. He was even prepared to admit now, for argument's sake at least, that he had been wrong in 1939 to oppose Canadian participation in the Second World War.[11] He was well aware too that during the long fight against Duplessism the most productive ideas, the most telling criticism, had come from those who at some point had left Quebec and could draw comparisons with other, more progressive environments. As late as 1963, he continued to deplore the fact that talented people had to make sacrifices upon returning to Quebec's inward-looking environment:

> we have covered quite a bit of ground in the last fifty years, and solid foundations have been laid in several disciplines. Still, the best of our returning expatriates, whether they are returning from the States or from Europe, know that in accepting repatriation they are amputating part of themselves. . . . They cannot escape an aftertaste of bitterness when they find themselves hedged in by obstacles and when ill will prevents them from accomplishing even the things that are possible.[12]

French-speaking Quebeckers, he contended, would never fully grasp the meaning and potential of the Quiet Revolution if they failed to acknowledge its 'universal' dimension.

One issue that allowed Laurendeau to illustrate this point clearly was the threat of nuclear war. He was convinced that the new attitudes characterized by the sudden impetus for radical reform, the frenetic demand for the immediate satisfaction of desires, and the brushing aside of Victorian sexual morality arose in part from a repressed fear of nuclear holocaust. The realization that there was no safe haven left on earth, and that the imagination could not truly comprehend the 'collective death' and devastation that nuclear war would bring, meant that people carried on with their daily lives—what else could they do?—with a subconscious anxiety that manifested itself in covert ways. But French Canadians could not pretend that the threat wasn't there. Isolation in the modern world was foolhardy. Laurendeau conceded that as a small country Canada had little real influence, 'except to witness by our actions that we refuse to participate in the collective folly'.[13] He maintained that Canada should oppose the proliferation of nuclear weapons first and foremost by refusing to accept them for its own military. Though he detested the Diefenbaker government in Ottawa for its indifference, if not hostility, towards French Canada, on the eve of the 1962 federal election he considered this issue too important to withhold his praise for the Conservative External Affairs Minister Howard Green's stand against accepting nuclear weapons on Canadian soil. At the same time he condemned Lester Pearson, the Liberal leader and Nobel peace laureate, as a false man of peace who first rejected and then accepted nuclear weapons. The Liberals, he argued, were 'the party of two flags'.[14] By these arguments, and by writing so extensively on such issues, Laurendeau demonstrated that in the modern world there were considerations of greater magnitude than local or even national problems.

A somewhat less tangible 'universal' issue that Laurendeau frequently discussed was the generational conflict of the 1960s. This to him was a catalyst that increased both the pace and the volatility of societal change and was part of a phenomenon spreading throughout the Western world. The generation born during and immediately after the Second World War was reaching the age of majority in the 1960s and, because of its sheer size alone, wielded enormous influence; though too young to hold power, it was capable of opposing those who did while supporting liberal and radical alternatives. Demographics apart, moreover, the baby-boomers in Quebec as elsewhere had very different values from their parental generation. They accused their elders of being, in Laurendeau's words, 'dogmatic' and 'conformist'. He acknowledged the differences between the two:

> Certainly it makes a difference to have been young during the Depression, during the war, or during the post-war period; to have been twenty under Duplessis or under Jean Lesage; to have read Malraux, Camus, or Sartre at

twenty rather than at forty. That marks you. You don't react the same way to the same facts or the same ideas. You can't possibly have exactly the same perspective on things. . . .

So here is a new generation. It casts a greedy and yet somewhat nervous eye on the world. It wants to do things. The things that have already been done leave it cold. It's looking for new tasks. It amplifies the importance of the goals it discovers for itself, and is exasperated to be constantly told about things that are being done now, which it considers to be as good as finished. This is the way the face of the world is changed. Like all creative people, the present generation is intoxicated with the discoveries it foresees, which block further discoveries yet to be made. It seems to be at odds with every-thing that is not itself.[15]

Laurendeau had many reasons for wanting to bridge the 'generation gap' to communicate with this age group. Some were personal. Like every middle-aged parent in this period, he worried that his own children might drift off into radicalism or the counter-culture. The youngest, Olivier and Geneviève, were not yet a concern, but Sylvie and Yves were destined to be 'sixties people', while Jean and Francine were still young enough, in their early twenties, to set themselves apart from their parents' ideas. They had been raised in a cultured home, one that in its general ambience could be called elitist and even conservative, while much of what the new generation applauded seemed loud and gauche. Laurendeau, for all his liberal views, was never a man who enjoyed North American popular culture. His son Jean stated that he was essentially a French elitist even in his musical and literary tastes; for example, the only French-Canadian novelist who was likely to have made it into his pantheon of greats was Gabrielle Roy.[16] For him it was too large a cultural leap from Debussy to rock and roll.

But he endeavoured to reach out in other ways. He wrote very sensitive and quite liberal articles during these years on subjects ranging from birth control to censorship[17] and he tried hard to understand when Francine, a strong feminist, wrote scathing letters from Paris about the backwardness of Catholic schools and the debilitating effects on the young of Quebec's taboo against sex education. While Francine went further than he would in her apparent willingness to toss out the baby along with the bathwater, he was able to sympathize with her. In fact, by 1965 he would write very critically on the same subject, noting, for instance, the sinking feeling he experienced when he enrolled his youngest daughter, Geneviève, in a Catholic girls' school. He wondered if it would start all over again; if she too would hear the nuns denounce '"women who smoke" as perverted women, and those who wear "shorts" as more per-verted still,' or if her Canadian history lesson would consist of enumer-ating the virtues of Bishop Laval.[18] But he conceded that he did not speak to or for young people generally to the extent that he once had, and that 'it's quite possible . . . I fail to grasp all of the real originality of the generation that is just beginning to express itself; that I don't take their negative attitudes seriously enough.'[19]

Indeed he was more prone to lecture them than to listen, though he claimed that was because they rejected dialogue. This, in his view, was their greatest error. He too had once been a radical young man, and he admitted that an amazing number of his elders and contemporaries had bored him to death, but there were some who were worth listening to. It was vital for the young to understand the conditions under which their forefathers laboured—not to exonerate them from all responsibility, but to learn from their mistakes. He pointed out that those who were just beginning to read would one day be the 'young generation' and the cycle would start again: '. . . it is the continuity of thought that is striking. And that is a good thing. I believe in generations. But I believe even more strongly in the solidarity of like-minded men.'[20] As he saw it, 'one shouldn't think of the new generation as an enemy army destined to overthrow their predecessors, but rather as a team which, in its own way, will occupy most of the positions filled by the team they replace.'[21] He was clearly afraid, as the sixties progressed, that the most radical and unthinking elements among the younger generation might take charge of the revolution and push it to unacceptable extremes. This would constitute a regression to the same sort of closed, intolerant society that he, for one, had been fighting to eliminate:

> There is no end to their grumblings of disgust and anger. And there is a kind of ritualistic magic in their protestations, just as the religion of their predecessors was tainted with superstition. Matching the svelte theologians of a conservative era, we now have the sulphurous theologians of a radical age. The affirmations of the former lacked backbone, the latter's negations are just as flabby. If you take an antique stone column and stand it on its head, you may think you're an innovator, but it's still the same old column.[22]

Laurendeau was determined, even if it meant opposing the young, that the era of reform just under way would reflect the liberal values he cherished, with a healthy dose of respect for the best of French Canada's past.

Yet another international trend that helped to spur the Quiet Revolution, and that set him apart from many in his own generation, was the spectacular advance of secular over religious values. Although he grew up believing that 'Catholic' and 'French Canadian' were inseparable, he had later striven to link French-Canadian nationalism to the progressive form of Catholic social thought embodied in personalism. At that time personalism seemed to be a way of reconciling religion with the materialist and secular trends that were an inescapable part of modern life. But as he pointed out in 1961, '. . . in almost every occidental country, the industrial revolution has produced a retreat . . . of religious faiths.'[23] It had become difficult, moreover, for a lay Catholic in the 1950s to defend the temporal role of the church in Quebec society. For many of those who thought the way he did, the church was indelibly stained by its close association with Duplessism, even if a handful of clerics had been in the front ranks of those seeking reform. Add the closet agnosticism that had led Laurendeau himself into an agonizing personal hypocrisy, and it is not surprising that in the 1960s he wrote less and less about the Catholic background of the nationalist cause.

Instead he agreed that the church deserved, in some measure, to be one of the major targets of reform. Nor was this a question merely of reforming the church as an institution, for society was embracing the secular religion and its make-up was changing. Laurendeau acknowledged in 1961 that a wave of agnosticism was sweeping over Quebec that could not be simply dismissed as an alien intrusion: 'In the face of such a disconcerting phenomenon, the most futile reaction consists in running to the ramparts and crying treason.'[24] French Canadians would have to start getting used to a definition of themselves that was cultural and linguistic, but not religious. This was even more the case, he observed with considerable foresight, because a wave of 'New Canadians'—yet another external influence--was about to swell their ranks; along with non-believers, these newcomers had a perfect right to expect Quebec's institutions, which were mostly confessional, at least to provide 'neutral' alternatives. While Laurendeau was not prepared at this early date to embrace the secularist onslaught unequivocally, he saw the necessity of accommodating it.

His views on education, however, constituted a much more radical rejection of the church's institutional role. His criticisms of the stifling impact of clericalism in education dated back to the 1930s, when he made it plain, on the basis of both his own experiences in the school system and the lamentable failings he observed at every level, that major reforms were imperative. After years of inaction on the part of Quebec's Catholic hierarchy, largely because of the cosy arrangements struck between it and Maurice Duplessis, his editorials had become fiercely acerbic. In 1959 he pointed out that a school system that prided itself exclusively on its classical humanist character while Quebec sank more deeply into scientific and technical backwardness was not even capable of teaching its students to speak decent French. Instead they spoke what he considered the lazy substitute called 'joual'—a version of French named for its pronunciation of the word *cheval* (horse), and a term that in the years ahead was to become synonymous with the need for educational and linguistic reform.[25] He also noted that many clerical teachers wrote to *Le Devoir* protesting about the atmosphere of fear they worked in, never daring to open their mouths with constructive criticisms in the certainty that reprisals would rain down from their Catholic superiors. To one such correspondent, Jean-Paul Desbiens, Laurendeau suggested that he publish his criticisms under a pseudonym, as Brother Anonymous.[26] Desbiens's caustic wit and sarcastic exposure of grievously low educational standards, past and present, sparked a major debate over the church's role in education. The publication of his book *Les Insolences du Frère Untel* in 1960, with an introduction by Laurendeau, was an overnight publishing sensation. This earned Laurendeau the enmity of Cardinal Léger, Archbishop of Montreal.

The Cardinal wrote him to complain that he had abandoned *Le Devoir*'s traditional allegiance to the church and placed in doubt his own trustworthiness as a Catholic; by initiating the debate over education and publishing a favourable review of Desbiens's book, even though the author had been disciplined by his religious community, he had contributed to the unfounded accusations that the intellectual climate in Quebec was poisoned and stifled by the church.[27] Laurendeau must have been amused by Léger's inability to see that his accusations were a blatant example of the very thing he was trying to deny. Nevertheless he took great care in framing his reply, revising his remarks several times. The result was a definitive statement of where Catholicism now fitted into his conception of the French-Canadian nation, as well as a brilliant analysis of the church's rapidly declining institutional role in Quebec. He placed himself squarely on the side of those who believed the church was overextended in areas such as social services and education, which it had dominated in one way or another for three centuries. He urged Léger not to resist the state's entry into these areas where the levels of competence were unacceptably low: the church should retire gracefully. He also called for less religious intolerance and for a more positive attitude among church authorities with respect to individual liberty and freedom of thought.[28] Although it was more painful for him than for younger reformers, Laurendeau had come to grips with the fact that the church's leadership role in Quebec society was nearing its end. It had failed, after centuries of successful adaptations, to meet the needs of Quebec's modern, urban reality.

No single issue better illustrated this trend or confirmed more clearly the strength of Laurendeau's conviction than his support for the creation of a Ministry of Education. Because he believed that the educational system as a whole, from normal schools through the classical colleges to the universities, was seventy-five years behind the times, he favoured nothing less than complete overhaul. It was the necessary first step towards the long-term success of other initiatives, for as he bluntly stated, 'the province lacks competent men and the reforms are waiting.'[29] In 1960 he was the first to call upon the new Lesage government to appoint a commission that could make the necessary recommendations for a massive restructuring.[30] When the Parent Commission, appointed in 1961, made the keynote recommendation to establish Quebec's first education minister, Laurendeau strongly endorsed the measure. By implementing Bill 60, the state would effectively take control of education:

> I, like my contemporaries, was long submerged in this fear of political intervention in education. Thirty years ago, twenty years ago, fifteen years ago, I would have undoubtedly been among the adversaries of Bill 60. We scarcely recognized, then, the rights of the state in this sphere: we more readily affirmed those of the church and of parents, without realizing that:
> — Parents exercised scarcely any influence at the structural level.
> — By necessity, the state weighed more and more heavily on administrative decisions, because, more and more, it funded teaching. And this influence ran the risk of being all the more arbitrary because it was officially denied.[31]

When several high-ranking Catholic ecclesiastics fought a rearguard action to limit the effectiveness of the new minister, insisting he be advised by a Superior Council of Education that would include clerics, Laurendeau unleashed a tirade. He noted that while almost every modern country, including some emerging Third World states, had a minister of education, Quebec, after waiting so long to have one too, was prepared to hobble it over the objections of a few bishops. They wanted a minister who 'is not a Minister like the others'. In other words, they were prepared to accept the existence of a minister provided he wasn't really a minister, and they were trying to get their way, as always, through undemocratic lobbying and high-level intrigue. In his editorials during this period he heaped scorn on 'the closed little universe' that the church preferred. 'I know,' he wrote in 1963, 'that French Canada entrusted the direction of public and private education to the church. It did well for itself: moral security, low salaries and disinterest. At the same time, it participated in the patronage and abuses of the party in power. . . .' The church, he recalled, had opposed every progressive measure—compulsory education, free education, and now the creation of a minister—as the diabolical inventions of freemasons. 'Unfortunately,' he pointed out, 'a part of the national community still feels as it did in the past.'[32] Even though his strong stand alienated many conservative nationalists and involved him in nasty exchanges with long-time friends like François-Albert Angers of L'Action nationale, he enjoined the Lesage government to steel its courage and resist those who wanted to turn back the clock.

In taking into account those broader influences—nuclear weapons, generational change, secularism—that were 'part of the times we live in', Laurendeau was careful to avoid a strictly political interpretation of the Quiet Revolution. Indeed, in his view the Lesage government was being driven by those influences as much as it was providing the impetus for change itself—and perhaps more. As he remarked in 1961, 'it's too soon to judge this [the Liberal government's] effort. I would rather measure its strength.'[33] While he applauded such long-overdue initiatives as the Parent Commission and pension reform, he was fearful that the government might shy away from the most important political problem of all: corruption. It was natural, he explained, for politicians to talk about this issue when in opposition, only to work all the patronage levers once they had gained office. One had only to remember Duplessis in 1936, the wolf who came disguised in the sheep's clothing of political morality. Laurendeau's many years fighting the corruption of the Union Nationale government had shown him that unless this cancer was cut out once and for all, other gains might prove ephemeral. Furthermore, such a change could only begin in the 1960s, for it would require a long-term transformation of an entire political culture. French Canadians would have to be taught to hate corruption if there was ever to be a truly democratic life for them.

If it is true, as some have claimed, that Laurendeau was Canada's most brilliant political journalist during the late 1950s and early 1960s, part of the reason was his fearless analysis of this issue. He brought to it a genuine zeal for reform, a probing investigative intelligence, and the courage to subject his own people to no-holds-barred criticism. He argued forcefully, for example, that this was no passing contagion associated with a particular party or leadership style. It was endemic to Quebec:

> We have patronage in our blood. We regard the position of civil servant as a perfectly legitimate political reward. We see elections as a great popular game whose rules escape the most common moral imperatives. We have a religion of the electoral fund. . . . And in [this] we only accentuate vices that flourish everywhere.
>
> It was therefore a matter of giving back to the party faithful their role in the party, and to the party, its role in the State.[34]

Laurendeau considered the many explanations offered by learned professors. These ranged from theories based on Quebec's interminable rural poverty and its corrupting impact on public morality to the hypothesis, best argued by Pierre Trudeau, that French Canadians did not fully appreciate the responsibilities of democracy because they had never had to fight for democratic institutions.[35] No single cause accounted for it adequately, in Laurendeau's view, but he had an explanation of why it continued: 'because we suffer it, we tolerate it. . . .'[36] Why, for instance, did the legal profession, supposedly devoted to justice, complacently accept a ruthless regime of patronage in its own ranks? In Quebec, where pious, moralistic rhetoric had been so much a part of public life, members of the general public seemed indifferent to the rottenness that ate away at their institutions. It served no purpose, he contended, to get angry at every 'Mr Smith' from outside Quebec who dared to criticize them, if they could not first prove that they were capable of participating in 'clean politics'. And this would have to begin with a different attitude towards the state. 'This conception of the state [as] a remote "monster" that one plays no part in, but that one tries to exploit, comes to us no doubt from deep in our past. It is tenacious. But we'll have to wring its neck if we want to enter into the contemporary era.'[37]

Since the Quebec state was clearly destined to become more active in society and therefore more central to French-Canadian life, Laurendeau insisted that politics had to become more participatory; it could not remain the tool of entrenched oligarchies. He had fought against the financial oligarchies under Taschereau and Duplessis and he would fight them again under Lesage if the government failed to take action on electoral reform, patronage, and influence-peddling. He was mildly heartened when the Liberal government introduced a major reform involving public tenders for government contracts in 1961. The howls of outrage from loyal Liberal supporters who, after years of being on the wrong side politically, now expected their 'just' rewards but who found instead they would have to compete for contracts, were music to his ears. He went so far as to attribute the remarkably strong showing of the Social Credit party in the federal election of 1962, when it elected twenty-six members from rural Quebec, at least in part, to a reaction against the drying-up of provincial government patronage in the countryside. Nonetheless, he would have to reserve final judgement on Lesage's political regime until some time after the implementation of the electoral reform law proposed for 1963. It promised to limit electoral expenses, to introduce government funding of election expenditures, and to circumscribe the role of legislators as distributors of patronage. 'All this is very fine,' he wrote, 'we'll find out in a few years if it's true. . . . that we're even able to pose the question without joking is a sign of progress we hardly dreamed of. . . .'[38] Although the process would take decades, Laurendeau's influential pen played its part during these years in Quebec's transformation from what was perhaps the most corrupt to what is now the most democratic electoral environment in Canada.

He was equally adamant about instituting a competitive civil service in which ability rather than party affiliation would be the basis for hiring and promotion. The absence of competent professionals in government, he pointed out, was a serious obstacle to carrying out the reforms of the Quiet Revolution:

> It's a complaint that should be levelled against previous governments, Duplessism carries particular responsibility: distrusting intellectuals and specialists, he did not renew the civil service, by opening up enough new careers. Now, this is a domain in which, except for brilliant exceptions, collective effort, social and political support, is absolutely essential. Adolescents will not embrace a specialty whose very existence is unknown to them, or that offers too few prospects; university students will not push their studies far enough if they don't receive sufficient moral or financial support from the society to which they belong. In the end, their knowledge or art will not be enough if they are not given the opportunity to exercise them on a vast enough scale. Everywhere the incentives were missing.[39]

Laurendeau had often been appalled by the strong current of anti-intellectualism in Quebec society, and in 1963 he implied that the Lesage government was showing signs of catering to a conservative backlash against the sudden ascendancy of men of ideas. Nothing, he maintained, could be more retrograde, for it was precisely the intelligentsia who had the ideas and competence to accelerate the catching-up process and in time, perhaps, make Quebec a society of the future rather than the past.

Laurendeau's faith in intellectualism and his defence of the concept that every progressive society should make full use of its intellectual elite was both personal and a mark of the 1960s. We have seen how he was shaped from childhood in the classic humanist mould, and how isolated he felt, coming home from Paris, in Quebec's stagnant and vacuous mental environment of the 1930s. From that point on he felt himself to be a rebel and leaned heavily on other, occasionally maverick thinkers whom he regarded as enlightened allies in the struggle to surmount the prevailing sluggishness. Since he had never regarded himself as a particularly original thinker, but rather as one who could listen to, absorb, fuse, and perhaps popularize the best ideas of others, he considered contacts with intellectuals his mind's lifeblood. The telephone link and regular meetings with professors like Léon Dion and Pierre Trudeau, as well as media figures like Gérard Pelletier and René Lévesque, had been vital during the anti-Duplessis years and continued to be so during the early days of the Quiet Revolution.[40] After the long years of darkness when the term 'intellectual' was ridiculed, he welcomed the more favourable attitude of the 1960s.

But Laurendeau's vision of 'engaged intellectuals' was of people who valued many types of wisdom and used their superior knowledge for the benefit of society. He could be contemptuous of the arid scientific mind— though he knew such people were required—and he positively despised the arrogant certificate-holders who sought only to advance themselves in the new order:

> I have known Quebec farmers who never went beyond the rural school and who were magnificent human beings: rational, colourful, capable of assuming considerable responsibility, and penetratingly intelligent. The best had something royal about them. You could talk to them for hours and draw from their conversation a fund of human experience which they had long meditated and could express eloquently. They struck me as healthy and joyous individuals. . . .
>
> And I can't help remembering something I have often thought about them. I have always wondered how such rich personalities became transformed in our matriculation factories into such a weak-kneed 'élite' who seem to be practically milked dry of all their original juice and joy. I am forced to conclude that we make a better job of our habitants than of our intellectuals.[41]

It was perhaps fortunate for Laurendeau that he did not live to see the displacement of the intellectuals, after their brief moment in the sun, by the bureaucratic professionals and business elites from the 1970s on.

While the greater part of Laurendeau's attention between 1960 and 1963 was devoted to analyzing those factors, both external and internal, bearing upon what were clearly revolutionary times, he was also drawn into the heated debate among French Canadians themselves regarding Quebec's relations with the rest of Canada. By 1963, in fact, this was the pre-eminent issue and one that literally took over his life. It was a debate that involved him in sharp conflicts with close friends and forced him to publicly chastise fellow nationalists who, he believed, were either resisting change or pushing the Quiet Revolution towards misguided goals. The debate was spurred by the Lesage government's growing nationalist tendencies, particularly with regard to federal-provincial fiscal relations, and led Laurendeau into confrontations with federalists, separatists, and revolutionaries over how the impasse was to be resolved. It was inevitable, of course, that the Lesage program of reform would lead to a financial crisis. If Duplessis had been able to balance his governments' budgets, it was because he did the absolute minimum in education, social services, and other fields. With only marginally improved revenues, the Liberals not only were doing more but were trying to overcome past deficiencies. Taxes could only be raised so high, and before long outspoken ministers like René Lévesque, who needed money to carry through with his plan to nationalize the last of Quebec's privately run hydro companies, complained vociferously that Quebec required greater fiscal autonomy vis à vis Ottawa. Before calling an election in the fall of 1962 on the nationalist slogan 'Masters in our own House', Lesage made a number of speeches stating Quebec's case for more tax dollars, demanding control of all inheritance taxes, one-quarter of income taxes generated in Quebec, and the renegotiation of federal-provincial shared-cost agreements.[42] Coupled with the Liberals' resounding electoral victory, these demands created the strong impression that nationalism was alive and well in Quebec.

Although Laurendeau suspected that the Lesage government didn't have an overall strategy for the renegotiation of federal-provincial relations, he backed its demand for more fiscal autonomy. After all, this had been his position with respect to Ottawa's usurpation of provincial powers since the 1930s. It had cost him dearly during the Duplessis years, when his autonomist stand offered succour to a socially retarded provincial government. It made far more sense now, however, when an effort was under way to modernize Quebec's institutions and fields of responsibility. Why shouldn't the federal government return those taxing powers it had appropriated during the Second World War? When asked in an interview when his patience would run out on Confederation, Laurendeau replied:

Even given the imperfect system under which we live, we have work to do in Quebec City. We have only just recognized this and we are improvising for the first while because competent people are lacking; this is natural, in any case, since it is the great tasks that call men to begin giving their best. Particularly in education and the civil service, in the economy and in the undertakings of cultural life, we have goals to reach. This will be the work of a generation.

The political environment in which this will be achieved is a restricted one. Especially in the fiscal area, we will come up against its limits. The environment must be opened up, which, in particular, means securing the provincial state's financial resources. If the natural growth of the provincial state is blocked by the central government's attitude, then that is when 'my patience' [with Confederation] will run out.[43]

It was a cornerstone of Laurendeau's thinking during this period that the terms of federal-provincial relations would have to be renegotiated. The Quiet Revolution made patchwork solutions unacceptable and constitutional changes mandatory.

This position brought him into direct conflict with Quebec's federalists, especially those at *Cité libre* who had been allies in the fight against Duplessism. The federalists opposed constitutional reform on the grounds that under the British North America Act Quebec had always had sufficient powers to build the kind of society it wanted, and that the demand for more powers, of the sort being pushed by Lesage, were actually an expression of all-too-familiar nationalist rhetoric. These neo-nationalists could, as they had done so often in the past, distract French Canadians from sustaining the liberal-minded internal reforms that were the real essence of the Quiet Revolution. In 1962 Pierre Elliott Trudeau, the most incisive spokesman for the federalist view, wrote a scathing article, entitled 'The New Treason of the Intellectuals', in which he warned that the progress of recent years was being betrayed by those reverting to the empty ritual of Ottawa-bashing.[44] Laurendeau, as we have seen, admired Trudeau's intellectual power, and during their frequent meetings at Gerard Pelletier's house to discuss current affairs he often found himself agreeing with the younger man's clear and intensely rational arguments. He praised Trudeau's writings on Quebec for these same qualities[45] and he made use of Trudeauisms, particularly in the struggle against separatism, in his own writings. Trudeau also had an admirer in Francine, with whom he was acquainted. Nevertheless, Laurendeau had never accepted Trudeau's scathing denunciation of virtually all of Quebec's past, nor his opposition to every form of nationalism. Considering Trudeau too legalistic and categorical in his thinking, he believed that the younger man lacked a feel for the social. Laurendeau once remarked to a fellow journalist that if Trudeau had been an artist, he would have painted very clear and colourful images; they would have been bold and distinct, but without much subtlety. His own paintings, on the other hand, would have had to feature many shades and hues to accommodate the nuances of which he was constantly aware.[46] In the years ahead, the differences between these two men over the need for a restructuring of Canadian federalism where Quebec was concerned would shift to the national platform in Ottawa, where they would have stunning repercussions.

But Laurendeau's conviction that the government in Ottawa would have to face up to the requirement of fundamental change was also based on the federal politics of the day. This was the era of John Diefenbaker's Conservative government, 1957 to 1963, and it is doubtful that a panel of hand-picked political sadists could have chosen a leader who would exacerbate the 'Quebec situation' more flagrantly. Just as the Quiet Revolution began to set free French Canadians' long-dormant energies, spawning a whole range of challenges to the Canadian political fabric of which Jean Lesage's autonomist belligerence was but one, Canadians elected a prime minister who was, from ignorance as much as ill will, deeply insensitive to French Canadians. This remained the case even after the Conservatives' landslide victory in 1958, with strong support from Quebec—a first for that party, Laurendeau was quick to point out, in political eons. The story of how Diefenbaker frittered away his mandate while alienating even the staunch Conservatives among his French-Canadian supporters, succumbing finally to Lester Pearson's Liberals in 1963, is the stuff of Canadian political legend. But for Laurendeau and Quebec's nationalists at the time, it was Diefenbaker's style perhaps even more than his policies that thoroughly alienated them. Laurendeau suggested that there really hadn't been a prime minister in the twentieth century whom French Canadians could love, not even Laurier or St Laurent, though this was very likely in the order of things for a minority. Yet there had been leaders, such as Mackenzie King, who had tried, even if in rather patronizing ways, to take their sensibilities into account. Diefenbaker was a horse of a different colour. His speeches in Quebec were usually sprinkled with condescending references to French explorers and punctuated now and then by gravel-voiced linguistic contortions that were a godsend for comedians (his frequent rendition of 'Mesdumbs et Messoors' even had unilingual anglophones doubling over). Such speeches were insulting reminders of a past when Quebec could be appeased by a few meaningless gestures. Was this prime minister likely to respond to the entirely new circumstances in Quebec? Where, Laurendeau asked, were French Canadians expected to fit into Diefenbaker's vision of unhyphenated Canadianism?

> A Westerner, a champion of New Canadians, and a man marked by rather painful experiences in his youth, Mr. Diefenbaker likes to assert that we are all Canadians. But does he believe very firmly in bilingualism or in the role of French Canada in our history? For a long time it has seemed rather doubtful. I believe he thinks of us as the most important minority group in the country. As such, and because the constitution guarantees us certain rights, we must be treated with special consideration. But never as partners on an equal footing.[47]

Laurendeau's idea of equal partnership was heavily weighted towards a cultural definition of nationality. This, as we will see, set him apart in terms of priorities from many of his fellow nationalists in the 1960s, who stressed political and, to a lesser extent, economic factors. As strongly as he argued for new powers for Quebec and for greater fiscal autonomy in the political-constitutional field, for him the ultimate test of federalism's legitimacy lay in the development of a truly bilingual and bicultural Canada. It is worth recalling that he became a nationalist in 1932 over the insensitivity of R.B. Bennett's Conservative government with respect to French-Canadian representation in the federal civil service. The issue had bristled with symbolic importance for him ever since, and he rarely missed an opportunity to remind Canadians that the government service in Ottawa was a wasteland for French Canadians. It was astounding to him that thirty years had passed without any substantial improvement. There had been gestures such as the printing of bilingual money and more use of simultaneous translation, but the fact remained that French Canadians could not hope to work in their own language in Ottawa, nor could they expect as a matter of course to receive services from the federal government in French. Here, he argued to an English-Canadian audience, was an anglophone swamp where separatism could breed and multiply:

> I know French Canadian Civil Servants who are separatists, and they probably are separatists because they are Civil Servants. In practice, [they] speak, write and work in English, on ideas and projects which originated in English minds. For, in the Federal . . . administration of a so-called bilingual country, French is a foreign language. In order to serve his country, a French Canadian often has to forget what he is; if he does not, he is kicked out, or perhaps tolerated, but his individual future is doomed.

Laurendeau often pointed out, too, that linguistic discrimination was even a problem in Quebec, where there was a growing fear that unless something was done soon bilingualism would continue to be a synonym for both assimilation and exploitation. He often used specific examples to illustrate the larger problem:

> The other day, a big company held in Montreal a meeting of its administrative board. This corporation has five vice-presidents, one of whom is a French Canadian. They all asked this man why, for heaven's sake, is there a separatist movement in Quebec. He answered: 'In each company, each vice-president has the ambition of becoming president. Here, we are five. The only one who knows he has no chance at all of becoming president is me: because I'm a French Canadian. Well, that's the best explanation of separatism that I can give.' Which is a crude way of expressing the desire of real equality of chance that you will find presently in all walks of life. . . .
> I could multiply examples of this kind—often very small, day-to-day details. For instance, in a Montreal restaurant, if I ask for some *café*, I am

still surprised to hear a waitress answer: 'Sorry, Sir, I don't speak French.'
I am surprised because, in Montreal, French happens to be the language of
the majority.[48]

While still some distance from visualizing a comprehensive solution to linguistic and cultural inequality, he could not accept the blithe assertions of
French-Canadian federalists that these issues could be dealt with in the
sphere of individual rights and without significant constitutional change.
As a minimum starting point, in any case, the government in Ottawa
would have to undergo a profound awakening. He found it almost impossible to imagine John Diefenbaker, the man he referred to as the 'babbling
prophet',[49] suddenly embracing the concept of Canadian duality. Was it
any accident, he asked, that the Conservative government's period in
office coincided with the rise of separatist feelings in Quebec?

During the early 1960s Laurendeau was often accused of exaggerating
the threat of separatism in order to bring pressure to bear on English
Canadians to grant sweeping concessions to French Canada. Some argued
that he was a closet separatist himself, while others—the more charitably
ignorant—suggested that he was contributing to separatism by writing
about it so much. Although these charges seem bizarre in light of the subsequent growth of separatism, it is true that the movement was quite small
during this period. In 1960 and 1961, when Laurendeau began analyzing
it in earnest, he described the separatists as few in numbers—a few thousand at most—politically fragmented into small parties across the right-left
spectrum, and limited to the middle classes. Like so many extreme nationalist movements before it, this one had not 'reached the masses'. As late as
1962, he commented: 'I still have the feeling that the movement is very
weak among workers and farmers, who constitute the bulk of the population. But it is only a feeling.'[50] Why, then, was he already raising the alarm?
The answer is that on this issue he was prophetically insightful. He could
see the fire in the match because he understood the potential, in the circumstances of the Quiet Revolution, for separatism to grow rapidly. As
he pointed out more than once, he had been a separatist in another volatile period, the 1930s, and he knew how it could fire the blood of the
young especially. As a lifelong nationalist he also recognized that in a sense
'. . . all French Canadians are separatists',[51] in so far as they were determined to protect their distinct culture and dreamed of doing so in a state of
their own. In fact, most separatists now insisted on calling themselves 'inde-
pendentists' because they wished to stress, in the progressive language of
the day, their constructive, nation-building purpose. But Laurendeau
insisted nonetheless that the movement was fuelled by French-Canadian
alienation from Canadian federalism and would spread in proportion to
the failure of English Canada to understand and deal with the problem.

He often elaborated on the reasons why separatism had such potential in the context of the Quiet Revolution. For one thing, it seemed the logical next step for the many French Canadians whose attention and loyalties had become focused on Quebec City since 1960:

> After the arrival of Paul Sauvé in power, followed by the victory of Jean Lesage, we became prodigiously interested in what was happening within Quebec, for and against: educational reforms, the war on patronage, the liquidation of Duplessism, vast economic projects, etc. The Quebec government was becoming more active, more vigorous and enterprising, more lucid and intelligent, at the very moment when the government in Ottawa was losing its dynamism. Quebec was the centre of attraction: French-Canadian public servants emigrated, therefore, from the federal capital to the provincial capital. From now on it was in our own home that things would happen.[52]

Among young people, for instance, there was already a tendency to refer to themselves as *Québécois* rather than *Canadiens français*. Members of the generation coming up were interested in instant solutions, and they were sometimes led by people, only a little less young, who had breathed the stale air of the 1950s: '. . . the first generation to free itself from the morass of Duplessism was starved for absolutes.'[53] Seeing many former colonies in Africa and Asia achieving nationhood, they naturally asked why the same principle of self-determination shouldn't apply to Quebec. And there were intellectual theorists, most notably in the historical field at the Université de Montréal, who had been popularizing an interpretation of the past according to which Quebec was decapitated socially by the British Conquest and had lived an essentially parasitic existence ever since. The only solution offering a prospect of dignity, if one followed this theory to its logical conclusion, was for Quebec to achieve sovereignty. The sovereign state had thus become, Laurendeau observed derisively, a 'condition of life'.[54] But he was not at all dismissive of the less hypothetical position taken by Marcel Chaput, a civil servant turned separatist, in his 1960 book *Why I am a Separatist*. A best-seller, it was the closest thing to a manifesto for the separatist movement until René Lévesque published his *Option for Quebec* in 1967. Chaput started from the proposition that French Canada was the best-treated minority in the world, but went on to argue that it was this minority status itself, which could never permit a full life, that was the problem. For Chaput and for many others, according to Laurendeau, the almost daily reminders of their minority status were what made the prospect of independence so alluring.

But Laurendeau also made it very clear that he opposed separatism. Many nationalist-leaning writers, looking back on these years, have tried to cast him as a separatist-in-waiting; as someone, in other words, who viewed it as an idea worth considering if and when conditions were right and after its exponents had polished up their arguments satisfactorily.

Their aim apparently has been to prepare the ground for the assertion that as the sixties wore on he became more sympathetic to separatism, and that had he lived longer he would have endorsed it openly. But the evidence does not support this notion. Those who would read their own political agenda into the early 1960s must downplay the numerous spirited denunciations of separatism in Laurendeau's own writings. In March of 1962, for example, he wrote an open letter in *Le Devoir* explaining that the insights he had acquired in Paris in 1936-37 had extinguished his separatist idealism: 'It was there . . . that I had lost my separatist faith; I have never recovered it.' Some of those insights, moreover, he considered to be still relevant: '. . . I am afraid,' he wrote in the same letter, 'of our becoming a closed system.' Although he could list as many examples as the next person of the price to be paid for remaining a minority, separatism threatened to revisit upon French-speaking Quebec a greater evil: xenophobia. As he argued in 1961:

> Still engraved on our collective subconscious are all the contradictory impulses of the minority complex: towards love or rejection; towards cowardice or fanaticism; towards building those long-cherished walls around ourselves that must be preserved at any price, or towards closing ourselves in behind odious walls that prevent us from seeing and breathing, walls that certain of us hurl ourselves furiously against in an attempt to bring them down. . . .[55]

To those like the separatist Pierre Bourgault, who maintained that Laurendeau had indeed lost the faith and was refusing as well to accept the 'logic' of independence, he replied that they were confusing logic with reality: in fact, a number of formidable realities reduced the separatist argument to what he branded a 'utopian fantasy'.[56]

The most important of these, in his view, was the threat of American economic and cultural imperialism. This had been decisive for him in 1937, and it still was. While liberal Canadians might consider the presidency of John F. Kennedy to be an inspiring example of America at its best, a society worth emulating, and while conservative Canadians might support John Diefenbaker's jaundiced anti-Americanism, Laurendeau looked beyond the present moment to the long-term vulnerability of Quebec:

> What bedevils our existence is the presence of the American colossus at our side. Our real and current problems arise not from our being a third of Canada, but from the fact that we do not account for even a thirtieth part of North America. Attaining sovereignty would not alter our geographic or demographic situation; it would not essentially change our relations with the North American world.
>
> Or rather, it would; it would weaken us. The non-US mass would fall to six million from the eighteen million it was before. Our economy would become

still more fragile, still more vulnerable, still more subject to the economy of the United States: we would be a 'banana republic', a status for which Duplessism . . . may have given us a foretaste.[57]

When he did write about contemporary America, Laurendeau saw little to justify the view that a Quebec independent in name only would be better off as a minority in an Empire characterized by its Cold War paranoia, its bullying of Cuba, and the racial problems in the south. Then too, he asked, what made the separatists think that English Canadians would stand by passively while their country was dismembered? 'Never would Canadians accept such butchery. It is chimerical, absurd.'[58] For those who might be putting their faith in English fair play, he pointed out that he had lived through the conscription crisis and had seen few traces of it then. Not even the 'witticisms' of René Lévesque[59]—who, Laurendeau knew, was the most radical of Lesage's ministers and one he often suspected of separatist tendencies—had provided an answer to this problem.

And it wasn't just English Canadians who would refuse to accept that the principle of self-determination, so glibly tossed around by separatists, justified an independent Quebec state. Neither did he:

. . . I have other reasons for keeping away from independentism.

I do not totally believe in the principle of nationality. The right to self-determination seems to me to be an anarchical agitation liable to challenge most of the existing states. Rare indeed are those without one or several national minorities. Except in the case of actual persecution, I refuse to insist on the application in our own case of a principle of which I do not recognize the universal validity.

Moreover, independent feeling begins with an ambiguity. We are always talking about the former European colonies in Africa and Asia that have just gained their independence. Now a large number of these states are in no sense nations: former administrative divisions of the old colonial empires, they are inhabited by extremely diverse groups. Let us not even look at the Congo or Katanga. India is a subcontinent, a civilization, but no nation at all. Twenty tongues are spoken; there are various cultures, often hostile to one another. Apply the principle of self-determination to India and the country falls to pieces. Similarly, how can we speak of nations in Africa, with the tribal system and the multiplicity of languages and ethnic roots?

I believe French Canadians form a nation, at least according to the meaning we give the word. To my way of thinking, however, the existence of a nation does not presuppose the strict and automatic right to complete independence.[60]

As a cultural nationalist, moreover, Laurendeau was not as ready as the separatists evidently were to throw away the French minorities in the rest of Canada. It seemed bizarre to him to argue that because they had been ill-treated and were in a state of rapid decline, they should be jettisoned rather than fought for.

By 1963, after Laurendeau had made the decision to fight for them on the Canadian Royal Commission on Bilingualism and Biculturalism, he was attacked as a traitor by the separatists. For someone who had devoted most of his life to the defence of French Canada, such accusations were difficult to stomach, especially since they often came from neophytes half his age who had so far done nothing positive for the nation. The separatist ideology was a legitimate option worth discussing, he wrote, but not with fanatics. 'When the normal reflex is to call a man a traitor, or more politely "collaborator", because his beliefs are contrary to yours. . . . When such practices become generalized, they signify a refusal to see things as they are and a refusal to dialogue with others.' He maintained that separatism had become more extreme and that now its entire appeal was negative. 'Its beginnings were generous, but the nervous jitters soon set in, and now condemnation succeeds condemnation, anathemas roll up to heaven, and we are once again besieged by moralists.'[61] Wounded to the quick, he became a formidable adversary who used his sharp reasoning and keen sense of irony to confront the separatists at their own level. If, he argued, they were so dedicated to Quebec's future, why hadn't one of them been able to summon the energy to join the debate on Bill 60, the legislation creating a minister of education? He had been assailed over this issue by the very conservatives that separatists claimed to hate, while they sat mouthing grievances on the sidelines:

> That's what I call courting sterility: only looking at one side of things; starting up witch-hunts; paying more attention to form than to content; ignoring day-to-day reality; practising a nationalism that is rigidly formalistic in conception; and every day ceasing a little bit more to belong to the nation they claim to be saving.

Intolerance, he maintained, was merely crossing the street from where it had once lived, and 'it could very easily go wild'.[62]

Given the rise in separatist militancy and the infusion of more and more youthful adventurism into the ideological climate by 1963, Laurendeau was not as shocked as most Canadians were by the sudden appearance of the FLQ. One evening at Gérard Pelletier's house in Westmount, during another of his semi-regular gatherings with other Quebec luminaries, he heard explosions go off as he drank his coffee. He, Pelletier, and René Lévesque 'had reporters' reactions' and began driving around the district, following the sounds. More explosions went off as they drove, while pyjama-clad citizens rushed into the streets. 'What struck me,' he wrote subsequently, 'was the absurdity of that kind of action.'[63] In the articles he wrote on this outbreak of terrorism, he recalled that such violence had not been seriously considered even in the far more oppressive circumstances of the Second World War and the plebiscite campaign of 1942. He thought of the terrorists themselves as 'dangerous animals escaped from their cages'. And he dismissed as ludicrous any comparisons that the FLQ, who claimed to model themselves on the Algerian urban guerilla movement FLN, might attempt to draw between Quebec's anti-imperialism and that of the Third World. 'Armed with some poorly digested Frantz Fanon,' he contended, 'they preach the necessity of hatred. . . .'[64] But violence was justified only when it was the last weapon left to use against an intolerable government. That was not the situation in Quebec, where those seeking independence had the right to do so democratically.

He deplored the fact, brilliantly demonstrated by Léon Dion in *Le Devoir*, that many French Canadians had softened their outrage at the terrorists after finding out that they were mere youths, 'improvisers'.[65] He, by contrast, had nothing but scorn for these 'fledgling converts to nationalism, amateurs whose convictions appear to be as absolute as they are flimsy and artificial'. It was no excuse to claim that they set off bombs just as other young people ran away from home or engaged in thrill-seeking sports. Violence was a 'human regression', and those who indulged in it were no less cowardly because they were young. Laurendeau wrote admiringly of those who instead chose the path of non-violent civil disobedience. Long an admirer of Mahatma Gandhi, he looked to the American south and argued: 'American blacks who let themselves be fire-hosed and insulted and bitten by dogs are, in my eyes, higher on the human scale and truer servants of their nation than bomb planters and the perpetrators of terrorist acts.'[66]

Yet, as profound as Laurendeau's repugnance was for the most close-minded of separatists and for all manner of terrorists, he also warned that it would be a mistake to misinterpret their actions as anything more than a sign of growing frustration in Quebec. The authorities should be wary of making new converts for the extremists by overreacting; 'acts of savagery bring out the brute in others, and the rancorous bourgeois strikes back with borrowed claws.' He worried especially that politicians would use the FLQ to imply that all separatists and nationalists were fanatics, and that reform was unnecessary. 'The fanaticism of those in power is secretive,' he observed, '. . . it consists of not moving, in not listening, in mechanically repeating the gestures of yesterday. . . . So we must also speak of fanatics of law and order and of sectarians of moderation who remain blind and deaf to the movement of history.'[67] He was convinced more than ever that the Quiet Revolution had released energies in Quebec that called for fundamental changes in Canada as a whole. 'I side with those who find the status quo intolerable, although I belong to a generation that has tolerated and sometimes even glorified it. My stand is that Confederation is better than separatism, as long as it is made over.'[68] He had already given speeches to English-Canadian audiences in 1962 making the point that French Canadians would no longer accept 'piecemeal concessions . . . a few humiliating crumbs to keep us constantly in mind of our situation as a cultural minority.'[69] Indeed, he called for a moratorium on changes such as the introduction of bilingual currency because they created a false illusion of progress. It was high time English Canadians came to accept that Quebec was not 'a province like the others', that it required more autonomy than Prince Edward Island, and that bilingualism could not continue to be a sham, a magician's trick: now you see it, now you don't. His message to French Canada also pointed in the direction of a last chance—the first of what would turn out to be a long string of 'last chances'—for Confederation:

> What remains for us to do is to use what we have—the provincial state of Quebec—but to really use it and not just go on shouting like children about everything we could do if only we lived under ideal conditions. What also remains for us is the task of patiently widening our powers and establishing the foundations of a new federalism.[70]

On 20 January 1962 Laurendeau had written what would, in retrospect, stand as his most important *Le Devoir* editorial. In it he stated that, having examined the Diefenbaker government's speech from the throne, he could only conclude that Ottawa had no intention of addressing the major issues facing Canada. While nuclear defence and economic conditions ranked high on such a list, the most pressing concern was the state of Confederation. The government's continuing search for a formula leading to the repatriation of the constitution from England and other minor tinkerings in the constitutional field showed that it was unaware of the dimensions of the crisis at hand. He called upon the government to create a Royal Commission on Bilingualism and he outlined what such a commission should do. First, it should find out what Canadians from coast to coast thought about bilingualism. 'That would be perhaps a good way to lance the abscess. We might as well stop kidding ourselves: there is nothing to lose from knowing the truth.'[71] Second, it should study other countries, like Belgium and Switzerland, that were similarly obliged to deal with linguistic problems. Third, a very careful investigation should be launched into the use of English and French in the federal civil service.

Only when this was done, he believed, would there be a real basis on which to create the bilingual country that Canada's prime ministers had so often claimed it to be. While some would later argue that Laurendeau's highest priority was a new constitutional deal granting Quebec more powers, it seems far more true that language and cultural issues were higher on his priority list at this time. He followed this editorial with another in March. 'What does making over Confederation consist of?' he inquired rhetorically. 'To me it seems that it consists of this: Canada proclaims itself a bilingual country, but it barely is one. It is therefore essential to make it truly bilingual. I am speaking, of course, of the political institutions and not of individual citizens.'[72] Diefenbaker's response was, as he might have guessed, a categorical 'no'. But it was far from the last word that Canadians would hear on the subject.

In the tumultuous climate of 1963, when the Quiet Revolution seemed to be fracturing into a half-dozen ideological directions, André Laurendeau felt called upon once again to defend the French-Canadian nation he had fought for throughout his career. He was hurt by the criticisms aimed his way and still looked longingly at the creative writer's sanctuary, but he was also challenged by the task of sustaining Quebec's liberal reforms and finding a new formula for Quebec's role in Canada. There was now no question of handing over this responsibility or nationalist leadership to the younger generation. They were too extreme, too unaware of the pitfalls. It would take a steadier, more experienced hand to run the rapids of societal change without spilling everyone into the torrent. 'It is normal, or in any case perfectly acceptable to be a separatist at twenty-five,' he observed. 'At thirty-five, it is more problematic.'[73] At fifty-one, it appeared downright foolish, especially since hatred seemed to be the separatist movement's main source of energy. The revolution that had taken place in 1960—and for one who had waited so long, it did indeed seem revolutionary—was all to the good. But for it to yield the best results for the greatest number of French Canadians, and to preserve their distinct culture, reform would have to take precedence over rupture. Who was to say that English Canadians could not also be found who saw the wisdom of a new, equal partnership? Laurendeau approached English Canada with a veteran's caution but also with the sincere hope that Confederation could be revitalized. It was an overture in the tradition of Henri Bourassa, and, like Bourassa, he was gambling his reputation as a defender of his people on the result.

10
Bilingualism and Biculturalism, 1963-1968

I remain a French-Canadian nationalist who doesn't believe in separatism and who wonders how two nations can live together, in what kind of federation—two nations of which one dominates, and the other no longer wants to be dominated. . . . I believe in a biculturalism which grows out of two productive nationalisms . . . that aim to modify the balance of power.

André Laurendeau, 1964[1]

The distance from Montreal to Ottawa in the 1960s was largely a matter of perspective. For a crow, flying sober and straight, it was measured in miles. For a car driver the distance was calculated in hours and depended greatly on whether or not the Quebec *sûreté* were in a rare anti-speeding mood. For President Charles de Gaulle of France, on the other hand, this final leg of his journey from Paris during Canada's Centennial celebrations of 1967 proved to be out of the question. After he had trumpeted his famous '*Vive le Québec libre*' from the steps of Montreal's city hall, thus appearing to encourage separatism, the government made it clear he was no longer welcome in Ottawa. Yet in that same year of so many symbolic images Montrealers would also be reminded of their pan-Canadian historical background when a group of hardy young canoeists retraced the far western route taken by the voyageurs of the *ancien régime*. In the waning days of France's North American fur-trade empire, the river journey from Montreal to Ottawa had been merely the opening gambit— a chance to warm up and get the paddling songs in tune for the stupendous trek as far as the forks of the Saskatchewan River. In part, at least, it was to revivify this expansive vision of French Canada's destiny that in the summer of 1963 André Laurendeau made his own pilgrimage from Montreal to Ottawa. For him it would be the voyage of a lifetime.

Laurendeau's adventure began officially on 11 July 1963, when he arrived at 24 Sussex Drive to have lunch with Prime Minister Lester Pearson. Thirty-one years earlier, as a furious young French-Canadian nationalist, he had demanded to see the prime minister of that day, R.B. Bennett, in order to present the Jeune-Canada youth movement's petition protesting the government's treatment of French Canadians in the federal civil service. His demand was refused and, after keeping up a steady barrage of criticism over the same issue ever since, he was rebuffed again in 1962 by another Conservative prime minister, John Diefenbaker, when he called for a federal inquiry into the issue of Canadian bilingualism. But in December 1962 Pearson, as Liberal opposition leader, had seized upon the idea and made it his party's policy. In a speech to Parliament on 17 December, which he described in his memoirs as the one he was most proud of, he stated:

> . . . I believe, that we have now reached a stage when we should seriously and collectively . . . review the bicultural and bilingual situation in our country; our experiences in the teaching of English and French, and in the relations existing generally between our two founding racial groups. In this review there should also be, in my view, every opportunity and every encouragement for Canadians, individually or in their associations and organizations, to express their ideas on this situation. . . .
>
> Are we ready, for instance, to give to all young Canadians a real opportunity to become truly bilingual? If the answer is yes, . . . what concrete steps should be taken at the different levels of our educational system to bring about this opportunity, having regard to the fact that constitutional responsibility for education is, and must remain, exclusively provincial?. . . .
>
> Then, there is the question . . . of specific and inescapable federal responsibility. What are the reasons why there are relatively so few French-speaking Canadians in the professional and administrative jobs of the federal civil service, including crown corporations and federal agencies? How can that situation be improved as it must be improved?[2]

Through his Quebec colleague Maurice Lamontagne, who had the greatest input into the Liberals' policy on bilingualism,[3] Pearson consulted Laurendeau in advance of the speech. Having no ties to the Liberals and precious little faith in politicians' promises, Laurendeau suggested that Pearson commit his party, if and when elected, to a federal inquiry even if the provinces refused to co-operate on education. To his surprise, Pearson added this pledge at the last minute. It was the first of many surprises. After hearing over the next several months from well-placed friends like René Lévesque and Jean Marchand that he was not being considered for membership on the Commission, he was contacted by Marchand on behalf of Lamontagne asking how he would feel about serving. Soon after, following the Liberals' election victory in April, Pearson phoned him at Le Devoir and, acknowledging that he was the 'father' of the Commission idea, asked him to serve on it. The following day Lamontagne offered him the position of co-chairman. The purpose of his visit to the prime minister's residence in July was to discuss the terms of the

Commission's mandate and make-up before giving formal acceptance.[4]

Laurendeau anticipated an awkward meeting, partly because he had been known as a strong critic of the federal Liberals since the days of Mackenzie King, the Rowell-Sirois Commission, and the conscription crisis of the Second World War. Not long after Pearson became Liberal leader he had written: 'Mr. Pearson appears to be a statesman who is trying, without much success, to metamorphose into a politician. The party hasn't reformed itself. It hasn't succeeded in renewing its Quebec personnel. The "great [Quebec] lieutenant' hasn't appeared on the horizon.'[5] He certainly didn't consider Lamontagne, who was also present at the meeting and whom Pearson had recruited in Quebec, along with Maurice Tremblay, to renew the Liberals' prospects there, as someone who could fill the shoes of an Ernest Lapointe or a Louis St Laurent. While advising Quebec's voters to reject the Liberals in 1962, Laurendeau let it be known that he personally would not vote for Lamontagne in Outremont riding. He made it clear to Pearson now, moreover, that he would not surrender his editorial freedom at *Le Devoir* to become the proposed Commission's co-chairman, and that both the resources and the time necessary to investigate thoroughly the potential basis of a bilingual and bicultural partnership would have to be made available. Pearson agreed on all these points, even joking that Laurendeau would be free at *Le Devoir* to discuss matters such as the nuclear issue; this was a subtle jibe at his severe criticism of Pearson's earlier flip-flop on the question of whether to accept nuclear warheads for Canada's military. When it was all over, Laurendeau had mixed feelings about the meeting. He was pleased with the absence of rigidity, which he always anticipated from the federal government, but he was a little taken aback by the uncertain, pressured atmosphere:

> I felt a little dizzy, and I felt for the first time, along with a feeling of sympathy for Mr. Pearson, that in Ottawa it was possible on occasion to improvise, the way it's done in Quebec. I arrived there full of reverence for the federal administration, and I was a little disappointed with the 'amateur' way things were being set up.[6]

Why did the federal Liberals push forward with Laurendeau's idea of a federal inquiry, and why did Pearson choose him, of all people, to help run it? It is not too difficult to understand the purely political motives for Pearson's adoption of the proposal back in the autumn of 1962. It had been one thing, after all, for him to lose badly to Diefenbaker in 1958, allowing the Conservatives to make a historic breakthrough in Quebec: that could be blamed on the errors of his predecessors, the St Laurent team. Considering Diefenbaker's ham-handed dealings with his Quebec caucus and French Canada generally over the ensuing years, there was every reason to anticipate a reversion of the Liberals' traditional Quebec support at the next election. But in June of 1962 much of that support, twenty-six crucial seats, went instead to the Social Credit party, thereby allowing Diefenbaker to cling to power with a minority government. As the Liberals thought wistfully about what might have been and gazed down the opposition benches at those rustic interlopers, the Social Credit MPs, it was obvious that they needed a new strategy in Quebec.[7] As a result of separatist rhetoric, FLQ bombs, and the Lesage government's escalating demands for more fiscal power, English Canada was becoming increasingly aware of the explosive potential of the Quiet Revolution, and this awareness made it feasible to consider innovative, even radical initiatives. It became clear too, in November 1962—when Donald Gordon, the President of Canadian National Railways, raised a furore in Quebec by stating publicly that there weren't enough competent French Canadians to fill senior management positions—that the issue of bilingualism in the federal civil service would have to be addressed sooner rather than later.

Indeed, when Pearson came to power in 1963, at the head of another minority government, he was well aware of the impatience among the Canadian voting public. The fast-growing youth cohort, the 'now' generation, were especially contemptuous when it compared the reform-oriented pizzazz of the Kennedy administration in the United States with the indecisive leadership in Canada. While Diefenbaker suffered most from these comparisons, aging five years politically for every one he spent in office, Pearson's incurable bow-ties, chirping voice, and unprepossessing looks were anything but tailor-made for the new 'image' politics. He needed a winning program, and during the election campaign he promised 'sixty days' of decision immediately upon assuming office. The strategy got off to a rocky start, however, when his finance minister Walter Gordon presented an 'anti-American' budget that proved to be unsellable to the Canadian business community.[8] Pearson needed to get the momentum back, and the Bilingualism-Biculturalism Commission could help. The beauty of royal commissions, moreover, was that they took so long to embarrass you—or so it was said.

In his public speeches and, much later, his memoirs, Pearson quite naturally referred to his more idealistic reasons for appointing the Commission. He contended, for instance, that national unity was the linchpin issue of his political career, and that while it encompassed many fields, including the Constitution, federal-provincial relations, and tax-sharing, '. . . in the long run, I am convinced that the problems of culture and language are pre-eminent.' He added that the most critical cultural concern for him was 'the recognition of the French language.'[9] And that involved more than merely acknowledging the right of the minority to use its maternal tongue in certain special circumstances; it called for a far-reaching attempt to make French an 'equal language' in Canada. Recognizing that there were distinctly different French and English interpretations of what was meant historically by French linguistic and cultural rights, he sided with the French-Canadian view, which stressed the words 'equal' and 'partnership':

> To French-speaking Canadians confederation created a bilingual and bicultural nation. It protected their language and their culture throughout the whole of Canada. It meant partnership, not domination. French-speaking Canadians believed that this partnership meant equal opportunities for both the founding races to share in all phases of Canadian development.[10]

Pearson, it seems, genuinely believed that the creation of a cultural compact implied in this interpretation would not only ease the immediate tensions in Quebec stemming from the Quiet Revolution, but would also provide a framework for a unique, dualistic Canadian identity.

The Liberals' term in office coincided with an unprecedented outpouring of Canadian nationalism that was deeply rooted in a traditional fear of American domination. But in this period special attention was focused on American economic imperialism, which threatened Canada's independence far more than, say, the military aggression, under the cover of Cold War necessity, that the United States was inflicting on Vietnam. On the positive side, Canada's approaching centenary was arousing both a patriotic fervour and a rebirth of the old pastime of defining the Canadian identity. John Diefenbaker's neo-Macdonaldism, with its emphasis on renewing historic ties to Britain, left the massive wave of post-war immigrants to Canada cold and only aggravated French Canadians and the young who were on the side of decolonization. (The British certainly didn't care, since they were looking towards the Common Market.) The public yearned for more distinctive 'Canadian' symbols, and Pearson strove to accommodate them with the adoption of the maple leaf flag and the unification of the Canadian armed forces. At the same time, however, he was aware that both economic independence from the United States and a 'melting pot' identity (which would run counter to French Canada's rising aspirations) were unrealistic. The promotion of a bilingual and bicultural identity, on the other hand, offered the promise of uniqueness *vis-à-vis* the Americans and an expansive future for French Canada. If care was taken in getting English Canadians used to the idea, they would soon recognize benefits in the form of cultural enrichment, an identity distinct from that of the United States, and the prospect of an end to the 'Quebec problem'. A Royal Commission seemed just right for the purpose. 'This was to be the grand inquest into relations between Canada's two main language groups,' Pearson recalled in his memoirs, 'with the purpose of recommending measures to establish a better relationship in the future.'[11] And who could give the enterprise more credibility in French Canada than the nationalist intellectual, free of political ties, who had demanded it in the first place? From Pearson's point of view, persuading

André Laurendeau to become co-chairman was worth swallowing all of his previous editorial insults.

But while all of this helps to explain the federal government's motives, it leaves Laurendeau's decision unaccounted for. He had spent most of his career opposing one Canadian prime minister or another, and for decades his able pen had titillated French Canadians with barbs aimed at unprincipled politicians from Quebec who 'sold out' in Ottawa. His defence of provincial autonomy against what he saw as a continuous federal onslaught had remained firm even under the do-nothing Duplessis regime. Why then, when Quebec City was taking great new initiatives in so many areas while defending autonomy more aggressively than ever, would he be attracted to the federal level? At that very moment he was intensely involved in the purely provincial issue of educational reform and was prepared to quarrel with old Catholic friends to see it through. And he had recently been appointed to Quebec's new Arts Council, a position that offered the prospect of greater involvement in the cultural world for which he had always longed. What would his nationalist intimates think, especially those, like René Lévesque, whose good opinion he valued? Would they call him *vendu* behind his back? And what would this mean for his family? Could Francine, the radical *Québécoise* in Paris, be expected to understand? Ghislaine would have no illusions either about the amount of time he would have to spend away from Montreal. Even if he would be mostly in Ottawa, that was enemy territory; it meant living behind the lines and working with a federal bureaucracy that he, above all people, knew to be English in thought, word, and action. There was also *Le Devoir* to consider. He had spent sixteen years helping to turn it into an intelligent and respected nationalist voice, and only recently his partner in that task, Gérard Filion, had resigned, leaving an editorial board of three—Paul Sauriol, Claude Ryan, and himself—to run things. For him to go now would be chaotic. As he explained in his diary of 1965, 'My refusal was the only course possible in the context of the situation at Le Devoir.'[12] But didn't Ryan also have a point when he speculated that it would be difficult for the man who called for the Commission in the first place to refuse to serve on it?

With respect to this last question, Laurendeau was deeply concerned as to whether his original purpose could be fulfilled by joining such a Commission. How far would he and his colleagues be permitted to go in recommending fundamental changes? Would there be sufficient financial and human resources to undertake the extensive research that would almost certainly be required? What guarantee was there that the provinces would in fact co-operate in the vital educational sphere? And, still more to the point, how much faith could be put in the willingness of Pearson and Lamontagne to implement the Commission's recommendations? His distrust of politicians even led him to have contradictory thoughts. While he

had originally demanded and would continue to pursue the widest possible terms of reference for the Commission, he was also suspicious in the
early stages that the Liberals might simply be planning to make it into a
publicity exercise, a great chunk of face-saving fudge, as so often seemed
to be the fate of royal commissions. 'I even worry about the ambitiousness
of the inquiry Pearson wants to set up,' he conceded, 'and, always wary of
politicians, I wonder, if anything so vast isn't likely to fade away into generalities.'[13] He knew the Liberal party was notorious for its tactic of
absorbing rather than defeating its critics by offering them federal positions and taking only those of their ideas it deemed politically expedient.
He commented on the Liberals' duplicity towards French Canada in 1962,
before they adopted the idea of a Commission:

> These people know us better. They know how to talk to us. But basically
> they have exactly the same reservations. They showed themselves, in power,
> to be the greatest centralizers; now suddenly they are autonomists; does
> that inspire confidence in you? They are experts in the art of confusing the
> issue. They aren't the ones who would say 'no' to the idea of a Royal Com-
> mission on bilingualism; they will content themselves, politely, with not
> having one.[14]

Now that the Liberals were in office they were going to conduct an inquiry,
but for what reasons? Was René Lévesque onto something when he
pointed out that 'a commission reduces its participants to silence'?[15]
Hadn't Lamontagne previously offered Laurendeau a seat on the Canada
Council?

With so many questions to consider, Laurendeau decided to consult
widely among his friends and associates. He started off with his colleagues at Le Devoir, telling them that he had no intention of accepting, but
would simply lead Lamontagne along in good journalistic style to see how
far the Liberals were prepared to go. But, as he reported in his diary, everyone there was 'favourable; or rather, no one could see how I could
refuse.'[16] Meeting René Lévesque at a Chinese restaurant, he found that
Lévesque had made a list on one side of a napkin of reasons why it was a
bad idea to accept, and on the other side he appeared to have jotted
down the one positive result he could foresee: 'Laurendeau could resign
with a bang.'[17] Lévesque was not the only one who argued that the way for
Quebec to get what it wanted was by pursuing federal-provincial negotiations, not by trying to reform the federal bureaucracy along linguistic
lines or pretending that English Canadians would embrace biculturalism.

In late June, Laurendeau met at Quebec City with Léon Dion, who was
a fairly recent confidant, and several Laval professors. Their attitude was
lukewarm, with Jean-Charles Falardeau, a prominent academic figure in
the Quiet Revolution, stating that he for one was tired of reaching out to
English Canada. Later that evening, at Jean Marchand's place near Cap

Rouge, Laurendeau sat admiring the beautiful setting, almost forgetting his reason for being there. Also present were Claude Morin and Michel Bélanger, both of whom were destined to play key roles in Quebec-Canada relations in the decades to follow. Although Marchand was hesitant, Laurendeau recalled the Quebec visit as the moment when he decided to accept the co-chairmanship: 'My decision became final at Quebec.'[18] Ironically, both Marchand and Dion would later join the Commission as well. If Laurendeau's family seemed to play a marginal role in his decision (though they would have much to say about it after his death), it was perhaps partly because his two oldest children, Francine and Jean, were in France, while Ghislaine was the type who spoke her own mind and then supported whatever he decided. No doubt Jean was correct when, in a letter to his father of 16 April 1963, he touched upon Laurendeau's irrepressible idealism as a prime motivation:

> The more I think about it the more I like this idea of an inquiry on biculturalism. . . . I suppose that for you this must be the biggest thing, or, as one says in music, the 'solo of your life' . . . , 'the role of your life'. . . . the thing that would please you the most while serving the greatest number.[19]

Although Laurendeau never did get the opportunity, beyond his diary entries and personal letters, to explain his decision in detail—the way he did with respect to his role in the conscription crisis of the Second World War in a book published in this very year, 1963—he did offer a brief accounting to the readers of *Le Devoir* on 23 July, the day after the official announcement of his appointment. He drew particular attention to the balanced linguistic make-up of the Commission, with its two co-chairmen representing French and English Canada, three French-Canadian and three English-Canadian commissioners, and two New Canadians, one of whom was French- and the other English-speaking. This he regarded as a good sign for advancing the idea of equality. 'As I see it,' he explained, 'the commission's job comes down to studying and trying to resolve, in the basic area of language and culture, the problem of the friendly co-existence of the "two nations".' He reassured readers that while his activity at the newspaper would be reduced, 'the main thing is that I have no intention of leaving for exile far from my own people. I want to maintain connections with life here. I am accepting the commission's charge unreservedly . . . but I am not "emigrating".' It seems clear that Laurendeau's fundamental motivation, despite his numerous misgivings and fears, stemmed from his sincere belief that the Commission offered an opportunity to begin a process whereby French Canadians could achieve linguistic and cultural equality in Canada. 'What is at stake,' he wrote, 'is the destiny of a people.'[20] Moreover, the one-step-removed-from-politics character of the Commission suited his desire for a true dialogue between English and French Canada—something he had believed to be impossible in politics ever since leaving the Quebec legislature in 1948. The prospect of digging in and doing the sort of research that was needed, of both the personal and the scientific type, also appealed to him intellectually. He wanted to be more convinced himself of the potential for a bilingual-bicultural Canadian identity, and then to convince others with proofs in hand. Having always believed that Confederation's failings were due more to ignorance than to malice, he relished the chance to do something concrete in the area of public education. 'I have been fighting for equality now for thirty years,' he reminded Le Devoir's readers, 'I have been calling for an investigation since January 1962. . . . I believe in it. I am diving in.'[21]

Laurendeau paid for his decision. To begin with, it alienated a number of nationalists. Paul Lacoste, who became co-secretary of the Commission and later a commissioner himself, described various nationalist responses: 'the polite scepticism of some, the sarcasm of others, the accusation of deserting nationalism.'[22] André had expected such reactions; nor were they entirely unprecedented. He had been parting company with fellow nationalists ever since the late 1930s: the extremists at La Nation, maverick politicians in the Bloc Populaire, conservative traditionalists after the war, Duplessists in the 1950s, separatists and ultra-Catholics in more recent days. If a few more could not grasp that he was going to Ottawa to pursue, not abandon, the nationalist cause, so be it. Father Georges-Henri Lévesque, who had suffered similar criticism when he joined the federal Massey Commission on the arts in 1949, had warned him it wouldn't be easy.[23] But the obvious distrust of long-time friends like Abbé Groulx and François-Albert Angers was harder to bear. He wrote to Groulx in 1965, drawing attention to the fact that they rarely communicated: 'Perhaps I also believed that you don't agree with the role that for the last year and a half I have felt I must play. . . . I hope to see you again despite the evolution in my thinking—not on nationalist ground but by returning to the artistic ambitions of my youth.'[24]

In 1964 Laurendeau felt compelled to resign from the Ligue de l'Action Nationale, after more than three decades, because of his ideological differences with Angers in particular. '. . . I've given too much of my life to this work to leave it with a light heart. But the divergences in thought . . . have become so strong and so constant that it seems to me quite ridiculous to belong to a movement that holds several central ideas at opposite poles from mine.'[25] Even those who supported him, like J.-P. Desbiens, could not help expressing certain doubts. Although Brother Anonymous, ever the satirist, teased him—'After Lafontaine-Baldwin, Cartier-Macdonald, Rowell-Sirois, Massey-Lévesque . . . , there will be Laurendeau-Dunton. They'll talk about you in the history books'—in a more serious tone he stated that bilingualism wasn't as easy as it looked in Switzerland, where there was at least an equilibrium in numbers. In Canada it seemed utterly utopian. The Swiss had only to drive an hour in any direction to get some practice in another language; but what of people in Winnipeg or Vancouver? In his view there were only about five years remaining to stem the tide of separatism, and he doubted that the Bilingualism and Biculturalism Commission would be enough. 'You don't patch up a house in such danger. You rebuild beside it, and differently.'[26]

In the years ahead Laurendeau would have good cause to recall the reservations voiced by his friends. But he began the great enterprise with high hopes; and having made his decision he would persevere. During the summer of 1963 he kept in frequent touch with Lamontagne, who was clearly the politician in charge, and with his English-speaking co-chairman Davidson Dunton concerning the staffing and official launching of the Commission. Although he knew Dunton, a fellow journalist and former chairman of the CBC, only vaguely, he soon came to have a high regard for him. Nor was this merely a public posture designed to maintain harmony. As he observed in his diary: 'I found Mr Dunton to be truly an ideal co-chairman, and still find him a pleasure to work with. Of course, a joint chairmanship is a difficult task . . . ; this being said, I couldn't have dreamt of a better colleague. . . .'[27] Most of those associated with the Commission appear to agree that, considering the serious problems they encountered, they were fortunate to have such compatible, even-tempered, and remarkably patient leaders.[28] While the co-chairmen were, in Laurendeau's words, 'neither one the assistant, nor the associate of the other',[29] he was named Chief Executive Officer, and by dint of this, as well as his prodigious capacity for work, he became the more-than-equal-partner. It would be going too far to agree with the remark of one commissioner that 'it was Laurendeau's Commission'[30]—especially after 1965, when he lost his share of the internal political battles—but it is true that at times he seemed to be keeping things on track through the force of his will alone. He also had a say, at his meeting with Pearson on 11 July, in naming the other commissioners. This was a very delicate balancing act, as Pearson recalled later: 'It was a difficult Royal Commission to organise. The problems were analogous to those of selecting a Canadian cabinet. As with a jigsaw puzzle, it was imperative to put the right people in the right place.'[31] By the 'right people', he meant at minimum a group of bilingual commissioners who had an appreciation of both 'founding cultures' and who were prepared to devote a good deal of their time, over a period of what most expected be two or three years, not only studying the issues but extolling the potential benefits of bilingualism and biculturalism. Whatever the rhetoric for public consumption about the 'investigative nature' and 'learning' aspects of the Commission's work, it was assumed that the commissioners, like the government, supported the concept.

Laurendeau discussed the Commission's composition with Pearson at their meeting in Ottawa on 11 July. It is not clear just how much leverage he had with the politicians in this matter and they of course had their own

priorities. Certainly he was familiar with two French-Canadian nomi-
nees—Jean Marchand, leader of the CNTU Quebec union and someone
he regarded as a personal friend; and Jean-Louis Gagnon, a journalist-
editor whom he credited with having made a quality newspaper out of
Montreal's French-language daily *La Presse*.[32] Laurendeau pointed out to
Lamontagne that the three of them would give the Commission a very
left-wing appearance 'since Jean Marchand, Jean-Louis Gagnon and I
had, without much effort, acquired that reputation.' It was a relief, therefore, that Father Maurice Cormier, an Acadian who was first President of
the University of Moncton, was also available, for his 'priestly attire
would cover us all'.[33] He commented further in his diary that he did not
know the English members: Royce Frith, a long-time Liberal party sup
porter from Ontario; Gertrude Laing, a professor from Alberta and the
only woman on the Commission or, indeed, in its upper bureaucratic
echelon; and F.R. Scott, the poet, McGill professor, and former president
of the League for Social Reconstruction during the 1930s.

In Scott's case, Laurendeau appears to have overlooked their period of
contact just prior to the Second World War. Perhaps their relations then
were more those of fellow members in a group, rather than one-on-one;
perhaps he was trying to repress the memory of his profound disappointment with Scott and the other English-speaking members of that circle over
their failure to stand shoulder to shoulder with him against Canadian
participation when war broke out. The final two members were Professor
Paul Wyczynski, a literary expert on French-Canadian culture from the
University of Ottawa, and J.B. Rudnyckyj, Professor of Slavic Studies at
the University of Manitoba and a rather obvious representative of what
the commissioners referred to as Canada's 'ethnic groups'. Laurendeau
was very satisfied with the Commission's linguistic balance and its general
sensibility towards French Canada, joking privately that 'during those
first months it was often said that the commission was made up of
francophones and francophiles'.[34] For the moment he was less concerned
about the strong centralist bias of English-Canadian members like Scott,
which would become a factor in the Commission's internal debates.

As Chief Executive Officer Laurendeau was responsible overall for the
day-to-day functioning of the Commission, and all the more so during
those periods when other key members such as Dunton, Marchand, and
Gagnon found themselves heavily engaged with their regular jobs. He
therefore had considerably more input than others into the selection of the
committee's senior staff and he worked closely with the latter in establishing agendas and internal policy and in directing research. Commission
members flying from great distances were at times reduced, after some
perfunctory questioning, to rubber-stamping the plans of the inner corps.
There were two Commission secretaries. That one was French- and one
English-speaking goes almost without saying in this world of exquisite

balancing: Paul Lacoste, a philosophy and law professor at the Université de Montréal, as well as a television moderator at the CBC, where Laurendeau first met him; and Neil Morrison, one-time Director of Public Affairs at the CBC and, in 1963, Dean of Atkinson College at Toronto's York University. Morrison could be described as Laurendeau's first English-Canadian friend, dating back to the late 1930s, and while he maintained in his diary that Morrison's name simply came up, he must have leaped at the chance to appoint such a strong anglophone ally. The other two personalities who loomed large at the staff level in the days that followed were the Co-Directors of Research, Léon Dion and Michael Oliver, who having recently completed a term as President of the NDP was hired in December 1963 to run what would become a veritable research industry; it seems Oliver was appointed because Lacoste and Morrison could not work well together.[35] Considering the nature of Laurendeau's previous ties to Dion, Lacoste, Morrison, Marchand, and Gagnon, it's not difficult to see why some people considered it to be his commission. As someone who valued long-term acquaintanceship, especially at the intellectual level, he probably could not have hoped for a better team. This, however, was not in itself a guarantee of success.

Laurendeau missed the Commission's first meeting, on 5 September 1963, because of illness and met his fellow commissioners collectively for the first time from 16 to 19 September. Although the Commissioner-General of Montreal's Expo '67 offered his organization's well-appointed meeting hall at Place Ville Marie for their meetings,[36] Dunton and Laurendeau chose the politically safer course and spent their first several months at the decidedly 'uncomfortable' Daly Building, opposite Ottawa's Château Laurier Hotel. The first meetings were concerned chiefly with defining the Commission's mandate clearly, launching its research program, and deciding how best to pursue their initial goal of consulting Canadians about their views on bilingualism and biculturalism. With regard to the mandate, the commissioners began with the Minute of the Privy Council passed on 19 July 1963, establishing their terms of reference, and authorizing them to:

> Inquire into and report upon the existing state of bilingualism and biculturalism in Canada and to recommend what steps should be taken to develop the Canadian Confederation on the basis of an equal partnership between the two founding races, taking into account the contribution made by the other ethnic groups to the cultural enrichment of Canada and the measures that should be taken to safeguard that contribution.[37]

This was a broad mandate indeed, and the commissioners had immediate problems defining some of the terms. Laurendeau and Dunton would have to meet again with Pearson on 23 November to seek clarifications. The Commission preferred, for example, to use the phrase 'two founding peoples' rather than 'races' in referring to the 'undisputed role played by Canadians of French and English origin in 1867, and long before Confederation'. Although this phrasing largely ignored the role of aboriginal peoples, a more acute concern in the mentality of the 1960s was how and on what basis to include the non-British and non-French peoples that the Commission lumped together under the name 'ethnic groups'. It wouldn't take long for these minorities within English-speaking Canada to make it clear they would not be so easily disposed of. The Commission also clarified early on what it considered to be the key element in its investigation: 'Language is the most evident expression of culture, the one which most readily distinguishes cultural groups. . . . In terms of our mandate, this statement means that the problems of bilingualism and biculturalism are inseparably linked.'[38]

For Laurendeau, however, the pivotal word in the Commission's terms of reference was 'equality'. It was for this that he had made the leap of faith and come to Ottawa. He therefore took the lead in pressing for as broad and unfettered a definition as possible, so that the Commission could enter any sphere that might relate to linguistic or cultural equality. His influence was apparent in the Commission's assertion that

> What we are aiming for . . . is the equal partnership of all who speak either language and participate in either culture, whatever their ethnic origin. For us the principle of equal partnership takes priority over all historical and legal considerations, regardless of how interesting and important such considerations may be.[39]

Laurendeau was particularly adamant in underlining the urgency of finding ways to achieve this equality. Having emerged from the hothouse of Quebec's Quiet Revolution, he stressed that a federal response to the threat of separatism, including the Commission's contribution, had to be produced expeditiously—within two or three years. For him, as indeed for Pearson, the Commission was driven by the 'Quebec problem'. That was one reason why the commissioners launched an ambitious research program to run parallel with rather than follow upon their own first-phase activities. It was a program that would be expanded again and again, finally becoming the tail that wagged the dog. Because the research was so expensive (it eventually cost more than $3,000,000, an unprecedented sum for any Canadian Royal Commission) and because it was the major reason the Commission took so long to report, it became a subject of unending controversy.

It is sufficient to point out here that while Laurendeau was by no means solely responsible for the magnitude of the Commission's research program (seven broad categories, with ten section heads under the supervision of Oliver and Dion), he did establish the flexible parameters that allowed it to grow. From his first meetings with Lamontagne—when he had the advantage of knowing he was being courted—he insisted that sufficient research funds would have to be made available to do a proper job. He was well aware that in some of the areas that the Commission would be investigating there was no information available, and if all he wanted to produce was 'impressions', he could have done that on the telephone at *Le Devoir*. According to Laurendeau, Lamontagne's response was, 'No limit!' In his meeting with Pearson on 11 July 1963 he reiterated the point and Pearson was swift to agree. Later, in fact, he recalled putting the prime minister to the test on that occasion by successfully arguing that it would be necessary to investigate large companies where the two languages met face to face and where there was friction: 'In this way, in the twinkling of an eye, we added at least a million dollars to our research budget.'[40] As Paul Lacoste observed, looking back on the Commission's research activity, 'on this point, Laurendeau was intractable, maintaining his intellectual rigour in the face of all objection.'[41] And yet Laurendeau was also suspicious of scientific researchers and number crunchers: 'I'm a believer in the religion of research . . . which is honest and disinterested —but I'm not a believer in every opinion of the researchers: . . . especially when new disciplines are involved, science contradicts itself.'[42] There were times when he chose to disregard some of the Commission's research and other times when he deliberately excluded the scientific contingent from policy deliberations.[43] Even those who worked closely with him were not always able to assess the impact that the results of some research projects had on his views. The charges, by critics of the Commission, that on most issues his mind was already made up before he began were unfounded, but it does seem that he gave at least equal weight to the episodic, highly personal observations he gained from the Commission's meetings and hearings.

These meetings—the result of the Commission's determination to consult widely—occurred between January 1964 and November 1966 and consisted of three separate types. As a first important measure it was decided that delegations, with the co-chairmen always present, should visit each of the provincial premiers to gauge how they felt about the Commission's mandate; whether or not they were likely to co-operate in providing educational and, in some cases, civil-service data; and, of course, how serious they considered the threat of assimilation to be for the linguistic minorities in their own jurisdictions. These meetings also quite frequently involved sessions with selected 'interested parties' in each provincial capital. The second type were regional meetings, twenty-three of them from March to June 1964, that allowed more than 11,000 people to voice opinions and to answer specifically the primary question: whether these two peoples, English and French, had the ability and the willingness to live together. The commissioners split up for these hearings and different teams criss-crossed the country in what became an exhausting marathon. Finally, in 1965-66, public hearings were held at which more formal briefs were presented by individuals and especially organizations. Although he hated the travel, the boredom, and the terrible parochialism he encountered everywhere during the regional meetings, in the end he saw them as the most worthwhile exercise:

> Have I stressed elsewhere an important aspect of these trips we make? In a short space of time, we come into contact with a large number of individuals, we hear many things that touch and move us, often in contradictory ways, and the next day the same experience begins again in a new place. It is exactly like being subjected to machine gun fire. It's easy to see why the weaker members give in immediately, and why the stronger ones go through moments of great emotion. It's rough going for everyone, and at the same time I believe it is profoundly useful.
>
> This form of inquiry has no scientific value: it is impossible for us to take true samples of opinion, and thus our meetings are based on incomplete facts. . . .[44]

The public hearings, on the other hand, came close to being a colossal waste of time what he referred to privately as 'a necessary evil'.[45]

The sessions with the ten premiers, which began with Duff Roblin in Manitoba and ended with W.A.C. Bennett in British Columbia, proved to be both depressing and mind-altering with respect to Laurendeau's conception of English Canada. He found most of them unimpressive as individuals, narrow-minded on language and cultural issues, and in most cases concerned only with how the Commission might impinge on their turf. Stanley Lloyd of Saskatchewan seemed open-minded and aware, Robert Stanfield of Nova Scotia was impressive intellectually, and Joey Smallwood of Newfoundland was gracious and co-operative. But the leaders of the larger English-Canadian provinces were much less forthcoming. Of Roblin Laurendeau wrote, '[He] will do all he can for cultural equality in Canada, but . . . he will carefully measure the implications of each of his acts; and . . . in the final analysis, unless there is a major change in the cultural climate, he won't be able to do much.'[46] Ernest Manning of Alberta, straight-laced and self-important, was by far the worst: 'What we have to say doesn't interest him in the slightest. He recognizes the existence of a grave and dramatic crisis in Quebec . . . and moves on to other subjects.' Manning clearly believed that the Commission would cause more problems than it solved. Bennett too appeared pleasantly uninterested and uninformed and firmly believed that French-speakers in his province had no major problems.[47]

Ontario's John Robarts was the most disappointing of all. He had acquired a reputation for willingness to quietly improve the lot of French Canadians in his province, but Laurendeau found him dull, practical, and unquestioning. He was not someone to be counted on for brave symbolic gestures that would really help the cause of bilingualism, such as making

French an official language in Ontario: 'He is typically "English", he controls the conversation and reacts very little; one doesn't get through to him, or else he hides it. . . . On the human level, he's someone with whom I wouldn't know what to exchange: but the problem doesn't exist because he gives almost nothing of himself.'[48] Although each of the premiers pledged his co-operation, Laurendeau was convinced that they didn't believe there was a national crisis; to the extent that they did recognize a serious problem, they thought it should be handled by the political leaders of Quebec and the federal government. As for the French minorities, they were just fine, thank-you.

These impressions were driven home with greater force in the sessions with academics, businessmen, and journalists, arranged in conjunction with visits to the premiers, as well as at the regional meetings. As Laurendeau stated after one seance with some western businessmen, '. . . you'd think the Commission was creating an artificial problem, and that French is fated to disappear . . . that biculturalism is an old quarrel between Ontario and Quebec and that's the end of it.'[49] Such opinions were magnified the farther west he went. Laurendeau had negative comments to make about the Maritime provinces too: notably, their complacency with respect to the sad state of Acadian minorities and their 'astonishing' provincialism.[50] But it was in the Canadian west that his hopes plummeted. He had been to Winnipeg in 1939 and, as we have seen, he had visited the rest of the western provinces in 1955. On the latter occasion he had written a good deal about the jaundiced western view of French Canada. But he was still unprepared for the degrees of ignorance and mindless ill-will he encountered in the public hearings there:

> Provincialism is strong everywhere. They call themselves Canadians, but they look at things first and foremost as Albertans and Manitobans. The only way to make any headway with them is to remind them that they *are* Canadians, that Quebec is part of Canada, and that if separatism split the country apart they would feel the effect.[51]

Indeed, Laurendeau commented several times in the personal diary he kept during his travels for the Commission that separatism was a valuable thing if only for use in cutting through the complacency and blindness of English Canada with regard to the problems threatening the country as a whole. He was required to explain again and again that bilingualism did not mean everyone would be forced to speak French; that its main thrust was to make it possible for French-speaking citizens to deal with the country's institutions in their own language and to ensure fair treatment for the French minorities where their numbers warranted. He was distraught when the media, whose representatives he found with few exceptions to be ill-prepared, small-minded and lazy, failed to explain this point, but seized instead on isolated statements by 'maniacs' and professional whiners who of course could not be prevented from also having their say before the Commission. There were plenty of these types in Quebec too, he admitted; but how could anyone take them seriously or expect to build a reasonable national consensus out of such material?

When he had an opportunity to reflect more deeply on the situation in the Canadian west, Laurendeau dwelt heavily on the threat posed to English Canada by the United States. Upon leaving Vancouver in 1965, he wrote, '[We are] much more convinced that English Canada, especially British Columbia, is going through a crisis of which we are only a secondary part: the big problem is the United States.'[52] The American cultural threat to French Canada had been a seminal theme in his own thinking since the late 1930s. His vision of biculturalism was grounded in the idea that there was another nation, called English Canada, with its own distinct identity and therefore its own solid reasons for working with French Canada to resist the American onslaught. Prior to the creation of the Commission he had been distressed to read that, according to the celebrated English Canadian journalist and historian Pierre Berton, French Canada was the main thing that English Canadians had to distinguish them from Americans:

I must admit my uneasiness on reading these lines. For us to be the sole source of originality for the rest of the country makes even less sense than Canada without Quebec. When one social group can define itself only in terms of its relation to another group, that means that the first party doesn't really exist. As for the second, it's like feeling the hand of a drowning man clutching your shoulder.[53]

But his travels now were confirming that English Canada's identity was indeed fuzzy. It became apparent that the so-called 'ethnic groups', particularly the Ukrainians, saw themselves as part of English Canada linguistically but not culturally. Culturally they considered themselves to be vibrant minorities in their own right, with claims the equal at least of French Canada's. For this reason they were often stronger opponents of biculturalism than were anglophones of British origin. It seemed to be the sad case, as Laurendeau had earlier speculated, that English Canadians, especially in the west, became more unified in opposition to French Canada. 'It is possible to imagine that to protect itself against the troubles in Quebec, English Canada might forge a new sense of unity and learn to define itself. . . . Then we would have *someone to talk to*.'[54]

Laurendeau was so dismayed by the negative views and lack of understanding in English Canada, which sometimes degenerated into personal attacks, that he was forced to wrestle with his own separatist feelings:

> On the one hand, English Canada is more involved in the discussion than we had foreseen; and that is excellent. For the moment, its negativism is much in evidence: a negativism about the Commission, which doesn't matter much, but also in many cases a refusal of French Canada itself. . . . I feel several times each week, and even several times a day, real inner urges towards separatism. These are elementary reactions, of an emotive character, to which I don't pay more than passing attention. But the density and the depth of the ignorance and prejudice are truly immeasurable, and even if the sociologists could explain to us the reasons for such things, the fact remains that they are difficult to accept and to live with.[55]

These feelings passed when the regional meetings reached Quebec and the real separatists were encountered up close. Laurendeau's anglophone colleagues were shocked. At the Sherbrooke meeting, for instance, they witnessed first-hand the degree of frustration among French-speaking Quebeckers who were obliged for economic reasons to learn and speak English in the province where they constituted the majority—a long-term problem that had led many of them to favour unilingualism. Their testimony also led the Commissioners to wonder how a strong base could be sustained in Quebec to nurture the wider influence of the French language and culture. It came as a blow for some of the anglophone commissioners to have to confront the apparent need for unilingual policies in Quebec to achieve this goal.

In Chicoutimi, an emerging separatist stronghold, and in Quebec City the French-Canadian commissioners were vilified as *vendus* by radicals and separatists who loudly dominated the meetings. Laurendeau, who had been called a traitor before, was not unduly upset. In fact, during these years on the Commission he continued to carry on a dialogue with separatists and at one point met with the editors of the left-wing journal *parti pris*. He also corresponded with Pierre Vallières, a revolutionary propagandist linked to the FLQ and author of *White Niggers of America*, when Vallières was jailed with Charles Gagnon at the United Nations in New York for protesting Quebec's 'oppression'.[56] He wished, as always, to keep in touch with all shades of Quebec opinion. But the fierce confrontational rhetoric of the Quebec meetings did go a long way towards convincing his fellow commissioners (those who still required convincing) that Canada was in a state of crisis and that much of its citizenry, in English Canada especially, was deaf to the danger.

Hence at a meeting on 4 September 1964 the Commission decided to issue a preliminary report that would outline the nature of the crisis and point towards the recommendations to come in subsequent volumes. This idea had been in the air for some months, with Laurendeau one of those favouring an interim report tied to a specific topic (the Army), which would dramatically illustrate the degree of linguistic and cultural discrimination against French Canadians in the civil service. But the sense now of a broader, more immediate crisis seemed to call for a general report focusing on the need for dramatic actions. Pearson, at the head of a minority government that seemed to stagger from crisis to crisis, needed something clear-cut and tough-minded from the Commission to justify his flexible policies toward Quebec in the cause of national survival. He let it be known he would like to have a preliminary report.[57]

There were other pressures too. Criticism from several sources, politicians and the media being front and centre, was building with respect to the Commission's costs and the projected time required to produce recommendations based on its research. Here again, a preliminary report would take some of the pressure off. Although some of the research staff, Oliver in particular, were reluctant to issue a document that would draw many of its conclusions from the highly subjective impressions gained at the regional meetings,[58] Laurendeau and a majority of the commissioners felt that the problems would be outweighed by the report's shock value. Laurendeau, who wrote some sections himself and supervised the report's preparation, agreed that its title should be 'The Canadian Crisis'. This decision angered Pearson, who said there was no precedent for giving a title to a Royal Commission report and who clearly feared the inevitable accusations from John Diefenbaker that he had simply manufactured a politically motivated justification for his policies. Even so, when Dunton and Laurendeau presented the document to him on 11 February, he called it 'a good report, though somewhat gloomy. . . .' Laurendeau wrote in his diary: 'I got the impression that he found our analysis lucid, but he's not unaware that this lucidity may cause him some problems.'[59]

This was a certainty, not only because of the preliminary report's graphic portrayal of a Canada in crisis—an idea that had serious doubters, and not just among federal politicians—but because its analysis and recommendations seemed to be based on what was described during the 1960s as the 'two nations' theory. This theory was rooted in the notion that the two languages and cultures described in the Commission's mandate actually constituted two nations, both of which had to be represented equally in federal institutions and enshrined across the country in education, the media, and legislative protection of English and French minorities. While it was always a point of dispute as to where the differences lay between 'culture', 'nation' and 'national culture', the report was aggressive in advancing the view that the bilingual-bicultural ideal was the key to solving the crisis, even though the Commission had found a very limited basis for that view in reality.[60]

Laurendeau had cause to be both pleased and pained by the reaction to the interim report. The fact that it proved an overnight best-seller (for a government publication), eliciting widespread media and political comment, was an indication that it had achieved its primary goal of awakening the country to the problems at hand. A substantial cross-section of opinion, moreover, was positive—strongly so in French Canada, with a somewhat broader mix of praise and criticism in English Canada. Several provincial premiers seemed to feel that it had done a sound job of analyzing the 'what' and the 'why' of Quebec's and Canada's crisis of cultural identity; they would suspend further judgement until the Commission offered more specific recommendations on 'how' to remedy the situation. But while the critics were in the minority, they were loud and effective. Diefenbaker, not surprisingly, dismissed the report as a collection of 'generalities and platitudes' that offered no solutions. The criticisms that wounded Laurendeau most, however, were those that implied it was a 'French Canadian report'. Some of the western newspapers, for instance, suggested that the Commission was manufacturing a crisis atmosphere where none really existed before, all because of the troubles in Quebec; worse still, it was trying to change the country's cultural make-up artificially and at unconscionable expense. For most of these observers there were neither two nations nor two equal cultures in Canada, but one predominantly English-speaking culture with a significant French minority in Quebec that might or might not be given special privileges to placate it, but that should not be raised up, at the expense of other minorities, to the level of an equal partner in a dual culture. Charles Lynch, in the *Ottawa Citizen*, charged that the French-Canadian commissioners had won out and that the Commission should therefore have been called 'Laurendeau and Co.'.[61] There were high-ranking civil servants who were rumoured to feel this way too, and who clearly resented the Commission's expansion of its mandate into a state-of-the-nation formula. Laurendeau wrote in his diary on 9 March 1965:

> All this makes the possibilities look pretty bleak as far as eventual implementation of the recommendations of the final report by the central government is concerned. But what strikes me the most is that a presentation, in which we've all tried to be objective, should be considered a priori a French-Canadian victory—a victory in the strictest sense of the term, that is, where some forces win out over others, all questions of convictions aside.[62]

Although a complete history of the Bilingualism and Biculturalism Commission has yet to be written, the partial studies produced so far, along with the personal reminiscences of participants, suggest that 1965 was a turning-point. Difficulties arising outside and inside the Commission not only undercut its importance as a vehicle for the resolution of Canada's identity crisis, but reduced its ability to move beyond the preliminary report's brave diagnosis to the production of the six volumes of analysis and recommendations that were supposed to offer a cure. The Commission lost its *élan vital*, its permanent staff began to drift off, and it acquired the reputation of an expensive 'white elephant'. Although in view of the Commission's long-term contributions, this criticism was unjustified, it affected Laurendeau deeply. His deteriorating health, his increasingly preoccupied state of mind, and his almost manic work habits all suggested a bleak awareness that the preliminary report might well be the climax of the Commission's work, to be followed by an interminable unravelling. Even Pearson, who had been a solid supporter throughout, became more critical, urging both Dunton and Laurendeau to make haste and get it over with. At the Commission itself there was more talk about the wonderful legacy of research it would leave to posterity and less about its transforming institutional and cultural impact in the near future. In fact, the whole idea of a cultural solution to Canada's internal problems was now beginning to decline in relation to the more traditional emphasis on political and constitutional negotiations between governments.

This change in the political climate in the latter part of the 1960s was the most important of several factors contributing to the demoralization of the Commission and, coincidentally, of André Laurendeau. It is worth recalling that he came out of Quebec's Quiet Revolution of the early sixties convinced that if there was to be a Canadian answer to French-speaking Quebec's aspirations, two fundamental changes were required. The first and most important to him, we have seen, was the sort of cultural initiative undertaken by the Commission. The second was the negotiation of greater autonomy for Quebec. Because he was a cultural nationalist first and foremost, he chose the Bilingualism and Biculturalism Commission as his field of action, but he continued to observe and speak regularly with those involved in the seemingly endless battles between the Lesage government, especially its nationalist point man René Lévesque, and the federal government over what came to be known as 'special status' for Quebec. One of Laurendeau's greatest sacrifices in serving on the Commission was, precisely as Lévesque had predicted, the ethical responsibility it imposed on him to refrain from writing about this subject, which had been so important to him for decades. He did write articles for Le Devoir and he continued his monthly article for Le Magazine Maclean, but the topics he discussed were esoteric ones in which, he maintained, neither he nor his readers were interested.[63] He was a political journalist who could not write about politics at the very moment when Quebec's constitutional future seemed to be at stake.

One reason Laurendeau had believed, in 1963, that the time was ripe for long-term solutions on both the cultural and constitutional fronts was Pearson's commitment to what he called 'co-operative federalism'. Unlike Diefenbaker—who had not understood, let alone been willing to give in to, Quebec's autonomist demands—Pearson seemed determined on a more flexible approach. The prime minister explained the rationale for his policy this way:

> While I judged that there could be no special status for any one province . . .
> I was prepared to make substantial concessions to Quebec (and to the other
> provinces) in the interests of national unity. . . . By forcing a centralism
> perhaps acceptable to some provinces but not to Quebec, and by insisting that
> Quebec must be like the others, we could destroy Canada. This became my
> doctrine of federalism, I wanted to decentralize up to a certain point. . . .[64]

Some analysts have maintained that Laurendeau intended to take advantage of this position by using the Commission to recommend new constitutional arrangements for Quebec that would go beyond the issues of language and culture. Claude Ryan, who was consulted when Laurendeau was deciding whether to join the Commission, has argued that this was on his mind from the beginning and that he would not have accepted otherwise.[65] It is true that Laurendeau half hoped and half anticipated that constitutional matters would be dealt with. He had a number of disagreements with F.R. Scott in particular whenever the issue arose. But it is also true that in the early going it was not something he insisted upon. There was no bristling threat to resign placed on the table. Rather, as Dunton explained to Pearson in Laurendeau's presence in 1964, 'We have always interpreted our mandate in the following way: we aren't primarily a constitutional commission; but if our subject leads in that direction, we'll go into it as far as we can.'[66] While Pearson agreed, it was clearly not his intention that the Commission should venture far in this direction; certainly not so far as to usurp the politicians' role. As some analysts have pointed out, the only commissioner with any constitutional background was Scott, and he was the one most opposed to the idea.

Nevertheless, Laurendeau became more determined on this course as his discouragement concerning the prospects for bilingualism and biculturalism grew. His vision of two vigorous national cultures existing cooperatively within one federal state depended upon a strong and autonomous Quebec as the foundation for the French national culture. This loomed as a more important priority as the hostility in English Canada accumulated at the regional meetings. It was after those meetings that the Commission decided to move decisively into the constitutional field, intending to devote the final volume of its report, Volume VI, to this topic. As Laurendeau wrote in his diary:

> We made a decision to extend the field of research into the area of the Constitution, because less extensive reform may no longer be adequate to deal with the situation. This corresponds to my own personal belief from the beginning, one that I brought up several times, but men like Dunton and Scott resisted it more or less. . . .[67]

Paul Lacoste, the co-secretary who became a commissioner when Jean Marchand resigned to run in the federal election of 1965, has written that Laurendeau felt unable as co-chairman to carry on this struggle in too partisan a manner, but urged him privately to do so.[68] Laurendeau's major written contribution to the Commission's work, following the preliminary report, was his authorship of what became known as the 'blue pages' at the beginning of Volume I, which, while not exactly a minority report on the issue, did point to the need for constitutional change in the political as well as the cultural sphere.

But just as Laurendeau was feeling compelled to follow this path, even if it meant confrontation with his fellow commissioners, the Liberal government became less flexible in the constitutional field. Its clear majority in the election of November 1965 reduced Pearson's acute vulnerability to parliamentary criticism, especially the withering bombast of Diefenbaker. It also reduced the Commission's value as an indication that the government was dealing with the nation's problems. More significantly, the Liberals' Quebec caucus took on an entirely new look as Lamontagne was unceremoniously dropped from the cabinet and Quebec's 'three wise men'—Jean Marchand, Gérard Pelletier, and Pierre Elliott Trudeau—arrived to become Pearson's new advisers on French Canada. Laurendeau knew them all well, of course, and still met with them occasionally in Montreal up to 1965. But Pelletier and especially Trudeau had been among the most severe critics of the preliminary report, working behind the scenes at *Cité libre*. Laurendeau had no doubt that Trudeau was responsible for a particularly cutting article entitled 'Bizarre Algebra'; 'no-one in that group had his razor-sharp bite, his frenzy for logic.'[69] The article condemned the Commission for exceeding its mandate, for proceeding from *a priori* assumptions inspired by French-Canadian nationalists, and for presuming that there was any constitutional basis for dividing the country into two equal nations. Not only did these Quebec federalists reject outright the idea that constitutional change was needed beyond the tinkering required to enshrine linguistic rights, but they clearly believed the Commission had no right to meddle in that area. Laurendeau was 'irritated' especially by what he called the 'pseudo-scientific dogmatism' of the accusation that the preliminary report was based on journalistic impressions rather than good research. To him, Trudeau and his colleagues were guilty as always of a systematic underestimation of the cultural factor.

It was all too clear, therefore, that the arrival of the 'three wise men' in Ottawa boded ill for the Commission. As Laurendeau watched the election results with René Lévesque, both 'nationalists' realized that henceforth they would be doing battle, each in his own way, with a strong contingent of anti-nationalists in the federal government.[70] No wonder the only winning candidate he felt he could cheer was Jean Marchand—notwithstanding the fact that he had gone to Ottawa himself, in part at least, to pave the way for talented French Canadians to work there. In his view, not only had Pelletier and Trudeau abandoned the cause of social democracy in Quebec, dealing a mortal blow to the NDP in the process, but they now regarded French-Canadian nationalism as their chief target. Why else would Trudeau choose to run in the upper-middle-class Mount Royal riding?

> . . . strange soil for a leftist French Canadian, but one which will give its member of Parliament the possibility of fighting off French-Canadian

nationalism safely. That is what I believe was the attraction for Pierre, who is appalled by separatism and the lack of respect youth shows to him: he looked for a position of strength from which he could counter-attack a René Lévesque.[71]

Laurendeau's concern escalated when, a few months after the election, Marchand told him that Trudeau had become Pearson's golden boy; 'Jean knows Pierre is a poor informer when it comes to present day Quebec.'[72]

It is not clear to what extent Trudeau and his federalist colleagues from Quebec used their influence with Pearson from 1965 on to limit the scope of the Commission. Although Laurendeau felt that Pearson was somewhat ill at ease with him, the prime minister continued to support the Commission's work in the all-important budgetary area. But if he had always been impressed with Pearson's intelligence and good will, he did not see him as a strong leader. Writing in 1965, he offered this impression:

> I admire his clear-headedness. He has all the right qualities, except where leadership is concerned: a quick sensitive intelligence, common sense, apparently solid willpower, at least with respect to himself, the ability to take in information and consider a question in a new way, I mean to re-examine it in its new context, and a certain intellectual daring. He looks like a head of state, when he's at his best; but does he have the strength? Can he achieve his vision in spite of his colleagues, friends and adversaries? It seems to me we've brought almost nothing new to his attention; in a sense, he was ahead of most of us: but he feels unable to do what needs to be done.[73]

At one point Laurendeau asked Trudeau to intervene to help get officials and other critics in the government off the Commission's back. From Trudeau's point of view, there was no reason to hamper Laurendeau in his efforts to complete the Commission's research and meet its publication schedule: the report would prepare the ground for greater bilingualism in the federal civil service and in the country generally, which Trudeau favoured. It was enough to make sure that the Commission, or at least the Laurendeau faction on it, stopped short of offering an ambitious blueprint for constitutional reform. In fact, most of the political pressure brought to bear on the Commission appears to have come after Laurendeau's death and Trudeau's replacement of Pearson as prime minister in 1968.[74] It is significant that the Commission's final volume on the Constitution was never produced. Laurendeau was trumped by the new political reality, and his 'blue pages' for Volume I were more a testament of his thought in the political-constitutional area than a serious plan of action. By the time the first volume was presented to Pearson in late 1967, developments such as René Lévesque's open commitment to separatism and Quebec Premier Daniel Johnson's aggressive stance at the 'Confederation of Tomorrow' constitutional conference in Toronto had drowned out the Commission's voice.[75]

Nevertheless, as important as the increasingly polarized political scene was in dampening Laurendeau's hopes for the Commission, its long-term success was more seriously jeopardized by the absence of a true basis for biculturalism in Canada. He acknowledged this as early as 1964 when he wrote to Francine in Paris: 'Biculturalism as most of my contemporaries understand it is a huge joke (the modern version of the bonne entente). . . .'[76] It wasn't merely the hostility he encountered in English Canada towards French Canada's culture—the assertions that it was 'backward' and destined to disappear anyway. On that score he had even been forced to listen to anglophones who didn't speak a word of French offering trenchant comments on the quality of French spoken in Quebec. Nor was it primarily the result of intellectual distinctions between 'language' and 'culture'. Here again he had become so frustrated with the nit-picking professorial types that on one occasion he interrupted to say, 'I call a cat a cat.'[77] It had somewhat more to do with the French minorities outside Quebec, whose language and culture were in grim, perhaps irretrievable shape.

But in the final analysis the death of biculturalism had above all to do with the rise of multiculturalism. Before joining the Commission Laurendeau had been warned that the 'ethnic groups' would be a major stumbling block, but his limited experience with English Canada and his preoccupation with defending the two-nations brand of nationalism in Quebec had blinded him to their militancy and growing importance. It was during his travels in the west in 1963-64 that his eyes were opened:

> . . . we began to formulate for ourselves an understanding of the situation we were observing; that is, a multiculturalism that is an undeniable fact and must be taken into account, but which manifests itself differently according to locality. Over and above it is the great problem of English-French relations in Canada. How can we get across the point that an 'ethnic group', even one that is relatively large provincially, but only represents 3% of the total Canadian population, is not at all the same thing as an organised society like Quebec, with a large population, its own institutions, and a long and specific history?[78]

Pearson too, in looking back, identified this failure to recognize the strength of multiculturalism as a major oversight in the establishment of the Commission.[79]

While the political and bicultural problems were beyond Laurendeau's power to change, he must be given a share of responsibility for the other setbacks suffered by the Commission in its last years. One was the length of time required to present the final report. It took four years for Volume I to appear, and the Commission's program wasn't completed until 1971, eight years after it started. After issuing an alarmist preliminary report in 1965, stating that the nation's plight demanded immediate attention, it

moved at glacier speed in publishing its own analysis and recommendations. Those involved have pointed out that Laurendeau for one was
stung by criticism of the 'unscientific' conclusions contained in the preliminary report and yielded to the pressure of the research staff, the
English Canadians in particular, to be much more thorough where the
final product was concerned. The result was a comprehensive research
effort after 1965 that consumed massive amounts of both money and
time; it turned the Commission into what Jean-Louis Gagnon, Laurendeau's successor as co-chairman, called 'Canada's Super-University'.[80]
Laurendeau admitted that there was a loss of control: 'Of course, the
researchers have functioned like an independent organisation, and it's difficult to maintain links with them even intellectually sometimes.'[81]
Pearson, who was forced to take the political flak for the delays and con-
sequent costs, was less generous. Without pointing a finger directly at the
co-chairman, he concluded nonetheless that '. . . there was almost an
excess of esoteric research. Academics appear to have been irresistibly
tempted to get a job on the B&B Commission to get on with a research
project they had been wanting to launch all their lives, but for which
they could not find funds.'[82] Laurendeau's lack of administrative experience, coupled with his inability to distinguish between legitimate criticism
of the Commission and negative appraisals that were little more than
covert attacks on French Canada, left him incapable of getting a grip on
things as chief operating officer. His solution, apparently, was to work
harder himself.

Still, it is unlikely that by 1967 Laurendeau could have injected new life
into the Commission. An enterprise that had begun with such high hopes
and all-encompassing purpose simply petered out. This is not to say that
it failed to produce significant results. For example, Laurendeau himself
was so impressed by the studies produced for the volume on the work
world that he wanted it to appear first; for one thing it would give the lie
to those who had cast doubt on the veracity of the preliminary report by
demonstrating that French Canadians were economically oppressed
everywhere in Canada, including Quebec. But that volume did not appear
until after his death. Nor would he live long enough to see the Commission's recommendations take effect in the linguistic and cultural life of
Canada. Among its direct results were the Official Languages Act of 1969,
putting French and English on equal legal footing in Canada's government
and institutions; a greater role for French Canadians in the federal civil
service; advances in minority-language education in several provinces;
and the creation of more than thirty 'districts' across Canada where
French and English minorities received special nurturing. It was an
impressive legacy that, although it fell short of his hopes, might have
eased the despondency that overtook him in his final months.

Over the five years of travel, work, stress, and wounding criticism from

1963 to 1968, Laurendeau's state of well-being, if not his health, had declined sharply. He had always been subject to migraines and insomnia, and in recent years had experienced severe back pain. But he seemed to recognize too that his thirty-five year career at the centre of Quebec's affairs was about to end. As he wrote plaintively in his diary:

> The years ahead look like thankless ones. I am going to find myself allied with people I often have no respect for (the rich, the old parties, the masses, and even then we can only hope they won't be caught up in the independentist maelstrom). What's more, most of my friends, I mean those I feel the most natural and spontaneous affection for, will be in the opposite camp. The clearest example here is René Lévesque, and the young. There is only one thing that repels me more than being snubbed by the young, and that is to flatter them like demagogues. This is a new area where I will be condemned to solitude. Life is not going to smile on me much any more [83]

On 15 May 1968, after a press conference, André Laurendeau suffered a brain aneurism and was rushed to Ottawa General Hospital, where he hovered semi-conscious for fifteen days. Finally, on 1 June, he died. Three days later, over a thousand people followed the funeral procession in Montreal, including Mayor Drapeau, Premier Daniel Johnson, and Pierre Trudeau, who was only days away from being elected prime minister. Following the funeral in Outremont, his lifelong home, he was buried at Saint-Gabriel, that other place where he had learned to know himself as a French Canadian.

Epilogue

But it will not be easy to achieve a Canadian nation. Sometimes when I realize the extent of the problem I despair of ever building a united country.
André Laurendeau, CBC radio broadcast, 1939

He chose the very nick of time to go away in.
Molière, *Le Misanthrope*

There was a consistent theme to the expressions of shock and grief that greeted the news of Laurendeau's death in 1968, at the relatively young age of fifty-six. It was stated succinctly by former Prime Minister Pearson, who was in England: 'Canada, especially at this stage, can hardly afford the luxury of losing a man of André Laurendeau's quality.'[1] This view that Canada and Quebec had been unexpectedly deprived of an exceptional personality at the very moment when his unique insights and talents were most needed filled numerous obituaries over the following weeks, as well as a special series of articles by friends and associates that appeared in *Le Devoir*. But for some family members and nationalist colleagues these expressions of despair were accompanied by bitterness. To them, Laurendeau had taken a wrong turn in agreeing to co-chair the Bilingualism and Biculturalism Commission, and had literally killed himself in a vain effort to make it a success. Simonne Monet-Chartrand, a close family friend, recalled a visit from Laurendeau early in 1968, when she herself was in hospital. He was haggard, exhausted and suffering from terrible headaches. She urged him to find a replacement for himself at the Commission before it was too late, and in a bemused, prophetic voice he replied: 'You may be right. I'd better hurry. I don't know if I'll have time to finish the last report. I feel responsible for it.'[2]

Looking back on this time almost a quarter-century later, Francine Laurendeau still felt angry that her father became a changed man, nearly broken, in his last years—in her words, a 'victim of duty'. Returning at last from France in 1966, she listened to her mother Ghislaine speak derisively of the 'Commission B.B.', an allusion to Brigitte Bardot, the vacuous glamour queen of the day. Nothing could have testified more eloquently to her father's long absences than the disappearance of his famous 'sound system' from its honoured place in the living room of the house on Stuart Street. How much these changes had to do with Laurendeau's extra-marital affair is not easy to say, but Francine emphasized that it was his 'exile' in Ottawa that 'devoured his time and energy'. When she did see him, he seemed preoccupied with insurmountable problems:

> You will say that I'm exaggerating. That this brain aneurism which carried him off after fifteen days would perhaps have occurred even if my father hadn't got involved in this business. But at least he would have continued till the end to do what he loved, that is to react to each day's events, to function each day . . . in his role as a journalist. Certainly as an editorialist, André Laurendeau was in the habit of being discussed, even contradicted; this was surely stimulating. But how to live with the incomprehension, the hostility and, worse, the indif-ference that surrounded his thankless labour on this impossible mission?
>
> That is why I would find it profoundly unjust if all that posterity retains of my father is this last frozen image where the film stopped, the image of the co-chairman of the Laurendeau-Dunton Commission.[3]

Nationalist friends also insisted that Laurendeau had wasted his last years by trusting the 'jackals' in Ottawa, some of whom were fellow French Canadians, and by assuming that an oasis of goodwill could be found in the desert that was English Canada. To them his name would now be added to a long list of casualties—Adolphe Chapleau, Wilfrid Laurier, Ernest Lapointe—who had made the same mistake.

The sense of loss felt by those who did not consider Laurendeau's last five years a total failure went beyond personal considerations to the trou-bled times themselves. At a time when ideological positions in Quebec were hardening and when the late-sixties' penchant for confrontation and extremist rhetoric was at its peak, a voice of sanity and compromise had vanished from the scene. Laurendeau had demonstrated more than once in the past that he too could be inflexible and confrontational. His anti-Semitic activities with Jeune-Canada from 1933 to 1935 were a case in point, as were his fiery words during the conscription crisis of 1942 and towards the youthful separatists of 1963. But these were exceptional moments in the career of someone who held that scorn for others, rather than for their errors, was a grave failing. He erred more often himself on the side of being too considerate. As Jean-Marc Léger, a fellow nationalist and journalist wrote, Laurendeau was 'the exact opposite of a dema-gogue'.[4] It was this very quality, in fact, that prevented him from be-coming a great nationalist tribune, like René Lévesque, for the youth of the 1960s who considered compromise a sign of weakness. Jean-Paul Desbiens explained this to him in 1962: 'I owe you a great deal, but not as a "master". . . . Perhaps [this is] because your personality is so nuanced, so subtle. A master has to be a little heavy. . . .'⁵ Nevertheless, in 1968 Desbiens felt that Laurendeau's distaste for excess and dogmatism would be sorely missed: 'We lose him at a moment when we have a great need for guidance; when his level, his reliable voice would have helped us to hold steady.'⁶

Many people in Quebec also feared that with Laurendeau died his vision of French-Canadian nationalism. A vision, as we have seen, in the tradition of Henri Bourassa, it was based on an idealistic belief that through enlightened compromise a working partnership could be forged between the English- and French-Canadian 'nations'. Laurendeau's struggle to translate this vision into reality at the Commission had been slowly disintegrating since 1965, and it was his realization of this, as much as anything, that accounted for his depression during those last years. By 1968 the stage was set for a long confrontation between the more extreme separatist and federalist camps. That year René Lévesque managed to unite the previously fractious separatist groups in Quebec under the banner of the Parti Québécois, and he began to win a wider following for the middle-class brand of separatism represented in the goal of 'sovereignty-association'. This option would be further bolstered after 1970 by the collapse of the more radical, working-class separatist movements like the FLQ following the October crisis of that year and the rapid decline of revolutionary ideologies in the neo-conservative climate of the new decade. Meanwhile Pierre Trudeau's election as Canadian prime minister, also in 1968, ensured that Laurendeau's earlier prediction would come true: French-Canadian federalists would use their power in Ottawa to oppose all Quebec nationalists and in particular the separatists. The advances made in areas such as Canadian bilingualism from that time until the Quebec sovereignty referendum in 1980 tended to be offshoots of this battle for the minds and hearts of French Canadians, rather than the fulfilment of the Laurendeau-Pearson vision of a vibrant Canadian duality.

We have seen that Laurendeau's conception of the French-Canadian half of that duality evolved over time. In fact, his long career graphically illustrates the variety within French-Canadian nationalism as well as the ebb and flow of priorities from one period to the next. In 1932, while under the influence of Abbé Groulx, he embraced the traditional view of the French-Canadian identity based on the *survivance* historical theme, which sought to preserve the essence of those cultural characteristics derived from the distant past as well as a conservative Catholic value system. But just as his perception of Catholicism's link to French Canada's identity changed dramatically over time, so too did his view of history. By 1960 he rejected pat historical theories imposed on the past to suit current purposes:

> I am instinctively suspicious of the kind of history that is too clear, too easy to understand, too structured. Something tells me that these structures derive from the historian's ideas rather than from historical fact. History, after all, is complex; it branches out in many directions at once. Granted, the

historian must make a selection from the whole range of material which he is exploring: yet when he reduces history to an intellectual framework or outline, his selection seems too arbitrary, too deliberate.[7]

As his own intellectual sophistication increased, starting with his two years in France from 1935 to 1937, Laurendeau's nationalism was infused with more liberal and progressive ideas. He became conscious of the narrow, petty-bourgeois rigidity of his earlier clerical-cultural concerns and he sought to open French-Canadian nationalism to outside influences while providing it with a more credible social doctrine. He was attracted to the philosophy of personalism partly because, as at least one commentator has observed, it allowed its adherents to avoid breaking completely with Catholicism and past tradition: '. . . they were defenders of liberty without rejecting all authority; . . . they wished to subordinate political action to reason without denying all doctrine.'[8] During the late 1930s Laurendeau's respect for his old nationalist mentors—described by the historian Guy Frégault as a 'little gerontocracy'[9]—together with the siege mentality engendered by the approach of the Second World War, had a braking effect on his progressive orientation. But his experiences during the war with the Bloc Populaire gave it a fresh impetus, carrying it to the level of a practical awareness of political and socio-economic realities.

While Laurendeau was always an opponent of those who controlled the capitalist industrial system in Quebec—particularly foreign and Anglo-Canadian business interests—during the 1950s he split with those nationalists who refused to accept the full implications of Quebec's urban-industrial reality. Institutional modernization, improvements in the material life of the French Canadian working class, and the continuing fight for provincial autonomy, so that the state of Quebec could play a more aggressive role internally, were the main features of his nationalist ideology during his tenure at *Le Devoir*. This social nationalism—or, as some analysts have called it, neo-nationalism—helped to make him a key figure during the prelude to the Quiet Revolution. But in the early 1960s, when he sensed that the young generation of nationalists were tying the fate of French Canada too narrowly to a utopian vision of an independent nation state and to political and economic themes, he emphasized once again what for him was always the nexus of the French-Canadian identity: namely, its unique culture. As he stated:

> Nationalism as it exists here is founded on a particular culture which it loves, is determined to defend, and wants to be free to develop . . .
>
> Naturally, a nationalism which is primarily cultural seeks support elsewhere; it knows that culture doesn't live in the clouds but among men, and that men have economic and political interests. If these interests and the institutions that serve them are at odds with the culture, little by little the culture will be abandoned. So nationalism is led to examine such relationships very closely.[10]

It was this cultural nationalism that inspired him to propose the Bilingualism and Biculturalism Commission, and with hindsight it was perhaps fitting that he left the stage before its final death knell had sounded. Within three years of his departure the Canadian government adopted an official cultural policy of bilingualism and multiculturalism, and the new terms that accompanied it—'cultural mosaic', 'pluralism', and so on—were like nails in the coffin of Laurendeau's hopes for a genuine English-French duality based on equality.

In the years following his death Quebec's federalists and separatists both tried to claim him as one of their own. The former pointed to the fact that, despite his obvious discouragement in the last years, he never endorsed separatism as an acceptable alternative. At the most, they argued, he was forced to put more of his hopes in the presence of a powerful, autonomous Quebec within Canada to defend French-Canadian distinctiveness. Separatists, on the other hand, claimed Laurendeau had learned the hard way that English Canadians would never accept French Canada as a worthy partner, let alone as a distinctive nation, and that hence the only alternative was sovereignty-association, which his moderate disposition would in time have found acceptable. The two sides still pore over his private musings, in the diary he kept during his time with the Commission, searching for morsels to feed their ideological appetites. But both are undoubtedly wrong. Unlike them, Laurendeau never needed the security of a one-dimensional position. On the contrary, he lived his whole life between contending ideas, trying to reckon the value of each while finding ways to incorporate their best elements into his own point of view. It was this, according to Fernand Dumont, that made his thought so difficult to categorize in straightforward terms: 'a nationalist slowly evolving or a hesitant socialist? A reticent federalist or a timid separatist?'[11]

Dumont, like so many others, preferred to think of Laurendeau as the 'archetype' of a consciously involved intellectual. He was at once passionately committed and distant; the man at the centre and the outsider.[12] The polarities that characterized the tensions in his thinking—tradition and change; politics and art; openness and discretion—enriched his thinking in ways that are still revealing today. They made his contributions to French Canada diverse and deep but also, somehow, incomplete. Similarly, while he was a courageous figure of great intellectual integrity who was willing to run risks and take a stand in the face of conventional wisdom, at times a painful sensitivity prevented him from revealing his true beliefs. Perhaps Jean-Marc Léger summed Laurendeau up best when he described him as '. . . the perfect example of the contemporary humanist'.[13]

Notes

This book is heavily based, in the first few chapters particularly, on the manuscript materials by and relating to André Laurendeau at the Fondation Lionel Groulx in Outremont, Montreal. They include his letters, school records, manuscript drafts, diaries, etc., as well as those of his father, mother, wife, and other family members. The documents in the collections at the Fondation concerning the Ligue pour la Défense du Canada, the Bloc Populaire, and the Royal Commission on Bilingualism and Biculturalism are also extremely valuable for any study of Laurendeau's career. For a thorough summary of the various Fondation collections, including photographs, see Robert Comeau and Lucille Beaudry, *André Laurendeau, un intellectuel d'ici* (Sillery, Québec: Presses de l'Université du Québec, 1990), 299-306.

In addition, some chapters make extensive use of Laurendeau's writing for *L'Action nationale* and, of course, the hundreds of editorials, *chroniques*, and *bloc-notes* he wrote for *Le Devoir*, as well as the documents at the Public Archives of Canada dealing with the Royal Commission on Bilingualism and Biculturalism.

Except as cited below, all quotations are taken from these primary materials.

CHAPTER 1

[1] André Laurendeau, 'The Conditions which Govern the Existence of a National Culture', in Michael Behiels and Ramsay Cook, eds, *The Essential Laurendeau*, trans. Joanne L'Heureux and Richard Howard (Toronto: Copp Clark, 1968), 70-1.
[2] André Laurendeau, 'Réponse de M. André Laurendeau de la Société Royale du Canada', *Écrits du Canada Français* 35 (1972), 60.
[3] Laurendeau, 'Conditions', in Behiels and Cook, 71.
[4] Fernand Dumont, 'Preface' to André Laurendeau, *Ces choses qui nous arrivent: chronique des années 1961-1966* (Montréal: HMH, 1970), xvi.
[5] André Laurendeau, *Voyages au pays de l'enfance* (Montréal: Beauchemin, 1960).
[6] Fernand Ouellet, 'The Historical Background of Separatism in Quebec', in G.R. Cook, ed., *French-Canadian Nationalism: An Anthology* (Toronto: Macmillan, 1969), 49-64; also F. Dumont et al., *Le Pouvoir dans la société canadienne-française* (Québec: Presses de l'Université Laval, 1974), ch. 11.
[7] Susan Mann Trofimenkoff, *The Dream of Nation: A Social and Intellectual History of Quebec* (Toronto: Gage, 1983), 218-32; also G.R. Cook, *Canada and the French Canadian Question* (Toronto: Macmillan, 1967), 79-103.

[8] J.-J. Lefèbvre, *Généalogie de la famille Seerset, des familles alliées, Perrin, Delvecchio, Laurendeau, Brisset des Nos* (Trois-Rivières: éditions du bien publique, 1966); also Francine Laurendeau, 'André Laurendeau et la musique', in Robert Comeau et Lucille Beaudry, eds, *André Laurendeau, un intellectuel d'ici* (Sillery, Québec: Presses de l'Université du Québec, 1990), 116-20.

[9] 'Concerning an Illusion', in Behiels and Cook, 87.

[10] *Voyages*, 151.

[11] Denis Monière, *André Laurendeau et le destin d'un peuple* (Montréal: Québec/Amérique, 1983), 16; also, Yves Laurendeau, 'En guise de supplément au Laurendeau de Monière', *Revue d'histoire de l'Amérique française* 38, no. 1 (été 1984), 78-82.

[12] André Laurendeau, 'It All Began in a Theatre in the East of Montreal', in Philip Stratford, ed. and trans., *André Laurendeau: Witness for Quebec* (Toronto: Macmillan, 1973), 256-7.

[13] Jean Laurendeau, 'André Laurendeau, la musique et l'ambiance', in Nadine Pirotte, ed., *Penser l'éducation: nouveau dialogues avec André Laurendeau* (Montréal: Boréal, 1989), 124.

[14] *Ibid.*

[15] *Ibid.*; Monière, 33.

[16] 'Réponse', 63.

[17] Francine Laurendeau, 'André Laurendeau et la musique', 119.

[18] 'Réponse', 61.

[19] Susan Mann Trofimenkoff, *Action Française: French-Canadian Nationalism in the Twenties* (Toronto: University of Toronto Press, 1975), 18-26.

[20] 'Réponse', 61.

[21] Gérard Filion, 'Ce qui lui a manqué, c'est une enfance d'enfant', in Comeau et Beaudry, 11-12.

[22] Yves Laurendeau, 'En guise de supplément', 80-2.

[23] André Laurendeau, 'Is the Devil on the Left?' in Behiels and Cook, 165-6.

[24] Mason Wade, *The French-Canadians, 1760-1867* (Toronto: Macmillan, 1968), I, 1117-19; for background on the classical college system see C. Galarneau, *Les Collèges classiques au Canada français (1620-1970)* (Montréal: Fides, 1978).

[25] Jean Laurendeau, 'André Laurendeau, la musique et l'ambiance', 125.

[26] S. Monet-Chartrand, 'Depuis 1938 . . . un ami précieux', in Comeau et Beaudry, 26.

[27] Pierre Dansereau, *L'Ecologiste aux pieds nus* (Montréal: Nouveau Optique, n.d.), 29.

[28] Monière, 27.

[29] Pierre Dansereau, 'André Laurendeau: les options réversibles', in Comeau et Beaudry, 180.

[30] André Laurendeau, 'The Meaning of Present-Day Separatism', in Behiels and Cook, 227.

[31] Monière, 23.

[32] Dansereau, 'André Laurendeau: les options réversibles', 180-1.

[33] *Ibid.*

[34] Yves Laurendeau, 'André Laurendeau ou la culture comme mode de vie', in Pirotte, 22-3.

[35] Monière, 31.

[36] Dansereau, 'André Laurendeau: les options réversibles', 180.

[37] *Ibid.*, 181.

[38] 'Réponse', 62-3.

[39] *Ibid.*

[40] Jean Laurendeau, 'André Laurendeau, la musique et l'ambiance', 132.

[41] *Ibid.*, 126-7.

[42] *Ibid.*, 127-9.

[43] Yves Laurendeau, 'En guise de supplément', 81.

CHAPTER 2

[1] 'Laurentian Nationalism', in Michael Behiels and Ramsay Cook, eds, *The Essential Laurendeau*, trans. Joanne L'Heureux and Richard Howard (Toronto: Copp Clark, 1968), 43

[2] Pierre Dansereau, 'André Laurendeau: les options réversibles', in Robert Comeau et Lucille Beaudry, eds, *André Laurendeau, un intellectuel d'ici* (Sillery, Quebec: Presses de l'Université de Québec, 1990), 182; for the complete Jeune-Canada manifesto see *Le Devoir*, 17 décembre 1932.

[3] 'Manifesto of the Jeune-Canada Movement', in Behiels and Cook, 35.

[4] L. Groulx, *Mes mémoires* (Montréal: Fides, 1972), Vol. III, 282, Denis Chouinard, 'Des contestataires pragmatiques: les Jeunes-Canada, 1932-1938', *Revue d'histoire de l'Amérique française* 40, 1 (été 1986), 5-28.

[5] 'The Meaning of Present-Day Separatism', in Behiels and Cook, 227.

[6] Monière, 37-8.

[7] 'Réponse de M. André Laurendeau de la Société Royale du Canada', *Ecrits du Canada Français* 35 (1972), 61.

[8] Dansereau, 'André Laurendeau: les options réversibles', 118-19.

[9] *Ibid.*, 118; Gérard Filion, *Fais ce que peux: en guise de mémoires* (Montréal: Boréal, 1989), 115.

[10] André Laurendeau, 'The Conscription Crisis, 1942', in Philip Stratford, ed. and trans., *André Laurendeau, Witness for Quebec* (Toronto: Macmillan, 1973), 3.

[11] See for example G.R. Cook, 'In the Bourassa Tradition', *Canada and the French-Canadian Question* (Toronto: Macmillan, 1967), 104-18; Charles Vallerand, 'De Groulx à Laurendeau', in Comeau et Beaudry, 163-8; André Laurendeau, 'Independence', in Stratford, 124-6.

[12] Joseph Levitt, *Henri Bourassa and the Golden Calf: The Social Program of the Nationalists* (Ottawa: Editions de l'Université d'Ottawa, 1969), *passim*; André Laurendeau, 'Henri Bourassa', in Robert L. McDougall, ed., *Our Living Tradition*, 4th ed. (Toronto: University of Toronto Press, 1962), 135-58.

[13] Levitt, *Henri Bourrassa*; Susan Mann Trofimenkoff, *The Dream of Nation: A Social and Intellectual History of Quebec* (Toronto: Gage, 1983), 169-75.

[14] J.P. Gaboury, *Le Nationalisme de Lionel Groulx: aspects idéologiques* (Ottawa: Editions de l'Université d'Ottawa, 1970), *passim*; for the 1930s in particular see A.J. Bélanger, *L'Apolitisme des idéologies québécoises: le grand tournant, 1934-36* (Québec: Presses de l'Université Laval, 1974), 191-255.

[15] L. Groulx, *Notre maître, le passé* (Montréal, 1924), 263.

[16] Susan Mann Trofimenkoff, *Action Française: French-Canadian Nationalism in the Twenties* (Toronto: University of Toronto Press, 1975), 99-113.

[17] Groulx, *Mémoires*, III, 275-83; Lucien Fortin, 'Les Jeunes-Canada', in Fernand Dumont *et al.*, eds, *Idéologies au Canada Français, 1930-1939* (Québec: Presses de l'Université Laval, 1978), 215-23.

[18] Dansereau, 'André Laurendeau: les options réversibles', 180-1.

[19] Fortin, 216-18.

[20] Dansereau, 'André Laurendeau: les options réversibles', 181.

[21] André Laurendeau, 'Le nationalisme s'enracinera-t-il mieux qu'en 1936', *Ces choses qui nous arrivent: chronique des années 1961-1966* (Montreal: HMH, 1970), 51-2.

[22] Dansereau, 'André Laurendeau: les options réversibles', 182.

[23] Groulx, *Mémoires*, III: 274-5; Filion, *Fais ce que peux*, 23.

[24] 'Nationalism in 1936 and 1961', in Stratford, 234.

[25] Dansereau, 'André Laurendeau: les options réversibles', 182.

[26] Groulx, *Mémoires*, III, 274-5.

[27] Filion, *Fais ce que peux*, 117.

[28] Dansereau, 'André Laurendeau: les options réversibles', 182.

[29] Filion, *Fais ce que peux*, 115.

[30] Fortin, 217.

[31] Lionel Groulx à Arthur Laurendeau, 23 juin 1933, Fonds Laurendeau, Institut Lionel Groulx.

[32] Dansereau, 'André Laurendeau: les options réversibles', 182.

[33] André Laurendeau, 'Party Politics', in Behiels and Cook, 39-40; for the full text see *Politiciens et Juifs*, Les Cahiers des Jeunes-Canada, no. 1, 1933.

[34] *Le Devoir*, 27 avril 1933.

[35] Filion, *Fais ce que peux*, 117.

[36] André Laurendeau, 'Why Keep Reminding Us That He's a Jew?' in Stratford, 178; also Pierre Anctil, 'Laurendeau et le grand virage identitaire de la Révolution tranquille', in Comeau et Beaudry, 235.

[37] 'Nationalism in 1936 and 1961', in Stratford, 234.

[38] 'Avant le congrès, visitons le musée de l'Union Nationale', *Ces choses*, 35; see also *Le Devoir*, 14 novembre 1933.

[39] *Le Devoir*, 2, 18, 19 décembre 1933; also B.L. Vigod, *The Political Career of Louis-Alexandre Taschereau* (Montreal: McGill-Queen's University Press, 1986): 206-7.

[40] 'Nationalism in 1936 and 1961', in Stratford, 235.

[41] *Notre nationalisme*, Tracts des Jeunes-Canada, no. 5, 1935.

[42] Quoted in Denis Monière, *André Laurendeau et le destin d'un peuple* (Montreal: Québec/Amérique, 1983), 70.

[43] 'Why I'm not a Separatist Anymore' (1962), Fonds Laurendeau, Fondation Lionel Groulx.

[44] 'Laurentian Nationalism', in Behiels and Cook, 45.

[45] Filion, *Fais ce que peux*, 116.

[46] 'Nationalism in 1936 and 1961', in Stratford, 235.

[47] Patricia Dirks, *The Failure of the Action Libérale Nationale* (Montreal: McGill-Queens University Press, 1991), 26-45.

[48] 'Nationalism in 1936 and 1961', in Stratford, 235.

[49] L. Renaud, 'La Fondation de l'ACJC', in Dumont, *Idéologies*, 173-92.

[50] Filion, *Fais ce que peux*, 114.

[51] Dansereau, 'André Laurendeau: les options réversibles', 182-3.

[52] Filion, *Fais ce que peux*, 117.

[53] 'Nationalism in 1936 and 1961', in Stratford, 236.

CHAPTER 3

[1] This description of the rally at the Mutualité is based on Laurendeau's own account in 'Communistes', *L'Action nationale*, VIII (mars 1936), 155-61; see also D.J. Fischer, *Romain Rolland and the Politics of Intellectual Engagement* (Berkeley: University of California Press, 1988), 256-7.

[2] 'Communistes', 160-3; for a detailed review of the correspondence from Laurendeau's time in Europe see L. Chantilly, *L'Incunable* (Bulletin de la Bibliothèque Nationale du Québec) mars et septembre 1984, 7-15, 6-13; mars et septembre 1985, 10-18, 14-22; mars et juin-septembre 1986, 26-37, 36-47.

[3] B. Miller, *French Personalism and the Search for Community* (New Haven: Yale University Press, 1972).

[4] 'The Conscription Crisis, 1942', in Philip Stratford, ed. and trans., *André Laurendeau: Witness for Quebec* (Toronto: Macmillan, 1973), 4.

[5] Gérard Pelletier, *Years of Impatience: 1950-1960*, trans. Alan Brown (Toronto: Methuen, 1984), 16; Stephen Clarkson and Christina McCall, *Trudeau and Our Times*, vol. I (Toronto: McClelland and Stewart, 1991), 58-61.

[6] 'Further Notes on "Our Nationalism"', in Michael Behiels and Ramsay Cook, *The Essential Laurendeau*, trans. Joanne L'Heureux and Richard Howard (Toronto: Copp Clark, 1968), 47.

[7] 'Return from Europe', in Stratford, 214.

[8] R. Aron, *Fifty Years of Political Thought* (New York: Holmes and Mier, 1990), 3-110; Fischer, 236-66.

[9] B.E. Doering, *Jacques Maritain and the French Catholic Intellectuals* (South Bend, Ind.: University of Notre Dame Press, 1983), 24-83; Michel Barlow, *Le Socialisme d'Emmanuel Mounier* (Toulouse: Privat, 1971).

[10] J. Hellman, *Emmanuel Mounier and the New Catholic Left, 1930-1950* (Toronto: University of Toronto Press, 1981), 5.

[11] *Ibid.*, 4.

[12] *Ibid.*, 1-2.

[13] 'The Origins of My Social Catholicism', in Behiels and Cook, 125.

[14] Pelletier, 17-19.

[15] In Behiels and Cook, 125.

[16] *Ibid.*

[17] *Ibid.*, 126.

[18] J.A. Amato, 'Emmanuel Mounier and Jacques Maritain: A French Catholic Understanding of the Modern World' (Ph.D. thesis, Rochester, 1970), 143-90.

[19] Hellman, 19-20.

[20] Emmanuel Mounier à Madeleine Mounier, 19 décembre 1925, *Esprit*; cited and trans. in Hellman, 15.

[21] 'Mounier and the Origins of Personalism', in Behiels and Cook, 128; see also André Laurendeau, 'La fécondité de l'argent, mécanisme contre nature', *L'Action nationale* IX (juin 1937), 42.

[22] Quoted in Hellman, 11.

[23] (London: E. Nash, 1907).

24 (Paris: A. Colin, 1937).

25 Zeuge, 'Hitler, l'homme qui arrêta le communisme', *L'Action nationale* VIII (novembre 1937), 155-64.

26 André Laurendeau, 'Le "Birth Control" hier et aujourd'hui', *Ces choses qui nous arrivent: chronique des années 1961-1966* (Montréal: HMH, 1970), 324.

27 'The Conscription Crisis, 1942', in Stratford, 4.

28 Jean Lacouture, *Léon Blum* (New York: Holmes and Meier, 1982), 305-58.

29 'The Conscription Crisis, 1942', in Stratford, 4.

30 *Ibid.*

CHAPTER 4

1 Patricia Smart, ed. and trans. with Dorothy Howard, *The Diary of André Laurendeau: Written during the Royal Commission on Bilingualism and Biculturalism* (Toronto: James Lorimer, 1991), 79.

2 André Laurendeau, 'Return from Europe', in Philip Stratford, ed. and trans., *André Laurendeau: Witness for Quebec* (Toronto: Macmillan, 1973), 215.

3 Stanley Ryerson, 'Laurendeau, la commission royale, l'histoire', in Robert Comeau et Lucille Beaudry, eds, *André Laurendeau, un intellectuel d'ici* (Sillery, Québec: Presses de l'Université du Québec, 1990), 219.

4 François-Albert Angers, 'André Laurendeau, journaliste à *L'Action nationale*', in Comeau et Beaudry, 98.

5 Denis Monière, *André Laurendeau et le destin d'un peuple* (Montréal: Québec/Amérique, 1983), 109.

6 'Mounier and the origins of personalism', in Michael Behiels and Ramsay Cook, eds, *The Essential Laurendeau*, trans. Joanne L'Heureux and Richard Howard (Toronto: Copp Clark, 1968), 127.

7 Monière, 109.

8 Donald Smith, 'L'action française, 1917-1921', in Fernand Dumont *et al.*, *Idéologies au Canada Français, 1900-1929* (Québec: Presses de l'Université Laval, 1974), 345-68; also Mason Wade, *The French Canadians, 1760 to the Present* (Toronto: Macmillan, 1968), 2: 865-88.

9 Patricia Dirks, *The Failure of L'Action Libérale Nationale* (Montreal: McGill Queen's University Press, 1991), 99-114; also André Laurendeau, *Ces choses qui nous arrivent: chronique des années 1961-1966* (Montréal: HMH, 1970), 35-9.

10 'Notre nouveau directeur', *L'Action nationale* X (septembre 1937), 3-4.

11 'Exigences d'un mouvement', *L'Action nationale* X (octobre 1937), 89-91.

12 Monière, 109.

13 'Return from Europe', in Stratford, 213.

14 'Concerning a Recent Encyclical', in Behiels and Cook, 51; also 'The Meaning of Present-Day Separatism' and 'Introduction to the "Rosenberg Doctrine"', in Behiels and Cook, 225-6 and 50.

15 'L'Actualité', *L'Action nationale* X (novembre 1937), 190-1.

16 'An Anti-Fascist Crusade', in Behiels and Cook, 131.

17 *Ibid.*, 134-5.

18 Michel Brunet, *La Présence anglaise et les canadiens: études sur l'histoire et la pensée* (Montréal: Beauchemin, 1968), 113-66; André Laurendeau, 'Concerning an Illusion', in Behiels and Cook, 86-8.

[19] 'The Conscription Crisis, 1942', in Stratford, 5.

[20] Robert Parisé, *Georges-Henri Lévesque: père de la renaissance québécoise* (Montréal: Éditions internationales Alain Stanké, 1976); also G.-H. Lévesque, *Souvenances* (Montréal: Éditions Québec/Amérique, 1986), 283-369.

[21] G.-H. Lévesque, 'La première décennie de la faculté des sciences sociales à l'Université Laval', in *Continuité et rupture: les sciences sociales au Québec* (Montréal: Presses de l'Université de Montréal, 1984), I: 51-64.

[22] John English, Ian Drummond, and Robert Bothwell, *Canada, 1900-1945* (Toronto: University of Toronto Press, 1987), 272-4; also, André Laurendeau, 'A Warning to French Canadians', in Behiels and Cook, 64.

[23] Unpublished manuscript, Fonds Laurendeau, Fondation Lionel Groulx.

[24] G.-H. Lévesque à André Laurendeau, mars 1935, Fonds Laurendeau, Fondation Lionel Groulx.

[25] Pierre Dansereau, 'André Laurendeau: les options réversibles', in Comeau et Beaudry, 183.

[26] 'An Anti-Fascist Crusade'? in Behiels and Cook, 131-2.

[27] André Laurendeau, 'American Threat', in Behiels and Cook, 52.

[28] *Ibid.*, 53.

[29] *Ibid.*

[30] *Ibid.*, 54.

[31] *Ibid.*

[32] G. Ramsay Cook, *Canada and the French-Canadian Question* (Toronto: Macmillan, 1967), 81-2.

[33] 'Total Bilingualism', in Behiels and Cook, 127.

[34] *Ibid.*

[35] *Ibid.*

[36] 'The Conscription Crisis', in Stratford, 14.

[37] *Ibid.*, 15; Laurendeau also met with the Marxist Stanley Ryerson in 1939 (S. Ryerson, 'Laurendeau, la commission royale, l'histoire', in Comeau et Beaudry, 219).

[38] Sandra Djwa, *The Politics of the Imagination: A Life of F.R. Scott* (Toronto: McClelland and Stewart, 1987), 136-57.

[39] *Ibid.*, 183.

[40] Monière, 120-2.

[41] Gérard Bergeron, 'Celui pour qui nous avons tous rêvé d'un autre destin', in Comeau et Beaudry, 284; see also G. Frégault, 'Aspect de Lionel Groulx', in Maurice Filion, *Hommages à Lionel Groulx* (Montréal: Leméac, 1978), 91.

CHAPTER 5

[1] In Philip Stratford, ed. and trans., *André Laurendeau: Witness for Quebec* (Toronto: Macmillan, 1973), 1-2.

[2] Hector Grenon, *Camillien Houde* (Montréal: Editions internationales Alain Stanké, 1979), 249-50, 272.

[3] 'The Conscription Crisis, 1942', in Stratford, 43-4.

[4] *Ibid.*, 44-5.

[5] 'Concerning a Recent Encyclical', in Michael Behiels and Ramsay Cook, eds, *The Essential Laurendeau*, trans. Joanne L'Heureux and Richard Howard (Toronto: Copp Clark, 1968), 52.

6 André Laurendeau, 'The Conscription Crisis', in Stratford, 5-6; also John English, Ian Drummond, and Robert Bothwell, *Canada, 1900-1945* (Toronto: University of Toronto Press, 1987), 311-12.

7 'The Conscription Crisis', in Stratford, 5; see also Laurendeau's further musing on the subject, 'The Meaning of Present Day Separatism', in Behiels and Cook, 224.

8 'The Conscription Crisis', in Stratford, 8-9.

9 *Ibid.*, 23.

10 *Ibid.*, 24.

11 *Ibid.*, 17.

12 *Ibid.*, 19; Patricia Dirks, *The Failure of the Action Libérale Nationale* (Montréal: McGill-Queen's University Press, 1991), 137-41.

13 Conrad Black, *Duplessis* (Toronto: McClelland and Stewart, 1977), 193.

14 House of Commons, *Debates*, 9 September 1939, 64-9.

15 'The Conscription Crisis', in Stratford, 39.

16 Sandra Djwa, *The Politics of the Imagination: A Life of F.R. Scott* (Toronto: McClelland and Stewart, 1987), 183.

17 'Canada: A Country of Two Cultures', 3 June 1939, CBC Series, Young Canada, Station CBM.

18 'The Conscription Crisis', in Stratford, 18.

19 *Ibid.*, 28.

20 *Ibid.*, 23-4.

21 *Ibid.*; H.F. Quinn, *The Union Nationale* (Toronto: University of Toronto Press, 1963), 104-6.

22 'The Conscription Crisis', in Stratford, 30-1; also Dirks, 141-5.

23 Quinn, 104-6.

24 'The Conscription Crisis', in Stratford, 24-5.

25 *Ibid.*, 32-3.

26 *Ibid.*, 36.

27 *Ibid.*, 46.

28 Denis Monière, *André Laurendeau et le destin d'un peuple* (Montréal: Québec/Amérique, 1983), 130-1.

29 'The Conscription Crisis', in Stratford, 25-6.

30 *Ibid.*, 26; see also Laurendeau, 'A Warning to French Canadians', in Behiels and Cook, 66-7.

31 'The Conscription Crisis', in Stratford, 40.

32 *Ibid.*, 116.

33 *Ibid.*, 33.

34 Jean-Guy Genest, 'Vie et oeuvre d'Adélard Godbout, 1892-1956' (doctoral thesis, Université Laval, 1977), 376-429, 479-530.

35 'The Conscription Crisis', in Stratford, 36; Black, 235.

36 'A Warning to French Canadians', in Behiels and Cook, 66.

37 *Ibid.*, 61.

38 *Ibid.*, 63.

39 *Ibid.*, 68.

40 'The Conscription Crisis', in Stratford, 47.

41 *Ibid.*, 51.

42 *Ibid.*, 52.

43 *Ibid.*, 51.

44 English *et al.*, 323.
45 'The Conscription Crisis', in Stratford, 55; see Susan Mann Trofimenkoff, *The Dream of Nation: A Social and Intellectual History of Quebec* (Toronto: Gage, 1983), 259-60.
46 'The Conscription Crisis', in Stratford, 55.
47 Monière, 140.
48 Brian McKenna and Susan Purcell, *Drapeau* (Toronto: Clarke, Irwin, 1980), 41.
49 'The Conscription Crisis', in Stratford, 62.
50 *Ibid.*, 65.
51 *Ibid.*, 63.
52 Monière, 141.
53 'The Conscription Crisis', in Stratford, 69.
54 McKenna and Purcell, 42.
55 *Ibid.*, 45.
56 'The Conscription Crisis', in Stratford, 68.
57 *Ibid.*, 70-1.
58 *Ibid.*, 78.
59 *Ibid.*, 92.
60 *Ibid.*, 121.
61 *Ibid.*, 87.
62 J.L. Granatstein, *Canada's War: The Politics of the Mackenzie King Government, 1939-1945* (Toronto: Oxford University Press, 1975), 373.
63 'The Conscription Crisis', in Stratford, 114.
64 *Ibid.*, 120; also, André Laurendeau, *Ces choses qui nous arrivent: chronique des années 1961-1966* (Montréal: HMH, 1970), 221-2.
65 'The Conscription Crisis', in Stratford, 120; also, André Laurendeau, 'The Meaning of Present-Day Separatism', in Behiels and Cook, 229-30.

CHAPTER 6

1 In Philip Stratford, ed. and trans., *André Laurendeau: Witness for Quebec* (Toronto: Macmillan, 1973), 263-264.
2 P.E. Trudeau, *Federalism and the French-Canadians* (Toronto: Macmillan, 1968), 107-10; also 'Réflexions sur la politique au Canada français', *Cité libre* 6 (décembre 1952), 52-6.
3 Patricia Dirks, *The Failure of L'Action Libérale Nationale* (Montréal: McGill-Queen's, 1991), 84-105.
4 'The "Impossible" Third Party', in Michael Behiels and Ramsay Cook, *The Essential Laurendeau*, trans. Joanne L'Heureux and Richard Howard (Toronto: Copp Clark, 1968), 98.
5 André Laurendeau, 'The Conscription Crisis, 1942', in Stratford, 102.
6 *Ibid.*, 103.
7 Michael Behiels, 'The Bloc Populaire Canadien and the Origins of French-Canadian Neo-Nationalism, 1942-48', *Canadian Historical Review* LXII, 4 (1982), 488.
8 *Ibid.*, 491.
9 Paul-André Comeau, *Le Bloc Populaire* (Montréal: Québec/Amérique, 1982), 93-6.
10 *Ibid.*, 112-13; also Paul-André Comeau, 'André Laurendeau et sa participation au Bloc Populaire', in Robert Comeau et Lucille Beaudry, *André Laurendeau, un*

intellectuel d'ici (Sillery, Québec: Presses de l'Université du Québec, 1990), 49.

[11] Denis Monière, *André Laurendeau et le destin d'un peuple* (Montréal: Québec/Amérique, 1983), 153.

[12] Paul-André Comeau, 'André Laurendeau et sa participation au Bloc Populaire', in Comeau et Beaudry, 48.

[13] Michael Behiels, 'The Bloc Populaire Canadien: Anatomy of Failure, 1942-47', *Journal of Canadian Studies* 18, no. 4 (Winter 1984), 45-73.

[14] *Ibid.*, 53-64.

[15] Paul-André Comeau, 'André Laurendeau et sa participation au Bloc Populaire', in Comeau et Beaudry, 49-50.

[16] 'The Churchwarden', in Stratford, 265.

[17] Laurendeau, 'Programme provinciale, Bloc Populaire Canadienne', 11 octobre 1942, Fonds Bloc Populaire, Fondation Lionel Groulx.

[18] Fonds Maxime Raymond, Fondation Lionel Groulx; Marie-Louis Beaulieu, *Mémoire sur les principes, les idées maîtresses et les objectifs d'une politique canadienne-française* (Québec, septembre 1942), *passim*.

[19] Paul-André Comeau, *Le Bloc Populaire*, 208-12.

[20] Behiels, 'The Bloc Populaire Canadien and the Origins of French-Canadian Neo-Nationalism', 494.

[21] André Laurendeau, 'The "Impossible" Third Party', in Behiels and Cook, 99.

[22] Paul-André Comeau, *Le Bloc Populaire*, 302-4.

[23] Brian McKenna and Susan Purcell, *Drapeau* (Toronto: Clarke, Irwin, 1980), 49-62.

[24] 'The Conscription Crisis', in Stratford, 106.

[25] Stephen Clarkson and Christina McCall, *Trudeau and Our Times* (Toronto: McClelland and Stewart, 1991), vol. I, 42.

[26] McKenna and Purcell, 55.

[27] Jean-Marc Léger, 'L'Engagement et la distance', in Comeau et Beaudry, 242; on the other hand, see the opinion of Paul-André Comeau, 'André Laurendeau et sa participation au Bloc Populaire', in Comeau et Beaudry, 48.

[28] 'The Conscription Crisis', in Stratford, 106.

[29] McKenna and Purcell, 57.

[30] 'The Conscription Crisis', in Stratford, 110.

[31] *Ibid.*

[32] 'The Churchwarden', in Stratford, 263-70.

[33] Quoted in Yves Laurendeau, 'En guise de supplément au Laurendeau de Monière', *Revue d'histoire de l'Amèrique française* 38, no. 1 (été 1984), 75.

[34] 'The Conscription Crisis', in Stratford, 112; also Paul-André Comeau, 'André Laurendeau et sa participation au Bloc Populaire', in Comeau et Beaudry, 49-50.

[35] Paul-André Comeau, "André Laurendeau et sa participation au Bloc Populaire', in Comeau et Beaudry, 48.

[36] Behiels, 'The Bloc Populaire Canadien and the Origins of French-Canadian Neo-Nationalism', 503-4.

[37] 'Inaugural Speech', in Behiels and Cook, 123.

[38] J.L. Granatstein, *Canada's War: The Politics of the Mackenzie King Government, 1939-1945* (Toronto: Oxford University Press, 1975), 220-1.

[39] Michael Behiels, 'The Social and Political Ideas of André Laurendeau' (MA thesis, University of Alberta, 1969), 70-1.

[40] Monière, 161-2.

[41] Conrad Black, *Duplessis* (Toronto: McClelland and Stewart, 1977), 291; H.F. Quinn, *The Union Nationale* (Toronto: University of Toronto Press, 1963), 111, n. 2.

[42] René Lévesque, *Memoirs*, trans. Philip Stratford (Toronto: McClelland and Stewart, 1986), 155-60.

[43] 'The Conscription Crisis', in Stratford, 177; Paul-André Comeau, *Le Bloc Populaire*, 316-18; Yves Laurendeau, 'En guise de supplément', 88.

[44] S. Monet-Chartrand, 'Dépuis 1938 . . . un ami précieux', in Comeau et Beaudry, 28; René Chaloult, 'Souvenirs d'André Laurendeau', *Le Devoir*, 31 mai 1969.

[45] Paul André Comeau, *Le Bloc Populaire*, 387-9.

[46] Monière, 185-6.

[47] 'The Conscription Crisis', in Stratford, 104.

[48] *Ibid.*, 118.

[49] *Ibid.*

[50] Gérard Filion, *Fais ce que peux: en guise de mémoires* (Montréal: Fides, 1991), 208-10.

[51] Jean Laurendeau, 'André Laurendeau, la musique et l'ambiance', in Nadine Pirotte, ed , *Penser l'éducation: nouveaux dialogues avec André Laurendeau* (Montréal: Boréal, 1989), 122.

[52] Quoted in Monière, 193.

[53] 'The Conscription Crisis', in Stratford, 112.

[54] Behiels, 'The Bloc Populaire Canadien and the Origins of French-Canadian Neo-Nationalism', 489.

[55] Filion, *Fais ce que peux*, 208-9.

CHAPTER 7

[1] 'L'Heure du salut national', *L'Action nationale* XLII (décembre 1953), 4.

[2] Pierre Godin, *La Lutte pour l'information: histoire de la presse écrite au Québec* (Montréal: LeJour, 1981), 77-8; see also Michel Roy, 'André Laurendeau, journaliste au Devoir', in Robert Comeau et Lucille Beaudry, eds, *André Laurendeau, un intellectuel d'ici* (Sillery, Québec: Presses de l'Université du Québec, 1990), 89-90.

[3] Gérard Filion, *Fais ce que peux: en guise de mémoires* (Montréal: Boréal, 1989), 210; see also Pierre-Philippe Gingras, *Le Devoir* (Montréal: Libre Expression, 1985), 152-63.

[4] After 1963 Laurendeau continued his association with the paper, but his involvement with the Royal Commission on Bilingualism and Biculturalism limited his writing to a few articles and behind-the-scenes consultations. Claude Ryan was the new editor.

[5] Filion, 204-8; Godin, 77-88.

[6] Gingras, 152-8.

[7] Denis Monière, *André Laurendeau et le destin d'un peuple* (Montréal, Québec/Amérique, 1983), 206.

[8] Filion, 205-8.

[9] *Ibid.*, 219-23.

[10] *Ibid.*, 241-2; see also Michael Behiels, *Prelude to Quebec's Quiet Revolution: Liberalism versus Neo-Nationalism 1945-1960* (Montreal: McGill-Queen's University Press, 1985), 24-32, and Laurendeau, 'Is there a Crisis of Nationalism?', in Ramsay Cook, ed., *French-Canadian Nationalism: An Anthology* (Toronto: Macmillan, 1970), 270-5.

[11] Yves Laurendeau, 'En guise de supplément au Laurendeau de Monière', *Revue d'histoire de l'Amérique française* 38, no. 1 (été 1984), 76.

[12] *Ibid.*, 77-8.

[13] Laurendeau, *Ces choses qui nous arrivent: chronique de années 1961-1966* (Montréal: HMH, 1970), 256.

[14] Gingras, 118-25.

[15] Filion, 211, 248.

[16] *Ibid.*, 253; Gingras, 137, 160; see also Chantal Perrault, 'Oncle André . . .' in Comeau et Beaudry, 33-6.

[17] Claude Ryan, interview, 1988 (Waterloo).

[18] Dale C. Thomson, *Jean Lesage and the Quiet Revolution* (Toronto: Macmillan, 1984), 19.

[19] Michel Roy, 'André Laurendeau, journaliste au Devoir', in Comeau et Beaudry, 90.

[20] Gérard Pelletier, 'Profession: éditorialiste', in Comeau et Beaudry, 87.

[21] *Ibid.*, 85; see also Jean-Éthier Blais, 'André Laurendeau, ecrivain', in Comeau et Beaudry, 147-9.

[22] Pelletier, 'Profession: éditorialiste', in Comeau et Beaudry, 85; see also Michel Roy, 'André Laurendeau, rédacteur en chef' in Nadine Pirotte, ed., *Penser l'éducation: nouveau dialogues avec André Laurendeau* (Montréal: Boréal, 1989), 135-8.

[23] Jacques Guay, 'Les grandes étapes de la carrière d'André Laurendeau', *Le Devoir*, 3 juin 1968; see also François-Albert Angers, 'Andre Laurendeau, journaliste à l'Action nationale', in Comeau et Beaudry, 103-7.

[24] Thomson, 19.

[25] Gérard Filion, 'Ce qui lui a manqué, c'est une enfance d'enfant', in Comeau et Beaudry, 12-13.

[26] *Ibid.*, 13.

[27] 'Continuing the Struggle', in Michael Behiels and Ramsay Cook, eds, *The Essential Laurendeau*, trans. Joanne L'Heureux and Richard Howard (Toronto: Copp Clark, 1968), 136-7; see also Filion, 247.

[28] 'A Primitive Tribe Without Education or Culture', in Philip Stratford, ed. and trans., *André Laurendeau: Witness for Quebec* (Toronto: Macmillan, 1973), 219-20.

[29] 'A Few Tentative Conclusions', in Behiels and Cook, 147.

[30] 'The Ungava Fiasco', in Behiels and Cook, 161-2.

[31] Monière, 204; see also Laurendeau, 'A Growing Imbalance', in Behiels and Cook, 194-6.

[32] Gérard Pelletier, *Years of Impatience, 1950-1960*, trans. Alan Brown (Toronto: Methuen, 1983), I, 11-13, 69; see also Pierre Elliott Trudeau, *La Grève de l'amiante* (Montréal: Editions Cité Libre, 1956) and Laurendeau 'A "Fourth Estate" in the Nation', in Behiels and Cook, 139-43.

[33] 'What Do We Want in Asbestos?' in Behiels and Cook, 152; Pelletier, *Years of Impatience, 1950-1960*, I, 69; also *Le Devoir*, 1 juin 1948.

[34] Filion, *Fais ce que peux*, 244-5.

[35] 'A Few Tentative Conclusions', in Behiels and Cook, 143-4.

[36] *Le Devoir*, 9 septembre 1956; Moniere, 212.

[37] John English, Ian Drummond, Robert Bothwell, *Canada since 1945: Power, Politics, and Provincialism* (Toronto: University of Toronto Press, 1981), 66-8.

[38] 'A Few Tentative Conclusions', in Behiels and Cook, 146-7.

[39] Behiels, *Prelude to Quebec's Quiet Revolution*, 150.

[40] *Le Devoir*, 21 juillet 1950.

[41] See Laurendeau's articles on television in *Ces choses*, 187-91, 290-4, 339-43.

[42] Monière, 218-19; see also Paul-André Comeau, 'La banalisation télévisuelle', in Pirotte, 155-60.

[43] Lucille de Garie à André Laurendeau, Fonds Laurendeau, Fondation Lionel Groulx.

[44] Gabrielle Roy à André Laurendeau, 25 mai 1960, Fonds Laurendeau, Fondation Lionel Groulx.

[45] Trudeau, *La Grève de l'amiante*, 46.

[46] 'Is There a Crisis of Nationalism?', in Cook, *French-Canadian Nationalism*, 257.

[47] *Ibid.*, 269.

CHAPTER 8

[1] In Michael Behiels and Ramsay Cook, eds., *The Essential Laurendeau*, trans. Joanne L'Heureux and Richard Howard (Toronto: Copp Clark, 1968), 9.

[2] Jean Laurendeau, 'André Laurendeau, la musique et l'ambiance', in Nadine Pirotte, ed., *Penser l'éducation: nouveaux dialogues avec André Laurendeau* (Montréal, Boréal, 1989), 122-3; 129-30; also Chantal Perrault, 'Oncle André . . .' in Robert Comeau et Lucille Beaudry, *André Laurendeau, un intellectuel d'ici* (Sillery, Québec: Presses de l'Université du Québec, 1990), 32, 35.

[3] Yves Laurendeau, 'André Laurendeau ou la culture comme mode de vie', in Pirotte, 23.

[4] *Ibid.*, 25.

[5] Perrault, 32.

[6] Jean Laurendeau, 'André Laurendeau, la musique et l'ambiance', in Pirotte, 130.

[7] André Laurendeau, 'Réponse de M. André Laurendeau de la Société Royale du Canada', *Écrits du Canada Français*, 35 (1964), 59-60.

[8] Perrault, 31.

[9] *Ibid.*, 34.

[10] Yves Laurendeau, 22.

[11] Perrault, 33, also Yves Laurendeau, 22-3.

[12] *Le Devoir*, 8 septembre 1959; for a detailed study of Duplessis's long career see Conrad Black, *Duplessis* (Toronto: McClelland and Stewart, 1977); for this period in Quebec see J.-L. Roy, *La Marche des québécois: le temps des ruptures (1945-1960)* (Montréal: Leméac, 1976); C. Nish, *Quebec in the Duplessis Era 1935-1939: Dictatorship or Democracy* (Toronto: Copp Clark, 1970).

[13] Laurendeau, 'Concerning an Old Illusion', in Behiels and Cook, 86-8.

[14] Laurendeau, 'Not a Province like the Others', in Behiels and Cook, 207; see also Laurendeau, 'A Policy of Grandeur', in Behiels and Cook, 202-3.

[15] Laurendeau, 'Federal Forgetfulness', in Behiels and Cook, 205.

[16] Hubert Guindon, 'Social Unrest, Social Class and Quebec's Bureaucratic Revolution', *Queen's Quarterly* 71 (Summer 1964): 150-62; J.-C. Falardeau, 'L'origine et l'ascension des hommes d'affaires dans la société canadienne-française', *Recherches sociographiques* 6 (janvier-avril 1963), 33-45.

[17] Michael Behiels, *Prelude to Quebec's Quiet Revolution: Liberalism versus Neo-nationalism 1945-60* (Montreal: McGill-Queen's University Press, 1985), 37-60.

[18] *Le Devoir*, 24 février 1959.

[19] Dale C. Thomson, *Jean Lesage and the Quiet Revolution* (Toronto: Macmillan, 1984), 18-20; Gérard Filion, *Fais ce que peux* (Montréal: Boréal, 1989), 264-82.

[20] Perrault, 33.

[21] Black, 653-9.

[22] *The True Face of Duplessis* (Montreal: Harvest House, 1960); Laporte's series in *Le Devoir* was entitled 'Les élections ne se font pas avec des prières'; see the analysis based heavily on these articles in Herbert F. Quinn, *The Union Nationale: A Study in Quebec Nationalism* (Toronto: University of Toronto Press, 1963), 130-45.

[23] 'Is Quebec Led by a "Negro King"?', in Behiels and Cook, 178.

[24] Gérard Pelletier, 'Profession: éditorialiste', in Comeau et Beaudry, 86.

[25] 'Is the Devil on the Left?', in Behiels and Cook, 176-7.

[26] 'Is Quebec Led by a "Negro King"?', in Behiels and Cook, 180 -1.

[27] Behiels and Cook, 164-78.

[28] *Ibid.*, 172.

[29] *Ibid.*, 172-3.

[30] Pierre Anctil, 'Laurendeau et le grand virage identitaire de la Révolution tranquille', in Comeau et Beaudry, 236, 238.

[31] 'Is the Devil on the Left?' in Behiels and Cook, 172.

[32] 'French Canada Is at Loggerheads With Its Intellectuals', in Philip Stratford, ed. and trans., *André Laurendeau: Witness for Quebec* (Toronto: Macmillan, 1973), 201; see also 'Like Father, like Son' in Stratford, 205-8.

[33] Gérard Pelletier, *Years of Impatience 1950-1960*, trans. Alan Brown (Toronto: Methuen, 1983), I, 99-130.

[34] 'It's Hard to Talk Across the Generation Gap', in Stratford, 210.

[35] In Stratford, 162-3.

[36] 'A Policy of Grandeur', in Behiels and Cook, 202-3; see also Behiels, *Prelude to Quebec's Quiet Revolution*, 84-96.

[37] 'Anglo-Canadians and Canada' in Stratford, 158; see also 'Can a French Canadian Feel at Home in Canada?', 'French Canadians and the West', 'A Province that Turns its Back on Us', in Stratford, 144-56.

[38] Behiels, *Prelude to Quebec's Quiet Revolution*, 214-16; see also Mireille Ferlaud, 'Les éditoriaux du *Devoir* et le thème de l'autonomie', in Fernand Dumont, Jean Namelin, Jean-Paul Montminy, eds, *Idéologies au Canada Francais, 1940-1976*, I, *La Presse-La Littérature* (Québec: Presses de l'Universite Laval), 101-60.

[39] 'Is the Devil on the Left?', in Behiels and Cook, 176; see also 'Dividing the Inheritance', in Behiels and Cook, 198-9, and Laurendeau's numerous commentaries on education in this period in Suzanne Laurin, ed., *André Laurendeau, artisan des passages* (Montréal: Hurtubise HMH, 1988).

[40] Denis Monière, *André Laurendeau et le destin d'un peuple* (Montréal: Québec/Amérique, 1983), 223.

[41] 'Is the Devil on the Left?', in Behiels and Cook, 177.

[42] Francine Laurendeau, 'André Laurendeau et la musique', in Comeau et Beaudry, 117; see Thérèse Casgrain, *A Woman in a Man's World*, trans., Joyce Marshall (Toronto: McClelland and Stewart, 1972), 134-46.

[43] Quoted in Behiels, *Prelude to Quebec's Quiet Revolution*, 246.

[44] Pelletier, *Years of Impatience, 1950-1960*, I, 147; see also Pierre Dansereau, 'André Laurendeau: les options réversibles' in Comeau et Beaudry, 184.

[45] Thomson, 64-87; see also André Laurendeau, *Ces choses qui nous arrivent: chronique*

des années 1960-1966 (Montréal, HMH, 1970), 1-10, with respect to his caution about the Liberals.

[46] For a good discussion of Laurendeau's possible subconscious motives for not fully committing himself to higher cultural pursuits see Yves Laurendeau, 'En guise de supplément au Laurendeau de Monière', *Revue d'histoire de l'Amérique française* 30, no. 1 (été 1984), 81-3; Fernand Dumont, 'Préface', in Laurendeau, *Ces choses*, xvi-xvii.

[47] Gérard Bergeron 'Celui pour qui nous avons tous rêvé d'un autre destin' in Comeau et Beaudry, 285.

[48] Filion, *Fais ce que peux: en guise de mémoires* (Montréal: Boréal, 1989), 240.

[49] *Ibid.*, 242.

[50] Denis Chouinard, 'André Laurendeau, Voyages au pays de l'enfance', *Dictionnaire des oeuvres littéraires du Québec*, (Montréal: Fides, 1984), IV, 967.

[51] Hugh MacLennan à André Laurendeau, 16 juin 1960, Fonds Laurendeau, Fondation Lionel Groulx.

[52] Monière, 245-9.

[53] Filion, 242; for commentary on other negative opinions about the novel see Gilles Henault, 'Les avatars d'une vie littéraire' in Comeau et Beaudry, 128-9.

[54] (Montreal, HMH, 1965); see Chouinard, *Dictionnaire des oeuvres littéraires du Quebec*, IV, 922-3.

[55] 'It All Began in a Theatre in the East of Montreal', in Stratford, 256.

[56] *Ibid.*, 257; see also Alain Pontaut, 'Le Théâtre d'André Laurendeau', in Comeau et Beaudry, 123-5.

[57] Monière, 244.

[58] For a comment on this and an analysis of his theatrical work see Jean-Cléo Godin, 'André Laurendeau, dramaturge' in Comeau et Beaudry, 133-7.

[59] Monière, 256.

[60] *Ibid.*, 257-8, see Yves Laurendeau, 'En guise de supplément au Laurendeau de Moniere', 76-8.

[61] Contrat et Permis de Representation, Service des Textes, Société Radio-Canada, Robert Charbonneau, Directeur du Service des Textes, 15 septembre 1960, Fonds Laurendeau, Fondation Lionel Groulx; André Gascon, Administrateur, Le Théâtre du Nouveau Monde, 18 août 1961, Fonds Laurendeau, Fondation Lionel Groulx.

CHAPTER 9

[1] 'Quebec: Capital of French Canada', in Philip Stratford, ed. and trans., *André Laurendeau: Witness for Quebec* (Toronto: Macmillan, 1973), 232.

[2] Simon Schama, *Citizens* (New York: Knopf, 1989), xiii.

[3] Kenneth McRoberts, *Quebec: Social Change and Political Crisis* (Toronto: McClelland and Stewart, 1984), 128-72; see also Fernand Dumont, 'De Laurendeau à l'intellectuel d'aujourd'hui', in Robert Comeau et Lucille Beaudry, eds, *André Laurendeau, un intellectuel d'ici* (Sillery, Québec: Presses de l'Université du Québec, 1990), 261; André Laurendeau, 'A State of Our Own', in Michael Behiels and Ramsay Cook, eds, *The Essential Laurendeau*, trans. Joanne L'Heureux and Richard Howard (Toronto: Copp Clark, 1968), 181-3.

[4] 'It's Hard to Talk Across the Generation Gap', in Stratford, 210.

[5] 'Anti-Separatism', in Behiels and Cook, 218-19.

[6] Jean-Pierre Wallot, 'L'Histoire et le néo-nationalisme des années 1947-1970', in

G.-H. Lévesque et al., *Continuité et rupture: les sciences sociales au Québec* (Montréal: Presses de l'Université de Montréal, 1984): 111-16; see also M. Behiels, *Prelude to Quebec's Quiet Revolution: Liberalism versus Neo-Nationalism, 1945-1960* (Montreal: McGill-Queen's University Press, 1985), *passim*.

[7] Laurendeau's articles for *Le Magazine Maclean* are collected in *Ces choses qui nous arrivent: chronique des années 1961-1966* (Montreal: HMH, 1970).

[8] Yves Laurendeau, 'André Laurendeau ou la culture comme mode de vie', in Nadine Pirotte, ed. *Penser l'éducation: nouveaux dialogues avec André Laurendeau* (Montréal: Boréal, 1989), 24.

[9] Denis Monière, *André Laurendeau et le destin d'un peuple* (Montréal: Québec/Amérique, 1983), 263.

[10] 'Quebec: Capital of French Canada', in Stratford, 231-2.

[11] 'The Meaning of Present-Day Separatism', in Behiels and Cook, 228.

[12] 'Return from Europe', in Stratford, 216.

[13] *Ces choses*, 57.

[14] *Ibid.*, 65.

[15] 'It's Hard to Talk Across the Generation Gap', in Stratford, 211.

[16] Yves Laurendeau, 'André Laurendeau ou la culture comme mode de vie', in Pirotte, 23.

[17] See, for example, *Ces choses*, 79-84; 324-9, and 'Journalism's Duty is to Probe the Unknown', in Stratford, 283-6.

[18] *Ces choses*, 253-4.

[19] 'It's Hard to Talk Across the Generation Gap', in Stratford, 209.

[20] *Ibid.*, 210.

[21] *Ibid.*, 212.

[22] 'Like Father, Like Son', in Stratford, 206-7.

[23] *Ces choses*, 20; see also Dumont, 'De Laurendeau à l'intellectuel d'aujourd'hui', in Comeau et Beaudry, 259-63.

[24] *Le Devoir*, 21 octobre 1959; *Ces choses*, 17.

[25] Malcolm Reid, *The Shouting Signpainters: A Literary and Political Account of Quebec Revolutionary Nationalism* (Toronto: McClelland and Stewart, 1972), 16-19; Yves Laurendeau, 'André Laurendeau ou la culture comme mode de vie', in Comeau et Beaudry, 26.

[26] See Laurendeau's introduction to *Les Insolences du Frère Untel* (Montréal: Editions de l'Homme, 1960); see also Jean-Paul Desbiens, 'André Laurendeau, au diapason de son temps', in Pirotte, 255-8.

[27] Cardinal Léger à Laurendeau, 30 septembre 1960, Fonds Laurendeau, Fondation Lionel Groulx.

[28] Laurendeau au Cardinal Léger, 18 octobre 1960, Fonds Laurendeau, Fondation Lionel Groulx.

[29] *Ces choses qui nous arrivent*, 45.

[30] Léon Dion, 'Bribes de souvenirs d'André Laurendeau', in Pirotte, 39.

[31] *Ces choses*, 155.

[32] *Ibid.*, 156-7.

[33] *Ibid.*, 7; see also Dale C. Thomson, *Jean Lesage and the Quiet Revolution* (Toronto: Macmillan, 1984), 88-124.

[34] *Ces choses*, 14.

[35] *Ibid.*, 97-8; see also Pierre Elliott Trudeau, *Federalism and the French Canadians* (Toronto: Macmillan, 1968), 103-23.

[36] *Ces choses*, 75.

[37] *Ibid.*, 99.

[38] *Ibid.*, 15.

[39] *Ibid.*, 46, 78; see also Léon Dion, *Quebec: The Unfinished Revolution* (Montreal: McGill-Queen's University Press, 1976), 15-20.

[40] Gérard Pelletier, *Years of Impatience, 1950-1960*, trans. Alan Brown (Toronto: Methuen, 1983), I, 96-8.

[41] 'A Primitive Tribe Without Education or Culture', in Stratford, 218.

[42] Laurendeau, 'Too Little, Too Late', in Behiels and Cook, 211-12; see also Jean Lesage in Michael Oliver and F.R. Scott, eds, *Quebec States Its Case* (Toronto: Macmillan, 1964), 12-30.

[43] 'A Fatal Association', in Behiels and Cook, 221.

[44] Trudeau, *Federalism and the French Canadians*, 151-81.

[45] 'Anti-Separatism', in Behiels and Cook, 218-19, Pelletier, I, 97-8.

[46] Cited in Isabella Grigoroff, 'André Laurendeau. A Study in French-Canadian Nationalism' (MA thesis, Political Science, University of Waterloo, 1979), 102.

[47] 'Weak Representation in Ottawa Turns Quebec Away from Canada', in Stratford, 197.

[48] 'The Meaning of Present-Day Separatism', in Behiels and Cook, 231-2.

[49] *Ces choses*, 128.

[50] 'The Meaning of Present-Day Separatism', in Behiels and Cook, 226-7.

[51] 'Nationalism and Separatism', in Behiels and Cook, 214.

[52] *Ces choses*, 131.

[53] 'A Rebirth of Separatism', in Stratford, 221.

[54] *Ibid.*, 222.

[55] 'Independence v. Federalism', in Stratford, 224-5; see also *Le Devoir*, 4 juin 1968; Pierre de Bellefeuille, 'André Laurendeau face au séparatisme des années 60', in Comeau et Beaudry, 157-62.

[56] 'Nationalism and Separatism', in Behiels and Cook, 216.

[57] 'A Rebirth of Separatism', in Behiels and Cook, 222-3; see also Laurendeau, 'Logic and Realism in Politics', in Stratford, 184-6 and *Ces choses*, 66-7.

[58] 'Nationalism and Separatism', in Behiels and Cook, 215.

[59] 'Logic and Reason in Politics', in Stratford, 185.

[60] 'A Fatal Association', in Behiels and Cook, 223.

[61] 'Like Father, Like Son', in Stratford, 207.

[62] *Ibid.*, 208.

[63] Patricia Smart, ed. and trans. with Dorothy Howard, *The Diary of André Laurendeau: Written during the Royal Commission on Bilingualism and Biculturalism 1964-67* (Toronto: James Lorimer, 1991), 21, n. 2.

[64] 'The F.L.Q.', in Stratford, 245.

[65] Laurendeau, 'Freedom vs. Violence', in Behiels and Cook, 234; see also Léon Dion in *Le Devoir*, 21 juin 1963; Louis Fournier, *The F. L. Q.: The Anatomy of an Underground Movement*, Edward Baxter, trans. (Toronto: NC Press, 1984), 13-42.

[66] 'The F.L.Q.', in Stratford, 246-7.

[67] 'Fanaticism', in Stratford, 251.

[68] 'Confederation But . . .', in Stratford, 237.

[69] *Ibid.*

[70] 'Independence vs. Federalism', in Stratford, 227-8; see also 'The Meaning of Present-Day Separatism', in Behiels and Cook, 233.

[71] 'A Proposal for an Inquiry into Bilingualism', in Stratford, 188.

[72] 'Confederation But . . .', in Stratford, 237.

[73] 'Logic and Realism in Politics', in Stratford, 184.

CHAPTER 10

[1] Patricia Smart, ed. and trans. with Dorothy Howard, *The Diary of André Laurendeau: Written during the Royal Commission on Bilingualism and Biculturalism, 1964-67* (Toronto: James Lorimer, 1991), 58.

[2] Lester B. Pearson, *Words and Occasions* (Toronto: University of Toronto Press, 1970), 196-7.

[3] Pearson, *Mike: The Memoirs of the Right Honourable Lester B. Pearson*, John Munro, ed. (Toronto: University of Toronto Press, 1973), III, 239; also 67-9. It seems that Lamontagne read Laurendeau's editorials calling for a Royal Commission on bilingualism, and that after discussions with Laurendeau biculturalism was added. Lamontagne then developed the concept in a memorandum to Pearson. Pearson's speech of 17 December was heavily based on Lamontagne's proposal; see R.M. Fowler to M. Lamontagne, 31 Jan. 1965, Lamontagne papers, MG32, B32, vol. 10, no. 10 (PAC); also M. Lamontagne, 'A New Canadian Partnership', 10 Dec. 1962, Lamontagne papers, MG32, B32, vol. 7, no. 13 (PAC).

[4] Smart, *Diary*, 26-7.

[5] André Laurendeau, *Ces choses qui nous arrivent: chronique des années 1961-66* (Montréal: HMH, 1970), 132.

[6] Smart, *Diary*, 27.

[7] Peter C. Newman, *The Distemper of Our Times* (Toronto: McClelland and Stewart, 1978), 241-53; for a good account of the Commission's origins see J. L. Granatstein, *Canada 1957-1967: The Years of Uncertainty and Innovation* (Toronto: McClelland and Stewart, 1986), 243-9.

[8] John English, Ian Drummond, and Robert Bothwell, *Canada since 1945: Power, Politics, and Provincialism* (Toronto: University of Toronto Press, 1981), 272; see also Walter Gordon, *A Political Memoir* (Toronto: McClelland and Stewart, 1977).

[9] Pearson, *Mike*, III, 236.

[10] Pearson, *Words and Occasions*, 193.

[11] Pearson, *Mike*, III, 240; see also Denis Monière, *André Laurendeau et le destin d'un peuple* (Montréal, Québec/Amérique, 1983), 280.

[12] Smart, *Diary*, 23.

[13] *Ibid.*, 20; see also Laurendeau, 'A Proposal for an Inquiry into Bilingualism', in Philip Stratford, ed. and trans. *André Laurendeau: Witness for Quebec* (Toronto: Macmillan, 1973), 189.

[14] *Ces choses*, 67-8.

[15] Smart, *Diary*, 23.

[16] *Ibid.*

[17] *Ibid.*

[18] *Ibid.*

[19] Jean Laurendeau à André Laurendeau, 16 April 1963, Fonds Laurendeau, Fondation Lionel Groulx.

[20] 'Diving in', in Michael Behiels and Ramsay Cook, eds, *The Essential Laurendeau*, trans. Joanne L'Heureux and Richard Howard, (Toronto: Copp Clark, 1968), 256; Laurendeau outlined his goals in a private memorandum (undated). See the summary in Granatstein, *Canada 1957-1967*, 249.

[21] 'Diving in', in Behiels and Cook, 256.

[22] Paul Lacoste, 'André Laurendeau et la Commission sur le bilinguisme et le biculturalisme', in Robert Comeau et Lucille Beaudry, eds, *André Laurendeau: un intellectuel d'ici* (Sillery, Québec: Presses de l'Université du Québec, 1990), 208.

[23] Interview with G. H. Lévesque, May 1982.

[24] Laurendeau à l'Abbé Lionel Groulx, 10 janvier 1965. Fonds Laurendeau, Fondation Lionel Groulx.

[25] Laurendeau à François-Albert Angers, 19 février 1965, Fonds Laurendeau, Fondation Lionel Groulx.

[26] J.-P. Desbiens (Frère Pierre Jérome) à André Laurendeau , 22 août 1963, Fonds Laurendeau, Fondation Lionel Groulx.

[27] Smart, *Diary*, 29.

[28] Paul Lacoste, 'André Laurendeau et la commission sur la bilinguisme et le biculturalisme', in Comeau et Beaudry, 208.

[29] 'Diving in', in Behiels and Cook, 254.

[30] Sandra Djwa, *The Politics of the Imagination: A Life of F. R. Scott* (Toronto: McClelland and Stewart, 1987), 385.

[31] Pearson, *Mike*, III, 241.

[32] *Ces choses*, 257; see also Jean-Louis Gagnon, *Les Apostasies I: les coqs de village* (Montréal: La Presse, 1985), 85.

[33] Smart, *Diary*, 27, Granatstein, *Canada 1957-1967*, 248.

[34] Smart, *Diary*, 29.

[35] *Ibid.*, 28 9; the commission had over 200 full- and part-time employees by the end of 1965.

[36] Paul Bienvenue à André Laurendeau et Davidson Dunton, 20 août 1963, Fonds Laurendeau, Fondation Lionel Groulx.

[37] Davidson Dunton, André Laurendeau, et al., 'Terms of Reference', *A Preliminary Report of the Royal Commission on Bilingualism and Biculturalism* (Ottawa: Queen's Printer, 1965), 21-5, 151.

[38] *Ibid.*; see also Djwa, 388.

[39] *Ibid.*; see also Léon Dion, 'André Laurendeau: un intellectuel engagé?', in Comeau et Beaudry, 267.

[40] Smart, *Diary*, 26; see also Monière, 291.

[41] Lacoste, in Comeau et Beaudry, 210.

[42] *Ces choses*, 83.

[43] Dion, 'André Laurendeau: un intellectuel engagé?' in Comeau et Beaudry, 274-5.

[44] Smart, *Diary*, 89.

[45] *Ibid.*, 135.

[46] *Ibid.*, 33; see also Granatstein, *Canada 1957-1967*, 251-2.

[47] Smart, *Diary*, 37; 53-4.

[48] *Ibid.*, 39-40.

[49] *Ibid.*, 35.
[50] *Ibid.*, 42.
[51] *Ibid.*, 32.
[52] *Ibid.*, 49.
[53] 'The Anglo-Canadian Nation?', in Stratford, 240.
[54] *Ibid.*, 243.
[55] Smart, *Diary*, 89-90.
[56] Pierre Vallières à Laurendeau, 29 novembre 1966, Fonds Laurendeau, Fondation Lionel Groulx.
[57] Smart, *Diary*, 116.
[58] *Ibid.*, 64-5; see Granatstein, *Canada 1957-1967*, 252.
[59] *Ibid.*, 129.
[60] The phrase from the Report that was frequently cited to capture its overall tone was this: 'Canada, without being freely conscious of the fact, is passing through the greatest crisis in its history' (*Preliminary Report of the Royal Commission on Bilingualism and Bilculturalism*, 13); Smart, *Diary*, 50.
[61] Smart, *Diary*, 130.
[62] *Ibid.*, 130-1.
[63] Smart, *Diary*, 64. Occasionally Laurendeau couldn't resist writing an editorial in *Le Devoir* on Quebec's political affairs, but in general he remained scrupulously silent. His articles in *Le Magazine Maclean* were generally on more esoteric issues as well.
[64] Pearson, *Mike*, III, 239.
[65] Smart, *Diary*, 108, 119; Claude Ryan, 'Il a soulevé les vraies questions et réfuté les résponses toutes faites', in Comeau et Beaudry, 278-9.
[66] Smart, *Diary*, 112; see also Djwa, 388-9.
[67] *Ibid.*, 108; see also 34. At the same time Scott made strong arguments to Pearson that another commission should be appointed to deal with constitutional questions, leading eventually to the Goldenberg Committee on the Constitution.
[68] Lacoste, in Comeau et Beaudry, 211-12.
[69] Smart, *Diary*, 155. See also *Cité libre* XV (décembre 1965), 13-20.
[70] *Ibid.*, 152-3.
[71] *Ibid.*, 152.
[72] *Ibid.*, 154.
[73] *Ibid.*, 115.
[74] Monière, 319; see also Neil Morrison, 'Bilinguisme et biculturalisme', in Comeau et Beaudry, 217; Lacoste, 212. Trudeau had appeared before the Commission in 1963, when the terms of reference were discussed, and warned specifically against its getting involved in questions of the Constitution or federal-provincial relations; see Djwa, 389-90.
[75] Smart, *Diary*, 168.
[76] *Ibid.*
[77] Dion, 'André Laurendeau: un intellectuel engagé?', in Comeau et Beaudry, 274.
[78] *Diary*, 38; 47; 148-9; Morrison, 'Bilinguisme et biculturalisme', 216.
[79] Pearson, *Mike*, III, 240-1.
[80] Monière, 291.
[81] Smart, *Diary*, 73, 123, 136-7.

[82] Pearson, *Mike*, III, 241. The costs reached $6.96-million by 1967, an unheard-of amount in those days.
[83] Smart, *Diary*, 168.

EPILOGUE

[1] Fonds Laurendeau, Fondation Lionel Groulx.
[2] Simonne Monet-Chartrand, 'Depuis 1938 . . . un ami précieux', in Robert Comeau et Lucille Beaudry, eds, *André Laurendeau, un intellectuel d'ici* (Sillery, Québec: Presses de l' Université du Québec, 1990).
[3] Francine Laurendeau, 'André Laurendeau et la musique', in Comeau at Beaudry, 243.
[4] Jean-Marc Léger, 'L'engagement et la distance', in Comeau et Beaudry, 243.
[5] J.-P Desbiens (Frère Pierre Jérome) à Laurendeau, 28 octobre 1962, Fonds André Laurendeau, Fondation Lionel Groulx.
[6] J.-P. Desbiens (Frère Pierre Jérome), 'Temoignages', *Le Devoir*, 4 juin 1968.
[7] 'Concerning an Old Illusion', in Michael Behiels and Ramsay Cook,, *The Essential Laurendeau*, trans. Joanne L'Heureux and Richard Howard (Toronto: Copp Clark, 1968), 86.
[8] Marcel Fournier, 'André Laurendeau, la culture et la politique', in Comeau et Beaudry, 256.
[9] Guy Frégault,'"Aspect de Lionel Groulx', in Maurice Filion, *Hommages à Lionel Groulx* (Montreal: Leméac, 1978), 61.
[10] 'The Logic of the System', in Philip Stratford, ed. and trans. *André Laurendeau: Witness for Quebec* (Toronto: Macmillan, 1973), 182.
[11] Fernand Dumont, 'De Laurendeau à l'intellectuel d'aujourd'hui', in Comeau et Beaudry, 260.
[12] Chantal Perrault, 'Oncle André . . .', in Comeau et Beaudry, 35-6; see also Laurendeau, 'French Canada is at Loggerheads with its Intellectuals', in Stratford, 204.
[13] Jean-Marc Léger, 'L'engagement et la distance', in Comeau et Beaudry, 245.

Index